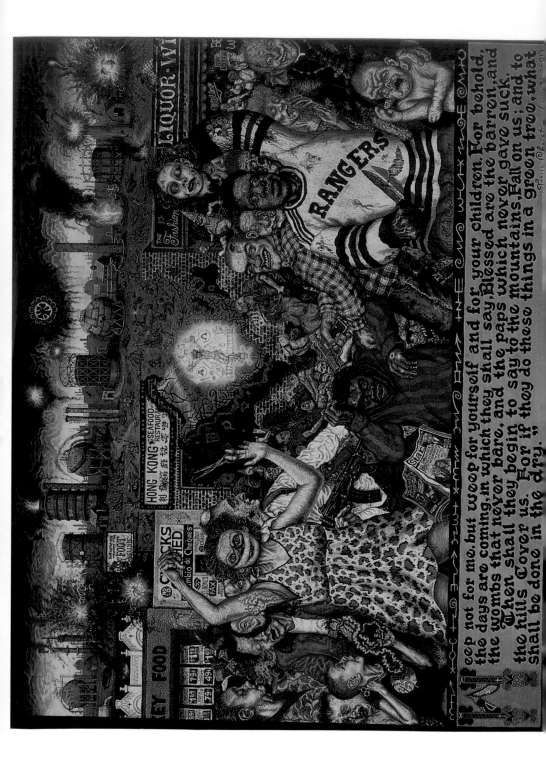

...eep not for me, but weep for yourselves and for your children. For behold, the days are coming, in which they shall say, Blessed are the barren, and the wombs that never bare, and the paps which never gave suck. Then shall they begin to say to the mountains, Fall on us; and to the hills, Cover us. For if they do these things in a green tree, what shall be done in the dry.''

CULT
RAPTURE

ADAM PARFREY

FRONTISPIECE BY
JOE COLEMAN

FERAL HOUSE

Feral House
PO Box 3466
Portland, OR 97208

Send S.A.S.E. for free catalogue.

Acknowledgements

Thanks to the following individuals and publications for the right to reprint and rewrite articles:

Jim Holman of the **San Diego Reader** for his generosity.
Allan MacDonell of **Hustler** for years of commiseration.
Jim & Debbie Goad of **ANSWER Me!**
Jim and Bill Redden of **PDXS**.
Lisa Kennedy and **Karen Durbin** of the **Village Voice**.
Don Myrus of **Penthouse** publications.

The following contributors deserve recognition and thanks:

Joe Coleman for his friendship and frontispiece, **Larry Wessel** for his amazing cover, **Crispin Glover** for his friendship and critical commentary, **Scott Lindgren**, **Nick Bougas** and **Ted Soqui** for their magnificent photographs, **Barry Krusch** for his deconstruction of *Time* magazine, **Linda Hayashi** for her cover design, **Michael Moynihan** for his friendship and helpful suggestions, **David Thomas** for the Feral House World Wide Web site (www.buzzcut.com/central/feralhouse), and my agents **Richard Pine** and **Lori Andiman**. Feral House could hardly carry on without the devotion and sympathy of **Charlie Winton**, **Gary Todoroff**, **Susan Reich**, **Anne Brooks**, and everybody else at **Publishers Group West**.

Throughout the years spent on this book, I have relied on many individuals for their aid, information, friendship and collaboration. The following people are due my heartfelt thanks:

Jerry A., Dwight Abbott, Carl Abrahamsson, Terre Baarlaer, Peter Bagge, J. G. Dallard, Blanche Barton, Dale Beyerstein, Greg Bishop, Bob Black, Steve Blush, Andy Boehm, Don Bolles, Ron Bonds, Robin Boyarsky, Jack Boulware, Len Bracken, Jack & Kathy Brewer, David Brothers, David Brown, Martin Cannon, Sean Carley, Jerry Casale, Monte Cazazza, Art Chantry, Rex Church, Dan Clowes, David Cole, Chris & Ruth Cooper, Tim Cridland, Matt Crowley, Georganne Deen, Rene Denfeld, Bob DeFord, George DiCaprio, James Shelby Downard, Katherine Dunn, Pat Eddington, Greg Escalante, Margaret Fiorino, Jim Fleming, Kris Force, Irene Forrest, Kathy Fors, Patrick Fourmy, Thomas Francis, Leonard Frank, Josh Friedman, Drew Friedman, Mark Frierson, Peter Gilmore, Jim and Debbie Goad, Ted Gottfried, Sue Greenberg, Karen Greenlee, Rudolph Grey, Todd Grimson, Bill Grimstad, Frank Grow, Michelle Handelman, Dian Hanson, Lars Hansson, Trent Harris, Ace Hayes, Tom Hazelmyer, Peter Hiess, George Higham, Warren Hinckle, Thee Slayer Hippy,

Michael A. Hoffman II, Jim Hogshire, Michael Hoy, Long Gone John, David Jones, John Judge, Margaret Keane, Jim Keith, Alison Kennedy, Don Kennison, Richard Kern, Jim Knipfel, Donna Kossy, Frank Kozik, Charles Krafft, Kristine Kryttyre, Greg Krupey, Johann Kugelberg, Paul Laffoley, Mary Lang, Joseph Lanza, Michael Lastra, Anton LaVey, Carol Lay, Christina Burks Lee, Johnny Legend, Herschell Gordon Lewis, Laura Lindgren, Miriam Linna, Jimmy & Natalia McDonough, Jim Martin, Larry Masset, Richard Meltzer, Howard Mittelmark, Judith Moore, Peggy Nadramia, Linda Nevin, David Normal, Keith Hammond, Steve O'Keefe, Tim O'Neill, Abe Opincar, Lawrence Osborne, Shaun Partridge, David Paul, George Petros, Edwin Pouncey, Monroe & Aimee Price, Gabriel Price, Ed Rehmus, Larry Reid, Vanessa Renwick, Boyd Rice, John Rier, Dan Rightmyer, Bruce Ritchie, Tom Roberts, Nick Rochford, Lou Rollins, Jim Rose, Melissa Rossi, Phil Sanchez, Cathy Seipp, Charlotte Sheedy, Daniel Sheehan, Billy Shire, Adam Siegler, Sarah Simons, Ratso Sloman, Ivan Solataroff, Peter Sotos, Phil Stanford, John Strausbaugh, Ken Swezey, Bob and Karen Taylor, Sean Tejaratchi, Kenn Thomas, Lindsey Thrasher, David Tibet, Nick Tosches, Greg Turkington, Bill Turner, Ron Turner, Sarita Vendetta, Robert Ward, John Waters, Leilah Wendell, Byron Werner, Robert Williams, Becky Wilson, S. Clay Wilson, Larry Wright, Peter Wright, John Zerzan, and at least several absent-minded and onerous omissions.

A few individuals have attempted to become a negative force in my life. Their expenditure of energy on my behalf cheers me. Even if their ruse is slander, they invoke my name more often than any publicist.

Maryanne Cassera became my guardian angel after a drunk driver plowed into my pickup truck, propelling my unconscious body through the passenger window.

MUCH LOVE to my wife Lisa and to the **Parfreys: Rosa, Jonathan, Jessica, Juliet, Rio, Paloma, Isaac, Morgan, Daniel, Stig, Juliet's new one & Bob Tolson.**

This book is dedicated to the memory of my father, **Sydney Woodrow Parfrey.**

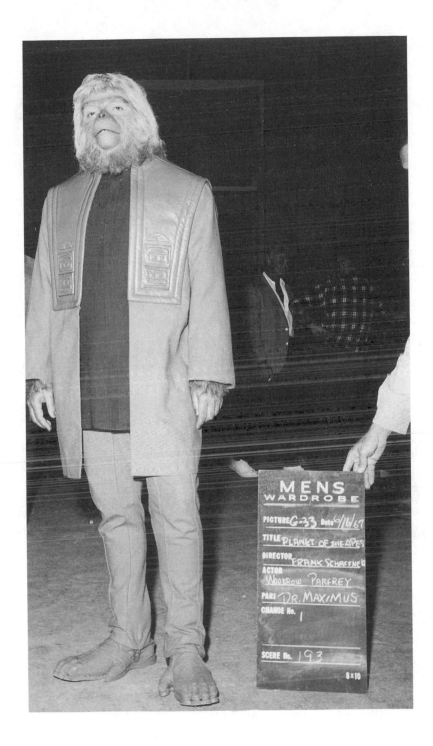

MENS
WARDROBE

PICTURE G-33 Date 6/16/67
TITLE PLANET OF THE APES
DIRECTOR FRANK SCHAFFNER
ACTOR WOODROW PARFREY
PART DR. MAXIMUS
CHANGE No. 1

SCENE No. 193

8 x 10

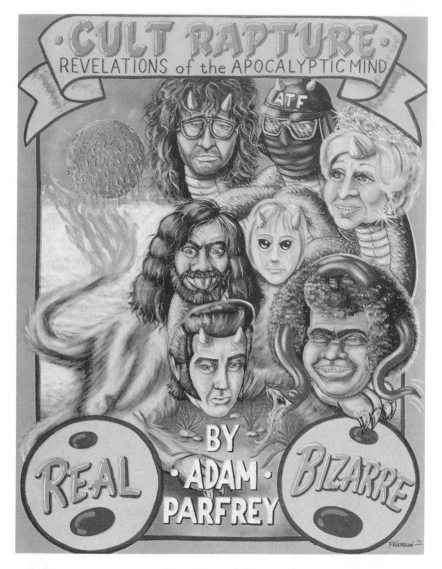

THE END IS NEAR
(THEY WOULDN'T MISS IT FOR THE WORLD)

Sideshow painter Mark Frierson's poster for the Center on Contemporary Art show which included work by Dr. Jack Kevorkian, Joe Coleman, Paul Laffoley, Robert N. Taylor, Dick Kramer, Leilah Wendell, Michael Moynihan, Charles Manson, George Higham, Charles Krafft, Rodney Vanworth, Shaun Partridge, and others.

CONTENTS

INTRODUCTION

This collection delves into the rapturously cultic experiences of groups you're going to wish you never heard of. How, why, did I sit with some of these characters long enough to not only obtain quotes, but glean their reptilian essence? Easy. My mind was on the payoff: thousands of people receiving an antidote to the Hallmark Card reality of America. Consider this book an emetic for the soul.

Cult Rapture is the result of years of toil in the cane fields of freelance journalism. My other career — as a publisher of outré books — affords me the luxury of writing about what I please for whom I please. It is a process not unlike serial monogamy. After I exhaust a subject (and it exhausts me) I throw all its components into a box, kick it into the basement and forget about it. Then my roving eye alights on some fresh topic. Such is the life of a freelance dilettante with money in the bank. Devotion, but with the promise of variety.

If journalism was my primary means of subsistence, I'd be forced to feign interest in the love life of celebrities. The political wisdom of Mr. Eisner, Mr. Rosenthal or Mr. Newhouse would necessarily become my own. Respectable newspapers or high-toned magazines are not interested, as I am, in maniacs, weirdos and bizarre social movements. I'm told that such things are not compatible with advertising. I'm grateful for the venues that have tolerated my interests and printed my work without leaning heavily on the red pencil.

If the articles in *Cult Rapture* share a common thread, they all describe how the panic-stricken middle class escapes its apocalyptic nightmare. Individuals seek secrets of their past lives from Pleiadian Space Brothers; paraplegics use their withered bodies to break the glass ceiling of orgasmic capability, launching their partners into a *petit morte* lengthier than a screening of *La Dolce Vita;* aging men disgusted by the shrewish examples of American womanhood seek sexual and emotional contentment by conjuring an appreciative *houri* through the mail; unloved girls throw themselves into the virtual reality of ecstatic fandom; materially successful upper-middle-class professionals abandon their entire cultural perspective by worshiping a Hindu Godman. Nowhere is middle-class anxiety so pronounced as in Jonathan Haynes, a BATF chemist who went so far as to commit two murders to prove that society had conspired from preventing him from taking an Aryan bride.

The American middle class is in the process of losing its security, its privileges, its clarity, its direction. Drifting out to sea, it grasps passing ideas as if they were life jackets. Before he first quit his candidacy for President, Ross Perot led all polls — a tantalizing indication of the extraordinary promise of the Populist paradigm. Gun control and the paramilitary adventures in Idaho, Waco and Oklahoma City have pushed this movement into pretzel shapes ever since. The new Populism is nostalgic, invoking the War for Independence as a battle cry against the "New World Order." It's also progressive, seeking an answer to the corruption and stasis of the two-party system. Populists rightly perceive Corporate America as abandoning domestic markets and domestic production for better prospects elsewhere. Enormous profits are waiting to be reaped in countries such as India, with a middle-class larger than our entire population, or Mexico, or Malaysia, or Taiwan. The Populist nationalism is not so much reactionary and warlike, as protectionist. Corporate allegiance is to Mammon, not to nation.

The middle-class foreboding over the triumph of capitalism is, in a sense, paradoxical. The threat of Communism has been trumped. This "victory" means, however, that American military adventurism must remain active on an international level, where the armed forces act in concert with the United Nations as a kind of international cop. These minor skirmishes don't justify Cold War-era expenditures, however. Prisons, police, SWAT teams, and the entire array of expensive spy equipment required to contain "domestic terrorism" has become the new life raft for the military-industrial complex. The Cold War paranoia has come home to roost within domestic borders.

As a rule, I never tackle subjects overwhelmed by media attention, such as the Oklahoma bombing. I made an exception in this instance because in all the coverage I've read, from the monotonous clamor of pundits bellowing about the "loss of American innocence," or the mom-and-apple-pie stories of individual heroism, or the unprincipled assignment of blame on the entire Populist militia movement, it has become clear the most compelling questions have not been addressed.

Why has it suddenly become necessary to dismantle so many constitutional rights? Why was the Posse Comitatus Act revoked, the law that once prohibited the military from attacking American citizens? Does the government expect civil war? Why has it become necessary for the FBI to snoop on every electronic, postal or vocal communication, even when the person spied upon is not suspected of committing a crime? Why must President William Jefferson Clinton create another anti-terrorist police bureaucracy when President Reagan put together a $3 billion a year program back in 1987? Who benefits most from Oklahoma City, and why? *Cui bono?*

I'm often asked, "Where did you find your subjects?" "Doesn't it get to you, all this strangeness, extremity and negativity?"

Remember the Indian who puts his ear to the train track in the movies? There's my inspiration for hunting down articles and sources. The usual journalistic sport of rewriting other people's work is cheating, and dull besides.

The best articles are like lightning: the revelations can only strike once. These usually become source material for professional "borrowers." After the publication of my article about Linda Thompson and the militia movement in the *Village Voice* (a prescient six months prior to the Oklahoma bombing), I was fascinated to discover a post-bomb piece on Thompson in *Esquire,* using my descriptions and even my turns of phrase. The *Voice* article netted me fifteen hundred dollars. The creative borrower from *Esquire* made something like ten thousand bucks.

The *New Yorker* magazine, meanwhile, accused Feral House of indulging in "fusion paranoia," a phrase conjured to castigate those who research conspiracies using information from both the Left *and*

Right. The *New Yorker* seemed flabbergasted that we weren't yoked to the Democrat/Republican, Right/Left paradigm like all "responsible" journalists. I am not alone in regarding the two-party system as a false stratification, a dumb-show concocted for the public as a means to distract attention from the ruling elite. This *New Yorker* piece proves why it receives so many ads for sixty thousand dollar watches and full-length furs. It's where the elite goes to confirm its preconceptions.

An excellent example of political theater inherent in the dumb-show was the July, 1995 Congressional hearing on Waco in which Kiri Jewell, said to be "deprogramed" from Branch Davidian teachings at the tender age of 10 by the so-called Cult Awareness Network, took the stand. Photos, videotape and testimony uttered by Kiri, now 14, were distributed by the mainstream media despite laws which protect the name and photo of juvenile victims of sexual predation from being published. Pundits wrote that Kiri's testimony effectively "paralyzed" the inquiry and "justified" the decision to spray equally paralyzing tear gas — banned from international warfare by the Geneva Convention — into an area where young children had no access to gas masks.

A few months after the fatal assault on Waco, I interviewed Kiri's grandmother at her suburban home in Orange County. Though her daughter, Sherri, was killed in the final conflagration, the grieving woman was concerned that Kiri's father, David, was working with "government psychiatrists" to expunge the memory of Sherri Jewell from young Kiri's mind.

It was strange indeed to see the woman's grandchild testify about sex crimes on national television; stranger still to realize that in so doing she justified actions which led to the murder of her mother in an explosive demonstration of Cult Rapture, in both its political and religious manifestations.

Adam Parfrey
August, 1995

THE GODS MUST BE CRAZY
THE LATTER DAYS OF UNARIUS

[This article does not attempt to address the truth or untruth of paranormal phenomena. It does, however, provide a glimpse of apocalyptic spirituality manifested by a group of misfists bonded together by the charisma of the elderly Archangel Uriel. More than just a grandmotherly figure, Uriel satisfies the longing of present-day nonentities in the belief that they are presently fulfilling a multi-generational destiny — their spiritual union with Ruth Norman, aka, the Archangel Uriel.

What makes this article different from several others surveying the cult was my good fortune encountering Stephan Yancoskie, a major mover and shaker of the cult, but who later had a falling out with the Archangel Uriel over his gay relations within the group. Yancoskie tells the remarkable story of Uriel's penchant for wedding dresses and marriage ceremonies with the fag hags who joined Unarius.

This, however, isn't the sort of thing that Unariuns want revealed about their group. The Archangel Uriel is supposed to be infallible. Shortly after this article appeared in *The San Diego Reader,* I was plagued with crank phone calls by people pretending to be all-powerful "Space Brothers." "C-S-3, 1-0-? TERMINATE!" the caller would yell in a high nasal monotone before hanging up. Unarius Academy members also blanketed the *Reader* with hectoring letters. Vice-President Charles Spaegel threatened a lawsuit because the article happened to create the perception that Unarius is "weird."

My first impression of Unarius was that it seemed an essentially benign organization, providing a needed sense of belonging for troubled and lonely souls. Total immersion in any eccentric philosophy can be stressful: anything that threatens the fragile logic of the belief system will result in extreme defensiveness.]

"Oh, no! Oh, no!" Joseph insisted. "You and everybody else will not refrain me from being God because I'm God and I'm going to be God! I was the first in the world and I created the world. No one made me." — an inmate from the Ypsilanti mental institution, from Milton Rokeach's *The Three Christs of Ypsilanti*.

Don't forget, if you have negative feelings against me, it is not me as a person because I am not an individual, I am the Infinite! — Uriel speaks, in *Effort to Destroy the Unarius Mission Thwarted*

Satan is alive and well and lives in a suburb of San Diego. Not to worry, though. The Archangel Uriel — the deity who resides in the body of 93-year-old Ruth Norman (at time of this book's publication, deceased) — tamed the Evil One. Satan now works unceasingly in behalf of all Light Beings as a "Doctor of Psychic Therapeutic Science" at the Unarius Academy of Science in El Cajon.

> URIEL
> You Came!
> You saw the Evil!
> You Conquered!
> You Healed Satan!
> You have set Man
> FREE!

I, Bonaparte: An Autobiography, in which the above poem appears, is periwig-pated Charles Spaegel's past-life testimony. For ten million years — from Spaegel's incarnation as the mind-controlling Tyrantus of the Orion Empire to Pontius Pilate to Napoleon — the Satan-spirit tortured and fretted his karma until he finally gave himself over to spread the gospel of Uriel. Today, the former Satan administers the day-to-day operations at Unarius World Headquarters in El Cajon, California, located near a nexus of thrift stores at South Magnolia Avenue and Main Street. He is also the primary Unarius "subchannel," who, by riding piggyback on Uriel's energy beam, is the human shortwave radio through which the Space Brothers (evolved beings

Ruth Norman (URIEL)

Cosmic Visionary
Founder-Director - Unarius
Spiritual Leader for the Earth

The Starmap of the 33 planets of the Interplanetary Confederation.

Background

from a higher astral world) answer the mystery of the cosmos. And they're never wrong.

"There is nothing that can't be explained by Unarius principles," says Spaegel, who is addressed at Unarius headquarters as Antares, a moniker that refers to his higher vibratory consciousness, which he regained after Satan's fall. And indeed, the glut of Unarius literature seems to cover all the bases. A three-volume set, to name one example, promises to reveal the *History of the Universe*.

The 125 books in the Unarius library largely consist of conversations with chatty astral luminaries eager to impart eternal wisdom to Eartheans. Unarius literature records discussions with Plato, Socrates, Herodotus, Freud, Pascal, Heidegger, Copernicus, Kepler, Karen Horney, Isaac Newton, Alessandro Volta, Hermann von Helmholtz, Gregor Mendel, Alexander Graham Bell, Albert Einstein, J. Robert Oppenheimer, incinerated astronauts Grissom, White, and Chaffee, the prophet Ezekiel, Kahlil Gibran, UFOlogist George Adamski, and ubiquitous electrical engineer and proponent of diathermy Nikola Tesla, who seems to divide his afterlife among free-energy aficionados and those who harmonically converge.

Though Unarius literature claims 300,000 students, the number of home-study students and active members would most likely be less than a thousand. An estimated 60 members attend local lectures and meetings. Other Unarius Star Centers (besides El Cajon) are reported to exist in North Carolina, Florida, Toronto, Vancouver, Australia, Bulgaria, and Nigeria.

In their civvies, Unariuns look no different from a coven of Amway salesmen. But when they parade about in their colorful Mylar space tunics as leaders of the Interplanetary Confederation, or when they enact past-life psychodramas from the antebellum South or the underground cities of Mars, for example, Unariuns are truly in their element.

The effect is like a community theater gone mad or a sustained and inspired Dada prank. Or so the nihilistic mind might reason. But irony plays no part in these ultra-kitsch spectacles. Rather, they are the gloriously gaudy expressions of a fantastic and hermetic belief system.

Taking the cue from Uriel, their flamboyant, purple-haired leader, Unariuns have successfully constructed a total environment in which their creed seems not only plausible but perfect.

Outsiders, as one might imagine, aren't just skeptical, they're stupefied. It wasn't a pretty sight when *Real People* and *A Current Affair* aimed their video blunderbusses at the earnest students of Unarius Science. Maury Povich followed a shallow, ridiculing *Current Affair* segment with a sneer and a comment to the effect that "we'll have to enter this on Stupid Pet Tricks."

The channeling community, whose proponents believe themselves to be in contact with astral avatars are uneasy with the Unarius style of consciousness. Reports Jon Klimo in his book, *Channeling: Investigations on Receiving Information from Paranormal Sources,* "For many in the channeling field, the Normans constitute somewhat of an embarrassment."

How do Unariuns react to such overt public ridicule? Charles Spaegel chalks it up to lower astral hordes drawing a veil of ignorance over men. Student Lianne Stevens claims that mockery has been solely in the domain of the media. "One-on-one," says Lianne, "people are incredibly receptive to the principles." And why not? If bestseller lists are any indication, Whitley Streiber's alien abduction nonfiction and Shirley MacLaine's metaphysical maunderings have seized hold of the mainstream American brainscape.

Even astronomer Carl Sagan, the mystical empiricist who persuaded NASA to spend a billion dollars on a satellite with schematic diagrams of a man and woman sans genitals, has been in touch with Unarius. He phoned one day with the challenge (as Spaegel recalls it), "If you guys are really channeling the eternal wisdom, then once and for all, prove Fermat's Theorem." (Seventeenth-century mathematician Pierre Fermat died without revealing the proof for one of this theorems. That proof was only recently solved.) According to Spaegel, the Space Brothers beamed down their answer. Unariuns transcribed it and sent it along to Sagan, who querulously responded with the demand that they translate the metaphysical verbiage into mathematical formulas.

"I'm no mathematician," admits Spaegel, who received his master of science degree from the University of Southern California, "so I couldn't do what Carl Sagan wanted, not that he would have listened anyway. He, like many other people who are first confronted with the Unarius teachings, their ego defenses get in the way. They've got too much at stake to listen to reason. If they would just understand that our problems are the result of our past lives, that we continue on after we discard this physical shell, then they'd lose that chip on their shoulder and begin to evolve."

In its rather grab-bag manner, Unarius teaching combines the channeling of discarnate entities, mystical geography, George Adamskian UFOlogy, Edgar Cayce, Swedenborgian commerce with angels, Theosophical and Rosicrucian mythology concerning lost civilizations, and Scientology's merging of sci-fi obsessions with psychological healing. "These other groups have an undergraduate understanding of consciousness. Unarius is the postgraduate course," claims Charles Spaegel.

Scientological and Unarius eschatology seem equally whimsical. According to one ex-Scientologist, L. Ron Hubbard wrote that Earth is the current prison for outcast souls of the Orwellian system of planets known as the Markab Confederacy. The Markabs keep life stirred up here on Earth with wars and disasters and phony religions that deny the truth of reincarnation. But Charles Spaegel cautions against commerce with the Church of Scientology. "We've discovered that L. Ron Hubbard was part of an Orion conspiracy to keep people controlled by robotizing them. I'm sure that Scientology bears out this proof of his past life."

> Unarius is not a cult. Jonestown was a cult. Unarius is a science based on the highest precepts of logic and reason. — The Archangel Uriel, Cosmic Visionary, Founder/Director of Unarius, Spiritual Leader for the Earth

Unariuns are especially insistent that their belief in reincarnation, extraterrestrial beings, and UFOs constitutes a science and not a religion. Unarius, an acronym for **UN**iversal **AR**ticulate Interdimensional **U**nderstanding of Science, is financially structured as a not-for-profit corporation and not as a tax-relieved religion. Their scientifically oriented books, titles like *Cosmic Continuum* and *Interdimensional Physics,* refer to modern science as an idiot mastery of a very limited dimension. Contemporary physicists, they assert, can learn from Unarius literature, which discusses heretofore neglected principles, such as oscillating vortexes in the etheric spectrum.

Cosmic Continuum was written by Ruth Norman's late husband Ernest, who claimed to have been the reincarnation of Jesus as well as the inventor of television. According to a Unarius press release, Ernest discussed his design for the orthicon tube, a forerunner of the television tube, with Philo T. Farnsworth during a chance meeting in Logan, Utah, in the 1920s. Farnsworth, they say, stole Ernest's design and parlayed it into a fortune. Ernest co-founded Unarius Science in 1954, the year he met Ruth Norman at a Los Angeles psychics' convention. "The Moderator," as Unariuns refer to him, died in 1971. His picture still appears alongside those of Ruth, Nikola Tesla, and Ruth's sister Esther as a frontispiece in Unarius publications.

Following her husband's death, Ruth Norman left Los Angeles and eventually chose the squat and dismal San Diego satellite of El Cajon as home for her Unarius academy, opening the Magnolia Venue headquarters in 1975. Two modest buildings house a meeting center, an attached art Star Center, offices, print shop, warehouse space, costume area, video and construction rooms. Her El Cajon neighbors congenially refer to Ruth as the Space Lady.

According to published accounts and the stories of her friends, the Archangel Uriel was born Ruth Anna Nields on August 18, 1900, to strict and abusive parents. She grew up in the Pasadena area and married a Mexican boy as soon as she turned 18. The marriage lasted only two and a half years but yielded a daughter who, to this day, shuns close contact with her mother. Uriel likens her Unarius students to the children she never had.

> Vaughn described what he was viewing at the moment. He said, "Oh, how lovely! I see you, Uriel, sitting in a huge golden throne. You are surrounded with literally thousands of little ones,

each one dressed in a different pastel shade. They have each brought to you, one lovely mind-created red bud. These countless roses have been formed in a huge heart-shaped wreath all about you as you sit. The great wreath seems about 20 feet high. The children are all so happy and bubbly to have you there, and a tremendous feeling of love exists. It all makes such a beautiful picture — you in the huge, golden throne, surrounded with the great heart or red roses, the many children gathered about, sitting at your feet. — From *Conclave of Light Beings,* by Ruth Norman and Vaughn (Charles) Spaegel

Ruth's full blossoming came late, becoming the Archangel Uriel (acronym of Universal, Radiant, Infinite, Eternal Light) only after her husband's death, when the Space Brothers channeled the information to her in the Unariun document *Conclave of Light Beings.*

At an early age, Ruth harbored theatrical ambitions, which might have been inflamed by her apparent blood relationship to the famous silent-film director King Vidor. Nothing came of this dream until she was 75, when she began playing ingenue roles in Unarius's improvised, videotaped psychodramas. These are an important component of Unarius Science wherein neuroses are healed by confrontation with one's past-life experiences.

Ruth Norman's brightest theatrical achievement came in the early 1980s in a past-life re-enactment titled *The Ballad of Annabelle Lee.* It's the kind of project that would make John Waters green with envy; a drag queen in blackface, pillow broadening his ass under a gingham dress, affecting a Hattie McDaniel look; two burnt-corked white girls mimicking Butterfly McQueen. The drag queen Nell fusses and flits around the recumbent Uriel, who is Annabelle.

> "Today's the big day," announces Nell. "Miss Annabelle Lee is goin' a courtin' on the riverboat!"
> "Oh, Miss Annabelle," coos the mammy, "you always my beautiful girl. You got mo' beaus up

and down the Mississippi than anyone can shake a stick at!"

"What's all that commotion, Nell?" cries Annabelle, the most ancient ingenue to fill out bloomers and a hoop skirt. "I'm sleepy!"

"Miss Annabelle must be tired, tryin' on all dose dresses and wigs all day long!"

A banjo twangs a Stephen Foster tune which inspires Miss Annabelle to go all misty-eyed as she heart-to-hearts with her faithful servant. "It is said, Nell, they don't treat you black people on the riverboat like I do — and you might have to take lodging down below, way down below."

"Miss Annabelle, you treats us black folks so good, so good!"

"God loves all God's chilluns!" replies Annabelle profoundly, a beatific smile on her face.

Segue to a riverboat scene. Shots of made up honky "darkies" singin' and spray-can-aged gamblers escorting Annabelle are intercut with pirated clips from *Showboat*. Now alone on deck, an outcast from the gay proceedings, faithful Nell is accosted by a slaveowner-type, who thrusts a mop into her hands, ordering her to swab the deck.

Soon the live action ends, leaving a Mark Twainish narrator to impart the climax and denouement. Apparently, Annabelle drowns in an accidental fall, and Nell is lynched by a mob as the scapegoat. There follows endless footage of swirling, muddy river water, over which Poe's "Annabelle Lee" is spoken in somnambulistic monotone. A Dixie melody twangs wistfully on a banjo, and the movie ends. Or does it?

In a videotaped colloquy following the dramatic events, Uriel contradicts all we have just heard. As she recounts the events, Annabelle is thrust into the steamships' paddles by Nell in a fit of pique. "Nell loved me so," reasons Uriel. "She would never have deliberately hurt me. I was born the same time as one of Nell's daughters, but she gave more attention to me than to her own little black pickaninny."

During the colloquy, now in street clothes, Stephan Yancoskie, the drag queen who portrayed Nell, expresses surprise that he would make such a good mammy. "I'd have never thought it true, but when I put on that skirt, I was she."

"You were she, you were she," seconds Uriel.

Uriel concludes with a blessing that appears to Unariuns as divine inspiration, but to an outsider it seems perhaps the onset of Alzheimer's disease:

> Looking back, all these things are most interesting, and fascinating, and only serve to prove the wonderful and never-ending and always factual, precise — and, oh, the farther we go the more precise and definite and defined become these principles. And we can go on and on and relate many of these principles, how defined they have become in this proving where one needs to prove.

Annabelle Lee is considered a keystone in Unarius's past-life psychodramas. Behind the scenes, however, a crisis reached boiling point when longtime Uriel companion and subchannel Thomas Miller reportedly refused to film the climactic scene unless the mammy (played by Yancoskie, then a rival for Uriel's affection) deliberately heaved Annabelle Lee overboard. According to her book, *Effort to Destroy the Unarius Mission Thwarted*, Uriel punished Miller with excommunication from Unarius Science for insubordination. In *Thwarted*, Uriel explains:

> I nurtured [Thomas] and nursed him, you could say, as a baby, gave him all the oscillations of my high frequency energies, constant teaching, pampering and lifting, pushing out his obsessions and helping him to overcome year after year after year, until he got to the point where he wanted to be me. He wanted to take over Unarius — he didn't make the attempt to destroy, he just wanted to take over. He wanted to be me!

Yancoskie, Miller's rival, coming to grips with his gay sexual identity, had been drifting around the West Coast trying to find an answer to his drinking problem and spiritual malaise. Entering the Unarius center, Stephan soon found himself wrapped in the comforting arms of Ruth Norman. "She looked at me and told me I was home at last. I was overwhelmed. I ate it up," reveals Yancoskie.

He soon replaced Thomas Miller as Uriel's favored companion. "I think Ruth was looking for a way to kick Thomas out of the group. She was getting tired of him, and after I came along, she got the hots for me," explains Stephan, whose own departure from Unarius several years later repeated a similar pattern. "The first time I left Unarius," he explains, "was after a television show. We got in a bitch-fight, and soon Ruth took off one of her crowns and was hitting me with it. She said, 'Here! If you want to be the Archangel Uriel, wear the crown! *Be* the Archangel Uriel!'"

Stephan quickly ascended the ranks of the Unarius hierarchy. "I did what I had to do to get to the top, and it wasn't that difficult. I didn't mind kissing Ruth's ass," he remembers, "and besides, the competition wasn't tough. The other members were weak ... washouts."

Dubbed "Arieson," leader of the ascended Aryan peoples, Stephan worked like a fiend at the Unarius center. Besides teaching weekly classes, he painted murals on the exterior and interior of the Magnolia Avenue complex, organized UFO pageants and appeared in a prodigious number of psychodrama and promotional videos. "Unarius allowed me to explore my creativity in ways that I would never have otherwise accomplished," recalls Stephan ruefully. "I'll probably never again have dozens of people at my beck and call to do what I tell them. In retrospect, I really appreciated the opportunity." (Yancoskie is currently a San Diego-based fine artist and designer specializing in pastel-colored mansion interiors.)

During the height of his power at the Unarius center, the "love oscillations" between Uriel and Arieson abounded. "I was with her constantly. I did her from top to bottom. When I first came, she looked like a country singer down on her luck. Then I designed her dresses, her wigs, the whole thing. She loved what I could do to her."

Yancoskie's ultimate split with Unarius came after it was discovered that he was "sleeping with one of the so-called straight members. Ruth yelled at me, called me a slut, and all kinds of names." Despite the drag travesties and, according to Yancoskie, the large number of gays in the group, Unarius philosophy paints homosexuality as a cosmic aberration. "It's the way Unarius keeps people in line. All the students are shown as being evil and against the spiritual hierarchy in past lives. Ruth was great at finding our emotional weakness and becoming the only solution for it."

Stephan's moment of truth came after he left the center for a second time and wrote Uriel a contrite letter, which was mistaken as an overture to readmission into the group.

> I came back to see Ruth because I wanted closure, to leave without all the bad feelings, to see things to an end without recrimination. As soon as I walked through the door, Ruth proposed that we get married.

In Uriel's closet hang more than a dozen wedding dresses. Reveals Yancoskie:

> Sometimes we'd drive down to town just to buy another wedding gown. She loved those wedding gowns. And she'd wear them in these symbolic wedding processions at the center.

> I was kind of shocked at Ruth's proposal. What could I say? I refused. She followed me to my car and seemed really confused. She kept saying, "Why? Why are you going?"

Yancoskie's rocky separation from Uriel and Unarius spawned the vindictive tome *Thwarted*, unique in the entire Unariun oeuvre for its concentration on the evildoings of an expelled member. But, like her other books, *Thwarted* consists of transcribed speeches and discussions among Uriel, her subchannel(s), and students. Here, Uriel claims that Stephan had hypnotized Unariun students with "lower astral forces" as he was actively reliving the time he had been a female named Shimlus on the planet Tyron, where he kept all the citizens

Proud students of Unarius science stand before a painting depicting the taming of Satan by the Archangel Uriel. (Photo by Adam Parfrey.)

Below: Morphed figure of Ruth Norman and the Mona Lisa.

"robotized." As documented in *Thwarted*, Uriel scolds and cross-examines her students as they attempt expiation of wrongdoing by dishing dirt on the ousted Yancoskie.

In the midst of the infighting, an article by Mike Granberry appeared in the September 29, 1986 edition of the *Los Angeles Times*. Though it provided few details, the article played up the Yancoskie excommunication, reporting that Yancoskie was contemplating "legal action for accusations made against him in the book." The *Times* article took the expected route by suggesting cultish behavior and fraud.

"Unarius students ... pay $5 almost every time they enter the door," wrote Granberry, suggesting that Unarius was extorting big money from the unfortunate. Actually, the pressure to contribute to Unarius coffers seems minimal, especially considering ever-churning printing presses and active video machinery.

Students do pay $5 at their weekly meetings and pay a small annual membership fee; other income derives from the sale of Unarius literature and voluntary contributions and bequests. From all appearances, Unarius is a benign though eccentric organization that provides context and meaning to those who would otherwise feel rudderless and adrift. Perhaps the most extraordinary testimonial is in a promotional video in which a young man tells how Unarius Science has made him a better surfer.

> Uriel is extremely humble and says that even though she is an archangel, she is only looking through a door at the Infinite. We don't look at her like a God, idolize her. She is just much further evolved than we are, and it is possible that we might be able to attain her great wisdom in future lifetimes if we adhere to the Principles. — Unarius student Lianne Stevens

It's not easy being a god, or even an archangel. Charles Spaegel: "They have tried to knock Ruth Norman off her pedestal or bow down to her just like they have done to Jesus." Well, she wasn't Jesus, but Uriel remembers being Mary of Bethany, Christ's virgin mum.

Biography of an Archangel and *Visitations of Gods and Men* are two Unarius titles chronicling the many lives of Ruth Norman: Dalos, leader of the Pleiadean peoples; Yuda, leader of the civilization of Yu; Poseid, the founder of Atlantis; Cryston, bringer of love to the Orion empire; Skott, light-bringer of the Scarpathian people; Ra Mu, spiritual leader of Lemuria; Isis; Ioshanna, priestess of the temple in Atlantis; Ensat, teacher of the Science of Life in Atlantis; Heliandra and Amon Ra of Atlantis; Queen Tiy, mother of Akhnaton; Pharoah Hatshepsut; Nada of Greece; Benvenuto Cellini; Akbar, Emperor of India; Peter the Great; Queen Maria Theresa; Queen Elizabeth I; Charlemagne; Johannes Kepler; Socrates; Quetzalcoatl; Annabelle Lee, Emperor Hsuan; Gautama Buddha; Zoroaster; Dalai Lama; Khadija, wife of Mohammad; Atahualpa, last Incan emperor; Darius I of Persia; King Arthur of Camelot; and 300,000 various and sundry other good guys.

It's been pointed out that several of Uriel's incarnations lived concurrently, but "Uriel lives in more dimensions and is beyond the realm of human understanding," says Spaegel, who has himself vibrated as the negative polarity to Uriel's light for many thousands of years.

Past and present lives of Uriel are commemorated in scores of student art work throughout the Unarius center, but the artist who has done her most proud was Leonardo da Vinci in his portrait of the Mona Lisa. The Unarius publication *Who Is The Mona Lisa?* tells the entire story, buttressed by a reproduction of the painting on the front cover and a photomontage on the back cover, which has Ruth Norman's head in place of Da Vinci's original model.

> Vaughn: I was at first taken back, simply amazed and flabbergasted when I saw how you took on the appearance of the Mona Lisa and actually became that epic lady in the portrait painted by Leonardo da Vinci! Then today when you came down the staircase with your wedding gown, your long red hair, the tiara and the great red rose you were holding, I simply had to blink my eyes and pinch myself! ... You appeared to be a woman of

30. Now, let it be said it wasn't makeup, for you
wore none. — *Conclave of Light Beings*

Perhaps it is difficult for the vulgar to believe an all-powerful, suprahuman force is wielded by a spacy granny from El Cajon. But for those who do believe, the testimony is vivid. View the psychodrama where Uriel lays on hands to heal the wayward Atlanteans — grown men blubber like babies, grown women spontaneously shake and rattle like leaves. There is the constant witnessing of the miraculous in multitudes of Unariun texts. Dorothy Ellerman:

> The typewriter was bathed in a beautiful color of purplish-red and I couldn't see my hands but I continued to type and shake and sob and tear, until the power became so intense that my head went down on the typewriter and I was taken out. When I came to on the cold, hard metal...I looked at the words on the typewriter, then a powerful ray-beam came down over my head as I continued to type. When I tried to get up off the chair, I had no legs and my body felt completely spent as though I had gone through a wringer, which I knew was a psychic purging of past-life dross. — *Conclave of Light Beings*

Charles Spaegel:

> The word "transcended" has to be put in capital letters ... It seemed as if all the muscles in my body had turned to jelly, and accompanied with this feeling in my legs was a great, intense power beam on my forehead. For the entire time of two hours, I was completely out of the body and, in this condition, I was viewing the ceremony of the city of Parhelion on the planet Eros! — *Conclave of Light Beings*

Now visited by a score of physical ailments, 93-year-old Ruth Norman struggles through her remaining days in a suburban home in the hills of El Cajon, Her speech slow and halted, as if by a stroke, the once-

energetic woman seems at last to be slowing down. On a recent afternoon, she greeted a visitor with her broken leg elevated, a bladder bag
hidden discreetly behind the Barcalounger. She's well taken care of —
her every whim is attended to by Spaegel and a couple of live in stu
dents.

Uriel points out her favorite paintings by Unarius students. "I'm very
proud of them, very proud," she says, adding that her students who
paint don't study technique, they study consciousness. (The flat,
metaphysical, naive style bears witness to this.)

Charles Spaegel becomes angry when Uriel was asked to discuss her
favorite food. "That's not a proper question. It's not important,"
Spaegel snapped. One does not clench the queen of England in a bear
hug. One does not ask Uriel about her favorite food.

Have you been in communication with Tesla, say, or anyone else, even
now?

"No, not since I've been off kilter, since I fell and broke my leg. No,
I haven't been interested ... When the famous people communicate
to me and it is transcribed onto a tape, it comes through perfect, just
perfect, it just comes through just like the water does."

No editing involved, then?

"No editing involved."

Do you feel any pain?

"What?"

Pain. Do you feel any pain?

"Uh?"

Does your leg hurt?

"Oh, pain. No. It doesn't much hurt, but they'll be putting the cast
on — When are they putting the cast on?"

Charles Spaegel speaks up: "Tomorrow morning."

"Monday?"

Charles: "Tomorrow morning."

"Yes. I might have pain tomorrow."

Charles attempts to reassure her. "The doctors will see to it that you don't have any pain."

"Surely, they have, uh, medication to, uh, deaden the pain now."

Many images of Ruth's late husband Ernest ring the room. I ask her if Ernest Norman will reincarnate into another body?

"Oh, no, he has completed his mission. They, the Space Brothers, have told me, too, that I have completed my mission on Earth and can leave any day."

Her mission completed, it's doubtful that Uriel will stick around to view the coming of the spaceships in (when else?) 2001 A.D. Little over a decade ago, Uriel purchased 67 acres of land in Jamul as the landing site for the Interplanetary Confederation. At this site, 33 spaceships, some a mile wide, will sit stop each other to form Earth's first interplanetary college. A model of this city/college is kept within the Star Center on Magnolia Avenue.

Stephan Yancoskie recalls the time in the early 1980s when Uriel awaited the arrival of the Space Brothers, excitedly pulling all-nighters with her favorite students. After the third night, Uriel threw in the towel, announcing that mankind was not yet prepared for the landing, that the lower astral hordes impeded their arrival. She pointed at a formation of unusual pink clouds at daybreak as the Space Brothers' signal to her that they had given it the old college try.

Uriel's "spiritual biune," Nikola Tesla, speaks about his relationship with a very special pigeon. The story is from John O'Neill's biography of Tesla, *Prodigal Genius,* and has been reprinted in Unarius's *Conclave of Light Beings.* Said Tesla:

> There was one pigeon, a beautiful bird, pure white with light gray tips on its wings. That one was different; it was a female. I would know that pigeon anywhere. No matter where I was, that pigeon would find me; when I wanted her I had

The Archangel Uriel at home, at time of our interview.

(Photo by Adam Parfrey)

only to wish and call her and she would come flying to me. She understood me and I understood her. I loved that pigeon ... Yes, I loved that pigeon! I loved her as a man loves a woman, and she loved me. When she was ill I knew and understood; she came to my room and I stayed beside her for days. I nursed her back to health. That pigeon was the joy of my life. If she needed me, nothing else mattered. As long as I had her, there was a purpose in my life. ... One night as I was lying in my bed in the dark, solving problems as usual, she flew in through the open window and stood on my desk. I knew she wanted me; she wanted to tell me something important, so I got up and went to her. As I looked at her, I knew she wasted to tell me she was dying. And then, as I got her message, there came a light from her eyes — powerful beams of light.

"Is not this story the greatest love story ever told?" wonders Uriel. "It must be said my infinite love has grown the more infinite toward this wondrous and beautiful soul, whether we term him Leonardo, Tesla, or any one of the hundreds of thousands of names he has used and carried during the eons of past millenniums?"

You can be sure that when Ruth Norman sloughs off this mortal coil, students of Unariun Science will remain vigilant for the space brothers to touch down in the year 2001. No doubt they'll keep an eye cocked for signs of Uriel's infinite love from the other side of the veil. Will she come as a cloud? A pigeon? A sunset? A ray of light? Perhaps one, perhaps all. But you can be sure it won't be the host of *A Current Affair.*

From Russia, With Love

The Business of Mail-Order Brides

[Written originally for the *San Diego Reader,* and reprinted in several other venues, my investigation of the mail order bride business concentrated on those inept and desperate men whose lack of success with American women inspired them to ante up thousands of dollars for the possibility of bedding and wedding the legendarily compliant Russian woman. According to the literature of matchmakers, Russian women have "respect" for older men. American cooze prospecting is said to be much easier in Russia, whose women are hungry for a ticket out of economic privation.

To my surprise, the mail order bride business confirmed feminist tracts pillorying the male's dehumanizing regard of the female as commodity. Those selling their services as matchmakers target men with the notion that they will be successful finding mates who are much prettier, younger, intelligent and compliant than their American counterparts. My interviews with the American boors in the market for a Russian sex slave revealed themselves as victims of an inferiority complex. The interviewees embodied the Reichian "Little Man" — prone to psychological overcompensation by acquiring women they can easily dominate.]

I t's a peculiar set-up. Strangers write strangers, attempting a mating dance despite cultural barriers so fierce that very little is communicated beyond the desire to communicate. Take Ed Burden (name pseudonymous by request), airline pilot, middle-aged, small tire around the middle. Between bites at Ed's favorite spot, a restaurant known for its gigantic portions, he pores over photos and earnest letters from young Russian women contacted through Scanna International, a foreign "pen pal" clearinghouse.

"I write each gal that she oughta send me more photos. That it's hard to tell what they look like in the books Scanna sends me," monotones Ed, as he presents me with snapshots of would-be immigrants doing their best to look alluring. He hands me a letter, painstakingly hand-written in English, which I read aloud:

> Very pleasantly capturing your lines of thought-fulness. Sensitive of your soul. My marriage not happen to be happy. Not experience mutual happiness and manifestation of tenderness for me. My husband is money only but he forgot about senses. I don't want it to be resemble bird in golden coop to feast one's eyes from far away. I want to have mutual understanding, intercourse, love from my husband. Many women see in Russian husband only tightly shut purse.

"I wrote her back and said I wanted to have intercourse with her," jokes Burden.

Ed Burden became interested in courting Eastern European women after seeing the mail order bride concept on a segment of *The Sally Jessy Raphael Show*. Dating services on both continents began in earnest at the start of the decade, when Glasnost pierced escape holes in the once impenetrable Iron Curtain. Soviet entrepreneurs dangled as its carrot a one-way ticket out of Perestroika hell to the Promised Land, where supermarkets overflow with gristle-free comestibles and the men aren't stinking drunk on potato vodka from before noon until existential day's end.

Nakhoda (translation: "Godsend") is one such Moscow-based agency that sends photos and vital statistics of aspiring Amerikanskis to state-side businesses like Scanna, which supplies North American men with spiralbound booklets displaying the exotic merchandise. Page after xeroxed page, Kohl-smudged nubiles stare uncertainly and even grim-ly at hope of a "better life." The pathos is even more overwhelming than a trip to the pound. A number, placed below each woman's photo, identifies her pitch on the facing page.

#28-R5. Irina M. 27 yrs, 5' 7", 132 lbs, gray-blue eyes, from Lugansk, NM. Is sociable, intel, kind, elegant, romantic. Partial to keeping house, needlework, books, travel. Seeks humorous, affectionate, finan. secure, intel, manly WM, 30-35. Writes Russian, English.

#108-F5. Irina B. 21 yrs, 5' 11", 153 lbs, brown eyes, student, from Sverdlosk, never married. "I am not a bore. I easily get on with people. I like order, neatness. I am fond of cycling, travels. I am beautiful and have a good figure." Seeks WM, well educated, family oriented, fond of children, over 28. Writes English, Russian.

Scanna lures its assortment of eligible bachelors in the classified ads section of popular magazines. Unlike the other come-ons that read, "Meet beautiful Asian women" and "Dream-girl introductions," Scanna promotes its wares with a bit more understatement: "Scandinavia — Russia — Great Britain, etc.: Sincere individuals worldwide seek correspondence for friendship, romance, marriage. Scanna International (since 1980), P.O. Box 4, Pittsford, NY 14534. (800) 677-3170."

Danish emigré Marie Helbog began Scanna in 1980 by arranging Scandinavian-American matches, but its most fecund female resource is Russia and Eastern Europe. In little over a year, nearly 10,000 Russian matrimonial hopefuls have been ogled and judged by an estimated field of 2,500 men. According to Scanna employee Chris Ensor, the American subscribers evince demographic peculiarities. The highest demand for Russian women seems to come from Alaska ("The Siberian women are used to the cold"), Dallas ("Members complain about the plastic people down there; that they can't find a down-home kind of girl"), and Southern California ("I suppose it's easy to get lonely driving the freeways"). For a while, the deluge of Warsaw Pact applicants forced weekly production of a booklet containing 200 women. It's now slowed to a booklet every other week. Though the 40 page booklets sell for $4, Scanna makes its money by selling addresses at $10, or for the volume rate of $8 apiece if 10 or more are bought at one time. Scanna Vice President Mike Hansen says that men tend to "play the numbers game and get a lot of addresses at once." A "Circulation Service," which costs members $40, places a photograph and profile of the men in Russia so that women can write the men cold. "It gets a great response rate. The down side is you don't know who's writing to you."

"The Russian women thing makes sense to me," claims Air Captain Burden. "I can fly over there for free. Soon I'm going to spend a month over there [in Moscow]. Have all these gals come out at one time or another from where they're at. Vladivostok, wherever. I don't know who I'm going to like, if any of 'em. You have to meet 'em."

Do you type out every letter you write?

"Are you kidding? The word processor's the only way. There's no goddamn way you can write individual letters to 'em. I don't know how I got through college without one. There's no misspelled words; there's no misspelled punctuation, there's a thesaurus. You can be a whiz-kid and not even use your brain."

What do you write the girls?

"Oh, you know. Bullshit stuff. Lot of the letters I compose while I'm flying across the country, describe the Grand Canyon, thank her for her letter, ask her for more photographs. If I really like them I'll ask them to write once a week. Because the letters take so long. Some of these letters take a month. So, she sent you a letter, it takes a month; you answer that letter, it takes a month, you're talking about one letter every three months. The ones I really want to hear from I told them write a letter every couple a weeks. Even though you haven't heard from me, write a letter. So you're not always waiting for a letter every couple a months."

Another young girl, 23 maybe, divorced, with a child of four, writes:

> I like to look films, read books, knitting, outing, and make merry with my friends. Well, now about my country. My country incadense political passion. Hardly don't happen...

Ed interrupts: "She's talking about the coup."

> But all for the present fine. Out will neutralize
> with supreme effort. Shed a blood and this afraid-
> ed of myself. I close my letter with dictionary.

Does the fact she has a child phase you?

"Yeah. I mean, that doesn't bother me. As a matter of fact, that would probably be a safer bet than having a single gal come over here that has no kids, you know."

Safer? In what way?

"With no kids, she might be inclined to wander. It's possible. I wrote to the Russian gals just to see what they were thinking. I wrote them that a lot of women in the United States will marry a guy because he's got money and [she won't] necessarily be real sincere about devotion and love. And what do you think about this? You know, I mean, hey, I don't want to be hoodwinked by one of these gals when all she wants to do is get the hell out of her country. And I wanted to get some sort of response back from them what they thought about the reasons American guys are reluctant to get married. Because of the fact women a lot of times, especially if you're making pretty good bucks, their interest is getting married and, uh, you know, they're going to get a lot healthier, financially, when they get divorced in the deal."

Do you have girlfriends over here?

"There's a couple I go out with but I basically told them what I'm doing."

What do they say about it?

"They'll say, 'What's the matter with American girls?' They'll take a real defensive posture." Ed proffers a birthday card greeting from Russia. "A real pretty gal sent that one."

How many do you correspond with?

"I'm writing to six or seven right now."

Do you address the matter of sex in your correspondence?

"No. I'm not worried about that because I've talked to guys who've been over there and they said don't just take a couple of condoms, take a fucking box. They'll be fucking your brains out."

∞ ∞ ∞

There's the distinct smell of lubricated condom as David Greenspan (pseudonymous by request) opens the door to his Orange County townhouse. He excuses himself as he finishes buttoning up his pants.

Sorry if I interrupted....

"No problem," says the bird-like, middle-aged Jewish lawyer from Philadelphia, who now labors for a Korean law firm in Garden Grove. He motions me over to a sofa by a large built-in bookshelf where many of the books remain shrinkwrapped. Screams and shrieks of terror echo from an upstairs television. "Russian lady upstairs," grins Greenspan.

What makes you interested in Russian women?

"See, we spoil them in this country. They all are looking for their superman, so to speak. They see tv, they see Kevin Costner, they see the heroes there. They're quite demanding, and there's so many people it's easy come, easy go. If you are one of the few who have very wonderful endowments, you're okay. It's difficult in a sense that I'm past my prime. It gets harder and harder to compete and you have to put up with so much stuff. The thing about this country, even if they're Gravel Gerties they'll make demands."

But what piqued your interest in Russian women?

"Scanna. Which concentrated originally on Scandinavia. I had a penchant, a predilection for that type. I found that Scanna — I hate to talk this way about human beings, but you have to — the real good stuff that was Scandinavian wasn't going through Scanna. I saw some of the Eastern Europeans and that caught my eye. So they sent out the booklets and I found that of all the countries they were promoting the one I saw the best source from was Russia. As I said, the other countries weren't getting the prime material; whoever was applying would be no better than what you might get over here in some of the [Singles] magazines."

Had you been through the Singles scene over here?

"I hadn't met anybody that I had a relationship with. At most it might have been a second date. And there was just so much baggage with all that stuff. Aside from the fact that nine out of ten of them you don't recognize in person from the photographs. It was such an ordeal. You lose a better part of an evening if you meet somebody after work. But Scanna, I was flabbergasted. There was just no place I know where you see the kind of quality. But, there are dangers. Motivation is obvious. People there are under the crunch. Although I will say this: the correspondence I've had have all been high-quality. They write very intelligently. They seem to be serious-minded. It's none of this like in America where a woman tells you what she likes. She wants to travel all over the world. She wants to go out in a sailboat. She wants to know what kind of car you have. She wants to know if you like fine dining. You don't get any kind of that stuff [from the Russian women]."

What do you tell the women in your letters?

"I tell them out front. I'm an older guy, I'm not going to kid you. And you're much younger. And so I say I'm going to be honest with you. I say I've got something to trade. If she's a young, beautiful lady, I say I have something that might be of interest to you. Where I can provide, make your life comfortable. I'm still pretty active, I belong to the tennis club, I ski. I offer these things, I offer myself, and while I realize that this is not the storybook situation I'm presenting, I'm presenting something that might be of interest to you. I don't claim to be in my prime or my peak of movement, but I'm still active, I'm going strong, and it's up to you. The ones who responded said that's fine, I want to meet you. The lady upstairs ... of all the ladies I sent invitations to, she was the only one who got a visa. Every now and then one gets through. It's hard to say why."

Is she going to stay or go back?

"She's going back. [*Sotto voce:*] At this point I haven't met any of the others, so ..."

Do you like her?

"I like her, but, you know, when you have a choice, you want to know what you're choosing from. In other words you want to know what's available and hopefully you can make the best choice."

Is she still in the running?

"Yeah, but uh, it's ... uh, it's really up in the air. Any human being has to select whether it's the best the can get. You can't pick what's not available, so you have to know what's available."

What will fit your criteria of the best?

"First of all, I have to be attracted physically. I have to see that there's a genuine interest in me on the other side. There's an intangible factor in life that I like to call vibration that occurs whenever you're interacting. I would also look for someone that speaks better English than this girl, that would be a factor. Someone who's a little more advanced."

How do you know what the women will be like once they arrive?

"If life were guaranteed, there'd be no divorces. There's a degree of chance. If you're clicking with somebody, that doesn't mean you're clicking every day. Even the one that's here, she wanted to go back earlier. Then we got to clicking a little bit. After she leaves I'm going to go over there. The people I've corresponded with, the people I've narrowed it down to, I'm hoping they'll show up, or some percentage of them. [*Greenspan lowers his voice to a whisper.*] This one, I'm very happy with this one. There's a problem because I go to work, and what does she do? Nothing. That's the problem. Now if I had an American girl, let's say from Florida, she'd be taking one of my cars. I don't know if it'd come back in a hundred percent condition. She might take off for a weekend. That's the kind of stuff you get with the American stuff. You get a little note: 'I had to go to Las Vegas, meet somebody there. Back Monday.' With my car and whatever. I get a feeling with these [Russian] people. You can trust 'em as far as any valuables. Most of them don't drive, which is nice, in a sense you don't have to worry about them commandeering anything. They're at home. The motivations are even worse for American girls because they're spoiled. I've had particularly bad experiences with American girls. I noticed a lot of the women had emotional problems. Their lives haven't turned out like they'd like them to. They've been living in a Pollyannish dream world, which is not reality. They take to drinking and don't have the kind of devotion that's necessary."

Why is that?

"I think expectations are too high. This is a country closer to mass media and so on. Everybody wants the cream. In other words, 90% is after 10%, there's obviously going to be a lot of disappointed people. And you see this whenever you go to parties or you go to clubs. There'll be a small percentage that will be fraternizing and assimilating and so forth, and the rest seem to stalk and reconnoiter and basically they go home without the bacon, so to speak. That's true for the Singles world. The Singles world, you're talking about a small percentage of success. What happens to the other 80%? They're left in a lurch. Now I may be in that 80% because I'm past my prime."

What do you mean, prime?

"Well, prime I'm talking about thirty, where you've got the most to offer in the way of health, life, future."

An immigration attorney I spoke to claims that Russian women are chaste, not prone to having sex before marriage.

"Using this one example [*Greenspan points upstairs*], I wouldn't say there's any problem. But when I was over there six or seven years ago, I was shocked how clean the country was. I didn't even see *Playboy*. Here was a country that denigrated religion and yet was more religious in the moral way than a lot of the religious countries. Because very frankly I had a couple *Playboys* that were confiscated. There's no discos. People go to sleep around 10:30 and there's just a few restaurants. Communism was not licentious. And I've studied communism. I've studied Karl Marx."

When are you going to Russia?

"January 12."

Does the girl know?

"No. Why tell her? This was something I felt was the only way for me to proceed at this point. I made contact with a certain amount, a couple dozen, and they couldn't get visas. In the meantime even a couple got married. There was one who was a real cutie, maybe she was too young for me, anyway."

Too young?

"Well, I'm not going to grieve over anyone who's 21 or 19. Although if you look at the contestants from Miss America, I don't think anyone's thinking they're too young. Like Justice Potter said about obscenity, you know it when you see it type of thing. I don't like the heavy-set side, I'll be honest with you. I've got a penchant for someone on the svelte side, but that's all got to go with the gestalt. Wherever my gestalt takes me that's where my gestalt's gonna be. If something in the abstract's gonna govern the realities, I'd be a fool. The reality will be that I will say to myself, I want this, I want her, or whatever. Which is like if you're shopping for a car or whatever, something will just hit you and you say, I want that.

"This could be the gold rush of social, let's say, intercourse. I'm really impressed myself. I'm laying the groundwork. Correspondence. So I got a little something going. So I'll hopefully make my choice. I don't want to put this in an Old World sense, like the King gets his pick. There's a certain kind of admiration for the guy who looks over a group and then can make his choice. It's something like a dream; in a way it's a dream of mine."

"Hey!" Greenspan ejaculates. "Do you want to meet her?"

Sure.

He bounds up the carpeted stairs, making loud pidgin English sounds: "SAY HELLO! SAY HELLO! FRIEND DOWNSTAIRS HELLO!" Bashful young thing peeks out behind a pillar. "SAY HELLO FRIEND!"

"Ha-Lo," the girl squeaks, embarrassed.

"HELLO FRIEND! HE FRIEND, SEE! SAY HELLO FRIEND!"
Greenspan turns toward me, shrugs. "She don't know too good
English."

∞ ∞ ∞

Letters are one thing; getting the men within kissing distance of the
women is another. Kearny Mesa immigration attorney Larry Holmes
points out the difficulty of getting the women over to the U.S. on a
travelers visa. "Only about one out of 20 can get over that way. It's a
real crapshoot." The only real alternative is to travel to Russia, meet
the girls there, make your choice and file for a fiancee visa. Holmes
says that it usually requires four months to get the fiancee visa
processed, and much longer for less competent attorneys.

"When they come over here on the fiancee visas, they got 90 days to
stay here and get married, or go back," explains Holmes, a compact,
conservatively dressed middle-aged gentlemen with Vietnam War
decorations and signed letter from "business hero" Ray Kroc on the
wall. "They have 90 days to get married, then they have to file
Adjustment Status, and then they have the interview some time after
that. It can be two months, or can be as long as 13 months, after fil-
ing. The INS doesn't consider that a real priority. The girl's here,
she's married, she's got work authorization, what's the rush? But the
thing is, that interview starts the clock when she can become permanent, which means if she gets divorced the next day she can still stay
here forever. Some will wait until they file a form 751 and the next
day, psssht!, she's gone. But will that happen? The men, they're pretty decent guys. They're not going to be alcoholics. Over there, it's
unbelievable."

Holmes' Russian bride business has really taken off the past year, handling referrals from Scanna International and American Russian
Matchmaking, a Studio City-based company that arranges tours to
the Motherland, where American men are set upon by hordes of desperate females at banquets and parties.

"Sometimes a guy will go to that first meeting [in Russia] and it goes
to his head. He thinks he's a rock star. Usually, he's the guy who's got
dates with three or four girls an afternoon and ends up with nobody.

Surprisingly, these girls don't automatically say 'yes, I'll marry you,' so they can come to the United States. They got to have something going. Some of the guys are surprised. They say, 'I thought they'd marry anybody.' Not necessarily. The Soviet women admire Americans because they smile easily. You and I wouldn't smile easily if we had to live over there. There are certain mannerisms the men have over there, that in the United States would be considered totally gross. The sidewalks are all covered with beetle juice, because they don't have dentists and when they get cavities they get this beetle juice as an anaesthetic, and they spit, it's gross. All over the place. Things like that the women over there don't like. The women over there are fantastic, they really are.

"I've raised a son by myself and now he's finally in college, and so I was going to be a free man and start a social life. On the way over to Russia, the guys were asking me, 'Are you looking for ... ' 'No,' I said, strictly business.' The first meeting I got to, Ron [Rollban, president of American-Russian Matchmaking] introduced me as the immigration attorney in case any girls wanted to ask any questions. There was about 75 women there. I panned from right to left with my mouth hanging open. The women were all so beautiful. I just couldn't believe it. And way in the corner there's a girl, she looks just like Brooke Shields, eyes about this big, she just smiled, and I smiled. She said, 'Are you tired?,' and that caught me off-guard. I said, pardon me? And she said, in English, 'Are you very tired?' And I invited her to dinner, and we've been together ever since. And you know, the thing is, she was born the same day, the same year, that Brooke Shields was."

"Ron [Rollban of American Russian Matchmaking] — he was the Hugh Hefner of the industry, and even he's getting married. He said to me, 'if I ever get married, take out a gun and shoot me.' He's fallen, too."

∞ ∞ ∞

The fallen 56-year-old Ron Rollban is one of those energetic entrepreneurs who seems to enjoy selling you something. The gist of his matchmaking pitch is this: "If a guy finds a wife through me there are three things I guarantee him. She's going to be younger, she's going to be prettier, and she's going to be far better educated than her Western counterpart."

The Studio City-based tour business avoids what Rollban perceives to be an endemic problem with some of Scanna's clientele. "There are people out there who go through their whole life ordering pictures and not doing anything about it. They're photo junkies." American Russian Matchmaking pares down the photo fetishism by providing a limit on photos and addresses, which are used primarily to whet members' appetite for regularly scheduled trips to Moscow.

"On my last trip there were some very nice guys and there's some playboys. Before the trip was over, every one of my playboys was engaged. And the nice· guys turned into playboys. What happens when we go over there, we assign each guy an interpreter. These interpreters are our personal secretaries, they make sure where we're supposed to be at all times. They're our brain and tongue; we can't communicate without them. They're like our mothers — they see we get to bed regularly. They're our confidant — we exchange information about the girls and get their opinion. They're our friend — because they spend all day with us. So it happened that my son, Rourke, was appointed an interpreter. After the first three or four

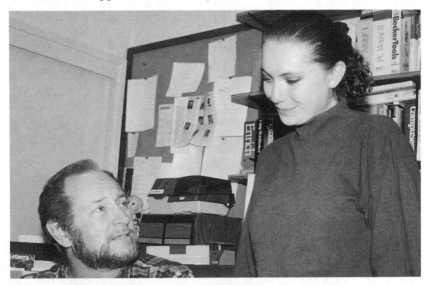

Ron Rollban of American-Russian Matchmaking, and foreign help.

days, he was meeting with all these women who had written him. After four days my son decided which lady he was most interested in. The interpreter."

Every man who signs up on a tour with American Russian Matchmaking is obliged to sign a contract stipulating a $3,000.00 payment to Rollban "after client has found a suitable mate and married them." The three grand lump sum does not include tour, attorney and correspondence expenses. The ARM kit to new members explains the high cost: "We realize three thousand dollars is a substantial sum but when you put it up against what you spend for a car and accept the limited utility and pleasure you receive for so many thousands more, a lifetime mate seems a bargain by comparison."

In a flurry of activity — barking orders to his Russian-born secretary, taking phone calls — Rollban parks me on a sofa to watch a video of all his television clips. There's a *To Tell The Truth* (only the prehistoric Kitty Carlisle guesses Rollban's identity), and excerpts from *Entertainment Tonight, Geraldo* and *Prime Time Live*.

The *Prime Time Live* segment tapes Rollban's Moscow banquets, where a flotilla of tarted-up females surround painfully ordinary American bachelors like starry-eyed groupies. Like David Greenspan put it, "it's a gold rush of social, let's say, intercourse." I ask Rollban about the response from radio talk shows, if he's run into any trouble.

"Trouble would be the wrong word. Flap would be a better one. People get the idea after talking with me that I may be too worthy of an adversary for them. If we start getting caustic with one another, I'm going to cut their heads off. Instead of attacking me, they attack my clients, saying, 'What type of person would go for a woman in Russian as opposed to one here if he wasn't a loser?' Yeah, right. Some of my losers are judges, doctors, owners of major corporations, heads of state ..."

Heads of state?

"Well, when I say heads of state, well, I got political people, which would be heads of state, and military, high-ranking military."

What do you hear from American women?

"On every show I've appeared on, I get attacked. I did a radio interview, and this woman calls in and says, 'Mr. Rollban, have you heard the expression of a communist under every bed?' And I said yeah. And she said, 'Now you're trying to put them in the bed. Does the FBI know about you? You should be arrested!' No one has come right out and said I'm peddling women because there are too many dating services to do that."

Never been accused of being a procurer?

"One guy said with a joking lilt in his voice, 'Ron, you're kind of like a pimp, aren't ya?' My whole line was, all my life I've strived for some degree of success so one day my father could point to me with pride and say, 'there goes my son, the pimp.' Of course I'm only a Russian pimp, a specialist."

With an "aha!", Rollban discovers a video taken from the previous Moscow excursion with footage of his fiancee, Lydia. He fast-forwards through an parade of would-be emigrants reciting their vital statistics to the camera. Suddenly a girl appears — big eyes, bee-stung lips. The enraptured old bachelor switches to extreme slo-mo in order to take in his young blonde dish one frame at a time. "Look at that face! Look at that face! If you looked up pig heaven in the encyclopedia, this would be it! Look at her mouth! She seems astonished at the world! I like to watch her when she turns and her hair whips out! Like that!"

The May/December man switches off the video after blonde Lydia sashays out of view, sitting in thoughtful silence for a moment or two.

"I have been very fortunate in my lifetime where women are concerned. More so than any five men have a right to be. Two trips ago one of the questions that was raised from the floor was, was I married? I said no. And she asked why not. And I said the day that I marry the two stupidest people on the face of the earth will have surfaced. And she says, what does that mean? And I said, when I have all this available, I could go out with you and you and you. So I said if I marry out of this, I'd have to be the stupidest person on the face of the earth. And the second stupidest would have to be the one who would marry me, because there is no woman who could handle this kind of competition. The temptations are out of this world. I won't go into the kind of propositions they've made to me, but they're multitudinous, and man, pretty tempting. Then I meet this little blonde and she torpedoes me with six direct hits. I sunk immediately. She's a doctor at 22. She's got the warmest personality you will ever encounter. Like she fell off a Christmas card. You say, why is she going to marry this fat old guy? It doesn't make any sense. So I have to admit I'm marrying her in anticipation of losing her. Why would I want to heap that kind of misery on myself? Because obviously this is going to be better than a puppy."

Now that you're betrothed to this woman, are you rescinding your playboy ways?

"I will do a little boasting here. I'll tell you that I've had the unusual. A female chief of police, the head of a major motion picture studio, a *Playboy* centerfold, two from *Playboy* pictorials, models, actresses, well-known actresses, doctors, lawyers. I've had the best, I've had the rest, and I'm old enough and experienced enough to know better. And then this little thing comes walking through my life and I'm doomed."

There's a big age difference ...

"33 years ... I've been with lots of women, none with 33 years difference with any serious intentions. I got a lot of flack with 15 - 20 years difference, but everyone is accepting the 33 years difference. Why? I don't know."

No conflicts?

"She spent the night the second night she was with me. She was very nervous. She's inexperienced. Grossly inexperienced. And she got up out of bed and went into the kitchen and sat there crying. I tried to find out what was wrong and she tells me she shouldn't be with me. She says astrologically, it was wrong. I said, I'm going to tell you this right now, if you think that I'm going to let astrology govern any aspect of my life, you're wrong. I make things happen, not the stars. And if that's what you believe, there's no relationship here. And she said, I think I should go home. I realized what hour it was and I wasn't about to put her on the streets at that hour of the night. We shared the bed that night. By morning things had not changed. And she said at 8:30, standing in the doorway, 'I not see you today?' I said no. Well, we got a double negative there, and about that time my interpreter walks in, and I ask her to tell Lydia that I will do everything in my power to find her the right husband. But she's not for me. I'm not for her. I will not be seeing her again. After Lydia was told this, she looked back at me and said okay, and it seemed emotionless to me. Maybe slightly pained, but that was the extent of it.

"Everybody was trying to get me to go back to her. I kept saying no. That night I lined up this blonde — you'd kill for this blonde. Great face, great body, fabulous boobs. She's in my apartment. And I had no interest in doing anything with that broad, I just wanted to hear from Lydia. My interpreter said she talked with her sister, who said Lydia had been there all day crying and she wanted to come back and beg me to take her back. It hurt me to think I caused her so much pain. Ordinarily I'm not quite this sensitive to other people but in her case I am.

"When I got back here I told my son I got engaged. He couldn't believe a die-hard bachelor, particularly with the [*coughs*] resources I have. I said, I'm going to show you a video, and you pick her out. I said you'll probably guess wrong, but you'll be dazzled when you see her. So he watches the comings and goings of all these women and he picks three, but she isn't one of them. When she did appear, he says, 'See, that's what I'm looking for. She's perfect.' He couldn't believe she was the one. He couldn't believe she would have said yes to me.

"Let me read you a letter Lydia sent me:

> Ron, how you've grown in my esteem, when I'd
> heard from you words of defense in my regard.

"With respect to that — Russian culture is much different than ours. There's a respect for age and authority. But I told Lydia I'm not seeking parental authority as far as she's concerned. I'm older than her parents! They should seek my approval more than anything else. When I called her one night, she couldn't talk to me because she said that any feelings of warmth for me would be laced by her father's epitaphs. I told the father through Lydia that he'd better watch his ass, that he should accord me respect because I was American, and if I had a wife, he'd have to give her the same respect. And she, Lydia, was going to be my wife, and so he better get accustomed to according her that kind of respect now. Otherwise, he's going to have to deal with me. So she said:

> In my life there were not a few men who aspired to the right of becoming my husband. Some of them were not bad at all, but I was never sure of the strength of their character and the ability to contradict my father. To stand up with me and take my side. But no, that was almost beyond their strength. They babbled before my father like stupid birds, and I gazed on each of them with slight loathing, and gradually understood that their simple compliance makes it impossible for any feeling on my part. Whereas you, you are simply the fulfillment of a dream into reality. Next to you, I'm not afraid of anything. Only near you do I feel perfectly at peace and see the beauty of life. Your words subside my fears and at the same time fill my being with energy and spiritual calm. How grateful I am for your words of respect and support. Such sincere, trustworthy solidarity is a rare quality, and is of incredible value in a person, and you possess it. I don't want to seem to make promises, but believe me, I will always abide by the point of view we will agree together on ...."

When is she coming over?

"Not 'til June."

Why so long?

"She has to finish school. Junior High. No, just kidding."

∞ ∞ ∞

51

"You should have seen this Russian gal's eyes when I took her into the Price Club," recalls Ed Burden. "Wide as saucers." Attorney Larry Holmes recounts an oft-told anecdote about newly arrived Russian women, how when visiting American stores, will throw everything they can grab into the shopping cart without regard to necessity, size, or price. "It's not that they're greedy. By reflex, the gal was hoarding because she thought the stuff wouldn't have been there even a few minutes later."

Though just a few marriages have been arranged so far; dozens more are underway. Ron Rollban is seriously considering producing late-night television infomercials, complete with 900 numbers. There's no telling how well the intercultural promiscuity will pan out. Holmes, a born-again Christian, believes Russian women will be less prone to divorce than their American counterparts. "They've been through a heck of a lot. They'll be grateful for what they have over here."

"The gorgeous women over here wouldn't give me a shot. Not so in Russia. I'm anxious to get over there and get it signed, sealed, delivered before it comes too well known," worries David Greenspan. "Maybe I shouldn't be talking to you. When there's a buyers market, you're not too anxious to get a lot of competition for the goods."

THE DEVIL AND ANDREA DWORKIN

[The initial version of my critique of separationist feminism, as epitomized by Andrea Dworkin's *Intercourse,* first appeared in the December 1990 edition of *Penthouse Forum;* a raunchier version found its way into the 4th issue of *ANSWER Me!* magazine in its maligned and misunderstood "Rape" issue. At base, my critique pays homage to a stimulating mind and fascinating writer. My uninformed equation of feminism with Dworkin's hysterical propaganda seems at this time a lazy, misogynist assumption for which I apologize. Many feminists, including Susie Bright and Rene Denfeld, have indeed spoken out against Dworkin's unreasoning fury.]

With a straight face and hysterical tone, Andrea Dworkin argues that heterosexual sex is the equivalent of rape. Pornography is considered something akin to the White Slave Trade, a Victorian-era concern that white women had become a prize commodity in foreign slave auctions or houses of prostitution. Their destiny, if escape remained impossible, was a life of prostitution and drudgery for the pleasure of muslim despots. White Slavery has been updated by the pornographic trade, where decent white women are lured into a life of objectification fulfilling male sex fantasies. Dworkin's rabid anti-pornographic stance is quite similar to a conservative agenda, so it was not at all surprising that Dworkin was quoted in Edwin Meese's inquisition on pornography, and supported Catharine MacKinnon's mission to prohibit pornography. Ironically, the first target of the Canadian law was a Vancouver alternative bookstore, whose titles by sado-maso lesbian Pat Califa, the lesbian comic *Hothead Paisan* and even (briefly) a couple books by Andrea Dworkin, were seized by customs.

Dworkin's novel *Mercy* no doubt aroused the curiosity of Canadian customs, for it remains the hardest porn that I have ever been exposed to. The pro-victim contextualization is supposed to rationalize every-

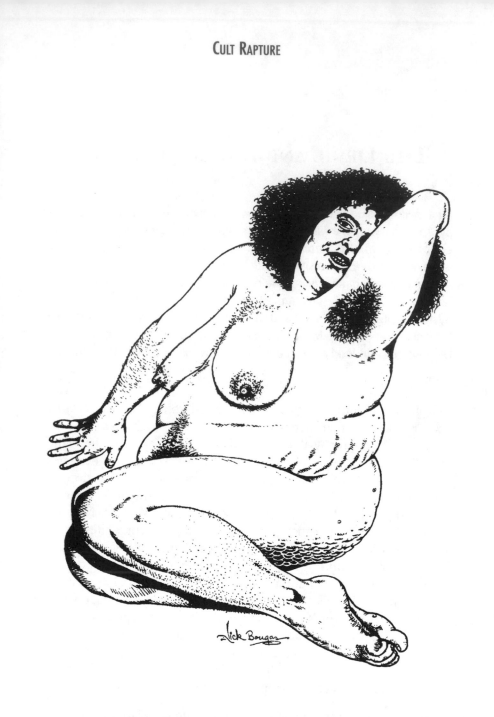

(Illustration by Nick Bougas)

thing. Peter Sotos, an unabashed fan of extreme violence profiled in *Apocalypse Culture,* told me that he seeks out Dworkin's literature, finding her among the most titillating literateurs in existence. Erica Jong has stated in print that her fondest wish is for Dworkin to confess her debt to De Sade.

In 1991 Feral House published an ersatz 1950s-style men's magazine entitled *Cad: A Handbook for Heels.* The book promised "The Forgotten Lore of the Red-Blooded American Male," reviving such outdated conceits as girl-watching, cigar-smoking, cocktail drinking, two-fisted tales, and photospreads of scantily clad beatnik chicks. CAD was nothing more than an exercise in cultural anthropology, but prohibitionary anti-porn feminists successfully demanded withdrawal of the book from the shelves of several college bookstores. The prohibition took place the same week displays for "banned book week" were displayed at these institutions for higher learning.

∞ ∞ ∞

You've seen the section in bookstores — Women's Studies, a jumble of lesbian propaganda disguised as clinical research into straight sex lives; the "blessed-be's" and hairy-legged tracts of so-called "white witches"; cunt coloring books; coy celebrations of menstruation and other uterine mysteries; spurious archaeology fabricating a golden, peaceful age of matriarchy; and, most entertainingly, violent screeds calling for male gendercide. Very few males blunder into this "pedagogy of the oppressed," fewer still actually ingest the suffocatingly righteous blithering.

Not that they're invited to. Women's Studies are by women for women, a gender exclusive club appropriating the wardrobe of third world rhetoric. This is the language of the victim, a screeching vocabulary of complaint and revolt against the despotic tyranny of men. Male despots are not welcome to enter into dialogue with the Women's Studies club unless they check their testosterone at the door, guiltily accept the "bad guy" rap, and cluck their tongues against the miscreants of their own gender who stubbornly deny female moral superiority. These de-juiced specimens can be viewed to best advantage in college towns, their concave chests cuddling the bastard offspring of Birkenstock-shod mates who are busy passing out petitions for the removal of *Penthouse* from convenience stores.

During my own college days, misspent in a feminist stronghold 90 miles south of San Francisco, I observed backsliding impulses among even the staunchest "sisters," a yearning, one might even say craving, for men who weren't (I often heard them use this word) wimps. Gloria Steinem would go ashen at the sight of this river of liberal arts cooze virtually throwing themselves at males who hadn't succumbed to the program and were thus capable of ardor in their fucking, men who were (by feminist definition) pigs. In fact, the weak-willed males, hang-dog looking with scraggly beards and wire-rimmed glasses, so sympathetic to the feminist struggle, received the major share of female contempt. They were tolerated as toadies and taken to bed as cut-rate dildos.

A dozen years have passed since those disheartening days spent under the specter of stentorian vaginas and pipsqueak penises. Since then, there seems to have been a gradual return to male and female archetypes, to scenarios of mystery and seduction. Of the former feminists, the more attractive of them got down to the business of finding and keeping a mate, while, in most cases, the less attractive grew more sophisticated and militant in their man-hatred. Do not presume, amidst these generalities, the disappearance of victimized rhetoric from the lipglossed mouths of erstwhile suffragettes. That would be asking too much. A feminist litany remains ever at hand to badger and browbeat husbands and boyfriends into sheepish admission of egregious maleness.

The browbeaters are what I term the Integrationist Feminists, those who like their cock on call. The Segregationist Feminists are harridans who don't like cock at all.

Pachyderm-like Andrea Dworkin may be the uncrowned queen of Segregationist Feminism in its present incarnation. Her book *Intercourse* has become the touchstone of contemporary feminist theory. Part literary criticism, part propaganda, and all elegant hysteria, *Intercourse* was written to further a simple program: to intellectually convince women to avoid the admittance of the male generative organ into connective friction with the vagina. And that's not all, fellas. Don't touch, but for God's sake, don't look either. *Pornography,* Dworkin's earlier tract, advanced her conviction that hardcore pornography and softcore men's magazines together fuel homicidal violence against women. And for all her leftist caterwauling, Dworkin's authoring of anti-pornography legislation with comrade Catharine MacKinnon has earned her ovations on the dais with the likes of Edwin Meese and Phyllis Schafly.

Don't make the mistake of confusing Dworkin's underdog vocabulary with empathy for anyone but her own kind. In *Intercourse,* Dworkin bases her equation of racism with heterosexual sex on the work of James Baldwin, a black homosexual. (The phallic braggarts of the Black Panther school she must, of course, pass by without so much as a word.) This is the same Dworkin who spells America with a "K" throughout her books, masking her own tyrannical will to prohibit other peoples' happiness with the argot of the oppressed. She descends to calling vital males "National Socialists," and the women who love them, "collaborators." "That collaboration," she rants in *Intercourse,* "fully manifested when a woman values her lover, the National Socialist, above any woman, anyone of her own kind or class or status, may have simple beginnings: the first act of complicity that destroys self-respect, the capacity for self-determination and freedom — readying the body for the fuck instead of for freedom." In other words, Dworkin denies the bond of the male-female relationship, taunting women as Nazi collaborators who value their boyfriend or husband "above any woman." What Dworkin wants is an inversion of loyalty, for women to run to the call of Sappho and Sisterhood and to tar and feather their male oppressors...

It is clear that the abolition of pornography will not suffice as the end goal of Ms. Dworkin's program. What will it take to calm Andrea Dworkin, to quell her tirades, to fill the yawning chasm of her sense of injustice?

Men, flop your tube steaks on the chopping blocks. Dworkin wants your cocks for mulch. Fucking, dilates Dworkin, annihilates the woman, overwhelming her with a sense of possession that ultimately leads to degradation and death. (That is, she allows, when the sex is good.) "That loss of self," writes Dworkin in the chapter entitled "Possession," "is a physical reality, not just a psychic vampirism; and as a physical reality it is chilling and extreme, a literal erosion of the body's integrity and its ability to function and survive... This sexual possession is a sensual state of being that borders on antibeing until it ends in death. The body dies, or the lover discards the body when it is used up, throws away an old, useless thing, emptied, like an empty bottle. The body is used up; and the will is raped."

Intercourse invokes the propaganda technique popularized by Julius Streicher. The enemy is portrayed as a vampire that is at once morally subhuman and yet preternaturally powerful and dangerous. Dworkin's full-tilt fictions are not some private exorcism of grief and rage, but rather a bellows to fan the flames of righteous hysteria in order to seize, ban, burn and extirpate. Because she plays the role of violated victim, Dworkin is given license to practice what she assails in the penised people, that is, unleash sadistic vengeance on an entire gender and sexual preference.

Remember that Dworkin contributed to the Meese Commission's inquest on pornography, and helped Catharine MacKinnon to enact Canada's Tariff Code 9956, to ban the importation and sale of all material "which depict or describe sexual acts that appear to degrade or dehumanize..." This incredibly broad and subjective code could be interpreted in such a way as to proscribe most books published, including the bible and Dworkin's own screeds. (A Canadian customs agent seized a shipment of one of Dworkin's books for several hours, and quickly released them, apologizing for the "mistake.") In practice, Tariff Code 9956 anally penetrates publishers too penurious to initiate costly lawsuits, and pro-sex lesbian bookshops that make a living selling the now-banned works of Pat Califa and Susie Bright.

According to the blurbs of praise that fill *Intercourse's* book jacket: "... Dworkin analyzes the institution [!] of sexual intercourse, and how that institution, as defined and controlled by patriarchy, has proven to be a devastating enslavement of women" (Robin Morgan); "Dworkin's prose is elegant, her passion for truth profound, her longing for justice both lyrical and unrelenting, her use of history and literature stunning, her understanding of racism, anti-Semitism and misogyny lucid, palpable" (Phyllis Chesler); "The book is outstanding, original, and an act of forbidden rebellion" (Shere Hite).

Shere Hite, perpetrator of *The Hite Report* on male and female sexuality, is described by Dworkin in *Intercourse* as "the strongest feminist and most honorable philosopher among sex researchers..." Dworkin is of course grateful for Hite's statistics which claim that only three women in ten attain orgasm during intercourse. Dworkin brandishes this statistic to underscore the uselessness of cock for women's pleasure. Later, she again quotes Hite's suggestion for heterosexual sex in which "thrusting would not be considered ... necessary... [There might be] more a mutual lying together in pleasure ... vagina-covering-penis, with female orgasm providing much of the stimulation necessary for male orgasm."

Hite's prescription for thrust-free, "mutual lying together," "vagina-covering-penis" sex demands complete passivity from the male. As Hite suggests in bold type in a late chapter of the *Hite Report* on women, "Intercourse can become androgynous." No thrusting and exploring for Hite's males, no sir, this is woman's eminent domain. A man is to lay on his back, hold his breath, and stay perfectly still until the woman has squirmed her way to a come atop a stationary and never threatening-to-be-dominant ding-dong. This is the only mention of a male-female sex-procedure that Dworkin even mildly approves of throughout the entire length of *Intercourse*. One must assume that Dworkin sanctions this ridiculous posture only as an interim measure designed to wean women of their desire for cock entirely.

One wonders, however, what porn-thwacking Dworkin must think of the nude, cunt-splayed photos taken in 1968 of the massive-muffed and Tampax-stringed Hite that were eventually displayed in *Hustler's* April, 1977 issue. Or what Dworkin had to say to Germaine Greer for her toes-to-the-ceiling, cunt-to-the-camera shenanigans in the Amsterdam sex paper, *Suck,* in the mid-'70s.

I suppose Dworkin was not about to split cunt-hairs over the issue, especially with ideological comrades. All this taken into account, how are we to take Germaine Greer's blurb on *Intercourse's* front cover:

"The most shocking book any feminist has yet written." Shocking in what sense? In the quality of its fantasy, its idiocy, or its hatred?

At the risk of contradicting Ms. Greer, the most extreme feminist tract has got to be Valerie Solanas's *S.C.U.M. Manifesto*, the manifesto of the Society for Cutting Up Men. Solanas, who shot and almost killed Andy Warhol in the late '60s, pleads for women to "destroy the male sex." Norman Mailer, who quotes from the manifesto in his meditation on feminist writing, *The Prisoner of Sex*, provides insight into why the *S.C.U.M. Manifesto* was reprinted in the popular feminist anthology, *Sisterhood is Powerful:* "... the *S.C.U.M. Manifesto*, while extreme, even extreme of the extreme, is nonetheless a magnetic north for Women's Lib." Though Dworkin neglects to list the S.C.U.M. in her extensive bibliography at the end of *Intercourse*, the spirit of Solanas's mandate is ever-present.

> Just as humans have a prior right to existence over dogs by virtue of being more highly evolved and having a superior consciousness, so women have a prior right to existence over men. The elimination of any male is, therefore, a righteous and good act, an act highly beneficial to women as well as an act of mercy. (The *S.C.U.M. Manifesto*, p. 67.)

Magnetic north of the women's movement? Consider the Bobbitt case, in which Lorena's psychotic episode was elevated to an heroic call to action by various feminist groups; consider that bootleg pamphlets of the *S.C.U.M. Manifesto* have been circulating in women's bookstores for more than twenty years. Dworkin doesn't have Solanas's humor or her damningly explicit methodology of attaining an anti-male utopia, but she possesses the ingenuity of a modern major-general. She knows how to employ all the weapons of a propaganda war; how to incite, persuade and most of all, bully.

Although Dworkin resembles the steatopygous Earth Mother, she doesn't pay much attention to the technology=patriarchy arguments of Wiccan feminism. For Dworkin, technology will provide the way out of heterosexuality and intercourse:

It is not that there is no way out if, for instance, one were to establish or believe that intercourse itself determines women's lower status. New reproductive technologies have changed and will continue to change the nature of the world. Intercourse is not necessary to existence anymore. Existence does not depend on female compliance, nor on the violation of female boundaries, nor on lesser female privacy, nor on the physical occupation of the female body. Intercourse is the pure, sterile, formal expression of men's contempt for women; but that contempt can turn gothic and express itself in many sexual and sadistic practices that eschew intercourse per se. Any violation of a woman's body can become sex for men; this is the essential truth of pornography.

It is indeed strange for the morbidly obese, pus-ugly Andrea Dworkin to localize sexual intercourse as man's greatest expression of contempt for women. If forced at gunpoint to fuck Andrea Dworkin my "contempt" for her would not reveal itself in a robust erection; to the contrary, my shrivel dick would require the services of a geek-like proxy, such as those seen servicing the glandular atrocities in the *Life in the Fat Lane* porn video series.

In one of those weird twists of fate, Dworkin's real life "platonic" live-in mate, John Stoltenberg, is rumored to be a biological male. Stoltenberg is infamous in New York City's publishing community as Dworkin's rabid lapdog, conveying threats and intimidation to those who do not indulge the whims of his tyrannical mentor. Dworkin's big-footed imprint is seen all over Stoltenberg's unintentionally hilarious books, *Refusing to be a Man* and *The End of Manhood*, which rather vainly inveigh against such biological verities as male genitalia and testosterone. Stoltenberg is the embodiment of Valerie Solanas's "Men's Auxiliary": "SCUM will conduct Turd Sessions, at which every male present will give a speech beginning with the sentence: 'I am a turd, a lowly, abject turd,' then proceed to list all the ways in which he is."

Perhaps it is unfair to lump Dworkin in the feminist category, for her turgid hysteria has more in common with Carry Nation or the Marquis DeSade than Susan B. Anthony. Nowhere in Dworkin's writings or public appearances does she argue for the accumulation of rights or opportunities. That would be too dull for her. Recently I enjoyed the opportunity of seeing Dworkin lecture at Portland State University, where she recounted atrocity stories, cried, and flapped her arms, screaming for vengeance. But the shrill passion didn't succeed in whipping up inquisitional hysteria in the pampered and comfortable middle-class femme contingent, probably for many of the same reasons why the JDL hasn't yet convinced Beverly Hills yentas to assassinate Holocaust Revisionists. Only a small portion of Dworkin's audience later participated in a march to a local jerk-off arcade, where a handful of bull dykes startled the raincoat rats with unlady-like epithets. Too bad Andrea was too circumspect to take the axe to the peep booths.

Those who most treasure Dworkin's hysteria aren't mainstream feminists but prohibitionist paper-pushers and the fundamentalist right. I've envisioned a scene fit for a Jodorowsky movie in which Richard Viguerie and Jesse Helms go down on Dworkin and MacKinnon on a bed of severed penises.

In the end, it is understandable for Andrea Dworkin to wield the cudgel of victim politics against men. In our "rape culture," women like Dworkin aren't worthy of the trivialization accorded sex objects. They are rejected utterly. This rejection has obviously left its mark on Andrea Dworkin; it has honed a vengeful and crusading intelligence bent on evening the score. Let us not weaken and pity the Gorgon; the figleaf of victimization is creating victims of us all.

THE GIRLFRIEND WHO LAST SAW
ELVIS ALIVE FAN CLUB

[The following article, which appeared in the *San Diego Reader,* ostensibly contains insights on the sociological bizarrarie of fandom. A little hindsight has filled me with shame over the article's laconic sadism. Little did I realize that the vicarious pleasures of fandom exist so that its practitioners can face impossibly bleak lives. Less-than-perfect existences are compensated for by fandom's insistence that perfection exists in human form. While the rest of us feel superior for trading in the pubescent stasis of fandom for an adult reality of compromise and disappointment, some people understand that they need reality like a kick in the teeth. While prisoners employ fantasy to kill time before they integrate themselves into the reality of the world "outside," nasty configurations of chromosomes are the same as life sentences for the ugly and socially inept. Why begrudge, even make fun of, the only escape route open to the genetically deprived?

Although I fully admit my culpability in the following article's sneering condescension, I offer it here uncut as an object lesson to unfeeling sadists. Those who laugh *with* the article, who share in my joy at clubbing easy targets, should consider themselves implicated in the crime of *schadenfreude.* Practiced by all self-proclaimed *übermenschen,* joy at other people's expense is the necessary first step in dehumanizing the "other," the psychological precondition for genocide.]

> G is for generous always giving of herself.
> I is for ideal, she's more perfect than anyone else.
> N is for newcomer, but a STAR she will be.
> G is for generous, her generous way to you and
>   me.
> E is for everlasting, our friendship will never end.
> R is for richness, now that she's my friend.
> — Jimmy Cooper, from the *Ginger "Lady
> Superstar" Alden Fan Club Newsletter*

S he loves him tender, she loves him true. But perhaps she did not love him true enough. Her considerable chest is heaving: maybe if Debby Wimer had been more devoted to Elvis before he — permit me to be blunt — expired, perhaps things would have turned out differently.

Bearing the entire weight of Elvis' demise on her defeated shoulders has been no easy task. You hear it in her voice: Debby has been second-guessing herself ever since the fateful day. I try to comfort her. Elvis, I tell her, was reclusive and, some say, stubborn. Even the tireless efforts of the purest-hearted fan couldn't have changed him. She sighs, nods, more nervous than moved. Guilt balls up in Debby's chest, then sloshes up and stings her throat with an acidic burp. Although she is deeply religious, Debby allows that when she heard that Elvis passed on, and the earth continued to revolve as usual, she began to doubt God's plan. Why hadn't she heard the horn of Jericho? Why hadn't the walls come tumbling down?

Life did not come to an end on August 16, 1977 … it just became more collectible.

The Rapture deferred, even Elvis' most sorrowful fan must seek contentment in life's little pleasures. Like eating. Not to say that Debby has a weight problem — a lot of men prefer gals with some meat on their bones, a truism that Debby is fond of repeating.

When I call to confirm my interview with this ambassador of the Ginger "Lady Superstar" Alden Fan Club, Deb asks if I wouldn't mind rescheduling for later in the afternoon. She needs the time to make up and look like a proper representative of a national organization — a national organization of fifteen, give or take a few. It isn't easy fixing yourself up on limited funds, you know. A hairdo's out of the question, so Deb must brush it back, bobbie-pinning the unruly and greasy strands. Clothes? Try finding something fashionable in the extra large sizes at the Salvation Army. Green stretch pants and a blousy shirt will have to serve. A smear of blush, a dab of eyeliner, a blot of lipstick, nothing too flashy — but a decent-enough excuse to finally make use of that spare package of Lee Press-On Nails gathering dust at the bottom of a bedroom drawer.

Debby allows that I'm the first reporter to visit her home, a drab and stuffy 1950's Escondido bungalow, tucked away at the perimeter of several new developments with unlikely rural names, like Mountain View Estates, all bedroom communities forty minutes away from downtown San Diego. The beige shag rug has seen better days; the walls are decorated with several thrift-store prints of Jesus in which the Son of God looks like a bewigged businessman. Family photos line a ledge near the dining room table. "Who's that?" I ask about a haggard-looking young woman with foggy black eyes. "That's my sister Barbara. She's retarded. They're taking care of her in a place in Ramona."

Deb's room is on the second floor, up the worn, carpeted steps, past Wiggleworm, a gassy, rheumy-eyed Cocker Spaniel yoked to the thin iron banister. Dad, laying on the couch watching football, just got back from the hospital (shhh! he had an aneurysm). It's a tough go, trying to make ends meet on mom's nurse's salary alone.

All of 35-years old, Debby allows that she tried to work once. She even trained to be a secretary at a business school in Escondido, where she graduated top three in her class. But this darn company stuck her in customer service. If they kept her in accounting, things would have worked out fine, but they just offered her to the customers, and customers can really be vicious! The customers blamed her, blamed Debby personally, for the problems they were having with their damn — excuse her French — appliances. Like she had any say so. She quit the third day, sobbing, vowing never to work again.

Now mom wants to lodge a boarder in Debby's room, which'll add another few hundred dollars monthly to the pot. Debby's got to move to a room half the size. The long and the short of it is that it's going to take at least three months to get all her stuff downstairs.

With finances in such a squeeze, Debby demoted herself from President to Co-President of the Ginger "Lady Superstar" Alden Fan Club, turning over the administrative reins to her friend, Darla Shaddock of Wisconsin. Darla's got a job and has more resources. A few members of the club had been getting on Deb's case for not sending out the newsletter on time. Members were only getting two newsletters a year when they should have been receiving four, which wasn't such a good use of eight bucks dues if you think about it. All in all, people are pretty understanding, but Debby is glad that Darla's "taking care of business" once again. ("Taking Care of Business" or "TCB," Deb reminds me, was the code phrase of Elvis' inner circle. Red, Sonny and all other members of the Memphis Mafia proudly wore gold-plated TCB pins, complete with Oswald Mosley lighting bolt.) Darla informs me that the newsletters are coming out on schedule now, and each one carries the imprimatur of Miss Ginger Alden herself as the one and only officially-sanctioned fan club.

(You say you've never heard of Ginger Alden? I mean, really, where have you been!? We're talking about the runner-up in the 1976 Miss Tennessee pageant, a nubile doxy who was rumored to become Elvis's second wife on Christmas Day, 1977. Ginger Alden, the very girl who discovered the constipated crooner freshly-croaked on the bathroom floor that fateful day in August, 1977. You may have also read at the supermarket checkout Ginger's acerbic comments in a recent *Star* about competitor Priscilla Presley turning Graceland into "Greedland." You might also see her obligatory tell-all Elvis memoir in bookstores before too long.)

Deb's lips tremble, withdraw like twin slugs over pointed little teeth. Swallowing her words, Deb speaks slowly, haltingly, as if someone was going to swat her for giving a wrong answer. "We love Ginger the best of all the women Elvis was involved with," gushes the woman who has devoted the past 13 years to keeping tabs on beauty queen/model/famous singer's girlfriend. Deb pictures herself Ginger's helpmeet, a special friend who daily provides Ginger a stepping stone to happiness and commercial success. "We're here to help Ginger. We'll only stop the fan club if she tells us to."

Debby feels that Ginger has not only become a victim of Elvis' untimely death but a scapegoat for gossipmongers. "Not many people like to admit this, but it's true that Ginger and Elvis were engaged."

Debby appreciates her modesty. "Ginger is very conservative what she models. She has a nice shape but she doesn't model bathing suits or anything unless they're one piece."

Debby values the purity of Ginger's heart. "Priscilla and Linda Thompson [longtime Elvis girlfriend] seemed to be out for the money. Ginger isn't. I never liked that kind of person. The greedy people. Greedy, selfish people, who are only in it to make money.

"I've got a couple letters from Ginger right here. Do you want me to read them?"

By all means.

"Okay." She unfolds the letter, clears her throat and begins to read.

> I believe that God has everyone's life planned out for them. And I thank God that I was able to share his last eight months with him. It all happened for a reason and I pray that I find why soon. It is so hard to understand. He was having so much to look forward to that Elvis got mad with his aides many times for not being where they were supposed to be and his aides were told when it was their time to be on duty to sleep on the white fur bed in the bathroom. I will never forget all the beautiful things that Elvis taught me about life. Most of the stories out now are by people who really didn't know him. I saw a side to him in these eight months that no one had ever seen before, and it was hard for me to accept at first when Elvis told me that he had loved before but had never been in love until he met me. He also said he had always been 60% happy or 40% happy, and the rest of him was still searching. He told me it even shook him up when he realized that the first time in his life he was in love. He said he had never planned on marrying again and never dreamed he would find somebody in his own hometown. I will love him always and pray that he will guide me and watch over me. I hope to still make him happy.

A lump comes to Debby's throat. She folds the prized artifact and slips it back into its envelope. She opens another letter, at least a decade old and limp from handling, the only other missive of substance she has received from Ginger Alden:

> In the coming months I hope to go into modeling or acting, but first I have to put the people together and get my head on straight. New Year's Eve I stayed home and watched television. I couldn't get interested in doing anything. No one has put me down for loving Elvis when he was twice my age. He did not act like a 42-year-old. Anyway, when love calls a person, you know it. Elvis always told me that if for some reason we ever broke up, then all the rest would be second best. There is only one true love in a lifetime and it is something that happens. A beautiful gift from God. Most people, I believe, are out to make money off Elvis. They know they have never seen anything like this in their lives. And won't again, so this is the only opportunity they'll have to make this kind of money the easy way.
>
> Quite a few imitators were imitating Elvis before his death. I think that Elvis would wish for them to get their act right, because I saw him root for an impersonator one time. I lived at home with my parents, and Elvis had the upstairs bathroom redecorated for me in turquoise and white. I got along with his family well, but didn't get to see them much because I was constantly with Elvis, and he was not into drugs, he had prescribed medication he had to take. The drug thing is trash and blown out of proportion. The first thing that Elvis read to me was 'A Case On Marriage' by Kahlil Gibran. That was what we studied the most. It is a beautiful piece, and one of my favorites.

Debby sniffles. "Elvis was very spiritual. That's how he got his Grammy Awards. Mostly his gospel music." As evidenced by the surfeit of Jesus prints on the walls, the entire Wimer family tends to be "pretty religious. We go to the Seventh-day Adventist Church whenever we can." Seventh-Day Adventism, like Jehovah's Witness, is an apocalyptic religion which relies upon heavy street-level recruiting. The SDA magazine, *Signs of the Times,* can generally be found in kiosks at airports and malls.

Debby doesn't see any irreconcilables in her worship of the man who has been dubbed Elvis "The Pelvis" Presley; rather than seeing it as a form of apostasy, she has devoted her life to transforming, in her mind at least, Elvis' checkered life into one of inherent goodness. She likewise safeguards the image of Ginger Alden as saintedly virginal and holy. Any book that reports the seedy elements of the Elvis myth are the perverted products of contemporary Judases. About *Elvis,* the infamous Albert Goldman book, Debby froths, "It's the pits. Trash, trash, trash! All lies. I was in the supermarket with my mother, and she asked me if I wanted that book, and I told her I'd rather see it burned. Burned!"

Though Debby pooh-poohs the notion that Elvis is still alive, he appears to her at night, in dreams. One vivid, recurring nightmare has Elvis materializing on the slope of her neighbor's driveway. Debby puzzles over its meaning. "I don't know why Elvis was in her drive way."

She tells me how Elvis and Ginger first met. "I'll tell you as much as I know. Well, one of his friends was a deejay in Memphis, he introduced them originally. But he originally found out about the Alden family through one of her sisters. She has two sisters. There's Rosemary, and Terry, her name is. She was a Miss Tennessee. And Ginger was the Runner-Up. You know, He'd just broken-up with his other girlfriend, Linda Thompson. Elvis asked his friend, George Klein, they're old friends, he asked if he knew anybody, you know. So he asked him to bring Terry Alden to meet him. And Terry asked if her sisters could come along; Elvis said yes, and they say that once Elvis had one look at Ginger he fell for her."

Really! Just one look?

"Yeah!"

Did she have her hair the way he liked it?

"I think so. I think so, yes."

So she knew in advance how to attract his attention. Was Terry mad that Ginger got the prize?

"No, I think she was pleased. For her. Yeah. He proposed to her January 26th, '77. And he kept saying he'd give her that ring, the one he gave her. It was out of one of his favorite rings."

How long were they together?

"They met in November '76, and he died in August of '77."

Did she like living in Graceland?

"She didn't generally live there. She was with him a lot there. He'd asked her to move in with him. But she wasn't into that sort of thing unless she was married."

Oh, she was principled about it?

"Yes."

She didn't have sex with Elvis?

"No no no. He probably would have liked that, but she wasn't into that sort of thing."

She was principled about it?

"Yeah, yeah. Yeah."

How do you know?

"I don't know but I know."

∞ ∞ ∞

> Humility is perpetual quietness of heart. It is to
> have no trouble. It is never to be fretted or vexed,
> irritable or sore; to wonder at nothing that is

done to me, to feel nothing done against me. It is to be at rest when nobody praises me, and when I am blamed or despised, it is to have a blessed home in myself where I can go in and shut the door and kneel to my Father in secret and be at peace, as in a deep sea of calmness, when all about is seeming trouble. — inspirational quotation from *The Ginger "Lady Superstar" Alden Fan Club Newsletter*

The first few Ginger "Lady Superstar" Alden Fan Club newsletters, pecked on a typewriter given to platen slippage, reflected the full range of Darla Shaddock's interests, including her fixation on a soap actor named William Espy and even Paul McCartney's brother, whose own fan club address Darla thoughtfully provides her readers. Darla makes it clear that she's more interested in facts than in fantasy, thoughtfully mailing me a "Ginger Alden Fact Sheet," which she promises to update real soon.

If Darla Shaddock is the organizational genius behind the Ginger "Lady Superstar" Alden Fan Club, Debby Wimer is its heart and soul. When Debby assumed the mantle of Presidency, the Ginger "Lady Superstar" Alden Fan Club newsletter blossomed with inspirational poetry and homilies plastered with stickers of cute animals, members' verse tributes to Elvis and Ginger or remembrances of pilgrimages to Memphis, xerox reproductions of Ginger's latest modeling assignments from advertisements or department store catalogues, Debby's beautiful pencil sketches of E & G, as well as newsy updates of Ginger and family's goings-on. Though she has relinquished newsletter mailing chores, Debby remains Co-President, a prestigious member still. We might add that Ginger Alden is an "Honorary Member" of the Ginger "Lady Superstar" Alden Fan Club, and receives a free lifetime subscription of the newsletter. (Alden, now married to Ron Leyser of Long Island, refused to be interviewed for this story.)

Recent newsletters are most notably graced with chapters from Debby's intimate novella, "Spanish Eyes," doled out in installment after juicy installment. Darla is the first one to admit that "Debby's got a way with words" — she had Debby ghostwrite her "Visit to

Memphis" some issues back — but feels a tad uneasy about Deb's story, which she reckons is a bit too — well, a bit touchy, too much of Deb's own fantasy. Darla is circumspect on the own reasons why she founded the Ginger "Lady Superstar" Alden Fan Club. "Ginger has dark hair," she offers, "I'm crazy about dark hair." Darla's squeamishness can perhaps be traced to that unmarked but definitive line that separates "wholesome" fandom from its more fervid expressions. The danger is not so much in the fantasy, but in believing the fantasy.

Debby doesn't register the least amount of shame over "Spanish Eyes," which may be the most revealing projection of fan mentality since John Hinckley's love letters to Jodie Foster. In "Spanish Eyes" Debby infuses herself into the Elvis saga in first person, becoming God's and Elvis's confidant, an extraordinarily attractive and resourceful woman who fends off Elvis' amorous advances while managing his life and career. At the end she mutates into a contemporary Virgin Mary, who carries Elvis' baby to term through the miracle of in vitro fertilization.

For all the hot and heavy softcore style of "Spanish Eyes," Debby disapproves of the "Slash" style of amateur science fiction, in which fans situate their favorite television stars in explicit pornographic situations. Circulated among cliques of lonely women fans, Slash fiction concentrates solely on homosexual couplings, Kirk buggers Spock or Starsky fudgepacks Hutch, in order that their beloved characters are not contaminated by female competition. "We have Kirk and Spock love each other because then we can have them for ourselves," said a pimply, obese Slash writer at a recent comic book convention.

Debby, was there any part in "Spanish Eyes" where you saw Elvis naked?

"No no no. No. He's a very modest person."

There are these books that say he had a nickname for his penis. He called it "Little Elvis."

"That's totally ridiculous. What I heard is that it's just the opposite."

What did you hear?

"I would say that he's quite well-endowed."

Oh, he is? Where did you hear that from?

"I don't remember. It's been a while. But I have. Heard."

Debby Wimer allows that she's thought about moving to Memphis ever since 1977, although, as she tells me, it's difficult to start one's life over in a strange place. Besides, she's been out of California only once in her life, a 1980 pilgrimage to Graceland after visiting Darla's house in Wisconsin. She recalls her trip as if it took place yesterday.

"We went to Memphis by bus. Took us about two days. And we arrived there Thursday, July 24th, around 7:30 in the evening. We found a room about a block or so from the bus terminal. And we had to wait until we got the luggage. Then we had dinner. And I called one of my friends in Illinois, telling her that I was in Memphis, and to tell the Aldens. I did this because at the time I didn't have their phone number. She did. So she called them. And her name is June, that's the one I called. Told me that Rosemary had told her I was coming, so in her letter I received just before I left she told me to call her. That she would call the Aldens and tell them. She offered to call them that night, but it was about 10 o'clock in the evening."

I'm sorry. I don't follow. Who told who you were coming?

"June told me that Rosemary [Alden, Ginger's sister] had told her I was coming. So in her letter I received, the one from Rosemary, just before I left, she told me to call her, then she would call the Aldens and tell them I was in Memphis. That was June. June would call the Aldens. She offered to call them that night, but I told them it was better to wait until morning because I didn't want to disturb them at 10 o'clock in the evening. I gave her the number at the hotel and the room number. So the next 8:30 in the next morning, Friday, Miss Alden called. And she said Rosemary was ill and that Ginger was in Mississippi, but would be back that evening. She also said that she would call me back. We could arrange a time to meet. She asked me too if I was planning to go to Graceland. I told her I was. At 12:30 that afternoon we boarded a bus bound for Graceland. We arrived there at 1 pm, and at the time Elvis' Uncle Vester was at the gate. We signed in and he showed us a copy of *The Presley Family Cookbook*. He seemed real likeable, but I was told not to say anything about Ginger to him. I didn't know why, but he didn't care for her. After that we went in and walked up the driveway. It's about 20 feet to the house. I got pictures of it. Then we walked to the meditation garden; that's where Elvis and his parents are. It was lovely. They had a fountain there; it was really nice. Then beautiful epitaphs on the gravestone. We left about 1:30 but I wouldn't have minded spending all day there. I loved it there."

Why did you leave?

"We were going to have lunch or something."

I see.

"We went across the street to the souvenir shop. And they all played Elvis music at the shop. And I bought about 20 bucks worth of souvenirs. If I had my way I would have bought more. They had a small coffee shop, "Hickory Log." We had lunch there. It had Elvis all over it. And they sold us souvenirs in there, too. I also have pictures of the gates. We got back to our room about 2:30. Mrs. Alden didn't call until about 9 o'clock that evening. She said Ginger was back, and they would be coming 2 o'clock the next day. In the afternoon. Saturday morning she calls again saying they'll be a bit late. Time passed. She called twice more saying she was sorry because Rosemary's doctor hadn't called, and they had to wait until he did. Finally she called and said they were leaving the house in ten minutes and they would be seeing us in about in another hour or so. Three and 4 o'clock came and went. They finally drove in about 4:30. I was really nervous. But I opened the door myself and they asked me who I was, and I told her who I was. She hugs me and she says hello, and Ginger's right behind her. She wore a short-sleeved blouse with a parrot on it here [points to chest], black slacks, and brown sandals. Had some rings on. I don't think there was the one Elvis gave her, I don't think, I don't know. One was like a black sapphire and the other looked like a dozen diamonds in an intricate setting. They might have been it, I don't know. She told me they were good luck rings. They stayed about two and a half hours. And they told us a lot of things that have never been published, about Elvis and Elvis's entourage. They were very interesting and informative. I wish I could say everything that was said, but there is no room. I could go on forever."

Over the years, have things changed in the way you see Ginger or the way you see Elvis?

"Somewhat. But mostly we back her all the way, we like her very much. We want all the best for her. She went through a lot when he died. She deserves what she's got now. And she's happy in her marriage. To that Jewish fellow."

Jewish fellow?

"Ron Leyser his name is. He lives in New York. We hope he's good enough for her. I'll know more when I write her sister, Rosemary. Ginger says that he didn't want her to be a martyr. When she was ready, that she should find somebody new." Debbie sighs, mumbles. "That's the last thing she'd want, but she did find him."

Why was that the last thing she wanted? Because she was still in love with Elvis?

"Yes. Yes, she was hurting too much over him. She didn't want anyone else at that point. She wasn't ready for anybody else."

If I'm So Wonderful, Then Why Am I Still Single? was one of several self-help books that Debby needed to renew at the Escondido library. "There are some good tips in there." Debby understands Ginger's heartbreak at losing Elvis: she tells me that she's been engaged three times. She almost tied the knot with an Escondido man who was thirty but still lived with his parents and tried to talk Debby into working while he'd lay about at home. Debby wasn't about to stand for that. It's difficult to sort out Debby's other erstwhile fiancees. Maybe one of 'em's a German pen-pal, a fellow Elvis fan. "He reads lips pretty good." The deaf guy wants to flop on the Wimer's couch when he visits the States sometime next year. Another pen-pal, from Oxnard, closer, but still no local, promises to visit any day now, but has so far stood Debby up. "He didn't come, that stupid! If he calls me I'm going to give him a piece of my mind."

On a drive through downtown Escondido, Debby makes me understand that any man must take a back seat to Elvis Presley. Even so, she lets on that I'm one of the most presentable gentleman to ever call on her. I neglect to tell her that I cannot fit her criteria for a love mate, who must, "One: Believe in God. Two: Not talk down to me. I have an I.Q. of 132 and men still kind of talk down to me just because I'm female. But they're the stupid ones. Three: Love old people. Four: Love animals. Good looking is a plus, but if he's just handsome, then it's like having a pretty box with nothing inside." Must he share an enthusiasm for Ginger and Elvis? "That goes without saying."

Chewing great hunks of a half-pound hamburger at the North County Fairgrounds' Red Robin restaurant, keeping a wary eye for overzealous busboys, Debby doesn't dare lay the mighty burger down between bites. She laps demurely at the suet and sauce that drips on her forearm: "I don't mind living at home that much. I look after my father while my mother's at work. He had a stroke and one side isn't working too good."

Back home, Debby allows me into the sanctity of her room. It's acrid with the fumes of an unemptied cat box. She locks the door behind me, then drops down all fours, calling, "Gin-ger! Gin-ger! C'mere, that's a good cat!" She proudly places the spotted, suppurating animal in my arms. "Ginger's got a skin disease." Which explains why the cat's belly is wrapped with a pair of dirty longjohns. I put the cat down and it heads to the befouled litter box, kicking up dust and excrement.

Debby begins to read a poem of which she is particularly proud, written on Elvis' birthday, in 1980.

> God Bless You, Elvis,
> Happy birthday,
> Wherever you are.
> We should not begrudge you
> the happiness you have found.
> You had so little here on earth,
> yet you gave us so much!
> I miss you so.
> I often wish I could join you,

so we could be together.
Yet if justice had been done,
you would be with us still.
I hate myself for wasting so much
time on other things; so unimportant
now when compared with the miracle of you.
I realized too just how precious,
how very rare and lovely a jewel I let
slip through my fingers.
You may forgive me, dearest Elvis,
but I'll never forgive myself.
I wish I could make it up to you.
I'm sorry I was such a fool.
God bless you, Elvis.
Happy birthday.
I love you.
I will for all eternity.
You will live forever in my heart.

"It was a rainy day when I wrote it," blushes Debby. "I had always thought of Elvis as an institution. He always seemed larger than life to me. He was always around as long as I'd remembered, and I always thought he would be around. And it was so hard to believe he was gone. I remember when I first heard about him dying. I was sitting in the kitchen listening to the radio and they said that Elvis Presley died about 2 o'clock that afternoon, and I thought, first of all, that it was a horrible joke. I felt like taking somebody apart, you know. It couldn't be possible. It was impossible. He was going to get married again, and stuff. And they said it later on, it was in the paper. That's when I had to believe it. I was in a store a couple days after that. They were showing his funeral on television. I couldn't watch it. It got to me. I thought I'd better get out of there or I'd disgrace myself."

Ginger — the cat — defecates into her neglected box, now a small skyscraper of turds. I swivel my head around Debby's room and am surprised to see but few images of Elvis and Ginger, yet a complete set of *Star Trek* videotapes line Debby's closet. "Oh, I'm a BIG *Star Trek* nut. I write *Star Trek* fiction, amateur fiction. No, I'm not paid. If I was paid Paramount Studios would sue me." Bosom heaving, Debby inches closer to me, revealing a spiral-bound book containing one of her *Star Trek* stories under the pseudonym "J. M. Lane."

You can almost hear Debby's thoughts as she shows me her Star Trek books: "This guy is interested in me. Why else would he be here? Didn't that book say that guys are lost these days. They don't know how to romance. They need for women to give them a signal." Debby bats her eyes at me. The room closes in on me like an old Batman episode. All I know is that I need to go through two doors to get outside, get beyond Debby and her all-too-real fantasies, her father lying on the couch, the skin-diseased cat, the Jesus and Elvis kitsch, the pictures of retarded relatives, the stained beige carpet, the Cocker Spaniel named Wiggleworm roped to the stairs.

I still don't remember if I literally ran from the house, or merely walked with swift purpose. Fleeing the smoggy Escondido twilight on Interstate 15, I turn on the radio. Elvis sings "It's Now or Never" — Debby Wimer told me it was her favorite song. A few weeks later I receive a note in the mail. Debby lists all the reasons why we would make a swell couple. She writes as if I'm both skittish and retarded, that the only thing preventing our romance is my exasperating shyness. She's willing to give our romance a shot, especially since a prospective suitor from the Ginger "Lady Superstar" Alden fan club flaked out on his plans to move to California. He was old and in ill-health anyway. With perfect cursive penmanship, she concludes her letter with reassurance that I won't need to worry about other competitors for her hand.

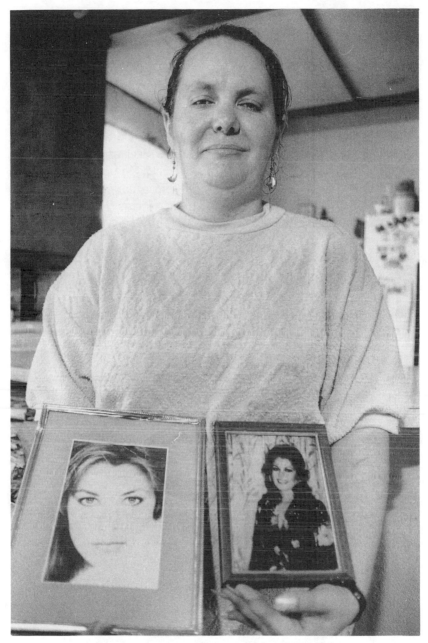

Debbie Wimer with photos of Ginger Alden.
(photo by Scott Lindgren.)

SPANISH EYES

[In which ultra fan Debra Wimer extrapolates on the second coming of Elvis. The main thrust of the fantasy is Debra's selfless donation of her womb so that Elvis and Ginger may have a child. Monogamy is saved by in vitro fertilization — though Elvis finds her sexually desirable, Debra need not cheat Ginger out of her perfect monogamous relationship to birth their child. Abridged from *The Ginger Alden Fan Club Newsletter*.]

The first thing I remember is crying over how tragically short Elvis Presley's life was, how he was taken so suddenly from all his loved ones — particularly the girl he loved and was to have married Christmas Day 1977. "Oh Lord, why couldn't You have at least let him remarry and father another child?"

To my astonishment I heard a soft and kind, yet authoritative voice reply, "Please don't cry. I know how the world was mourned since I took him August 16, 1977. How would you like to have him back?"

"That would be wonderful, but how could you do it?"

"You doubt the Almighty?"

"But he's been gone over thirteen years!"

"I am fully aware of that. Remember, I made Adam out of the dust of the ground. I can fashion another body for Elvis which will look exactly like the original ... with a few improvements, of course."

"Do you really mean it? We'd do anything to have him back!"

"On one condition."

"Name it."

"You must keep him entirely hidden from the public for a period of one year."

"That's a pretty tall order! How am I going to do it?"

"I will help you, don't worry ... but you must promise me that you will do this."

"Oh yes, Lord, gladly. I have always felt partly responsible for his death. I know I could have helped him had I known him."

"After this you will know him better than anyone except myself ... that is why I have chosen you to take care of him during the year in hiding. He has been out of circulation and is out of shape. It will be your job to prevent him from working as he did before. That was part of what killed him. The strain was just too much for his heart to handle."

"Thank you, Lord. I won't let you down." I sighed, then pointed out, "But you know how determined he is when he wants something. How can I alone convince him to take care of himself?"

"I have planned for you to be his manager. You will gently suggest that it would be wise for all concerned if he took care of himself. You have a way with words; you'll convince him."

"Lord, I'm afraid I am not worthy of the trust you have placed in me."

"I have deemed you worthy," he replied kindly but firmly. "You have nothing to worry about. I will guide you every step of the way."

"Where will we stay?"

"At his home in Palm Springs. It is currently unoccupied. ... He must be treated with utmost courtesy and consideration at all times, or I will take him away again."

"I understand, Lord, and I will go to the house now." I went out to my car, finding to my surprise that all my belongings had been mysteriously and thoroughly packed.

As I drove God told me, "I will return him to you halfway to Palm Springs. When you see a warm bright light beside you in your car, you will know I am sending him to you."

I still didn't understand why God had chosen me. Why not Ginger or a member of his family? I asked what would happen to the gravesite at Graceland. "Nothing, at least not for a year. It will look as it always has."

"Why couldn't we stay at Graceland? Elvis would be more at home there and we'd never leave."

"I have very good reasons for wanting you to keep him in Palm Springs. It is isolated, and Graceland is constantly overrun by his fans since it was opened. You will need all the privacy you can get." I hadn't thought of that! "He is impatient to return."

"You have him there with you?"

"Yes ... or more accurately, his spiritual body. He says he can hardly wait to come back, since he left a lot of unfinished business behind when he died."

I'll say he did, I thought ...

As I entered a deserted stretch of road I felt a warm bright light, as warm as the sun, and was told to slow down to 55 mph. I thought it was strange that I should maintain that speed, but complied — then something compelled me to look at the seat beside me.

I just wasn't prepared for the sight that met my eyes. He was sitting there in the white suit he had been buried in, the one his father had given him the Christmas of 1976. He had an almost unearthly beauty about him. I wanted to reach out and touch him, but was afraid he would disappear.

I also had an irresistible urge to see if he wore shoes, since people were usually buried barefoot. He indeed wore shoes! It was as if the Lord had said, "Say something to him. He's real, he will respond to you."

I finally said, "Welcome back."

His speaking voice was more beautiful than it had ever been. "Thanks. It's good to be back." It was incredible that Elvis was really here, really speaking to me! But I wouldn't believe he was real unless he touched me. At that moment he covered my hand with his. "Do you mind? I've missed the human contact of touch."

"Not at all." I strove to sound calm, yet knew my heart was pounding. His hand felt warm, firm, masculine. "Has God discussed the details of what we're supposed to do for the next year with you?"

"Thoroughly. I intend to cooperate a hundred percent." ... Now that I knew he was real, I could really talk. "My family doesn't know anything about this; no one does. I was told not to tell anyone. I will obey, of course, but they were understandably hurt. I could only say I'd have to move to Palm Springs for a year. I can't even contact them to let them know how I am. I'm supposed to isolate myself with you for a year.

"Not that I don't welcome the prospect — any woman would — but I have a job to do. I intend to do it well, too ... and don't think you're going to get away with murder just because I'm female. That Southern charm won't work with me — at least not where it counts."

"I might prove to be a handful. Do you think you'll be able to handle being alone with me for a year?"

"I think so. The Lord told me to call on him if I needed help."

"You'll need it, believe me," he laughed.

"That wouldn't surprise me, but I think I'll enjoy it just the same."

"I'm sure I will, too." He brushed the side of a finger along my cheek. Even as I felt a thrill shoot through my entire body, I told myself sternly NOT to become too attached to him. It would only make letting go that much harder on both of us.

"Elvis, I don't want to say this, but feel I must."

"Fire away."

"I feel it would be best if we stayed just good friends, with no romantic overtones."

For a moment he looked like you'd just hit him over the head, but smiled and said, "I understand, and I respect your decision ... but let me tell you right now, it won't be easy for me to abide by it...."

∞ ∞ ∞

I have to admit that he tried his level best to get romantically involved with me that year, but I gently reminded him, "As much as I'd love to, I can't. You already have a fiancee who loves you deeply. You must not break her heart for what could just be a fleeting thing." He had to agree that I was right and he did love her, although he was very much attracted to me.

He loved Ginger. I knew that all too well, and he fully intended to marry her when the year was up. Finally I could deny my feelings no longer.

Despite my resolve not to, I had fallen deeply, hopelessly, in love. What could I do? I could never call him mine, nor could I ever let him guess how I felt. He belonged to Ginger. If he ever guessed he would likely drop Ginger and stay with me because I knew he also cared for me. I couldn't risk that; I didn't want him to break her heart.

How I would ever hide my feelings, I didn't know — but hide them I must! I finally told God about it. "Lord, I have a big problem."

"You're in love with Elvis."

I sighed. "Yes, despite my resolve not to. What am I to do?"

"For once even I don't know." And if even God couldn't help me, what chance did I have?

∞ ∞ ∞

I had my chance and blown it. If I could only have known his lips, arms and body even once — you lose the chance. Still, loving him as I did, I could never give myself in marriage to anyone else. I even considered entering a convent but realized that that would be worse than staying around him.

He was now ready to return to show business. When we walked into the STAR offices everyone who seen him did a double-take. We asked to see the head of the outfit because we had the reincarnation story of the century! We were ushered into a plush office and told to sit down by a fiftyish man in an expensive grey suit.

"I'm Elvis Presley," Elvis said.

"Let's not play games," the man said. "I have no time for jokes."

"This is no joke," I assured him.

His face turned white. "But how? Elvis Presley died over a decade ago!"

"I'm not really sure. I can hardly believe it myself," Elvis told him. ... "Tell the world that I'm getting married next week — to the girl I was engaged to twelve years ago. It may not be Christmas, but it's been much too long. This time I'm going to be around to marry her!"

Before a week was out the STAR was all over the world: ELVIS PRESLEY REBORN ... REINCARNATED ROCK KING SAYS "I'M GOING TO MARRY MY FIANCEE GINGER ALDEN NEXT WEEK."

∞ ∞ ∞

They had been married just two months when Ginger's doctor told her that she was pregnant, expecting to deliver the baby the following April. She was happy, but Elvis was absolutely ecstatic! After she told him the news he called me and could hardly talk coherently, he was so happy.

Ginger wanted to know what all I'd done with him while we were isolated for a year.

"Nothing to what I wish I'd done," I quipped.

"Oh Debby, be serious!"

"I am. He was very attracted to me and asked me to have an affair, but I couldn't do that to you, though. I knew how you loved him and that I'd only spoil what you two had..."

"I can never thank you enough for giving him back to me."

Ginger just seemed to grow more beautiful as her pregnancy advanced. In the latter stages she really didn't care to have Elvis see her and I couldn't blame her — but assured her that she didn't have a thing to worry about, since to a man the woman they love carrying their child is always beautiful.

Since she had conceived so early, Elvis decided to wait until after the baby was born to resume touring. Incidentally, I had limited him to one show a night and three in a week — and his touring to two weeks a month. He didn't exactly love the idea, but knew it was for his own good.

∞ ∞ ∞

A nurse came in and asked, "Would you like to see the baby?"

"Yes, very much." I stood up. "Elvis is still asleep; please don't wake him. I will wake him when it's time." I left the room quietly and made my way to the nursery. The nurse picked up the baby and brought him to the window. He was so beautiful!

He had the beginnings of Elvis' firm chin, his classic nose and sensuous lips, but Ginger's brown eyes. I saw the adorable baby softness which would gradually mature into a firm chin, tall lithe body, and masculinity comparable only to his father's. The nurse then asked if I would like to hold him.

"Oh yes!" I had to put a mask and gown on, then she handed the child to me. I smiled and whispered, "Hello, baby Jess. Welcome to the world." I brought out one tiny, perfectly formed hand; he got a death grip on my index finger. I could hardly believe I was actually holding Elvis' son the child who would continue the Presley line!

∞ ∞ ∞

Elvis came out to where I was waiting. His face looked gray and sad. "What's wrong?" He didn't seem to hear; he just sat down and buried his face in his hands. "Elvis, what happened? Is there anything I can do?" I put a gentle hand on his arm. He looked up, eyes clouded with gloom.

"Not unless you have another child for me," he replied.

"I don't understand."

"Remember when Ginger said for you to leave?" He held my hands tightly.

"What did she tell you?" I asked as I gave them a reassuring squeeze.

"That she couldn't have any more children." ...

I knocked on Ginger's door.

"Come in, Debby." ... When I got closer to her I could tell that she also had been crying.

"I told Elvis we couldn't have any more children," she confessed. "I hated having to tell him that, especially right after Jess's birth, but I had to, and it breaks my heart, too. Well anyway the doctor told me that I have what is called an 'infantile' or 'tipped' uterus. The odds would be at least two billion to one against my having another child full-term and healthy, that I'm more likely to miscarry and have it kill me. Thank God for little Jess. At least we have him."

"But you said that Elvis wanted at least half a dozen kids."

"I know, and we still do — but how can we, now?"

"Aren't there any alternatives?"

"The doctor said the only way for us to have another child is either to adopt or have another woman carry it." She took my hand. "Deb, I want to ask a favor of you."

"Anything."

"He said that my tubes and ovaries were healthy, so if there was anyone who wanted to volunteer to carry my baby, she was to contact him and he would make the arrangements."

I was certainly taking a gamble, using my body for an experiment that might (or might not) work, and if anything went wrong, I could die in the midst of. Also, how was I going to keep it a secret from Elvis? Whatever else he was, he wasn't dumb.

∞ ∞ ∞

A few weeks later Ginger called: she was crying. "Oh Debby, I've missed my period!" She didn't sound happy.

"The doctor said it could kill me. We've got to do something. I didn't mean to have it happen, I swear. I was sure I'd taken my pill ... I'm not going to tell him. You're going to help me get rid of it."

"You mean — "

"Yes, I mean! I'm going to have an abortion! Thank God Elvis hasn't noticed yet. This way he'll never have to know. ... We'll go to an abortion clinic; I made a special Sunday appointment. ... Debby, you have to come. If you don't I won't be able to go through with it. You know how dead set against abortion Elvis is. He feels it's murder, and ordinarily so would I , but this is a matter of life and death ... mine!"

∞ ∞ ∞

The weekend went off without a hitch. Mrs. Alden was enraptured with seeing her new grandson Jess, and Ginger had the abortion with no complications. Her waistline returned to normal; it was as though the pregnancy had never been. We returned to Graceland Monday morning and Elvis was none the wiser.

A little later I had to go to the doctor and become implanted with a fertilized egg taken from Ginger a few days before. It was over before I knew it. Now all we could do was wait and see if the egg "took."

The time for the next scheduled period came and went, so I knew that that meant the experiment was successful — that Elvis and Ginger's child was now growing inside my body. I called Ginger and told her. She was ecstatic!

I told the doctor how sick I was. He said it was somewhat unusual but nothing was really wrong. He claimed it would disappear after the third month. I had to go through another six weeks of morning sickness? Oh lord!

Thank heaven I didn't have to hide it from Elvis after all. I could openly let him know about my pregnancy — and you may be sure that he could tell I was pregnant. After all, he'd had two children, he knew the signs ... and you may be certain that he asked plenty of questions!

"What's wrong, Deb? Don't you feel well?" Elvis asked when I barely touched my lunch.

"What makes you think I'm not well?"

"Something has to be wrong when you refuse your favorite foods."

"Remember when I said I had to be gone all night to secure a business deal for you?" (This had been just over six weeks ago. I had slept with the guy because he reminded me a lot of Elvis; he had been an excellent lover, too, but I hadn't gotten pregnant even though I hadn't used birth control — but what Elvis didn't know wouldn't hurt us.)

"How could you let him make you pregnant?"

"It's an occupational hazard in this business if one is female."

"You mean you really are pregnant?"

"Yes. I estimate between six weeks and two months along. I'm seriously considering giving the baby up for adoption because I could never care for it properly. Being your manager takes all my time."

Elvis exchanged a meaningful look with Ginger. "Are you thinking what I'm thinking?"

"You better believe it!" she declared ... and so it was arranged. I would give the child to them when it was born. Why shouldn't I? It was theirs anyway. I just carried the child, like a surrogate mother.

I just hoped to God I wouldn't get some crazy notion about keeping the child, because it wasn't mine to keep, though it had been a chance to carry the child of the man I loved. Unfortunately, it didn't belong to us — it belonged to Elvis and Ginger. It had grown inside me but truly belonged to them.

I had to laugh, but not in front of Elvis. He would have been furious if he'd ever learned of how his wife and manager had pulled off this amazing conspiracy! It wouldn't hurt him to think the child was mine, at least not until it was obvious to everyone (even him) that it wasn't.

Elvis and Ginger were ecstatic over their new daughter, swearing they would never be able to thank me enough for her, but Ginger and I exchanged a secret smile and look whenever he talked about the baby. Maybe someday we could tell him the truth about the "adopted" child, but in the meantime it was best that he remained ignorant of the facts.

What floored me was that the doctor told me that I could handle any number of pregnancies. Seeing how happy Elvis and Ginger were with their new daughter, I finally decided it wouldn't be so bad to carry their children for them. Maybe next time we'd suggest to Elvis hiring a woman to carry their children so they could have more. And who would be better suited than I?

WILL SOMEBODY PLEASE FIND A MATE
FOR THIS NICE, WELL-MANNERED,
ARYAN PSYCHO-KILLER?

A submission received by Feral House in 1990 got my attention. It was original — I'll give it that. Never before had I read a paean to the Third Reich as a sexual wonderland. The article chided Wilhelm Reich's *Mass Psychology of Fascism* as a traitorous attempt to quell the martial spirit of the German people.

The essay was too deadpan to consider satirical. It had all the earmarks of a true believer. The author, Jonathan Haynes, concluded that Hitler was not only a great warrior, but a great lover, too. He summarized Hitler's position as "Make Love! Make War!" In comparison, Wilhelm Reich's "Make Love! Not War!" seemed prudish next to Hitler's life-enhancing blessing of action.

For years Jonathan Haynes attempted to find the appropriate Aryan mate and copulate to his heart's content. But no Aryan would have him. If he couldn't make love, he'd could at least fulfill one-half of Hitler's equation and make war. Before he was caught by the Chicago Police in 1993, Haynes had murdered two people. In 1987 he shot a gay hairdresser who dyed dark hair blonde; the other victim, a Chicago opthamologist, fitted brown eyes with blue-colored contact lenses. Haynes considered long and hard about his lack of success with women. He lay the blame at the feet of Jews who have created an entire generation of racial impostors. Unfortunately for Haynes, his murders have puzzled fellow Nazis and have failed to gain him the respect and love of even one Aryan girl.

Soon after Haynes was sentenced to death in Chicago, I wrote to him, reminding the lunatic of the paper he sent me. He remembered the essay very well and still believes that it's true.

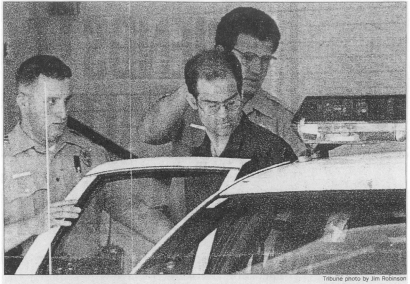

Tribune photo by Jim Robinson

Murder suspect Jonathan Preston Haynes is escorted by Wilmette police Monday to a bond hearing in Skokie.

Top: Haynes traveling from court (courtesy Chicago Tribune)

Bottom: Haynes photomontage from *Hakenkreuz*

Haynes makes the case that National Socialism encouraged a pragmatic sort of sexual freedom, unsullied by the interference of Jews, Blacks, Gypsies, Indians and every other racial group that have stolen the Aryan woman's soul since 1945. Nazi racial laws hold a lot of appeal for Jonathan Haynes, who has seen Aryan women turn away from Aryan men, brainwashed by talk shows and peer pressure to dally with blacks and Jews. Haynes backed his article sent to Feral House with murder as a desperate inoculation against racial suicide.

Haynes told me in a collect telephone call that his time will come. People will see the importance of his sacrifice and things will change. For example, Haynes predicts that a good Aryan will "kill that Jewish dwarf, Ruth Westheimer," who has proved to be poison for the race. Haynes says he's hard on Wilhelm Reich because he invented the idea that "military posture prevents the release of a strong orgasm." He would like to place a bet that Nazi soldiers were considered "extremely sexy" by their occupation nations. "French women couldn't keep their hands off of them."

Jonathan Haynes admitted to me that he was a fan of pornography until he discovered Jews were behind it. He's seen films where even Mexicans have blonde hair. "Things have gotten so out of whack that blonde girls — *natural* blonde, that is — do the scenes with the black porn actors." Haynes complains that he's never experienced the pleasure of dating an Aryan girl, yet he sees them on the arm of black athletes or drug dealers or in restaurants with ugly Jewish men.

"As for the Jewish girls, nearly all of them treat their own men like shit. They're really good finding a way to hook up with an Aryan man. The Jewish guys, with all their money, drug the Aryan girls so they don't mind getting molested at the end of the evening." Echoing Julius Streicher, Haynes filled me in about "Jews who blackmail their Aryan girlfriends to do porn. Sometimes the unlucky ones do private pictures sold to collectors, where they're tortured, amputated and snuffed. That's a Jewish enterprise."

"This is no lie," Haynes told me as the phone clicked audibly from prison. "Japanese businessmen buy 'em at a hundred thousand a print."

What makes matters even worse than the occasional snuff film is the brainwashing Aryan women undergo to avoid him. He knows just "who" and "what" is behind this avoidance factor. Haynes had gone so far as place personal ads in Nazi newspapers with nary a response. Just one middle-aged woman met him at a German restaurant. It seemed like they'd get on well, Haynes told me, so he started talking about his interests. He wanted to know if she knew much about the Jewish question. The woman pretended to heed the call of nature but sneaked out the back door of the restaurant instead.

He didn't like the way that woman acted. Not one bit. So hee contemplated why he could not find a mate. The reasons why he was having so much trouble "deeply disturbed" him. That's when he killed the hair stylist, Frank Ringi.

Haynes was free for six years after the hairdresser's murder. At the time Jonathan fancied himself a fixture in the world of subterranean publishing. His name graced the masthead of Re/Search's *Industrial Culture Handbook*. Haynes hated Boyd Rice, who was written up in the *Industrial Culture Handbook* for his artful noise music under the moniker "Non"; Haynes made phone calls Boyd described as "absolutely psychotic." Haynes told Rice that he shouldn't consider himself so "great" just because he gets girls. "If you think that I'm queer," Haynes inexplicably told Rice, "then you can hold a girl down for me and I'll show you that I can fuck her." Haynes then communicated a kind of death threat to Boyd. After all, it was he, Jonathan Haynes, who had killed, and Boyd, who got all the chicks and attention, never pulled a trigger. So who was the *real* man after all?

By 1991, Haynes self-published a book titled *Hakenkreuz: A Kaleidoscopic Vision of the Third Reich,* which collected his photomontages mixing Nazi imagery with religious iconography, or curious collages showing Nazi leaders casting a lewd eye on sexy models. The collages provided a forensic glimpse into Haynes' deep-rooted sexual inadequacy mitigated by feelings of grandiosity.

Hakenkreuz was peddled haphazardly through classified ads in right-wing newspapers. Soon he landed a job as a Chemist for the Bureau of Alcohol, Tobacco and Firearms (BATF). His BATF job spurred him on to frenzied study of Holocaust Revisionism as a way to pin culpability for every personal misfortune on Jews. He dedicated *Hak-enkreuz* to the Revisionist historian David Irving and, oddly, Communist propagandist John Heartfield. In his spare hours, he initiated conversations with every available Revisionist, leaving messages on their private answering machines if they weren't available to chat.

Haynes studied the career of Jewish Revisionist David Cole with fascination. Cole persisted in his Revisionism despite beatings and verbal rancor from Jews, and even from Revisionists who felt that he was "usurping" Revisionism from non-Jews. Haynes tracked down Cole's number through his associate Bradley Smith. I am indebted to David Cole for making a cassette copy of the strange, rambling message left one night on his answering machine by Jonathan Haynes:

> Uh, I find it ironic that ... you know David Lillienthal? [Jewish anti-Zionist author] ... uh, I find it ironic that I'm forced to read Semites to develop an anti-Semitic position. Gentiles, sometimes they're not accurate as ... uh, well ...

> I'VE GOT A RIGHT TO LIVE! Let me get to the point. I see a lot of black men going out with white women. I see movies like *Guess Who's Coming To Dinner* and I see who's behind it, and it doesn't make me comfortable. uh, uh, uh, uh, I look at the people who's producing that type of movie in Hollywood. *Guess Who's Coming to Dinner, Jungle Fever*, etcetera, ad nauseam, and I meditate on my own position. I DON'T THINK I'M A WORTHLESS PERSON! I DON'T THINK I DON'T DESERVE A WIFE. I THINK I'M A WORTHWHILE PERSON AND I THINK I DO DESERVE A WIFE! And if I can't get a wife, I'm gonna get angry and I'M GONNA LOOK FOR THE CAUSE OF WHY I CAN'T GET A WIFE. Why all these white women are going out with black men, I'm gonna look at the cause and I'm gonna try to eliminate them.

From what I gather from the interview with you [in Jack Wikoff's anti-Jewish Revisionist newsletter *Remarks*], you're not chasing after Aryan women, which I congratulate you on. I wonder about the spiritual capacity, your spiritual quality. The Jews think that Aryans destroyed a third of their race and yet for some reason they think that Aryans are very attractive sexually. Star in their pornographic films, not that I'm against that. It's fun to celebrate beauty, so I don't condemn you on that score.

I'm gonna search out the factors that deny me a wife, and I'm gonna deal with them. I don't think that you're that intellectually ... you know, there's different, there's different uh, *loyalties* that differ with each other. Too bad I couldn't talk to you personally, but this will give you an introduction to my kind of thought.

I don't want to give you my phone number because I live with Asians. Asians have always come across to me as hardworking honest people and some of their women in fact are quite beautiful, and I don't want to give you my work phone number [at the BATF] for fear of what you might do with it. It's gonna have to be a one way communication, but but but at some later date we can talk again. I've tried to discuss this subject with Jews before and I must admit I was the first to start shouting. I'm ashamed to admit that, but it's true, but they jumped my car. I hope you know the implications of what you're doing and the magnitude of it. I guess you're in a difficult position yourself, having been disowned by your family. Who knows? I might send you some money someday. I'm willing to stand on a streetcorner and let people blow me away. I feel like I'm in that position to my enemies. Either they're gonna

blow me away or I'm gonna blow them away. Ok,
bye for now.

The message seemed as if Haynes had deciding upon making David
Cole his next target. Instead he became fixated upon murdering the
President of a company that manufactures tinted contact lenses. He
traveled to Chicago, hung out near the executive's home, but lost his
nerve after eight nights of stalking. Perturbed at his failure, Haynes
picked an eye doctor out of the yellow pages, one with the biggest
advertisement for tinted lenses. He murdered Dr. Martin Sullivan in
August, 1993.

The murder made national news after Haynes was captured. The
name was oddly familiar to me. He was, of course, the same Haynes
who demanded I publish his "Make Love, Make War" article.

I wrote a letter to Haynes, then languishing in a Chicago jail. He
called collect, and persisted in making it seem that his murders were
a wonderful thing for the future of the world. He loaded me down
with the same statements he gave a Chicago paper:

> I condemn fake Ayran cosmetics. I condemn
> bleached blonde hair, tinted blue eyes and fake
> facial features brought by plastic surgery.

Did he regret his actions now that he will be executed?

> Not at all.

Did he now imagine a better way to get his point across?

> No.

Did he enjoy working for the BATF?

> It was fulfilling. They were a great bunch of guys.

Haynes reconsidered this statement, and then urged me not to speak
of his job with the BATF, not wanting to embarrass his former colleagues.

The following article is an exact replication of the article he sent Feral
House back in 1990.

Collage from *Hakenkreuz* by Jonathan Haynes

THE SEX ECONOMY OF NAZI GERMANY
A CRITIQUE OF WILHELM REICH'S
THEORY OF SEXUAL REPRESSION

by Jonathan Haynes

In Germany today, the events of 1933-1945 are often lumped under a phrase best translated as "the unsurmounted past." Just as the sun forbids a calm examination by the naked eye, that period of German history is so intensely luminous that few dare view it for fear of permanent retinal damage.

When meteorologists look at the sun, they do so through a filter which reduces its intensity. When historians look at the Third Reich, they require a filter no less real. Reality is too strong, so they view the events and personalities of that time through the calming lens of their own prejudice and preconception. Woe betide the historical fact which does not fit! That fact will be filtered out and quietly disposed of.

The worst offenders in this regard are undoubtedly the so-called "psychohistorians," those armchair quarterbacks with 20-20 hindsight who seek to explain the warp and woof of history through examination of the psychology of those who make it. We are told by practitioners of this art that Hitler was a coprophiliac, a latent homosexual, and that he had Jewish blood in his veins. As these theories spout from the mouths of those who profess to be friends of gays and Jews, we should question whether such stuff is a serious effort at understanding or simply mudslinging in the time-honored manner.

The psychohistorians make no attempt to deal with reality. Instead, they build up and knock down strawmen of psychoanalytic theory. Such strawmen do nothing to explain the past, and as long as our historians need such crutches the past will remain unsurmounted.

As an example of the aforementioned psychoanalytic strawman, consider the theory put forth by doctrinaire leftists that the Nazi *Weltan-*

schaung of masculinity and strength was a result of sexual repression. While many leftists have taken up this lie and shouted it across the rooftops in an effort to make Germany look as unappealing as possible, the most articulate and long-winded exponent of this calumny was Wilhelm Reich, an ex-associate of Freud who lived in Berlin when the Nazis took power.

This theory of genital frustration remains dominant, yet with a little research it can be seen to be absolutely false. It is only by intimidation of the scholarly opposition that this "big lie" of sexual repression in the Third Reich remains enthroned. After all, what serious academic could be sufficiently suicidal to break the news to the world that the Nazis were not sexually repressed? The myth is sacred, and anyone who dares to bring the cold crosshairs of truth to bear on this helpless myth deserves the heartiest condemnation. One is reminded of the bumper sticker that reads, "I have abandoned my search for truth, and am now looking for a good fantasy." This apparently was the attitude of many otherwise intelligent men in attempting to trace back Nazism to its psychological roots.

When we sift through the speeches and writings of Nazi officials and the accounts of foreign correspondents living in pre-war Berlin, we find that the Nazis actually put into practice many of Reich's concepts of sexual freedom. To be fair, there was a central divergence between the aims of Hitler and Reich. Both advocated and supported the full expression of the sexual urge, but they did so for quite different reasons. Hitler's aim was to populate the world with millions of blond-haired, blue-eyed Aryan Supermen by the year 1980: "Every child born means another battle won in Germany's struggle." To Reich, however, sex was an end in itself, and he emphasized its self-justification to the extent that he was ridiculed as "the prophet of the better orgasm" by his European psychiatrist colleagues.

"Know thine enemy" is a truism to keep in mind. Reich apparently did not, for his books *Sex Economy, The Sexual Revolution* and *The Mass Psychology of Fascism* all failed to come to grips with the realities of sexual life in the Nazi state. In *Mass Psychology,* we find statements such as the following:

> The possibilities of sex-economic work with chil-

dren are enormous because the children will show a burning interest. Once children and adolescents are reached on a mass basis through their sexual interests, there will be a powerful counterweight against the reactionary force: political reaction will be powerless.

When calling Reich's bluff, one is confronted with an embarrassment of riches. It is clear that the "reactionary forces" reached the adolescents through their sexual interests far more effectively than did the "progressives." Foreign-born observers saw the sex economic propaganda more clearly than the native-born Reich.

In *Riddle of the Reich,* Wythe Williams says:

> Hitler gives the youngsters more than a new faith, he gives them a new and daring freedom from the old moral code. To the restless, sex-bothered adolescents he says: "go and sin!" He appends a unique alibi — an unprecedented morality — to the new immorality For he tells them that their sinning is good for the German race and its Nazi state.

In *School for Barbarians,* Erika Mann reports the following:

> The Nazi party has always made a great point of the virility of its members. I have seen the sex instinct deliberately aroused in many ways. At mass meetings, speeches dwelling on the copulative prowess of the Nazi male would send the Storm Troopers marching out of the hall all set for demonstration. They never had to look far for a partner. German women would wait outside the meeting places. Very little preliminary courting was then required. At the movies I have seen pictures whose only purpose could have been to turn the spectators' thoughts toward procreation, with long love passages, and subsequent sequences depicting the joys of parenthood.

Hitler was no Victorian puritan. He was well aware of the powerful hold that sexuality has on the human mind. He went so far as to offer a blatantly sexual metaphor to describe the success of National Socialism in Germany: "We are an uprising of the strength of our nation; the strength of its loins, if you like." (One does not have to look very far for the sexual significance of the stiff arm salute.)

Not only was he aware of sexuality, but, as a master of mob psychology, he was able to harness its powerful psychic currents to drive the turbine of his movement. Eyewitness accounts of his oratorical rock 'n' roll abound with sexual sheens: "Down in the front row, adolescent girls sit tense, with facial expressions of those awaiting some supreme satisfaction...[afterwards] the girls dropped like slaughtered calves, sighing heavily. Joy and fulfillment."

In *Mein Kampf,* Hitler often refers to the feminine, passive nature of the mass audience, suggesting that the ultimate purpose of his speeches was not the delivery of abstract political information, but sweet-talk and seduction. Just as musicians are said to make love to the audience through their instruments, Hitler made love to the audience through his words.

Reich acknowledges, in a peripheral fashion, this subliminal aspect of Nazism in chapter four of *The Mass Psychology of Fascism,* entitled, "The Symbolism of the Swastika":

> The swastika was originally a sexual symbol. In the course of time, it took on diverse meanings, among others that of a millwheel, that is of work. The original emotional identity of work and sexuality explains a finding of a swastika with the following inscription: "Hail, Earth, mother of man. Grow great in the embrace of God, fruitful to nourish mankind." Here, fertility is represented sexually as sexual intercourse between Mother Earth and God-father. "Swastikas" in old Indian language means cock as well as voluptuary. A look at the swastika will show it to be a schematic by unmistakable presentation of two intertwined human bodies ... representing a sexual act.

It is almost comical to read of Reich's heroic efforts to save German youth from the supposedly repressive sexual attitudes of the National Socialist leadership. Sparring against the windmill of authoritarian sexual repression, Reich inveighed against the institution of the drafted Labor Services, best remembered for their massed appearance at the Nuremberg party rallies with shouldered shovels. The following paraphrase is true to the original:

> The inclusion of German youth in the labor service has interfered tremendously with their sexual life. Urgent questions have to be solved; there are serious conditions everywhere. What is the sex life of the adolescents in the camps like? The Labor Service youths are at the age of flourishing sexuality, yet there is no chance of getting together with girls. They are forced into abstinence or masturbation, which leads to disintegration of sexuality or to the development of homosexual tendencies, increased nervousness, irritability, neurotic states and physical complaints. In the course of the years, German youth, in a hard struggle against the parental home and the bosses of the system, have begun to establish their right to a healthy sex life. Youth has to fight, with all possible means, against the sexual hypocrisy, intolerance and indecency which results from the sexual oppression of youth. Their idea was that girls and boys are to live in good intellectual and sexual companionship, and that it is the duty of society to help them to do so. What is the attitude of the new German Reich?

It is truly astonishing how often wrong and how far wrong Wilhelm Reich could be. While the wind was blowing due north, he informed his loyal readers that it was blowing south. When the sun was beating down on his head, he broadcast the news that it was raining cats and dogs. If we are to accept the validity of reports from such correspondents as William Shirer, writing in the classic *Rise and Fall of the Third*

Reich, we find the attitude of the new German Reich to be surprisingly supportive:

> At eighteen, several thousand of the girls in the BDM (Band of German Maidens) did a year's service on the farms: their so-called 'Land-Jahr,' which was equivalent to the Labor Service of the young men. Their task was to help both in the house and in the fields. The girls lived sometimes in the farmhouse and often in small camps in rural districts from which they were taken by truck early each morning to the farms. Moral problems soon arose. The presence of a pretty young city girl sometimes disrupted a peasant's household, and angry complaints from parents about their daughters having been made pregnant on the farms began to be heard. But that wasn't the only problem. Usually a girls' camp was located near a Labor Service camp for young men. This juxtaposition seems to have made for many pregnancies, too. One couplet, a takeoff on the 'Strength Through Joy' movement of the Labor front, went the rounds of Germany: "In the fields and on the heath, I lose strength through joy."

It would seem that the official establishment of adjacent camps for "sex-bothered" male and female adolescents is enough to clarify the system bosses' attitude as to the desirability of sexual companionship. In fact, in their urgent desire to spark a population explosion in Germany, the system bosses set the stage for Reich's dream come true: utopian camps of youths living without adult interference or sexual repression, in which the naturally fertile sex economy would arise from the free expression of male and female attraction.

In Wilhelm Reich's philosophy of sexual freedom, there was no need to delay gratification: when the sexual desire was there, fulfillment should immediately follow. "If a boy of 15 were to develop a love relationship with a girl of 13, a free society would not only not interfere, it would affirm and protect it." According to Erika Mann, the Nazis agreed in theory and practice:

> The practical possibilities of becoming a mother are excellent, as early as 14 years of age. The 'State Youth' offers encouragement and opportunities, with its feasts, its farm years and hay loft nights. Parents watch their daughters from a distance, helplessly; they might object, but to whom? The number of illegitimate pregnancies and births among the members of the State Youth is enormous.

What we see here is a crisis of indecision among the critics of Nazism. One critic (Reich) said the Nazis' sexual morality was too restricted. Another critic (Mann) said that their sexual morality was too lax. It is as if two cartoonists tried to caricature the same politician: one thought his nose too large, and so drew a huge proboscis, while the other thought it too small and drew none at all. Seeing these critics at loggerheads, how can we know who to believe?

Many mothers and fathers, especially those of the Catholic faith, were alienated by the party's utilitarian sexual philosophy. Some parents tried to retaliate, writing and circulating underground pamphlets deploring the 'moral degeneracy' and 'un-Christian practices' which the state youth leaders encouraged their followers to indulge in. One such pamphlet, "An Open Letter to Goebbels," was pseudonymously authored by "Michael Germanicus," who charged that sex crimes were allowed and even encouraged in the camps by Hitler Youth leaders, crimes in which girls of 16 and even 14 years old had been morally and physically ruined.

While the document was officially dismissed as anti-German slander, it seems likely that every word of it was true. At the Nuremberg party rally of 1938, attended by 100,000 State Youth, it is known that more than 900 girls came home "bearing children for the Führer."

In Nazi high schools, female students would hear statements like the following from their teachers: "We shall all today or tomorrow be able to abandon ourselves to the rich emotional experience of procreating in the company of a healthy young man, without troubling about the impediments that encumber the antiquated institution of marriage."

The Ministry of Propaganda did its part in spreading the new morality, regularly briefing the editors of Nazi women's magazines on the correct line. "Lady Führer of the Reich," Frau Gertrude Scholtz-Klink, spoke to a gathering of editors in Berlin, holding up the shining example of the new German maiden who "returns to her basic urges by submitting to them humbly and with pleasure."

Some officials slipped into crude, explicit propositions in order to get German women marching, barefoot and pregnant, to the tune of "Kinder, Kuche, Kirche." Bavarian Gauleiter Paul Giesler made a long and impassioned speech to the student body of Munich University, dwelling on the duty of German girls to bear children for the Führer. He scoffed at their inhibitions and gave them an opportunity to prove themselves patriots on the spot. "If you have no one with whom to conceive children, I'll lend you one of my men," he said, proudly indicating his SS bodyguards. "I can promise that you won't be disappointed."

In their zeal to fan the fire of population growth, Nazi theorists set out after the institution of marriage, claiming it psychologically and biologically unnatural, as well as undesirable from a reproductive point of view. Reich proves himself a good German when he states:

> For a sexually intact individual, it is sex-economi-
> cally impossible to submit to the conditions of
> marital morality, only one partner, and that one
> for life. The very first prerequisite of marriage is a
> far-reaching suppression of the sexual needs...

Starting from the premise of reproductive fecundity Professor Ernst Berman of Leipzig comes to the same pro-polygamous conclusion in a Nazi-authored essay entitled, "Knowledge and the Spirit of Motherhood." He writes:

> Lifelong monogamy is perverse and would prove
> harmful to our race. Were this institution ever
> really enforced — and fortunately this is almost
> never the case — our race must decay. Every rea-

> sonably constructed state will have to regard a
> woman who has not given birth as dishonored.
> There are plenty of willing and qualified youths
> ready to fertilize the girls and women on hand.
> Fortunately, nature has made it possible for one
> stalwart lad to suffice for 20 girls. The girls, for
> their part, would gladly fulfill the demand for
> children were it not for the nonsensical so-called
> civilized idea of the monogamous marriage, an
> idea in complete contradiction to all natural facts.

Hitler laid down his justification for his break with monogamous tradition:

> A people never dies out for lack of men. After the
> Thirty Years War, polygamy was tolerated, so that
> it was thanks to the illegitimate child that the
> nation recovered its strength. As long as we have
> in Germany two and a half million more women
> than men, we shall be forbidden to despise the
> child born out of wedlock What harm is there
> in every woman's fulfilling her destiny? I love to
> see this display of health around me. The opposite
> thing would make me misanthropic.

Reich jibed with Reich in the distinction between marriage as a social convention and marriage as a natural bond between man and woman. Reich says, "Everybody knows that 'we want to get married' really means 'we want to embrace each other sexually.' A source of confusion and misery is the conflict between the legal and the factual concept of marriage. To the lawyer, marriage is a union of two people of different sex on the basis of a legal document. To the psychiatrist, it is an emotional attachment on the basis of a sexual union, usually with the wish for children."

In a move that would warm the heart of any practicing sex-economist, the State Youth leaders announced in mass meetings and on national radio that from October 1935 onwards, the state would grant recognition and support to "biological marriages" between Nazi youths of good race and correct ideas. Babies born as a result of these limited term contract arrangements would be listed as "legitimate" and the legally unwed mother could count on respect and not derision from Nazi society. Hitler speaks:

> Marriage, as it is practiced in bourgeois society, is generally a thing against nature. But a meeting between two beings who complete one another, who are made for one another, borders already, in my conception, upon a miracle...Nature doesn't care the least bit whether as a preliminary the people concerned have paid a visit to the registrar. Nature wants a woman to be fertile.

How would Reich respond to this long list of refutations and contradictions to his theory of Nazi sex repression? Perhaps he would try to slip out from under the mass of evidence by claiming that, while talking about sexual repression, he actually meant emotional repression. He might draw the line between sex and love, assert that Nazi sexuality was high in numerical quantity but low in spiritual quality. In this defense there is a grain of truth.

Looking over Nazi policy statements, it does sometimes seem that they looked at their population program as just another gear in their huge war machine. Himmler spoke of his strict selection process, how before admitting a man into the Order of the Death's Head, he examined their photographs with a magnifying glass attempting to discover racially alien characteristics: "I wanted the perfect German man, and him multiplied a million times."

The sex that transpired between men and women in the Third Reich was a part of the large scale manufacturing system that stamped out tons of bombs, tanks, guns, synthetic rubber tires and bouncing baby boys, all with replaceable parts, all shaped with only one goal: Victory!

Several sources point to a shocking, business-like coldness about the whole affair, an attitude not so much of seduction as recruitment, selection based on little else than pedigree and surface appearance. Liaisons were arranged with the same matter-of-factness by which we might make carpooling arrangements today. Consider the reasoning behind the following ads culled from the classified ads of wartime Berlin's newspapers:

> Pure, Aryan Girl, 24, strong, healthy and virile, is anxious to serve the Fatherland by being the mother of a soldier's child. Heil Hitler!

> Widow, 23, husband killed in the war, seeks to give the Fatherland a son. Father must be a serving soldier. Write…

> Young soldiers on leave can still serve the Fatherland. Aryan girl, 22, absolutely fit and strong, good position, university student, wishes to be the mother of a future soldier of Germany.

> I, too, would serve the Fatherland. I am 24 years old, unmarried and of prepossessing appearance. I seek a serving soldier of good family to be the father of a child who will fight for Germany.

In *Of Pure Blood*, Marc Hillel and Clarissa Henry give a good account of the "Lebensborns," so-called "Fountains of Life," which masqueraded as maternity homes while serving as stud farms and brothels for the SS.

Reck-Malleczwen, German aristocrat and anti-Nazi, recorded the following in his journal, which was found after his execution for treason and published under the title of *Diary of a Man in Despair:*

> A young couple in Munich recently discovered that a defect of vision, with recurrent blindness, seemed to be hereditary in the man's family. The young man had himself sterilized forthwith. But since as good Germans they were obligated to have children, the husband unflinchingly sent his wife to the Lebensborn. The Fount is an SS organization, with offices in the remains of the synagogue on Lenbachplatz … Available at the offices of the Fount is an album of the photos of guaranteed pedigree, Nordic blond SS men. The client

chooses one of these according to taste, and then indicates her choice of stud to the Fount official. Soon thereafter the client finds herself pregnant, and in due course the mother of a little Germanic pan. And this little fellow will grow up to strike down, with a completely new and unusual coldness, everything which dares to infringe on the New German Order of National Socialism...

One might start to wonder if this lust for efficiency knew no bounds. Was the act to be subjected to time and motion studies, women to be filled with Aryan babies like so many coke bottles to be filled with cola, then capped, crated and shipped? Apparently there were some boundaries which even a racial fanatic like Heinrich Himmler was reluctant to trespass.

Reichsgesundheitsführer Dr. Conti (his title is no joke — it translates "Reich Minister of Health") was, as a medical man specializing in gynecology, well aware of a technique known as "artificial insemination" developed by Russian and American scientists and applied to animal husbandry. Dr. Conti believed that this operation would be highly valuable to wartime Germany, as it would allow a war hero to do his patriotic duty without ever leaving the front. In addition, old-fashioned girls who had not fully accepted the modern Nazi attitude on sexuality might be willing to accept a pregnancy brought about by artificial insemination but not by a one night stand. He conceded a disadvantage: "There would be a rather soulless, mechanical element in the process of fertilization." But in the interests of national population policy he considered the proposition to balance out in favor of application.

Himmler checked his enthusiasm when he decreed his belief that the handling of sperm in this way degrades the quality of offspring. "I am firmly convinced that it is bound, sooner or later, to lead to the deterioration of future generations, and probably to impotence or sterility." Thus the sexual act did not quite make it from the haystack to the assembly line, but it came close.

Wilhelm Reich said "Make love — not war."

Adolf Hitler said, "Make love — make war."

> To deserve its place in history, our people must be above all, a people of warriors. This implies both privileges and obligations, the obligation of submitting to a most rigorous upbringing and the privilege of the healthy enjoyment of life. If a German soldier is expected to be ready to sacrifice his life without demur, then he is entitled to love freely and without restriction. In life, battle and love go hand in hand, and the inhibited little bourgeois must be content with the crumbs which remain. If the warrior is to be kept in fighting trim, he must not be pestered with religious precepts which ordain abstinence of the flesh. A healthy minded man simply smiles when a saint of the Catholic Church like St. Anthony bids him eschew the greatest joy that life has to give, and offers him the solace of self-mortification and castigation in its place.

Top: Michael Monagan and John of the Kids From Widney High
(Photo by Scott Lindgren.)

Bottom: Two-headed baby exhibit in Los Angeles, 1990
(Photo by Adam Parfrey.)

THE ENDANGERED FREAK

A local news show leads-in its 11 pm broadcast with an item about a baby flown all the way from Hong Kong to Portland. "Baby Kim," they say, will undergo several crucial operations within the next few days. What kind of operation? We're not told. However, a card displaying the address of a local charity for Baby Kim flashes several times while we're implored to give generously. On a nightly basis, we're treated to updates on the condition of Baby Kim, which always inspire coos, winks and goo-goos from the newscasters. A week passes. It's time, the newscaster reports excitedly, for Baby Kim to fly home to Hong Kong so that she can begin life anew. The auspicious departure at Portland Airport is captured by the betacams. For the first time, the cameras zoom in on the now-famous tyke, her face hidden under bandages and surgical tape. A newscaster beams as she reports that local contributions have saved Baby Kim from becoming a pariah in her homeland. Thanks to our generosity, Baby Kim can attend school, fall in love, marry, and have children, especially now that we've corrected her harelip.

Harelip? Is that all? I had imagined Baby Kim possessed three eyes, at the very least. No wonder the newscasters didn't mention Baby Kim's problem until the very end. Plastic surgery is no longer newsworthy, even if it involves Siamese Twins. But if the government wants hate sessions from the bourgeoisie, then we're treated to endless videotape of child amputees. When the child amputee footage is trotted out, you know we're being primed to embargo or go to war against a foreign state.

Incurables are treated in an altogether different manner. If we can no longer provide a cure, our answer is to provide "self-esteem" or the illusion of physical and intellectual parity for the handicapped. Humanist shame is expiated with nationally televised multi-million dollar events like the Special Olympics. For reasons unknown we're supposed to applaud the pluck of those poor children who run the

100-yard dash in a minute and a half. As the droolers hug Arnold Schwarzenegger on the dais, are we supposed to applaud because of the child's abnormality, or rather because of Arnold's sympathy? Would his sympathy be as acute for a child with an I.Q. of 90, or do kids really need to score closer to 50 for that special moment of affirmation from the Austrian Oak? "Self-esteem" projects are also the rage in the inner-city. What must economically disadvantaged children think when they see the same buzzwords used on them that last week comforted a legion of retards and spazzes?

Hollywood's hypocritical morality finds its most heartwarming expression in films like *Forrest Gump*, a conservative epic whose moral instructs us that the biologically deficient are compensated with a purity of heart and nobility of soul unattained by those of sound body and mind. Mother: "Who do you want to be when you grow up?" Boy: "Forrest Gump." Mother: "He was a good boy. He loved his mama."

"How do we bring back a sense of shame, of right and wrong?" quails the February 6, 1995 issue of *Newsweek*, blaming pop culture for the erosion of morality. *Newsweek* would have more profitably examined the entire feel-good posture of egalitarianism, a myth foisted on the have-nots to quell their sense of injustice. The most damaging myth of egalitarianism remains the false dichotomy of right versus left, left versus right. The amoral kids *Newsweek* cries about learn from reality — in this country, people with money are treated with respect and people without money are treated with contempt.

Newsweek's social theoreticians tell us that something is wrong when children's moral compasses cannot find magnetic North in a society that rewards Mammon. The differences between businessmen and gangsters are merely aesthetic; one prefers a business suit, the other a Raiders jacket. The latter is more flamboyant and less of a liar, and therefore is seen by children as a more desirable role model.

Now that the Cold War is directed inwardly at domestic threats, the State will bring tensions to a boil between the poor, the working poor and the lower middle-class. Those who challenge this particular stratification, turning culpability for the nation's problems on the government instead, are said to breed "terrorism." *Forrest Gump* and its New

World Order ethos regards intellectual acuity as a terrorist threat, or at the very least, a signpost of moral degeneracy.

The age of Tod Browning's *Freaks* did not stoop to portray monstrous specimens as moral Pollyannas but as a kind of Mafia that found solace and power in acts of brotherhood and retribution. Ruling this hierarchy were the true biological anomalies rather than the "gaffed" or faked freak; the value of the congenital freak was most clearly demonstrated in the size of the weekly paycheck.

Today, with advances in pre-natal science, only the rare parent would choose to bring to term such erstwhile royalty as half-man Johnny Eck, limbless Prince Randian or the cranially bizarre Koo-Koo the Bird Girl.

Faced with the decision to drain and reduce his new-born hydrocephalic child's head, Nobel Prize winner Kenzaburo Oe wished the surgeons Godspeed. The alternative was to allow the child to die. Saving the child's life would yield its own severe problem — a human being with the mentality of a two-year-old. Oe spared no expense lavishing instruction and love on Hikari, his "special son." After twenty years of patient instruction it is discovered that Hikari can scribble simple chamber music in the style of a brain-damaged Haydn. The compositions are regarded as a small miracle. A barrage of international publicity greets the retarded child's records, which become objects of curiosity that sell in the hundreds of thousands. As I listen to Hikari's simplistic compositions performed by a trio of accomplished Japanese musicians, it's difficult to conceive of either a complexity of emotion or complexity of thought; Hikari's efforts mimic early classical works in the same way a parrot mimics a voice. We're nevertheless told that Hikari's compositions are "inspirational," "moving," a connection to something ineffably deep within the human soul.

"Special Kids" at Widney High, a "special school" in Central Los Angeles, recorded an album for the folk label Rounder Records (their instructor, Michael Monagan, who provided the basic Casio-like rhythms and compositions, has nepotistic connections at the label). A full-length cd, eponymously titled *The Kids of Widney High,* contains the mangled-mouth magic of retarded children crooning ballads and screaming appreciative noises for a woman who runs the school's "primary reinforcement" program. Tiffany and other fading recording stars lend blurbs for the "good cause."

If the marketing department at Rounder exploited *The Kids From Widney High* as high concept weirdness, similar to freakish acts like the Geto Boys, the record could have been a hit. Sold as yet another "kudos for victims" project, no one could have imagined its extraordinary and irrepressible strangeness. Discovering the disc at a cut-out bin, I passed out tapes of the record for dozens of people. Inspired to further the innovation of "tardcore," I formed a pop band The Tards, recording discs for the Sympathy for the Record Industry, Man's Ruin and Amphetamine Reptile labels. The Tards have faced the same politically correct resistance in its marketing as did the brilliant *Kids from Widney High* album.

The imposition of egalitarian views is seen in the language itself. Individuals once called living skeletons are now said to suffer from anorexia; huge, ugly fat people are said to have acromegaly or elephantiasis. The once-strange sight of the bearded lady is now almost ubiquitous; women displaying facial hair are fighting "gender-based stereotype." The word "freak" has been expunged from usage altogether; the operant phrase is "physically challenged." As for the physically handicapped, we are told that using the phrase "differently abled" saves the deformed from linguistic oppression.

Even Tod Browning was forced to preface his film with an apology, his freaks exerted a fascination more personally satisfying and enriching than humanist pity. By cutting off the true source of the freaks' power, we subject them to a far more grotesque fate.

It wasn't long ago that freaks were allowed to profit from the sexual queasiness and curiosity of the normals. Pitchmen spieling in front of the midway's freak tent would play the rubes' curiosity, as he wondered if half-men (like Johnny Eck, born without buttocks or legs) possessed a cock. And, if he did, where the hell did he stuff it? The half-man, half-woman possessed an even larger question mark poised at crotch level. The rubes' desire to see an irrefutable example of the hermaphroditic mystery would leave them open to half-men, half-women acts, which raked in big money by "guaranteeing to show all" in private. Bruce Jackson, a transvestite carny, describes his transformation from man to "woman" in his book *In the Life:*

> When I was stripping with a carnival, I was billed
> as a woman. Paraffin injections for breasts and an
> elastic band for a gaff [carny term for man-made
> freakhood] ... You put a piece of Kleenex around
> the penis, just back of the head, and cinch-knot
> with three-quarter inch elastic ... And bring all of
> your equipment ... down between your legs and
> then push the testicles up into the stomach ... and
> bring everything else as tight as you possibly can
> up between the crack of your ass. Then you tie the
> elastic again so that there's another knot right at
> the base of your spine and the remaining elastic
> goes around your waist ... You can show absolute
> nakedness except you have to tweak a back panel
> .... The gaff with the elastic band makes the
> appearance of a vagina ... the bag which is now
> empty, brought forward, produces the lips of the
> vagina ... I've had men kiss and never know the
> difference.

Jackson, a gaffed transvestite, no doubt occupied a lowly position on the pay scale. The true freak was far rarer, dearer, and sought after. To compete with the true freak, the gaffs had to create an amazing act. One was described by William Lindsay Gresham in *Monster Midway* as the "crucified man," who bored holes in his hands and shot streams of water through them with the aid of small hoses. The entire skin of Fred Walters was a dark slate blue due to constant ingestion of silver nitrate.

All the big-top impresarios worth their sawdust found a lucrative biological freak. A side-showman named Slim Kelley spent years trying to track down a black logger who reportedly had only one eye in the middle of his forehead. After Kelly finally caught up with the shy prodigy, the logger turned down all the filthy lucre just to keep out of the freak circuit.

Freaks sometimes amassed small fortunes, investing in businesses or stocks before retiring in Bissonton or Gibsonton, the South Florida village that became the official community of Very Special People.

The "Ten-in-One," carny lingo for the freak tent, is where the attractions sat silently, or availed themselves of the opportunity to hawk photographs on the elevated stage. Marks milled about underneath, gawking and gasping until too spooked to look any more. A typical Ten-in-One featured pinheads, tattooed women, perhaps a crocodile-skin boy and a Thalidomide casualty Seal Girl, giants and dwarfs. "The Missing Link" or "The Wild Man of Borneo" were hairy hippies in a buzz-cut era. A couple non-freak acts, such as a sword-swallower, would round out the spectacle.

The culmination of the freak show, known as the "blow-off," required a separate admission. The blow-off usually featured the alcoholic low-life who'd chew a live chicken in exchange for a bottle of hootch and the remainder of his human dignity. Occupying the lowest rung of the carny ladder, the geek was the central image of William Lindsay Gresham's *Nightmare Alley*, a mythic story which repays the crime of hubris with the degradation of geekdom. In *Carnival*, Arthur A. Lewis describes a lady geek named Veronica Shant whose act consisted of swallowing "a half-dozen heads from live chickens and three or four field mice whole and maybe a garter snake or two." The strange and terrible saga of the geek might have originated with a Frenchman named Tarrare. According to Gould and Pyle in their 1896 classic, *Anomalies and Curiosities of Medicine:*

> Tarrare .... seized a live cat with his teeth, eventrated it, sucked its blood, and ate it, leaving the bare skeleton only. In about thirty minutes he rejected the hairs in the manners of birds of prey and carnivorous animals. He also ate dogs in the same manner. On one occasion it was said that he swallowed a living eel without chewing it; but he had first bitten off its head... He waited around butcher shops to eat what was discarded for the dogs. He drank the bleeds of the hospital and ate the dead from the dead-houses. He was suspect-

ed of eating a child of 14 months, but no proof could be produced of this. He died of purulent diarrhea, all his intestines and peritoneum being in a suppurating condition.

The Ten-in-One may very well have its origins in Babylonian Mystery Religions, where animal familiars were worshiped. The Elephant Man, the Monkey Girl, the Dog-Faced Boy, the Mule Woman all congregated there. Literary critic Leslie Fiedler pointed out in *Freaks: Myths and Images of the Secret Self* that Julia Pastrana, the so-called "Ugliest Woman in the World," was almost constantly propositioned and lusted after. Pastrana

stood only four and a half feet tall. Most of her face, including her forehead, was covered with a shocking growth of shining black hair.... Her ears were big and the loop earrings she wore made them look even bigger. Her nose was wide and squat, her nostrils enormous. Her lips, large and deformed, were surmounted by a heavy moustache. Her chin was prognathous, giving her an apelike appearance. Each jaw carried a double row of teeth, 'irregular and abnormal' (this according to Abe Lincoln's photographer Matthew Brady, who photographed Pastrana). The Ugliest Woman turned down many offers of marriage during her career and ended up marrying her manager, a man named Lent. A child was born to them, a child so hideous that it is said Pastrana died of heartbreak from the sight of it. The child died early in infancy, and was stuffed and exhibited alongside her taxidermied mother in many exhibitions up until the mid-1970s.

Grace McDaniels, the "Mule-Faced Woman," was, some say, misnamed. She ought to have more accurately called the "Hippopotamus Woman." In his memoirs, McDaniel's employer, Harry Lewiston, described her appearance so:

> Her flesh was like red, raw meat; her huge chin
> was twisted at such a distorted angle, she could
> hardly move her jaws. Her teeth were jagged and
> sharp, her nose large and crooked. The objects
> which made her look most like a mule were her
> huge, mule-like lips. Her eyes stared grotesquely
> in their deep-set sockets. All in all, she was a sick-
> ening, horrible sight.

Frederick Drimmer, of *Very Special People* fame, quotes circus hand Edward Malone to the effect that Grace "was always one of the most pleasant women I ever knew. She was attractive to a lot of men, too, believe it or not. I can't tell you how many proposals of marriage she received." The "Mule-Faced Woman" finally accepted a proposal from a handsome, younger man, with whom she had a son. She died in 1958, a contented, elderly woman.

The erotic attractions of the grotesquely ugly or immensely obese woman are as new as the Willendorf Venus, a statuette traditionally interpreted as a Stone Age fertility symbol. Latter-day adipose cults include NAAFA, the National Association for the Advancement of Fat Americans, and the OCO, a cryptic-occult organization whose rituals venerate Ceres, the Goddess of fecundity. Anton Szandor LaVey, High Priest of the Church of Satan, announced his preference for chubby women in his book *The Satanic Witch,* and was known to attend NAAFA meetings. LaVey states that today's predilection for the anorexic, boyish woman corresponds to the de-virilizing of the American male. In his teenage years, LaVey worked the carny circuit, which provided him an excellent school on the forbidden aspects of human behavior.

"The fat women," remembers LaVey, "had an appetite for sex that matched their appetite for food. They were simply voracious. And they didn't lack for suitors, either. The suitors all seemed to be thin, wiry men — fox terrier types."

Zap comics contributor turned fine artist Robert Williams recounts a youthful escapade with a fat woman:

> I saw this long line of guys in front of the Fat Woman's trailer. I asked one of the guys what it was all about. "We're standing in line for blowjobs," said the guy at the end of the line. Being young, curious and horny, I got in line myself. When it came my turn I went into the woman's trailer, saw this puddle of slime next to the Fat Lady's foot — all the spunk she spat out from all the other guys. Next, she was blowing me, and then I noticed that some of the guys were peeking in at me, so I started flapping my arms like a chicken and crowing, putting on a show for them, then wham! I slipped and fell face-down into that pile of spunk.

While plump people tended to signify an erotic element, the skinnies — with such names as the Shadow and the Living Skeleton — personifed death itself. It's interesting that there has never been a recorded instance of a Thin Woman exhibited in a Ten-in-One, though recent headlines and television movies give us freak content in docu dramas about Karen Carpenter's anorexia. As a publicity stunt, carnivals would often announce a marriage between the Fat Lady and the Thin Man, though in modern times there was been only one instance of such a mating. Peter Robinson, the stuttering Living Skeleton from *Freaks*, married the 467 pound Bunny Smith.

"Many women," muses Anton LaVey, "are attracted to unusual and different sorts of men, and freaks are certainly different. Johnny Eck, for example, though he lacked a bottom half, was handsome and talented and attracted the interest of many women. He aroused their sense of curiosity. Armless and legless Prince Randian, the Human Torso, fathered four daughters and a son. Some freaks, however, if they are too repulsive, cross over the threshold of curiosity. The Elephant Man, or Bill Dirks, for example."

Dirks was the phenomenally hideous prodigy who sported a wide cleft traveling down the center of his face like the San Andreas Fault. Within this cleft a rude third eye was painted. LaVey tells the story of Dirks going shopping, the brim of a large baseball cap pulled over his face.

A smartass bag checker razzes him with, "You trying to hide your face or something?" whereupon Dirks tears off his cap to expose his deformity. The bag checker faints dead away. Painter Joe Coleman got to know Dirks when visiting the Straits show near the P.T. Barnum Museum in Bridgeport, Connecticut. Coleman was sketching some of the freaks when Dirks informed Coleman, "Lookeee here, I'm an artist, too," and scratched out a stick figure on Coleman's sketchpad. "Poop-eye! This is poop-eye!" exclaimed Dirks, in some kind of quasi-conscious reference to the fake eye painted on his monstrous axe-face.

Midgets — not to be confused with dwarfs — are other examples of the oversexed freak. Well-formed but tiny, the self-appointed aristocrat of the Ten-in-One, midgets sneer at the malformed dwarf, whose head and torso might seem normal in size, but whose arms and legs appear foreshortened. LaVey informs me that

> Dwarfs have a quite ordinary level of sexual desire, but midgets are constantly on the prowl. It's interesting to consider that the male midget's taste is for the oversized — in cars, cigars and girls. I was once the object of a female midget's sexual advances, but I wasn't interested in fucking someone who looked like a fragile, bone-china kewpie doll. A word of advice: don't treat midgets like little boys or as people less than normal size. I learned my lesson when I once tried to help a midget move an elephant tub. He cursed me like a demon and kicked me in the shins.

The most complex sex lives of freaks are experienced by Siamese Twins. Many connected twins are able to feel the sensations of their partners. The pretty and demure Hilton Twins, Violet and Daisy, were finally able to individuate their sex lives by "getting rid of each other mentally." Violet took a husband, placing a cloth between her and Daisy while her husband consummated their marriage vows. The prim Daisy, despite all her best efforts, was mortified to discover that she could not blot out the experience of orgasm experienced by her sister.

The famous Siamese Twins, Chang and Eng Bunker, settled down in North Carolina after retiring from Barnum's traveling circus. Despite the rancor of local townies, Chang and Eng married local girls, Adelaide and Sarah Ann Yates. The Bunkers built houses a mile apart, setting up two different households. They spent three days in one house and three days in the other, a rigid schedule adhered to until death. They agreed to become masters of their own household, leaving their twin to a three-day period of absolute servitude. Eng fathered seven boys and five girls; Chang, seven girls and three boys. All were normal except for one boy and girl fathered by Chang, who were deaf-mutes.

The famous Tocci Twins, Giovanni and Giacomo, joined at the lower back, sported four arms and two legs. Their one set of genitals had to satisfy the two different women they eventually married.

Frank Lentini, on the other hand, was blessed with two functioning sets of genitals, but used them on one wife only, with whom he had three sons and a daughter. Lentini's greatest asset was a nearly full-sized third leg which grew straight out of his ass which he used to kick balls and dance. Myrtle Corbin sported four legs, two small ones growing inside of two normal-sized appendages. Myrtle had two sets of sex organs; out of one she bore three children, out of the other she had two.

Amputee Times, now defunct, was the fetishist networking paper for armless and legless women. The fetish was no doubt encouraged by Annie Sprinkle's on-screen cavortings with Long Jean Silver, who masturbated Sprinkle by inserting a pretty stump inside Annie's clam trap.

The infamous sage of sex magick, Aleister Crowley, took out the following advertisement in a Greenwich Village newspaper back in 1915:

> WANTED: DWARFS, Hunchbacks, Tattooed Women, Harrison Fischer Girls, Freaks of All Sorts, Colored Women, only if exceptionally ugly or deformed, to pose for artist — Apply by letter with a photograph.

Notice that this ad was posted seventy years before Joel-Peter Witkin got in the act. None of Crowley's biographers believe that Aleister used these freaks for anything other than twisted sexual *hors d'oeurves* on top of his usual diet of buggery, felching and self-abuse.

Since Crowley's time a change has come to pass to normalize the sex lives of the severely handicapped. A recently published book titled *Sexual Options for Paraplegics and Quadriplegics* comes complete with a forward by *Joy of Sex's* Alex Comfort that asserts, "Virtually nobody is too disabled to derive some satisfaction and personal reinforcement from sex." The textbook includes how-to photos complete with heart-rending snapshots of flaccid and cathetered crippled dicks yanked and sucked by blasé young women. The book also discloses complex, artificial methods by which seminal fluid may be tricked out of the cripple's body, thus assuring the handicapped their reproductive rights. This new concern for the reproductive rights of the malformed can be contrasted to the eugenic programs of the 1920s, in which many countries and American states practiced preventive sterilization of the "mentally and physically unfit."

Eugenic courts, inspired by American example, became the cornerstone of Nazi philosophical practice. It is interesting to wonder what German eugenic courts would have made of the claim found in Robert G.L. Waite's book, *The Psychopathic God,* that Hitler possessed only one testicle. Waite's theory may in fact have been inspired by a famous World War II period parody of the Colonel Bogey March: "Oh, Hitler, he only had one ball / Goering had two but they were small / Himmler was somewhat similar / But Goebbels had no balls at all."

The ancients believed that birthing a freak was nothing less than a portent of bad luck. The ancients would not understand the point of current films like *Mask* or *The Elephant Man,* which hold that freaks represent the noblest expressions of the human spirit. The enlightened attitude of *Mask* and *The Elephant Man* may be, in the end, a sop to the guilt pangs of our equalitarian culture. We must re-learn to gawk without shame, to admit our fascination with deformity, the biologic expression of the *fin-de-siécle*. If we aren't allowed to know the "other," we sure as hell will never understand ourselves.

B'bye!

David and Violet Brandenburger, founders of I CAN

(photo by Ted Soqui)

PLEASE MAY I TOUCH YOUR SCAR?
QUEASY HOURS AMONG I CAN:
A CULT OF SEX-OBSESSED CRIPPLES

The Brandenburgers — big fat David and tiny, quadriplegic Violet — whose sex therapy cult they call "I CAN," have no use for your pity. And despite being two very unlovely physical specimens, David and Violet claim to have attained Buddha's sense of self-perfection. Without, that is, all the mental-and-moral-self-purification folderol.

Bludgeoned with severe rheumatoid arthritis at the age of two, Violet Brandenburger's limbs are gnarled, wasted and practically useless, her bones shriveled and calcifying; a severed facial nerve has paralyzed one side of her face. Even sitting up is a painful chore. But that doesn't appear to restrict orgastic indulgence. "I tell you what, man," boasts Violet's hubby, David, "when I first met Violet, she was getting as much dick as I was getting pussy. I've never seen this lady want for male attention."

No mere sex object, Violet should be compared to a kind of Goddess, kind of like the ancient pagan temple prostitutes, or is it temple priestesses? David tells me that the ancient Goddesses served both roles. It was the Goddess Violet, after all, who first experienced the Orbital Orgasm, a heaven-and-earth shattering convulsion that remains I CAN's proudest discovery.

Violet: "I found early on that I can shut off the pain if I turn on the pleasure. The human body cannot feel pleasure and pain at the same moment. We're inspiration for *anybody* to know that they can have fulfilling sensual and sexual lives. 'If I Can, You Can,' that's my motto. The only limitations you have are in your mind."

The Brandenburgers characterize their non-profit corporation as a "human potential" or "growth" organization, in some ways similar to est, Scientology, Sandstone, or More House, in which a student's "tapes" are "reorganized" or "erased" by therapists or counselors to ostensibly create a happier or more fulfilled personality. The afore-mentioned human potential groups are comparative supernovas to the I CAN asteroid, which navigates its tenuous, loopy orbit in a modest three bedroom home in a rough East San Diego neighbor-hood near Lemon Grove.

The Brandenburgers, who can rarely afford to advertise their services, rely upon word-of-mouth and referrals for prospective students. The tithing scheme is flexible. Some students pay only for courses; others pledge their entire income to the Brandenburgers to prove their "love and devotion" to the cause. "The Hundred Percenters we consider family members," says David, "where we'd die for them or whatever."

A mere handful of students currently pay into the Brandenburgers' "Institute for the Realization of Human Potential." And despite some former members' grumblings to the contrary, David holds that "this isn't a money hustle. Whether it's More House or Scientology, they're all into some kind of money hustle. That's not our bag."

The I CAN bag accommodates three-parts More University teachings (David spent many years "training" at the San Francisco Bay Area-based sex therapy commune), two-parts learn-by-Violet's-example cripple worship, one-part Taoist Erotic Massage and a dash of para-psychology.

There's no address on the I CAN house, just a breadbox-sized paint-ed wood sign that says, "HERE." It's one of those squat low-middle-class stucco jobs with gravel instead of a front lawn. Chainsmoking David Brandenburger, capacious belly protruding beyond his t-shirt, testicles visible below his shorts, stands sentinel at the front screen door. White trash furnishings inside: worn shag carpet, glass case dis-playing ceramic figurines, unicorns and clowns. Stale, uncirculated air, the smell of mineral oil, sweat, farts and cigarette smoke.

Dwarfing everything else in the front room is a huge iron lung-like machine labeled VIBROSAUN, a five thousand dollar heat-and-vibration gizmo that services the I CAN members as a pre-orgasmic relaxation apparatus. Red L.E.D. lights and numbers flash on the front panel, reassuring its current occupant that the machine is doing something quite scientific and impressive.

"I don't use the heat when I'm in the Vibrosaun," says David. "My belly hits the overhang and the hot air doesn't circulate where it should. Hey, take your clothes off and take the Vibrosaun for a test drive."

No thanks.

"We want to invite you to experience a free bodywork session today."

Maybe later.

There's a crowd in the bedroom, doing touchy-feely things and giggling on the huge waterbed. Violet — known as "The Main Attraction" — has her twisted little hands massaged by erstwhile chiropractor and resident Hundred Percenter, Dean Nicholls. "You blow people's minds when you tell 'em a little cripply-wipply can do all that she can do," says Violet's proud hubby. "Let me show you the video of Violet hang gliding," enthuses David as he pops in a videocassette in the VCR. Footage from a local newscast rhapsodizes about Violet's achievement, a typical handicapped-person-beats-the-odds story. "Quiet!" shushes David, "here's the part where you can hear Violet cumming!" Sure enough, an "oooooooohh" is audible on the air as Violet is shown flying through the air with the greatest of ease.

David looks at his watch and bellows: "FUCK." Violet explains: "He's a wrestling freak, and he's missed a few minutes of the match."

You mean Hulk Hogan?

"I don't watch that WWF crap!" the fat man cries. "I watch the real stuff. WCW, World Championship Wrestling. It used to be called the NWA, which was the oldest sanctioning body of wrestling going back to the early 1900's."

Violet eyeballs a wrestler named Sting, a blond slab with crew cut and Indian war paint, whose poster is thumbtacked to the bedroom wall. "I got to meet him and get his autograph. He's better live than on tv. He's got a gorgeous body. Uhhnn, just to die for." The entire bedroom is, in fact, decorated with Violet's tastes in mind. There's more beefcake on display in a homoerotic print celebrating the Israeli athletes killed at the Munich games: long-distance runners, loins discreetly veiled by an Israeli flag, sprint down a rocky ridge descending from some heavenly Valhalla. Reproductions of clowns, clowns, clowns, wall-hangings of unicorns and dragons. Comedy and tragedy masks with the yin-yang symbol painted on them. Inexplicably, there's a velvet painting of a confused-looking Jesus sandwiched between a marijuana water pipe and a More House symbol. All "toys that make me happy," gleams Violet.

DAVID PUTS HIS MOUTH WHERE THE MONEY IS

Now in her early 40s, Violet, born Violet Martinez in San Juan, Puerto Rico, is the youngest victim on record diagnosed as having juvenile rheumatoid arthritis. Doctors were doubtful that she'd last five years. Daughter of a naval officer, she moved from Puerto Rico to Spain to England, and as a teenager to the island of Guam, where she conducted many dangerous liaisons with the band members and the Corpsmen at the Naval hospital. At Shaminade College in Hawaii, Violet directed and acting in student productions. "I played Mrs. Bramston in *Night Must Fall;* I hated her, a neurotic wheelchair case."

True to the time, Violet joined encounter groups and lectures of mystical topics throughout the 1970's. In 1978 she met David Brandenburger at the Aquarian Foundation, a Hawaiian Spiritualist Church.

"I saw him there, always flirting with the young females. I was saying, 'how are you going to keep it up, guy?' One day I was dragged out to a healing meeting on the subject of chakras. Then this funny-looking guy comes bopping over and we started talking. We got into a conversation, going higher and higher and higher. It was all loaded with sexual overts and it wasn't even subtle. And I looked at him and said, 'Do you want to put your money where your mouth is?'"

"Actually," David corrects, "you said, 'Do you want to put your mouth where the money is?'"

"I'm used to — as a disabled female — getting a lot of men coming on to me with, 'I could make your life so happy,' and then when you say, 'Okay, let's go play,' they go ... [*hacks, coughs*]. Or turn out to be absolutely dead in bed. [David] was bragging and carrying on and then when I busted him he said, 'I have to call the house.' I say, 'Fine, there's a pay phone at the end of the hall.' Then he stands there like a little boy shuffling his feet and says, 'I don't have a dime.' Well, I always carry at least a dime, so I whipped it out and he made the phone call. And my husband at the time, who was a gay male, and his lover, who lived more at our place than his — I told them David was coming home and these guys went crazy and tried to talk me out of it. When we retired to the bedroom, David actually sat there and asked me about every scar on my body, touching them, feeling them in a loving manner. He said 'If we're going to make out I want to know what your physical limitations are.' This was a novel idea. This is the way two people sexing and sensing each other should be. Instead of the find 'em, fuck 'em and forget 'em club, he stuck around."

David stuck around at first simply to collect Violet's social security check. "It made very good business sense. At that time, I hadn't gotten on social security yet myself. She was living with a couple guys who were taking all that money. I said, why don't I live with you and we can keep the money *in* the house."

"That made sense to me," remarks Violet, "especially since I wanted to get rid of my troublemaking housemates."

"So I moved in with her. One thing I'm really good at and that's money. I'm a master of deficit spending."

"I know I loved the guy. He wasn't quote, in love, unquote, in the romantic sense when we got married. But then he woke up one day and realized, 'Hey, I really do love this woman.'"

With all the sucking and fucking going on, isn't there any sexual jealousy?

"Humans aren't monogamous by nature," says Violet, as Dean the masseur fluffs up her pillows. "When we first got together I asked him for two things. Don't ever let me catch you in a lie, 'cause I'll walk and that's it. Two was, let's make it an open relationship and if either one of us sees something we're interested in *playing* with, then we go to the other and ask, 'Is it okay to have a date with so-and-so?' I was in the hospital one time and I got this phone call from David. Apparently, he picked up a hippie lady hitchhiker, and she was saying, 'I'll give you a blowjob if you drive me forty miles beyond where you're going. He actually told the hitchhiker 'It's fine with me but I got to get permission from my wife.'"

"Actually, Violet, the word was not permission, it was *agreement,*" interrupts David.

Violet giggles and coughs. A student lights a cigarette for her, stuffs it between one of her arthritic fingers. She cranes forward to lip the filter. "My mistake. He calls me up and tells me the whole story and I said 'go for it, 'cause it's almost over with visiting hours and I'm not in a good physical space. Go have fun and make sure it's a good blowjob."

David beams. "She was the first woman to have me *right*. Shit, I didn't care what the package was. She had me *right*. And I never made out with a cripply-wipply before. All those scars from all those operations. How would this move? How would that not move? So I could make love with her and not hurt her."

"It was what I always wanted. Then David put the cherry on the icing and said, 'There's a whole group of people who feel like I do. Then I met the higher-ups at More House and took some of their courses."

More House (now known as More University, a little-publicized but influential "growth" group that holds seminars and encounter groups on money, relationships and sex) provided the practical and ideological foundation for much of the Brandenburgers' work. Most I CAN cant (using such vocabulary as hexing, agreement, doing) has its origin in More House teachings. David credits his extended stint at the original San Francisco Bay Area More House for saving his life. Called the "Colonel Sanders of the human potential movement," More House's founder, Victor Baranco, profited off of real estate schemes, the kind suggested by the book, *How to Buy Real Estate With No Money Down*. Baranco would take out loans on undervalued property, order free labor More Housers to get out their dry wall and paintbrushes, and then re-sell the renovated real estate at inflated prices.

An entire chapter of the 1972 Rolling Stone book release, *Mindfuckers: A Source Book on the Rise of Acid Fascism in America,* profiles Baranco and his More House inspiration; the other mind-fuckers profiled are Charles Manson and Mel Lyman. It was about this time David Brandenburger put in heavy hours with the group, painting houses and "making out with at least four different women a day."

"More House saved my life. I'd been heavy into drugs, I was into the SDS, the Weathermen. I'd been in jail, I'd been in mental institutions. I was headed towards dying or being locked up and their teaching me agreement and perfection and total responsibility turned my life around. The sex stuff was a bonus."

Sometimes, David Brandenburger and fellow More Housers would do the "sex stuff" on camera. "They did a whole bunch of doing demonstration tapes at More House, and they were so controversial they couldn't get them released into the educational market so they wound up selling them to porn distributors.

"The movie I made was one of the ten minute black and white things on super 8. Me and a girl who was living at More House at the time were hitchhiking one day and we were picked up by this guy who took us to dinner, then took us out to his house. He had a crew cut, 45 or 50 years old, and though you could swear he was a redneck, he brings out a cardboard box with half a pound of dope in it. We'd smoke and then he asked us if we wanted to be entertained, and he brings out a bunch of those ten minute films. And they were so stupid. Me and that broad looked at each other and said, 'Hell, we can do better than that!' He said, 'Sure, yeah, show me.' So we did something right there in front of him on the floor. He went out the next day and spent two or three thousand dollars on film equipment and brought us over and had us make a movie. He made fifty thousand bucks on it.

"Pat Matlock [like David Brandenburger, Buddha-obese] ran the group I first attended," David recalls. "I went home with him the first night I met him." It was in a so-called Players Group, "where we did all kinds of weird things in the areas of sensuality," when David discovered his role in life, as an impulsive, mad-dog character named "Animal."

"We were always doing some really strange things. I remember one of the ladies, a housewifey type, said, 'I've always had the fantasy of getting up on a table and stripping in front of a group of strangers.' She jumps on the table and I crawl over to her and start pawing. Pat says, 'David, get down, David, get down.' I continue pawing at her. And then he says, 'Animal, go into the kitchen. So I go WHOOOOOO and crawl into the kitchen on my hands and knees and hide behind the counter, moaning and groaning while this woman finishes her strip.

"Then a hunky guy stands up, a guy who prided himself on being a real stud, and he said 'I'd like to do that, too.' And when he begins to strip, I go WHOOOO WHOOOO ARF ARF ARF! Pat goes, 'Go get him, Animal.' And so I run over there and completely strip him naked. Using my teeth, I pull his shirt off, get his belt, pull down his pants. And I thought if I kiss this guy at the head of his dick he'll fall over dead, so I just walked off. Pat says, 'Good Animal, good Animal.' From then on, Animal was the person who had less limitations than anybody else.

"Like that time in a sensuality course when we had this young stud who pulled up in his twenty thousand dollar Porsche and his silk tie and all that shit. Victor was teaching the course and I wasn't wearing anything more than I am now. The stud says to Victor, 'I don't understand what you're saying. I'm here to learn how to get more pussy. Vic looked at him and said, 'Animal, stand on the table.' He said to the guy with the perfect hair, 'Look at this guy. His nuts are hanging out of his pants. He probably hasn't brushed his teeth in a month. He's a slob. But he gets more pussy than anyone in this whole Institute. What did you say your problem was?' That shut him up."

Winded by the story, David pauses to huff on a cigarette, "So I get to boss everyone around because I got less limitations. I get to push their limitations."

"We get to push yours, too," reminds Violet.

"When you can find them," retorts David.

"I got a road map."

"You cheat. You've been married to me for thirteen years."

"That ain't cheating, that's doing time," says Violet with a laugh, and the other I CANers lollygagging on the waterbed roar appreciatively.

Behind the Green Door

The I CANers are anxious to meet the journalist. So I'm provided warm introductions all around:

(Blind) Mike Meehan: The senior I CAN member (nine years) who credits the Brandenburgers for giving him the self-confidence to keep his girlfriend and daughter happy. He now lives in his own home, minutes away from the I CAN house.

Dean Nicholls: Third in command, this New Age Hundred Percenter integrates Joseph Kramer's Taoist Erotic Massage and Light Touch therapy into the More/I CAN workbook.

Tony Roberts: Diminutive, dark-haired, axe-faced I CAN's "Director of Parapsychology" teaches courses on "Witchcraft and Demonology," "Developing Your Telepathic Abilities," "Para-psychology and ESP," among others.

Juanita Walker seems to be pushing 50. "Sexing" older women is an I CAN specialty, as David Brandenburger attests: "A big success story of ours was this 62-year old concert violinist who took our sensuality course. We took her to see *Deep Throat* and *Behind the Green Door*. She went home and masturbated for hours. She went from high collars and bras to short skirts. And she was really built! She looked like a woman of 40, really!"

I CAN reconstituted Mike O.'s sex life following a severe car accident. David: "His brains were falling out of his head, and then he went into a coma. He eventually came out of it and had to re-learn everything. How to talk, all of it. Now he's got his wife back thanks to us."

Top: Ain't they got fun! From left to right: David Brandenburger, Dean Nicholls, Tony Roberts, Violet Branderburger, Blind Mike Meehan, Alan Kohler, Juanita. (Photo by Adam Parfrey)

Bottom: Prelude to the three-hour orgasm: David works Violet's digits. (Photo by Adam Parfrey)

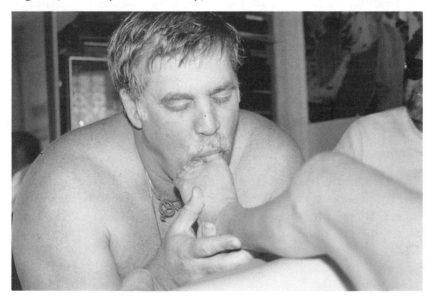

Alan Kohler: The newest house member, who is afflicted with AIDS, functions on the low end of the I CAN totem pole. "We call him our House Effect," David explains. "It's his job to take care of us, take care of the house. We're teaching him to have pleasure. You see, if you like to have a clean house, then cleaning a house should be pleasurable. We call it 'responsible hedonism.'" Apparently, the responsible hedonism also pertains to safe sex practices. An I CAN textbook, *The One Hour Orgasm*, suggests the use of Saran Wrap as a kind of viral screen.

By now, the entire I CAN gang is fondling each other, cooing, fingering and rubbing. Oily flesh starts to heat; there's nowhere for the exhalations to go except back up the nostrils again. Juanita rubs on Dean's back, provoking the objection of Dean's flyweight lover, Tony: "Juanita, I'm getting jealous." Violet, salaciously: "Juanita needs another man over there." Cheers, whistles from the peanut gallery. Violet continues, "Juanita doesn't only come over here for classes and private hours, she comes over here for lots and lots of hugs. She's a hug freak." Tony assents, "She's a hug monster."

The photographer snaps some candids. David projects his gut out even further than is natural: "I'm proud of my belly." Tony: "Yeah David, show 'em your triplets."

Howls of "yuck!" and "oh, gross!" as David propels the fake choppers out of his mouth, hamming for the camera. "I didn't want to fuck with real teeth. I deliberately let them rot. All my life I had oral surgeons, braces, constant fucking with my teeth and I finally got sick of it and let them go bad until I found a dentist who would pull 'em. Which they usually refrain from doing when you're thirty years old. I love dentures."

"I have a joke," offers Juanita. "A woman should have a menagerie. She should have a Jaguar in the garage, a mink on her back, a tiger in bed, and a jackass to pay the bills." Violet cackles.

Tony's a bit distressed: "What about for men? I'd like to have that."

"You would? I guess it's not a sexist joke after all," relents Juanita.

"Ah, shucks!" says Violet out the side of her paralyzed mouth.

Alan gets in on the fun: "What does a doe do on a Saturday night? Go to the Elks lodge and blow a few bucks." [*Lots of laffs.*]

Tony's goes one better: "Do you know the difference between a straight faith healer and a gay faith healer, don't you? The straight faith healer will say, 'Jaysus will save you, be healed.' Gay faith healer says, 'Well, get over it, Mary.' [*The gay guys giggle.*]

Juanita: "You know why women have two sets of lips? So they can piss and moan at the same time." [*Screams, people falling on the floor, beating the carpet with their fists.*]

"You see," says David, "We're crazy here. We call it functional insanity. We're all nuts. And Violet is Nurse Ratched." He takes another puff on the constant cigarette; the cigarette haze burns my eyes. "We don't trust air that you cannot see, taste or smell.

"Did I tell you how Blind Mike got confronted this morning? 'Nita came in and I told her that we all got adjusted, and she wanted to know if she could get adjusted, and I said, 'That's easy enough to arrange.' She said, 'I've got to take my clothes off.' I said, 'No, just your bra.' So I started unbuttoning her top, she pulls her top down, and I unsnapped her bra, and I'm sitting there holding her breasts and I said, 'Oh Mike, check this out,' and I grabbed Mike's hand, put it on her breast and both of them turned red."

"He's always pushing me beyond my limitations," explains Juanita, a little annoyed. "David's always trying to get me out of my bra when I come here." Adds Tony, "And he usually succeeds."

"Let me tell you something about sexual conditioning," lectures David. "A couple came to us, they'd been married for eight or ten years. She couldn't get off, she was frigid. They met when they were in high school. He was the jock, she was the cheerleader. Both of them of course were inexperienced. He's gonna have his first date with her and asked the guys in the locker room, 'What shall I do?' And the older guys said, 'When you get that bra off, thump her right on the nipple. Women go nuts for that.' And she's having her own conversation and saying, 'I really like this guy. I'll do whatever it takes to have this guy around.' And her girlfriends say, 'Just pretend to enjoy whatever he's doing. That's how you land him.'

"The date finally comes and they're making out in the back of the car and they're excited and he gets her bra off and goes thump. She jumps, then remembers what her girlfriends told her and she goes, 'Mmmmm,' and then he goes thump again. And again. Well, ten years later she can't cum. Guess why.

"When I finally got into doing sensuality with a woman, I figured the smartest thing I could do was whatever she told me. And I shut my ego up. You can't lose that way. I know now how to please any broad."

The Goddess Violet cuts in. "My pet peeve is that women are allowed the sensual aspect, but men are getting ripped off sensually and sexually. The normal male orgasm may be for a few seconds to a minute and a half. The woman can have an orgasm for as long as she wants. The creative side of the males has been suppressed by the females. Because we've lied, like David's titty thump story."

Through a cigarette haze thick and acrid, David pontificates: "Some people love liver. I throw up just to smell it. And if we're that different on taste, think of how we are that different on orgasm sensation."

"In rehab centers," says slow, brain-damaged Mike O. hiding at the far side of the waterbed, "they teach you that you are mutilated, not a whole human being. Especially in sensuality. They say, 'You're going to have to face it, that part of your life is over. And it's not. It doesn't have to be over."

How do you go about restoring a sex life to a paralytic?

"First you've got to build up people mentally," explains David. "If the nerve endings aren't working, we work on conceptual — that's mental — sex. It's what you call BADA or body memory. You can have a person work with the memory of sensation. It's not necessary to re-create these feelings physically."

But what if the genitals are not functioning?

"They can be more functional than a doctor will lead a patient to believe. I remember an anecdote by Vic Baranco, who said he would only be convinced that a patient was paralyzed from the waist down if he hit his penis with a hammer. If he felt anything, then he'd lighten up next time." David fingers the I CAN medallion around his neck, a peace sign turned on its side, with a circle, an arrow and a cross at the end of each line beyond the circle. "The I CAN symbol means you're perfect, it also means I exist to serve you, and you have to go through a special training process to wear one."

Violet, rolling in the waterbed waves, beseeches the nearest available student to insert a long drinking straw, attached to a clown-faced sports bottle, into her mouth. Juanita rolls around in the waterbed next to her, gazing fondly. "When I met Violet it was a fantastic experience."

"For a long time 'Nita stumbled over saying the words 'blind' or 'crippled' or whatever. She'd stop just before they came out," David recalls.

"It's really been incredible to me, that [Blind] Mike and Violet are human beings. Violet and I have an incredible mind link. For instance, we do the exact same things the same days. Yesterday, for example, was a blowout day for the both of us."

"I lay the whole day under the comforter and just vegged," says Violet. "Juanita had the same kind of day."

Dean: "We should mention something about the mind link, too. We discovered a new form of orgasm that only seems to happen between two males. Both of us feel it at the same time. Electric shockwaves. The one producing it feels the same way."

"We were wondering," Violet interjects, "if it would feel the same way man-man or female-man. I maintain that it would be more like a flavor difference than a total difference."

Tony's got the answer: "The first time it happened, Dean said, 'What are you doing, I'm feeling these electric shocks surging through my body.' What had happened was, fifteen seconds after I started blowing him he felt this sudden — like he was beginning to have an orgasm, but it didn't happen, but then he felt these electrical shocks going through him and he realized that I was the one producing them. Unconsciously, what I had done was make up a mind link with him. Then I became conscious of it and built up one of these charges, and I would send it to him, from my mouth to his dick. He would flail around and then he'd send it right back to me. And then it would make me jerk around a bit. My intent when I started to blow him was to have him reach an orgasm, but then all this started and we never reached the orgasm state but it was just as pleasurable."

"You missed a step in there," reminds Violet. "Tony had an attitude change from 'This is the best tasting dick' to focusing his attention on Dean and taking the maximum pleasure for himself, and when that bond is made, then you can establish a mind link. It was easier to establish with Tony because he has his telepathic capacities. That's the start of what we call the Orbital Orgasm."

Tony: "I'm producing in Dean what Violet produces in David."

"I can produce it in Violet," says David, in a gruff, defensive tone. "One of the major purposes of More University is to train a man how to cum like a woman. We've got four people in the room here now that can produce an Orbital Orgasm. To get there, one person must focus his full attention on the other person. The other key is that the person who is being rubbed on must totally surrender to the person doing the rubbing. Which is difficult, especially for a man. We're not trained to have attention put on us. So for a man to surrender his ego to another person is to give up quite a lot. If Violet is sucking on me, I'm not supposed to even reach up and do this [*mimes grubbing Violet's hair*] because it's distracting to the both of us. You've got to really clear your mind."

"The hardest part is the mind chatter," says Violet.

"You've got to be in a meditative state of receptivity," offers Dean.

"It took Violet and I three years to develop the Orbital Orgasm," says David."

Why so long?

"My resistance."

"It's hard for David just to receive. He'll get turned on and try to rub on my hair or rub on my clit. Generally put himself into a cause position. The only way I could break through his ego bullshit is tell him, 'You're not even allowed to move.' Once that was happening I could sense the difference in him and could then go through and create the orgasm experience."

"In the mind link, it's Violet's viewpoint of the orgasmic experience that she's creating in me. We're looking at using this mind link for something more than pleasure, using it as a diagnostic tool, to see what's wrong with someone, use it as a healing technique."

Another cigarette is stuffed into Violet's paw. She puffs and declaims, "Men have been led to believe that once you ejaculate, that's it, it's a downhill ride. We've found that it continues on the same height and can go higher and higher and higher through intent and attention. A little bit of coaching here and there, and well, there's your willing victim. Turn him into a puddle!"

"We've gone as long as three hours," blurts David.

"He was crying uncle at the end," laughs Munchkin-voiced Violet. "His cummer was stuck. Stuck on orgasm! pleasure! sensuality! for three hours. Finally he yelled 'uncle! uncle! uncle!'"

Three hours, I wonder. Isn't that an awful lot of fluid to lose?

"I didn't mind it," David beams.

Violet illustrates: "It's like a spurt spurt then dribble, dribble, dribble. And we always have our drinks nearby."

"When Violet was doing this to me for the first time," remembers David, "the pleasure would get so extreme that I would astrally project out of my body. I would do this to non-confront what was happening. And then I would come back from the astral plane and say, 'Gee, Violet, when will I start cumming?' and she'd say, 'You already did.' If you walk up to somebody and say you've just had a three hour long orgasm, they're going to say you're nuts."

The I CAN mystical component doesn't end at mouth-on-penis or mouth-on-clitoris mind-links. Tony Roberts reveals how he exorcised some mischievous spirits lurking around the house: "We've gotten some interesting entities around here. One that was erasing the memory in the word processor."

"And stealing pills and checks and papers," David adds.

"I'm a sensitive," relates Tony, "born with a Venetian veil over my face. I told the spirits that I was aware of their presence to cut out their shit, fuck off."

Alan, the House Effect, enters with a trayful of ice teas. He lingers, looking to Violet with mournful puppy-dog eyes, waiting for a stroke.

David's working hard to restrain himself, to allow everyone their say, but can't help cutting off Violet to move the conversation to ontological questions. "One of the things that I believed, and it comes from More training, is that the amount of good you can have is in direct proportion to the amount of bad you can have. Without good, bad has no value, there's nothing to compare it to. But here's the good part: At whatever age you are, you've already had enough bad in your life to have nothing but good for the rest of your life! I thought that maybe the amount of pleasure you can have is in direct proportion to the amount of pain. I thought that Violet could only have that extreme pleasure because she had that much pain..."

"Until I changed his mind," blurts Violet.

"Then I found out I could have that pleasure," says David. "One of the Violet-is-a-Goddess things that we've come up with is that Violet had the pain so I don't have to. Actually, my big belly is holding Violet's pain. The fun thing is that she keeps kicking the level of pleasure up. That gets to be a real mind boggle because I'll start having expectations of what it's going to feel like and she'll change the picture entirely, create a whole new orgasmic experience in me that will just blow my mind.

"More University had this contest going where they had six men working alternate shifts and they had kept this broad cumming for 72 hours and when they finally stopped she was yelling, 'More, more!'"

"I don't think I could go 72 hours," allows Violet.

FORMER CAGED BIRDS SING

House Effect Alan has prepared a dinner of barbequed chicken in the backyard patio, where I CAN caged birds and loose ducks make alarmed noise. David flags down a resident Mallard, holds the duck fast to his chest, and it shits on his hand.

Violet explains the purpose of caring for these animals: "If you're in a high level of stress and very fidgety, the duck will want to get away from you. So if you want to hold one of the ducks, you've got to slow yourself down and then they'll nestle right into you and get rubbed until you want to put them down."

"We took an ad out in the *San Diego Reader* a while back," says David. "It said something like, 'Is your therapist a quack? Why pay for lies when you can have the real thing from the Institute for the Realization of Human Potential, which offers duck therapy. Come and experience what H.E.D., Highly Enlightened Duck, and quacky wacky duck, S.E.D., the Slightly Enlightened Duck, has to offer. Relieve stress, soothe your mind, put yourself at rest. Call for further information...'"

"Donna was telling me about her little white cat," relates Juanita. "The cat had been fixed and she couldn't, you know, get it... After Donna took the Basic Sense [Basic Sensuality course, offered both by I CAN and More University], the cat is like, you say, the ducks. The cat just comes in there and lays on its back and waits to be rubbed. And that's all about sensuality."

"I can tell you about the dog that was trained to lick anything with vaseline on it that we used to have," says David. "Popular among the women."

"Not with me," says Violet. "I like the two-legged animals."

"You know how Violet came to be called 'The Animal Trainer?'" asks David. "It's when I first brought Violet along to a More group in Hawaii and one of the guys there said, 'Mmmmm, I've never been gummed by an arthritic before.' And Violet said, 'You might want to try it sometime.' That really flattened the room. From then on, Violet was called the Animal Trainer. They really treated her like a queen."

Discussion turns to memories of the first sexual experience. David declares, "My first one I remember as a child was mother running out of the room to answer the phone in the middle of vacuuming, and me putting the vacuum cleaner on my dick and finding out at three that it was really incredible.

"If you have a group of babies together, they're all naked, they're all rolling around touching each other, playing with each other, they do whatever feels good. We're born cumming! Male babies are born with an erection, female babies are born with a fully engorged pussy. Fully engorged! A baby feels things everywhere. A baby can have an orgasm just by putting your finger on his palm. His little legs and arms will all kick up, feel the sensations all throughout his little body. [*David presses his finger against his palm.*] With our methods of teaching, you can have an orgasm doing what I'm doing now....

"I'll tell you another thing. The hymen, that's a bullshit Christian concept."

How do you know?

David pauses: "Well, I've had two babies. I had to check that they were born with everything intact, and I've never seen a hymen! ... If you're checking a hymen with a finger and you can't get the finger inside you probably think that there's something in there stopping it. When I've de-virginized women and screwed them with one finger, there's a lot of vaseline, a lot of gentle physical preparation and coaching and talking and *safeporting*. I do a lot of things ever before my cock ever gets near her vagina.

"They just don't teach women things about her cycle. There's the old saw about how a woman doesn't want to be touched when she's having her period. Well, that's exactly when she should be touched. Rape studies have shown that rapists will hide behind a bush, see a woman, let her pass, see another woman, let her pass, then they just sense something and pounce on the next woman who walks by. Ninety percent of the time she'll be in cycle, a period of tumescence. Even if the woman is old or a real dog."

David drags on a coffin nail, exhales, his sunken eyes drifting off on some faraway place, beyond the confines of the smoky little bedroom.

"It's the sick people in the world who don't have a good cum. Hitler, you know, fucked and then killed his mother."

I didn't have any idea....

"Yeah, it's true. There's a lot written about that. If you control a person's sex life, you control the person.

"We had a lady come to us, Paula, with her 13-year-old daughter, Emily. Alcohol abuse had turned Paula's body off. And she came to live with us because she wanted her daughter to get some good clean sexual information. Not anything from out of the gutter. It's a real success story. Now Emily knows how to take care of herself and control the sexuality of the kids around her."

The girl was 13 years old?

"We just gave her information. I never laid a hand on her."

David Brandenburger speaks the truth. When mother Paula and daughter Emily, then 13, came to live with the Brandenburgers, she was never forced to have sex with any of the I CAN group. But, as Emily now recalls, she was under pressure to masturbate daily and report her orgasmic progress with the household.

Paula and daughter Emily, 15 at time of interview, live in Santa Fe, New Mexico, and were contacted by phone. Paula, a veteran of the More commune, found the I CAN experience to be enriching. "I learned to be honest with myself and my feelings, not feeling guilty, not hesitating. Violet is one of the most powerful individuals I've ever met. I got it easy compared to what she's got. She's a very sensual woman."

Emily had another perspective on their stay with the Brandenburgers. "Everyone had to, uh, get off every day by using a vibrator. I'd get hassled about doing my exercises, which meant that I was supposed to use it — the vibrator. They'd make me feel bad, or at least they'd make me think something was wrong with me for not using it. After a while I just told them that I was doing it just to get David off my back. Then he'd praise me and tell me how wonderful I was.

"David was my big problem. Living with him was real hard. We'd get in huge raging fights about little things. I remember a time when there was no food in the house and David bought two sheets of acid. His habits disgusted me. It seemed all David would eat is bologna, and he'd do something disgusting with it, like fry it."

There were good things about living in the I CAN house, Emily allows. She wasn't shocked about the nudism or an occasional encounter with people engaged in oral sex, but "hated the whole idea of living there." She was most distressed over the power the Brandenburgers had over her mother: "They grounded me for a bad report card. I threw a tantrum, but they were able to convince my mom that they were doing the right thing. I think the reason I wasn't doing well in school at the time was because of the stress of living with them. I think one of the reasons we came out to Santa Fe was because of them. They ran up my mother's credit cards, maxed them out."

David Brandenburger believes that Emily may have been most distressed by the embarrassment of having her mother "demonstrate to Emily how to do herself." Although she still lives with her mother (and since joined by a new stepfather), Emily has since decided to retain her father's last name.

The Brandenburgers continue to phone Paula, though Emily claims to shun contact: "When [David] calls up he wants to know every detail of my life. Every detail. After a while I got the feeling he was just a dirty old man."

A San Diego-area singles counselor, Shellie Greta Fraddin, still listed on The Institute for the Realization of Human Potential's letterhead as one of the Board of Directors, contacted the *San Diego Reader* to "expose the Institute's practices. I don't think they should be allowed to teach any more." Fraddin claims to have been sucked into the I CAN group by a process they call Sanctuary, in which prospective members, in David Brandenburger's words, "take three days to do whatever you want. We'll pamper you, and you can avail yourself of whatever it is we do. It's a total no-pressure situation."

"They call you up, keep in constant touch with you, ask if they can help you in any way they can. I got into some financial trouble and I took them up on their offer." Fraddin claims the experience was a nightmare in which her every wish was overruled by David Brandenburger. "He kept making comments about my breasts. He asked me to masturbate in front of everybody." Finally, Fraddin whines, "David Brandenburger took my stuff out of my room in a violent manner, and threatened to throw it out on the street. It was against my contract with them."

Denying the latter charge, David Brandenburger counters that Shellie Fraddin ran up a bill she never bothered to pay, and that the rest is sour grapes: "She's a three time loser in the marriage racket, a singles counselor who couldn't succeed in a relationship if she tried. She's got the body of a 25-year-old but the face of the wicked witch. I did that broad once. When I put my lips against her clit, she resisted an orgasm more than anyone else I've ever done."

Yet another former More University student ("their classes are just fabulous"), Fraddin was reluctant to admit her "training exercise" with David Brandenburger. "I'm a sensuous, responsive woman. I made a mistake repressing all my thoughts and feeling about how repulsive this man is. But the More University people said he was trained there, so I looked on him as a teacher. I found him too repulsive and I'm ashamed about that experience with him."

When asked to enumerate his negative traits, David Brandenburger admits, "I'm an asshole with the ego the size of Texas. It comes from life experience. Can you imagine what it would be like to get a blowjob from your wife in the morning and then come back from work that night and find your wife and kids are gone?" (Brandenburger's first wife and two daughters now reside in a suburb of Detroit. "I've not been allowed communication with them for 15 years.") "But I'm a very caring person," insists David. "I'll give anything to you to take care of you even if it looks like I'm losing on the deal. I don't care as long as you're winning."

It's More philosophy and Violet's opinion as well, that it's the woman who pulls the strings in her relationship. "Dave gets to play the big bad wolf. He gets all the attention on, 'He's the bad guy.' Where in reality, it is like a marionette puppet. I'm the one who's setting him up to take the flack. I'm actually much nastier, much heavier to deal with, than David."

David: "But people aren't willing to have that viewpoint. They're not willing to have it that they were victimized — "

"By a crip!" hoots Violet.

"We like to make everyone a friend," continues David. "Which sometimes causes problems when you're trying to make money. Your friends act like 'why should I pay if you're my friend?' The answer is we won't be here if you don't. If I'm in a *teacher valence,* you don't have to like me and I don't have to like you."

Alan, the newest paying guest of I CAN house, weakened by AIDS and annoyed at having to fetch drinks for everyone, takes the opportunity to interject, "David's on my case a lot. It can be really exasperating."

"I got an asshole thing to say about that," ejaculates David. "That you're desperate, and I've got a lot of patients."

"And maybe you're an asshole and I'm convinced you don't have to be one," Alan rejoinds. "I know David's deep dark secret," laughs Alan. "Did you know that he's a Republican?"

David maintains that he's proud to be one.

"We've got a word around here that is sacrosanct," continues Alan, "and that is 'stop.' When David gets going, the word stop means stop."

"It took me a long time to get that one," says Juanita.

David bursts in: "But I remember one time when I had my face between some lady's legs. She said 'stop' but her pussy was saying 'go.'"

Everyone turns to stare at Juanita. She blushes.

Alan: "That's an aha!"

Violet: "Because 'stop' in a sexual environment can mean 'don't stop,' we pick a word that's totally out of concept. My favorite one is 'mouse.' It doesn't come up in ordinary conversation, and if I want someone to cease all motion I'll say 'mouse.'"

GOODBYE *HOUSE EFFECT*

Living arrangements were shifting fast in the I CAN household. Dean cleared out of his room to go live with Tony several miles away. Alan, the beleaguered House Effect, suddenly found another gentleman to move in with. Another man, tall, gangly, asymmetrical swipes of hair tufting his forehead, relaxes in the patio doing Sanctuary. "He's got a brain tumor," David remarks helpfully. A crack-thin Appalachian-type woman wanders through the house.

Are you doing Sanctuary, too?

"I'm with him," she says, pointing to Brain Tumor.

Grunting, David lifts Violet out of bed, depositing her in the wheel-chair. She discusses next week's surgery with disconcerting objectivi-ty: "I'm going back to the hospital, get my lung pushed back in place. They took out a rib from under each breast to form my jaw when I kept rejecting implants. Through time the lung herniated through the missing ribs. I ended up in the E. R. three nights in a row. They got an x-ray and it looked like a very large tongue was sticking out right underneath my breast. They put a patch of synthetic material over it, and now it's peeking out a corner, and I'm going back in for the doc-tor to stick me back together again."

Dean's regimen for Violet now includes thirty minutes of crutch-walking between erotic massage sessions.

"Picking her up, Violet feels ten pounds lighter. After erotic massage, after vibrosaun, after hot tub," claims David.

As far as his future plans are concerned, David Brandenburger is working on legitimizing such I CAN discoveries as the *Orbital Orgasm*: "One of the big challenges is to get the medical equipment involved. EEG, EKG, sphinctanometer, etcetera."

Sphinctanometer?

"A sphinctanometer is a thing that's put in you anally or vaginally to measure contractions. We'd like to get these different kinds of diagnostic equipment so that we can start recording this quote, unquote, scientifically."

Wouldn't it change one's sexual experience to have a scientific measuring device shoved up the rectum?

"Oh, shit no," dismisses David.

Violet: "We've gone beyond a lot of horrible limitations. The sphinc-tanometer is not a feel good tool. If it was going to be done to a brand new person there would have to be a lot of *safeporting*. So you tell them it's not exactly going to be pleasant, but relax and you'll get used to it."

David: "It's nothing like a sphygmoidoscope."

What's that?

"The thing they shove up your ass and it's got a camera and every-thing else. I had that experience. They stuck in so much stuff."

Violet: "He was such a baby about it!"

"Thirty fucking inches long! It's the only tool on earth that in order to use it you have to have an asshole on each end."

Violet props her head against the waterbed pillows to view the prints of unicorns and clowns that are arrayed against the wall. She sighs, uvularly intones: "When something is not going quite right, I'll look up at the picture of the unicorn and I'll get a little smile on my face, take a deep breath and I'll feel better."

On my way out, Violet requests a hug. David follows me out the front door, presses my flesh, says, "We'd like to have you down. Not as a reporter, but a friend. We'd really love for you to have Sanctuary with us.

"Let us take care of you!"

CITIZEN KEANE
THE SORDID SAGA OF THE WEEPY WAIFS

Eyes. Enormous eyes, the size of headlights. They belong to a waif, a very waiflike waif, barefoot, button-nosed, a large tear spilling down her cheek. The waif has evidently wandered into an archetypical waifish haunt, here a claustrophobic alley; she looks at the viewer with a presentiment of abuse.

Little Miss Goggle Eyes is not a teratological specimen that escaped from a pathologist's pickle jar. She is Keane's "The Runaway," and like the other big eye Keane oils that achieved such monumental popularity from the 1950s to the early 1970s, the style is thrift store expressionism. As for the content ... well, let's ask art critic Kenneth Baker: "Keane paintings are just as manipulative and just as formulaic, and also as impervious to irony as most pornography is."

But as cultural archeologist Jim Morton points out in *Pop Void*, Keane kids were the true Pop Art, much more a mass phenomenon than Warhol's Brillo boxes or Lichtenstein's exploded comics Keane waifs appeared on collectable plates, were re-created as "Little Miss No Name" dolls, sold by the million as greeting cards, and hung inside the United Nations as well as the salmon-colored bathroom walls of the booboisie. Spurious big eye prints sprouted like toadstools. A hack named "Gia" specialized in moony-eyed mongrels and alley cats. "Eve" transformed big eye kids into precocious go-go dancers.

Now the saucer eye orphans have lost their original paternity.

For over 30 years, ex-realtor Walter Keane sold himself as the progenitor of the *sui generi* Keane kid. But as a result of a concatenation of acrimonious trials, Walter's ex-wife Margaret has been judged the true and lawful originator of the beloved kitsch creations. If Margar

Keane and the judicial system are right, Walter Keane has perpetrated a humbug of monumental proportion. The legally disgraced Walter Keane avows that he is the victim of an international ring of art forgers, a devious religious organization and a crooked and spiteful ex-wife.

Throughout the 1960s, Walter Keane was wealthy and famous, the toast of entertainers and politicos with sublime aesthetic aspirations. Hardly a week passed by without Walter Keane devising a way to get his name and photograph in the news. All he'd have to do is call an old "school chum" at United Press International, and a photographer would hurry by Keane's home to snap a few of Walter posing Gauguin-like in front of a half-completed canvas or hobnobbing with the likes of Joan Crawford, Dinah Shore, the Beach Boys, Dean Martin, Eve Arden, Jerry Lewis, Kim Novak, Natalie Wood, David Rose, Don DeFore, Wayne Newton, Red Skelton and Nelson Rockefeller. All became proud owners of dearly-bought oils of Keane kids.

Today, Walter Keane lives alone in a rented La Jolla cottage, a rheumy-eyed and arthritic man in his late '70s (a self-published art book vainly reduces his age by five years). He intersperses winking remembrances of "painting, drinking and loving" with vitriolic accusations against ex-wife and nemesis, Margaret Keane.

"I knew all the big shots. Dali, Picasso, they were all my friends. One time in Paris, Picasso was throwing a big party and I was there. I took a canvas and put it up on an easel and I laid down ten 100 dollar bills. I said, 'Master, that's for you and your girlfriends. All I want you to do is put X, Y, Z on there and write Picasso.' He thought I was making fun of him. Joan Crawford, she introduced me to one of my first great loves, Miss Chivas Regal. And she threw parties for me, introduced all the Hollywood stars to my work. I had this long bar in my Woodside home, it came around the horn, Red Skelton tried to buy it for four thousand bucks once. Seventeen people could sit around my bar room. The Beach Boys, Maurice Chevalier were guests there. Howard Keel and all those guys. We'd have parties until four in the morning. Dinner, drinks, anything they wanted. Always three or four people swimming nude in the pool. Everybody was screwing everybody. Sometimes I'd be going to bed and there'd be three girls in the

The Keanes paint-as-they-go in their halcyon days
at their San Francisco apartment.

(Photo courtesy UPI/BETTMAN)

body. Sometimes I'd be going to bed and there'd be three girls in the bed. I took a photo once of three of the girls there. Crazy, wild..."

Although he claims a nagging shoulder injury prevents him from painting, Mr. Keane has spent the last decade writing and rewriting an a vanity press memoir titled *The Real Love of Walter Keane*. The book is an extraordinary mixture of sexual braggadocio, mystical communications with the dead, monumental self-pity about the torments of the artist, and astonishingly delusional patches of self-inflation, culminating in Michelangelo's necromantic election of Walter Keane to the Elysian Gallery of Artistic Immortals.

AUTOHAGIOGRAPHY OF A DEFEATED MAN

(Please note: the following description culled from Keane's autobiography reflects only Walter Keane's version of his life story. A story, we should add, that is shot through with plagiarism, bizarre supernatural episodes, faulty chronology and certain claims that have been successfully challenged in court.)

The Real Love of Walter Keane begins in rural Nebraska during Walter's childhood, as he vies for parental attention among 14 siblings. He fondly remembers his grandmother, who instructs Walter at the age of five how to paint a rose. The autobiography suddenly skips thirty years — barely a mention of Walter's schooling or ten year career in real estate speculation, except for his epiphany away from the world of business signaled by the onset of crippling stomach pain.

> As I listened to the birds sing, staring fixed-eyed and watching them fly freely away, I lifted my arms toward them and cried out, "Please wait; I am one of you!" I closed my eyes. Then came the spark. My dazed, feverish request was answered. I realized that my innate artistic talent had been locked in my brain and my body for all these years. Feeling a sudden strength and conviction, I knew that a new life had begun.

Walter flees like the bird to Paris in 1946 with his first wife Barbara, who soon returns to the familiar comforts of California, leaving Walter to pursue a bohemian life of drinking, loving and painting. On a significant side trip to Berlin Walter discovers the sight of "frightened, neglected, and often abused children."

> Nothing in my life until then, or since, has ever made such an impact as the sight of those children fighting over garbage. As if goaded by a kind of frantic despair, I sketched these dirty, ragged little victims of war with their bruised, lacerated minds and bodies, their matted hair and runny noses. Here my life as a painter began in earnest; Paris had been only a lighthearted apprenticeship. The insane, inhuman cruelty inflicted upon these children cut deeply into my being. From that moment on, I painted the lost children with the eyes that forever retained their haunting and haunted quality.

Walter returns to Paris with "single-minded" resolve to alert the world to the plight of his starved children. Distraction comes in the form of a prostitute-with-a-heart-of gold named Colette, and her gamine daughter, Renee. Colette ("a perfect part for Cher," says Keane) lives an idyllic life with Walter, procuring little-girl models for him in her spare time. On a trip back to California in the summer of 1947, Walter is chagrined to find that his cheated-upon wife does not welcome him with ardor, and so he repairs to a houseboat in Sausalito to do the bohemian rhapsody: wine, women and song. In a moment of unguarded self reflection, Walter reveals, "I am probably the only man alive who washes his hands before unzipping his pants and then washes them again after zipping up."

In between perfecting his trademark waifs, he has a child, Susan Hale, by the ordinarily unresponsive Barbara in December 1948. The family sets sail to Paris, and Walter sets up a studio in Montmartre. As his marriage begins to unravel, Walter sojourns to Hong Kong, taking up with yet another prostitute-with-a-heart-of-gold named Mai Ling, who he sets up in business. The rambling man sets sail once again and is saved by a lithe young thing named Dana in a shipwreck. Walter savors the delights of postwar Japan, and from there flies to Tahiti, where he spends his time painting waifs while comparing himself to Gauguin.

Back with his Colette in Paris, Walter decides to keep her occupied as his art dealer. Accompanying Walter on a business trip to Tokyo, Colette hears that her young daughter Renee was run over by a car fleeing a rapist. Walter flies back to Paris with the traumatized Colette and discovers Renee's diary. Three pages of Walter's autobiography is taken up with gruesome details of remembered entries, though Keane admits that his knowledge of the French language remains sketchy at best.

> Wednesday: Jacques picked me up at school a few minutes early. As soon as we walked into the apartment he removed all his clothes. He drew a hot bath for the two of us and asked me to wash his back. I laughed and told him Mama did Walter's. When we got out of the tub, Jacques asked me if I would kiss his hard penis. I said, "No." He took my hand and with violence in his voice demanded I hold it and kiss it or he would hit me across the face. I was, and still am, terrified. I told him "No" and begged him to go away. All the time his fingers were tickling me between my thighs.

Overcome by rage and despair, Colette drops out of sight. Distraught and lonely, he returns to Barbara, who at last asks her philandering husband for a divorce. On his Sausalito barge he produces "Alone," a painting of a waif sitting on a vast cosmic stairwell. Walter Keane describes it thus:

> Here, is my symbol of humanity "Alone" with infinity but in the company of the always here and the constantly now. The child represents the isolation and stresses of humankind as she perches precariously on the vast stairs of life. The distant side of the stairs is the brink of the universe; the near side, in muddy reflection, is the edge of the abyss of human degradation. The spheres in the

> beyond draw us irresistibly by gravitational forces,
> pulling us back through the eyes of the child
> which are but sights into the blue-black of space
> and time.

He asks himself, "Was my eternal romance to be with a pallet and a brush? Would art forever be my only real love?"

Walter spends the next few years basking under the light of success, living it up in the jazz clubs of New York and North Beach hangouts like Vesuvio's, where he drinks until the wee hours with beatniks like Jack Kerouac and movie stars like Kim Novak. On a fateful day in the summer of 1955, during the annual outdoor exhibition of the Society for Western Artists near Fisherman's Wharf, Walter meets a "slender, young blonde woman" named Margaret, the soon-to-be Mrs. Keane. On a whirlwind first date, she surprises Walter by emerging naked from his bathroom. He admonishes her, "I like to unwrap my women." In the midst of their lovemaking Margaret hurries out of Walter's apartment to return home to husband and daughter.

Two weeks later, Margaret shows up at Walter's door suitcase in hand, begging to become his disciple. Almost against his will Walter offers to buy insecure Margaret orthodontia and plastic surgery. Stymied by the lack of visitation rights with his daughter Susan, an attorney advises Walter to remarry in order to convince the family court of a family-like atmosphere. Walter sets a marriage date with Margaret and throws himself into the task of "improving" her.

> The transformation of Margaret into a complete
> person whom she, herself, could live with and like
> loomed as a monumental task. There was, however-
> er, something enticing about the challenge. I
> envisioned myself as a sort of Henry Higgins with
> Margaret as a modern day version of Eliza Doolit-
> tle.

Walter's instructions include the social graces:

> To accompany Margaret's new wardrobe, I sug-
> gested a list of greetings and topics for conversa-
> tion on specific social occasions. I encouraged her

to practice them with certain graceful gestures in front of a mirror.

Then came painting:

> To give Margaret instruction at the most basic level, I bought her a projector, then you place a photo or a page out of the artist's book in the projector and project it onto a canvas. Trace it on the canvas. Next step, fill in the colors much like a numbered painting designed for a child. This was her beginning of copying other artists' work. She worked at this method steadily, copying great works of Modigliani and El Greco.

On their wedding day, Walter discovers Margaret *en flagrante delicto* with several parking lot attendants. Walter consults his attorney, who cautions that an annulment will endanger visitation rights with Susan. Walter reluctantly decides to follow through on his marriage to Margaret and simulate the appearance of a happy marriage. Walter sets up a gallery in the Hungry I nightclub, where he is the subject of a scandal when the jealous owner Enrico Banducci sees Walter having a drink with Banducci's girlfriend. Banducci takes a swing at Walter. He ducks and Banducci knocks Walter's girlfriend cold. Headlines in the daily papers read, "Artist Beats Up Girl in Bar." Though Banducci and henchmen finger Walter for the crime, the court exonerates him.

Walter sets up other galleries in New York and San Francisco, and the Keane kids meanwhile win over the world. Married in name only, Walter and Margaret make the divorce official. Afterward, he woos and romances a pretty stewardess, Joan Marie, in grand style, kissing her for minutes in a revolving door during a busy shopping day on New York's Fifth Avenue. Autograph-seeking fans shout, "That's Walter Keane, I saw him on the *Jack Paar Show*," "I saw you on the *Today* Show," "And in the Sunday *Parade* section."

Walter finishes work on "Tomorrow Forever," the most ambitious big eye painting yet. Like the Ripley illustration of the marching china- men, "Tomorrow Forever" delineates a horizon of endless big eye waifs. After completing "Tomorrow Forever," Walter's deceased grandmother "appears" to him and speaks:

> My Little Walter, we have seen your masterwork. Please tell us in your own words what was in your mind and in your heart when you created "Tomorrow Forever."

> "I will try, Grandmother." My mind reaching back into many yesteryears, I began.

Walter's memoir suddenly takes flight with a mythopoetic sermon on the painting's evolution, from initial sketches to the completed "masterwork."

> Over the horizon of the infinite past — out of the ages lost even to the pin-pointers of time — they come, as they must have been coming in my unconscious ever since that deeply etched day in Berlin.

> They come in multiplying numbers from the first moment of creation, down to the moment that is now — a moment that is a restless fraction of eternity — a moment that must move on into tomorrow, on into tomorrow's tomorrow, and the tomorrow of that morrow, on into tomorrows forever.

> But they are only children! No, not children: mankind. For the child, in the words of Wordsworth, is the father of the man. Somewhere in unrecorded time, eons before the earliest civilization, a man planted a seed that became one of these children, and that man owed his being to a seed planted eons before him. The timeless river of Life; or, in Kahlil Gibran's phrase, Life's longing for itself.

> They stand witness that this longing will not be denied, for they journeyed down to the moment

161

that is now through a glacial waste and deluge, through plagues on end; yea through the most devastating of all malevolent forces, man's own evil.

Blessed with a fiber so sturdy — and midway in the passage toward another tomorrow — they should be full of scamper and laughter, as were those children who were their ancestors. Yet their eyes — eyes that reflect the ecumenical soul — hold an arresting gravity: a wonder ... but an ominous wonder; not the innocent, enviable wonder that is the heritage of childhood. Their eyes, so somber and unblinking, may seem to accuse; but no, the case penetrates deeper. Their eyes speak a query — a query all the more unmistakable for its weighty silence: What are the bequeathers of their tomorrow up to?

... Studying the faces of these children — that one on the right, has he not the features of tomorrow's Gandhi? And this one, the look of Moses? Over there, another Socrates? And here, Maimonides? Those others — a Galileo? ... a Linnaeus? ... a Pasteur? ...

Who is that? Caesar? No, the shadow passes; an illusion only. For these children — the children of today's universe — given the right response to their mute query, will reclaim their heritage and start scampering toward TOMORROW FOREVER.

Walter's ectoplasmic Grandma rejoices at the lofty description of "Tomorrow Forever," and crows:

At our last meeting of the artists', writers', painters' and poets' group, Michelangelo put your name up for nomination as a member of our inner circle, saying that your masterwork

"Tomorrow Forever" will live in the hearts and minds of men as has his work on the Sistine Chapel. You were honored by the unanimous vote of all our members and you will officially join us in the year 2007.

Accolades continue to pour in from the angelic afterlife. A spirit named "Bernard" compares Walter to Leonardo, Raphael, Tiepolo and Veronese:

With "Tomorrow Forever" Keane reaches such an extraordinary level of achievement that the mind boggles at the thought that this still young artist has within him the potential to achieve even greater levels.

Validation from the greater world beyond is shattered by John Canaday's article in *The New York Times*, ridiculing the selection of "Tomorrow Forever" as a theme painting for the Pavilion of the Hall of Education at the 1964 New York World's Fair:

Keane is the painter who enjoys international celebration for grinding out formula pictures of wide-eyed children of such appalling sentimentality that his product has become synonymous among critics with the very definition of tasteless hack work. "Tomorrow Forever," as the painting is called, contains about 100 children and hence is about 100 times as bad as the average Keane.

Without regard to such stifling literary conventions as chronology, Keane's autobiography continues with bucolic idylls with Joan Marie and tortured moments with Margaret. Walter attempts to convince her to destroy her forged copies of Modigliani. Walter is soon robbed by gunmen in his Woodside home, and he blames the heist on Margaret: "Only Margaret and the Swedish installer of the safe knew where I kept my money. When questioned by the FBI, Margaret admitted that she might have told someone about my safe while she was drinking."

Walter marries for the third time, exhausting third wife Joan Marie with a *bon vivant* lifestyle. They see the Pope, the governor of California, Liz and Dick, and Madame Chaing Kai-Shek. After daughter Chantal is born, the loving couple fly to Martinique, where Walter charms the pants off the native girls, and from there to Paris, where Walter sets up a beautiful young girl in law school. A son, Sascha Michael, is born in June 1973. Then tragedy strikes. "The twenty-two oil paintings I had done in Martinique plus the eleven oils from my California studio had been lost at sea." (It should be pointed out that all of Walter Keane's art production since his divorce from Margaret has been "lost at sea" or salted away with "private collectors.") Although he claims a happy marriage, Walter drowns his physical and mental pain in pills and ever-increasing amounts of Chivas Regal scotch.

Fast forward eight or ten years. Walter blacks out on his way home from the Whaling bar of the fancy La Valencia hotel in La Jolla.

> I was sinking down fast, sinking down, down, down. Head bashed in, blood dripping on my body. Soon, I lay in my own splattered blood, having fallen in the turning circle. I was dazed, lost, confused, with my bloated and throbbing nose, a complete mess in the solitary darkness. I had drunk away my family, my health, my wealth, and now I was drinking away what little remained of my life. Then a sound like angels' wings fluttered above me.

> From out of nowhere, two strong arms wrapped around my tired, limp and almost lifeless body, lifting me to my feet. A familiar voice, becoming more and more clear, embraced me with loving words: "My little Walter, you can now walk through the wall and continue your drinking until death. Or you can steady yourself in the turning circle, turn around and walk to freedom."

The concluding chapters of *The Real Love of Walter Keane* are outraged descriptions of the libel, slander, copyright infringement, bankruptcy and other suits that occupied him in the 1980s. He concludes with a voice from beyond, the cry of the wide-eyed waifs.

> Today, my mind is like a parachute; it works only when it's open. Now I hear again, I see again, I feel again, I touch again. Now I love the rain, the breeze and the calm. At close of day, I sing again, strolling one step at a time along my path at the water's edge. As the sunset colors flashed in my eyes, came a whisper, "Walter, the Sunrise and Sunset are REAL. You can trust us."

MARGARET'S VERSION

Margaret Keane has not written an autobiography to exonerate herself. She hasn't the need. Since her Keane Eyes gallery opened on San Francisco's Market Street in Fall, 1991, in which originals sell for as much as $185,000, major articles in *The San Francisco Chronicle* and *The New York Times* played up Margaret's newly-crowned status as the fountainhead of big eye art.

It wasn't always that way. During, and even some years after the dissolution of her marriage to Walter Keane, Margaret was the big eye artist's shadow woman, a mere portraitist. Near the end of their marriage, Walter produced a two-volume vanity monograph under the imprint "Tomorrow Masters Series." Printed in Japan, editions were published simultaneously in English, French, Spanish and Japanese. One of the two volumes is devoted to Walter's waifs, complete with posed shots of Walter holding five paintbrushes as he daubs a reflective highlight on a saucer eye. "The child seems so real that one wonders why she does not blink at the approach of the brush," reads the caption. Margaret's companion edition is devoted solely to her mysterious, long-necked almond-eyed women, painted in a style that might best be described as thrift-store Modigliani with occasional Magritte-like effects ("Torn" — three-dimensional woman's face on a piece of torn paper; "The Puzzle" — slender woman as jigsaw puzzle).

Today, Margaret Keane lives in Sonoma County with her middle-aged daughter, Jane. Her version of events contradicts almost every part of the legend that Walter Keane so aggressively sought for himself. In a phone interview, Margaret recalls her life with Walter in a soft, dreamy voice.

"Walter Keane didn't paint any of the paintings of the children. I did them, all of them. When he was out drinking and promoting I was home painting."

How did you come across the style of the big eye art?

"I always enjoyed doing faces. I used to scribble and doodle in my textbooks in the margins. Scribbling and drawing all the time. Used to always draw faces. When my daughter was a baby I started doing her portrait and then my neighbors wanted me to do their children's portraits, and I did them with larger eyes than normal. Eyes were always large."

Are there any paintings still existing from that period that you know of?

"Yes, a few. When there was the trial in Federal Court in Honolulu two or three of the people that I had painted their children back then had lent me the portraits for the trial."

When did you meet Walter Keane?

"1954 I guess."

He impressed upon you as being an artist?

"He still had his real estate business. But when I first met him I thought he was an artist. I met him at a San Francisco Art Festival, a yearly thing. I was there doing portraits and he was showing these Paris street scenes. By the way, the Paris street scenes did not have any faces in them. Done with a lot of palette knife, thick paint, entirely different from the way I paint."

Some of the big eye paintings have that thick paint kind of background in them. Did Walter contribute any kind of artistic input?

"He did try and sometimes put a little paint on the backgrounds when it was like a stucco wall or something like that. He also had a good color sense, helping me pick out colors one time."

In a photograph taken by UPI, you were painting graceful, long-necked women and he was doing the sad-eye waifs. He claimed he taught you how to paint by teaching you how to use a tracing machine.

[*Laughs.*] "Well, I did go through a period where I did elongated ones after he was claiming that he did the children with the large eyes and I finally gave in and let him claim them. So I tried to develop another style so I could at least be known as some kind of a painter. I can show you an earlier picture taken by the *Berkeley Gazette* when we lived in Berkeley, where I was sitting in front of an easel painting a large-eye painting and he was painting the background of a clown painting. This was an earlier one before he took over and insisted that he was the one doing the children. In the beginning I had hoped that he'd learn how to paint. He kept saying he was going to try and if I would help him, he would do it. I just finally gave in and let him — it was a very bad thing to do."

Seeing as how Keane is Walter's name, why do you still use it?

"I wish I didn't, but the paintings are known by that name."

The big eye children have an abused quality to them.

"I was reflecting my own deepest feelings in the paintings of the children. I was really putting myself, my feelings, into the child. I was bewildered and hurt and searching for answers, really deep questions, why we're here, why God allows wickedness, why there's so much injustice in the world. All of these things. I was very unhappy at the time. I was putting all my feelings into them."

It was pretty much the high life for you and Walter for a while.

"He was a tremendous promoter, and he had a marvelous personality. He could sell anybody anything and he could really turn on the charm. And he was a businessman. For years he was very very charming and he just swept me off my feet and I thought he was an artist who painted these street scenes and I was totally captivated by him."

But you say he wasn't really who he said he was...

"A couple of years after we were married, I really found out the truth. I was beginning to suspect it after a year of marriage, I guess. He kept saying he was rusty, he hadn't painted in a long time. So I thought he was just rusty and he would soon get back into painting to the level of the street scenes. We were married about two years and I came across this big box in the back of the closet one night when he was at the Hungry I selling paintings, and I opened it up and there were all these street scenes, about ten of them, just like the ones he'd been selling. Only these were signed S-E-N-I-C. As soon as I saw these I knew he hadn't done the other ones. When he came home I confronted him with them and he said that those were the teacher's paintings, he had done the ones with Walter Keane signed on them. But I know he didn't. From then on I knew the truth, but he'd kept saying he'd learn to paint if I could help him, teach him. And when he couldn't paint he'd say it was my fault, practically had me convinced it was my fault he couldn't paint. If you can believe that! He just drilled it in me constantly, it was my fault he couldn't paint.

"I finally got up the courage to leave Walter after ten years. I got a separation to begin with and went to Honolulu to get as far away as I could. When I got more courage, I came back and filed for the divorce. I was just happy to get out alive."

Get out alive?

"Uh huh. He was threatening to kill me and my daughter. One thing I stood up for: he hit me once or twice and I made such a to-do about it that he didn't do that again. That's the one thing I stood up for, but it was certainly emotional and psychological abuse. I was really very much afraid of him."

When you got out to Honolulu, what then?

"I put my daughter in summer school there, and I tried to rest, get my thoughts together, and decide if I was going to stay there or not. I'd been in Honolulu about a month when I met Dan McGuire. And by the end of summer I decided I was going to stay there. I didn't paint much that summer, I was so shook up. After I filed for divorce I painted a few paintings and mailed them to Walter. I was so afraid of him I thought if I kept mailing paintings to him then he wouldn't have me killed. That's how mixed-up I was."

The big eye kids you now paint are smiling. They don't have that haunted look.

"That's due to my conversion."

When did you find your new faith?

"I was baptized as Jehovah's Witness in August, 1972. About six months before that somebody knocked on my door, and I usually shoo them away, but this time I asked them a couple of questions. She opened up her bible and answered questions, and I was amazed that the questions were right in the bible, and she knew where to find the answers. And she left me a little book, *The Truth That Leads to Eternal Life*. She came back in about three days and for every question I asked her she showed me the answer in the bible. I was totally amazed."

How did your baptism affect your art?

"It took a little while but the paintings gradually started not being so sad. They started getting happier and happier and the colors started getting lighter and brighter and now I paint many happy paintings. Even laughing. My inner feelings come out in the paintings, and I'm so much happier. I found the answers I was looking for. I think many people are very upset and very disturbed by the things that are going on. The bible shows in the Book of Revelation that God is going to bring ruin to those ruining the earth. It promises all through the bible that the earth will be restored to paradise conditions. There will be a time when we'll be able to live eternally on paradise earth, which was God's purpose for earth. We're living in what the bible calls the Last Days. It's the Last Days of this wicked system, of Satan's system of things, where we're under the condemnation of death. The people who are living now are living in the Last Days when God steps in and cleanses the earth."

∞ ∞ ∞

In the days following our initial interview, Margaret Keane sent me a Watchtower tract book, *You Can Live Forever In Paradise on Earth*. The Jehovah's Witnesses, with their kitschy tracts promising a multi-cultural K Mart utopia, seem a wholly appropriate aesthetic environment for the latter-day big eye waifs, their tearful countenances now turned into smiles.

On a follow-up interview, Margaret was anxious to learn if I had read the JW book. She was alternately bemused and exasperated by Walter's continuing accusations.

Walter says that you copied Modiglianis for an art forgery ring. He says you're so good at copying by now that you could forge a Rembrandt.

"Well, I don't know what to say about that. It's just so ridiculous."

What about the Jehovah's Witnesses bribing witnesses?

"The staff of the Jehovah's Witnesses don't even make a salary. It's against the tenets of the religion. That's just the most preposterous thing. It's sad, really."

Did you hear about what he said about your wedding night, about you and the parking ...

[*Interrupts.*] "He tried that in court, and the judge threatened him over that one."

Can you explain all the photographs that have Walter at the easel painting the big eye children. And the ones with him painting Kim Novak and Natalie Wood?

"That was all a pose. I painted Kim Novak from a photograph and did Natalie Wood as a big eye kid myself."

Walter claims that he can no longer paint due to a bad shoulder.

"Sad, isn't it?"

By the way, who is this Eric Schneider, who wrote the introduction to Walter's self-published book? Walter first claimed that it was his own writing, then he called me back to say that Schneider was a Swiss art critic.

"It wasn't like that. Walter hired a writer to do it."

Who?

"He's pretty famous now. I'm sure he wouldn't want people to know."

From the style of it, it sure sounds like Tom Wolfe.

"How did you know?"

BONFIRE OF WALTER'S VANITY

In 1964, when Walter Keane hired Tom Wolfe to write the introduction to his vanity art book project, Wolfe wasn't yet the white-suited avatar of New Journalism. His first book was not yet published, and he was still drawing a stipend from *New York Herald Tribune*. Wolfe's pseudonymous blow job may be the loopiest bit of mercenary rhetoric ever placed between the covers of an art book. He mocks the pedantry of art criticism and the infinite pretension and pomposity of his subject by elevating Keane kids into visual expressions worthy only of the great masters:

> ... Indeed, in retrospect, Keane's short Business Period appears almost as a fortuitous ritual of purification. So complete was Keane's isolation, in terms of the world of art, during those crucial years that his own art and his own artistic instincts were able to develop on their own terms. Thus, whereas the average American art student of that period, or for that matter, of our own times, went to Paris already a somewhat slavish devotee and cult worshipper of French Modernism, Keane was able to examine it as a possibly useful tool and then discard it when he saw the very specific limitations it would impose upon an artist of his own limitless ambition.

... Keane paints the eyes with the same fullfaced perspective of the primitives but with complex, mysterious, almost oracular combinations of thick and thin pigments, and highlights that seem to come, as it were, from an unseen world beyond the immediate image, so that the eye as a thing of depth, of penetration, of admission to the secret self, attains a power that not even the primitives, in simple acts of faith in the eye symbol, could feel.

The end result, of course, is the Keane vision, seen by the viewer as the subjective content that gives Keane's work an emotive fission that explodes, continually, almost in the manner of an infra-red flash, from the very firmness of line and contour that give that work, as form, an unparalleled sense of formal structure. Alternately pouring forth from, and seen within, these eyes are consummate summation of the anguish, the fear, the despair, and yet the flame-like hope, of a world wracked not only by momentous political cataclysms but assaults on former seemingly immovable investments of simple religious and intellectual faiths, buttressed, at the time, by cultural frameworks that seemed then so unflinchingly imbedded, and now merely terrifyingly evanescent.

... With "Tomorrow Forever" Keane reaches such an extraordinary level of achievement that the mind boggles at the thought that this still young artist has within him the potential to achieve even greater levels...

Wait a minute! Isn't this the angel Bernard's spiel from Walter's autobiography? Seems so, word for word. Walter borrows many other purple effusions of "Eric Schneider" and jarringly inserts them among his stuttering prose as if they are his own. Sometimes, he has trouble even copying. A Wolfeian coinage, "cenophobiac moon," becomes in Walter's book a Malapropish "xenophobic moon."

WAIFS ON TRIAL

During a contempt of court proceeding in his bankruptcy trial, two San Diego-based psychiatrists, Gail Waldron and Katherine Raleigh Di Francesca, examined Walter Keane to assess his mental health. They reported that Mr. Keane suffered from bladder incontinence and a paranoid delusional disorder consistent with heavy, long-term alcohol intake. Throughout the weeks he was interviewed for the *Reader*, Mr. Keane's moods fluctuated from friendly to suspicious to hostile to friendly again, sometimes within the same minute. Recollections rambled in the dusty caverns of his memory, changing content in their disjointed retelling.

"I shouldn't be talking to you. They've gotten to you already," cried Walter.

Who?

"The Jehovah's Witnesses. They no doubt bribed you with a hundred thousand dollars. That's nothing, that's a drop in the bucket to them. They can get to anyone. Anyone."

Why would they want to bribe me?

"The Jehovah's Witnesses make a million dollars a month selling prints of my paintings and ones that Margaret copied and still copies. It's big business. That's why they bought all those rent-a mouths at the trials."

Margaret Keane hadn't yet joined the Jehovah's Witnesses when she first came out of the closet to claim the big eye waifs as her own. In a 1970 *Life* magazine interview she challenges Walter Keane to a "paint off." "I never heard of the article," says Walter. "I was overseas and nobody knew where I was. I didn't read anything." Walter points to a Property Settlement Agreement that Margaret signed at the time of their divorce as proof of his authorship of the big eye paintings. Paragraph C of that agreement clearly states:

> The parties hereby agree that the fair market value of all the statutory and common law copyrights to Margaret's paintings is equal to the fair market value of all the statutory and common law copyrights to Walter's paintings, and that each hereby exchanges their respective community property interests in all copyrights to the paintings of the other, and each further waives and relinquishes to the other any and all right, title or interest he or she may have in the copyrights to the paintings of the other.

Exhibit A-2 of the document lists paintings by Walter Keane, including "Alone" and "Tomorrow Forever"; Exhibit A-1 lists Margaret's paintings, all of the long-necked variety, and none of the so-called big eye kids.

Was the property settlement agreement entered as evidence in his court battle?

"I don't know, I don't know," mutters Walter. "I was living on caffeine and adrenaline. The judge didn't allow me to enter a lot of pertinent evidence. And I don't remember."

Walter and Margaret's eight-year court battle began on April 16, 1982, when Walter files a $1.5 million dollar copyright infringement suit in Santa Clara County over a July 11, 1981 article in the *Peninsula Times Tribune* in which Margaret claims authorship of the big eye waifs. The suit is dismissed with prejudice in February, 1984. Walter blames the dismissal on his attorney for forgetting to file proper paperwork.

Next it's Margaret's turn. A 1985 article on Walter Keane in *U.S.A. Today* states, "Thinking he was dead, the second of his three ex-wives (also a painter) claimed to have done some of the Keane paintings. The claim, vehemently refuted by a very much alive Keane, is in litigation." Margaret files suit in Hawaii against Gannett Co., Inc., for libel and Walter Keane for slander and malicious prosecution due to lack of merit in Walter's earlier case against her. Walter counter-sues Margaret for copyright infringement once again.

Walter's attorney, Seymour Ellison, soon drops out of the case when his personal life careens out of control. Now retired from the Bar, Ellison characterizes Walter Keane as "not the best-liked man. He was very contentious." He adds, "I never received a cent from Walter Keane." Walter is forced to use Gannett's attorneys. A lengthy presentation by Margaret and her attorneys includes her now-famous 53-minute painting of a big eye kid in the courtroom. Walter begs off from the painting competition complaining of a sore arm, remarking bitterly, "Margaret can copy anything, even a Rembrandt."

Thirteen days into the trial, Gannett asks for a directed verdict, which District Court Judge King grants. The Gannett attorneys flee, leaving Walter to fend for himself as his own attorney in a "bifurcation of trial." Judge King often lectures Walter on proper courtroom conduct, labeling him "vitriolic." Walter calls a long-time friend, John May, to testify under oath that he'd seen Walter's big eye kids long before Margaret became acquainted with him. Under cross-examination, May admits that he had never actually seen Walter paint. In a mind-boggling judgment, the court awards Margaret Keane $4 million in damages.

Fearing that the huge judgment will remove all possible financial avenues for appeal, Walter files for bankruptcy on May 29, 1987 in the United States Bankruptcy Court in San Diego. Former millionaire Walter Keane shows assets of only $5,702.50.

Finally, in January, 1989, The United States Appellate Court in the Ninth District of San Francisco cancels the $4 million judgment against Walter Keane as excessive, though they uphold the original verdict. Margaret Keane must initiate another trial in order to collect any damages. She declines to do so.

Meanwhile, in Bankruptcy Court in San Diego, Walter's legal wrangle continues. An exasperated Judge John J. Hargrove finds Walter Keane in contempt of court on November 3, 1988 for concealing his assets. Walter blames the contempt ruling on his Newport Beach-based attorney Herbert Niermann. Walter is convinced that Niermann is "a plant."

Judge Hargrove's contempt ruling is largely based on a deposition by one Janice Adams, a woman who came to the aid of Walter Keane after hearing of the $4 million judgment against him. Walter claims Adams was yet another "plant," a mouth hired by the Jehovah's Witnesses to do him in: "Jan Adams gave me three blow jobs a day. Morning, noon and night. I couldn't fuck her, you see, she didn't want to be touched. She thought I was rich, tried to open her own whorehouse in Reno. She was a woman of the night, if you get my meaning." Counters Margaret Keane: "Janice Adams is a very nice, respectable woman whose father bought a Keane painting. She thought Walter was in distress and lent him money. Ultimately she discovered the truth about him."

Contempt hearings finally come to a head on June 4, 1990, a day when Judge John Rhoades lectures Walter:

> Mr. Keane, if you refuse to answer any question,
> you will be incarcerated in the future. I will not
> hear any further argument as to whether you can
> or cannot answer the questions. I think the only
> way we are going to get your attention, and to
> refresh your memory is to put you in prison.

Fearing a prison term, Walter calls in his entertainer friend and avid Keane-collector Wayne Newton to testify upon his behalf. Newton flies in from South Dakota to deliver an impassioned defense of Walter Keane, who, aptly enough, has often been characterized as the Wayne Newton of the art world.

> I became acquainted with Walter Keane some
> years ago upon viewing some of his paintings in
> Hawaii. Those paintings inspired me. They
> inspired me in such a way that I then became
> interested in working for children's causes
> throughout the country, and throughout the
> world... The "Keane Eyes," if you will, became
> kind of a standard phrase that I used in describing
> my own daughter.

I had the pleasure of introducing Walter Keane to an audience in Las Vegas. That audience stood up with a standing ovation for him. So the effect that he has had on people throughout the world, regardless of the fact that maybe he is a little eccentric, which at times has certainly been significant. One must only look into Walter "Keane's eyes" to understand Walter Keane, and to look into those eyes is seeing the same eyes that he paints on his children.

And at a time in this country when we are dealing with four letter words on television on a regular basis and movies full of rape and dope and child molestation and every other crime against mankind, his subjects remain exactly the same, your honor. They remain innocent and bewildered children. Is it possible that this day has been brought about by the wrath of an ex-wife, which for eternity some of us might be a part of, from myself all the way up to the great former president of the United States?

What you see before you, your honor, is not an arrogant man, as he has been portrayed and maybe come off that way in prior hearings. He is a giver. He has given his entire lifetime. He is financially broke. He is scared. He is vulnerable and most of his friends have passed away. The rest of us who are his friends are here today. He is not beaten because he still has his dignity and his honor. I would beg Your Honor to not incarcerate Walter Keane, but that would be demeaning to His Honor and to Walter Keane. So I ask Your Honor, in the name of human justice and human compassion, don't incarcerate Walter Keane. Give him back to his children.

In response, Margaret Keane's attorney, Nancy Perham, goes on the offensive:

> Margaret Keane was the artist. She is the one who suffered with the children. She is the one who painted the children. While Walter Keane was out meeting all the Hollywood stars in San Francisco, Margaret Keane was spending 16 hours a day painting all those children.... And so you talk about a spirit of the law and the spirit of justice, Mr. Newton cares for Walter Keane because of the big eyed children. Margaret Keane painted those big eyed children, and this man, who is supposed to be so warm and compassionate, stole that from her.
>
> I have known Walter Keane since 1982, and when I look into his eyes I see the eyes of someone who is a liar, a fraud, and someone who is trying to hurt a person who is a wonderful person, Margaret Keane, who is being vilified here today.

Shortly after the San Diego court hearing on the morning of June 4, 1990, Wayne Newton flies to North Dakota to perform. Troubled by the evidence he heard in the courtroom that day, Newton takes a jet to Honolulu several months later in order to personally apologize to Margaret Keane for his "uninformed testimony." "He didn't have to do that," says Margaret. "He's just one of the nicest and most honorable men I ever met."

Despite the best efforts of Ms. Perham, Walter Keane escapes a prison sentence at his contempt hearing. Wayne Newton's attorney, Mark Moreno, takes up Walter's case, urging him to sign an agreement releasing both Walter and Margaret from pursuing further litigation against one another. Walter signs the agreement under protest. The legal show grinds to its conclusion at last in September, 1991, when Bankruptcy Court vacates all claims by and against Walter Keane.

Though Walter claims the private support of his ex-wives Barbara and Joan Marie, and children Susan, Chantal and Sascha, none of them were willing to testify in court. "My daughter didn't want to get involved in that," he says. "For seven generation they've never done anything public. Not to go out to a bar, never to a public restaurant, never to a public anything. My daughter's mother is worth eight to ten million bucks. She doesn't want to get involved." Neither does Kim Novak, though she sent Walter Keane's the following handwritten testimonial early in the court battle:

> Artist Walter Keane and I have been friends for over 20 years. This note is to inform you that Walter painted two pictures of me — one as a child and one of me from my Hollywood years. I also did a portrait of him which I believe he still has and enjoys. I do not wish to get into any lawsuits or publicity but wanted you to know this fact. I'd appreciate your not involving me in this as I will not be available.
>   Sincerely,
>   Kim Novak Molloy

YOUR BIG EYES MAKE ME FEEL SO SMALL

Along with platform shoes, smiley faces, and the indomitable Peter Max, Keane paintings are making an inevitable comeback. So sentimental and deficient in irony, they become ripe targets of contemporary satirists. Church of the Subgenius' Paul Mavrides executes a big eye Mao portrait. *Rolling Stone* magazine publishes a big eye Nancy Reagan. The Keanes rate a full entry in Jane and Michael Stern's *The Encyclopedia of Bad Taste* (1990, Harper Collins). The Franklin Mint is currently producing big eye kids collector's plates. And Margaret's Keane Eyes gallery is booming with an onslaught of publicity.

Walter Keane meanwhile is trying to salvage a career upon the ruins of his reputation. He peppers the press with strange, disjointed letters, as in his 14 page epic to Jane and Michael Stern admonishing them for taking part in the "LIE OF THE CENTURY — your connecting me and my life's work with one of the MAJOR ART FORGERS and fabricators of our time, a woman called Margaret." He concludes on a menacing note: "If your LIES were told in China in the late forties, when Chiang Kai Shek fled to Taiwan in December, 1949, You two STERNS would be cut in half, or They would cut your heart and eat it, their way to demonstrate Revenge. Your unzipped lips went too far. Why did you do it? WHY??????"

Come July Walter will be forced out of his rented La Jolla cottage to make room for the landlord's vacationing children. "I don't know where I'm going to move," he frets. "Maybe to Paris. They appreciate me in Paris."

"Walter is truly a remarkable man," admits Margaret Keane. "But I think he missed his calling. He should have been an actor."

Postscript

After this article originally appeared in the *San Diego Reader,* Walter Keane wrote a long, rambling letter in reply. Rather than refuting any specific points, he resorted to using *ad hominem* attacks against the integrity of the reporter. Other letters came to the *Reader* speaking of victimization by the confidence man techniques utilized by Walter Keane. These letters supported the substance of my article. Mr. Keane told at least several individuals that Jehovah's Witnesses had paid me off to the tune of $300,000,000 for the above article. Mr. Keane is apparently a very important man.

Walter Keane in his La Jolla flat prior to eviction.

(Photo by Adam Parfrey.)

GOD, CHRIST, SATAN OR CON?
Westerners Worship a Hindu Godman

Technology is Occidental magic, and though Disneyland's Tomorrowland has suffered a great fall, we are likely in the thrall of microchips and nanotechnology. Sai Baba is a magician of a different sort; his predistigitation is taken by many — millions — as literal demonstration of godhood. It seems strange, perhaps a little out of place, that many of his American followers are professionals like psychiatrists and engineers, who yearn for the spiritual verities from the ultimate father figure, the omnipotent Sai Baba who demonstrates his godhood through the conjuration of gold rings, watches and the ubiquitous ash of cow dung.

> It is like baking a cake. I stir, I knead, I pound, I twist, I bake you. I drown you in tears. I scorch you in sobs. I make you sweet and crisp, an offering worthy of God. — Sathya Sai Baba

Sai Baba makes holy *vibhuti* appear from his hand during *dar-shan*.

With his blond, curly hair and clear blue eyes, New Age musician Richard Del Maestro embodies the archetype of the *bhakta*, or devotee. He's sweet and crisp, and hollow as a reed — to enable the breath of God to whistle between the ears. From his Cardiff Hills home, with dilated-pupil candor, Richard explains that his spiritual discovery began while musing heavenward from his crib. "I've always wanted to know why the stars are in the sky. I look at the sky and wonder, where did this come from? And how did this arrive? How is this possible?"

Richard knew at a very young age that someone, something, somehow, would answer his questions, satisfy his longings. He found this force in a dark-skinned, afro-headed individual from South India named Sathya Sai Baba. To his devotees, Sai Baba is the Avatar descended. In a word, God.

For the moment, Richard is high on God. The weekly North San Diego County Sai Baba meeting had just concluded in his tract home. The atmosphere is charged with the singing of *bhajans,* which Richard accompanies on harmonium, and the ritual use of *vibhuti,* or holy cow dung ash. Upon the wafting fumes of jasmine incense he rhapsodizes about his discovery of the prime mover.

> I stumbled upon Sai Baba though my sister. She had his picture up. I felt very threatened; I felt like, oh my god, what is happening to my little sister? Is she involved in a cult? She said that she didn't know very much about him but handed me an article out of a New Age magazine. I read the article.

> It talked about when he raised his hand, thousands of people before him would have their consciousness raised, merely by the motion of the lifting of his hands. It talked about him knowing the present, past and future of everybody he sees. About him materializing ash and rings and things. As I read this article I thought, my God, if this is true, then this is what I've been looking for.

I ran into a woman who had his picture on her wall. I asked, "Do you know who this is?" And she asked, "Do you know who this is?" She took me to the Sai Baba Center, where I bought some books. I got home, would look into a book, burst into tears, close the book, and say, this is nuts. There's no logical explanation for my bursting into tears. Then I'd do it again. Open the book, burst into tears, close the book. I cried through one book, I cried through another book, deep, sobbing, crying, absolutely inexplicable to myself. I thought, my God, man, are you mad? What's with you? Pull yourself together, it's just a book. But it wasn't just a book, it was the story of Sai Baba, and I was so moved and touched by it I was overwhelmed.

I heard that you could have a dream of him. That you can't dream of him by your own will. He must choose to come to you. I yearned to have a dream of him. These are visions, not dreams. They're real spiritual experiences.

Before long I had some very profound dreams. *Very* profound dreams, where he would be talking with me as if he knew me better than my own mother. Until you experience talking to someone who knows you better than your parents know you, you can't fathom what it feels like. There's no way of describing that.

I would listen to His 43rd birthday discourse [from November 23, 1968] over and over again until I memorized it. "For the protection of the virtuous, for the destruction of evil-doers and for establishing righteousness on a firm footing, I incarnate from age to age."

Anyone who makes a claim like that has got my attention. I'd question the discourse, I'd question these dreams, and I'd put two and two together. "If you take one step towards me, I shall take a hundred steps toward you. Shed just one tear, I shall wipe a hundred from your eyes ... If you waste this chance of saving yourself it is just your fate." Anywhere you go in this speech, it's just so powerful. After I took that one step towards him — "Baba, I want to have a dream" — Boom! I'm having this dream and it is blowing my mind *wide* open. I mean *completely* right out the top of my head! Waking up from this experience and glowing for three days. And I'm in love. And I'm fulfilled, and I'm happy. And I don't know why. And I can't describe it to a human being. I can only say, I hope I have another dream, and I want to go see him.

THEY BELIEVE IN MIRACLES

Little known in the United States, Sai Baba is acknowledged India's most revered *sadhu,* overseeing a following estimated this year by *India Today* as 50,000,000 strong internationally. The estimate includes "millions in Europe and the US." Exact numbers are difficult to determine since devotees are not compelled to sign up with any organization or even participate in communal worship at any of the thousands of Sai Baba centers worldwide. Nevertheless, there are 150 Sai Baba centers in the U.S., each servicing a handful to hundreds of devotees. The diminutive, furrow-browed godman's most distinguishing feature is his nimbus-like afro. Born in 1926 to pious, middle-class parents, his given name was Satyanarayana Raju. At the age of 14, after a dire illness precipitated by the sting of a scorpion, he announced to his family and the world that he was the reincarnation of the Muslim saint Sai Baba of Shirdi, and from then on went by the name Sathya Sai Baba. At the first he claimed not to be your workaday *sunnyasi, yogi,* or *guru,* but an *Avatar,* an incarnation of Godhood descended. Jews await the Messiah, Moslems, Mahdi, and Christians, Christ. Sai Baba claims to be all these incarnations.

Omnipotent and omnipresent, Sai Baba pronounces that he pities the person who does not believe that he has the power to transmute earth into sky and sky into earth. Since he is God, no one can comprehend him. His ways must remain inscrutable. "Talking about Sai Baba," writes devotee Howard Murphet in *Sai Baba: Avatar,* is like putting the ocean in a bell jar." Recalls N. Kasturi, Swami's official biographer, "When [a devotee] heard himself ask Baba, 'Are you God?' Baba replied, 'How can an ant measure the depth of the ocean or a fish discover the truth of the sky?'"

San Diego County is a power node of Sai Baba worship, accommodating devotional centers in the tony Sunset Cliffs area in addition to the North County organization. The Sunset Cliffs center is run from the expansive home of Dr. Samuel Sandweiss, a practicing psychiatrist who wrote *Spirit and the Mind* and *Sai Baba: The Holy Man and the Psychiatrist,* the latter being a well-distributed title that has been for many their first taste of the godman. San Diego native Dr. John Hislop, still an active devotee at the ripe age of 88 years old, wrote two books, *Conversations with Sathya Sai Baba* and *My Baba and I,* published by Dr. Sandweiss's Birth Day Publishing Company. Hislop is considered by his followers as one of the most evolved devotees, whom the Avatar has showered with sustained intimate contact.

Despite his large international following and the astounding claims surrounding Sai Baba, no major article had ever been undertaken by this country's secular press. The American Sai Baba organization was caught thoroughly unprepared for my inquiries, repelling and inviting them in turn. Although dozens of English language books have been published, and a proliferation of videotapes rented and sold in New Age shops, devotees shun publicity, an aversion articulated on many occasions by Sai Baba himself.

Exposés have dogged the trail of self-styled gods who made inroads into the pocketbooks of American followers. Guru Maharah Ji of the Divine Life Temple was the pudgy, teenage, Mammon-enriched avatar worshipped for a time by disgruntled hippies, such as '60s radical Rennie Davis. Maharah Ji's teachings, like that of the sequel to the horror movie *Re-Animator* centered around activation of the pineal gland. The Rolls-Royce enthusiast, the late Baghawan Shree

Rajneesh, later known as Osho, for whom the star-crossed Rajneesh-puram in Central Oregon was erected, attracted red-robed dropouts eager to indulge in primal screams and orgiastic sex. Fellow tantric Da Free John (aka Da Love-Ananda and Franklin Jones) author of *Easy Death*, proclaimed in 1990 to be the apocalyptic incarnation of Kalki. The balding, love-handled avatar is still building his temple in the Fiji islands primarily with the aid of American worshippers.

Unlike Rajneesh or Maharah Ji, Sai Baba doesn't seem interested in setting up camp in the U.S., preferring instead appearing to devotees in the ether. By his decree, no monetary demands are made on his followers. Tithing is prohibited. To discourage ostentatious displays of philanthropy, any contribution to the communal kitty is supposed to be done out of sight of others. Devotees are encouraged to contribute to local needs rather than service the central authority. All books and audio tapes are distributed at cost. Sai Baba has directed that his devotees use their homes for worship in order to avoid public or private collections of money for temples and a bloated bureaucracy.

And unlike Rajneeshees and Hare Krishnas, Baba *bhaktas* do not don ochre robes and drop out of society. They are urged instead to observe strict moral practices within their respective communities, with an emphasis on public service projects. Richard Del Maestro's North County center organizes weekly distribution of burritos to field workers; Sandweiss's South County group has its own burrito project twice a month, and helps out at the Joan Kroc Center for the Homeless. Baba devotees seem so apparently benign and well-integrated, you wouldn't know that they hold such an unusual set of beliefs.

Sai Baba's ashram, located in the small town of Puttaparthi, India, is an evolving empire of hospitals, temples, universities, schools, hotels, and even an airline landing strip. These expensive services, provided to the public at low or no cost, are said to be funded though blind contributions to a central trust.

It is not for his good deeds that Sai Baba is famous, but his miracles. With the spin of his hand he materializes *vibhuti,* which he dispenses to crowds receiving his darshan. *Vibhuti,* which is actually cow dung reduced to ash and perfumed with jasmine, produced by the ton at the Sai Baba ashram, is eaten and swabbed on the forehead by all devotees in every devotional meeting. At once a sacrament and a cure-all, *vibhuti* is said to symbolize the fragility of material existence and the transcendence of the spirit: from ash you have come and ash you shall become.

In private interviews Sai Baba's miraculous performances take on, as devotees tell me, a rather desultory air. He apports gold watches and jewelry, medallions, statues, jappamalas, necklaces, rings and other knick-knacks. Some of these materializations have been captured on film and videotape. Dale Beyerstein, affiliated with the Canadian chapter of the Committee for the Scientific Investigation of Claims of the Paranormal (CSICOP), responding to requests by concerned relatives of Baba devotees, self-published an investigation titled *Sai Baba's Miracles: An Overview*, in which professional magicians analyze Sai Baba's materializations frame-by-frame, noting classic sleight-of-hand and misdirection. At present, according to Mary Keene of the Sathya Sai Book Center of America in Tustin, official sale of video-tapes has been discontinued until Baba puts his imprimatur on them. Videotapes that were previously sold through the center, such as those filmed by devotee Richard Bock, and, incidentally, scrutinized by Dale Beyerstein and CSICOP, can only be sold through private parties.

Anecdotal reports from believers overwhelmingly make the case for Sai Baba as the genuine article. San Diego resident Mike Congleton, a four-eyed magician by hobby and computer engineer by trade, is an uncritical believer after seeing Sai Baba in person:

> I've always had a good understanding of sleight of hand and misdirection, like Houdini or Dun-ninger. I know about mentalism and all that stuff. Outside of Banaglore I visited an orphanage that had medallions exuding *amritha* (a nectar-of-the-Gods like substance). Here's something with no strings attached, no tubes. A medallion sponta-neously oozing *amritha*, right into my palm. It was at the orphanage where ash was appearing on religious objects. From a statue of Jesus, red ash was coming out of his hand and heart. The fellow

who ran the orphanage held up a *lingam* [for Sai Baba, not a phallus but egg-shaped object, a ritual object said to symbolize the birth of the cosmos] and asked me what I saw. I looked and saw an orange robe and Sai Baba. He said not everyone saw Baba inside the *lingam*.

When I arrived at Puttaparthi the ashram was practically deserted because of a strike. Baba had his hand in front of me, then says, "Okay, 500 rupees service charge." He reached into the air right in front of me and grabbed ten one thousand dollar bills, American money. He said, "Money doesn't mean anything to me; it's your love and devotion to God." Then he turned his hand over like he was dropping the money, and then it disappeared.

In his first pilgrimage to Sai Baba, after spending months being ignored in *darshan* among thousands of other worshippers, Sai Baba finally invited devotee Richard Del Maestro to a personal interview:

He asked, "What do you want?" I said, "I want to be as close to your heart as possible. I want to be as close to your physical presence as possible." He said, "Where am I?" I said, "You're everywhere." He said, "How do you know?" At that point, I didn't know how I knew, except from the books, or just believing what I heard, and not because of any real experience. He said, "You know from your imagination." He's teaching me to be discriminating. He said, "I am God; you are also God." I said, "Yes Swami, I feel more like God every day." He said, "That feeling is Good. Follow that feeling." Then he waved his hand and materialized this ring for me. He slid it on my finger and said, "Ah, perfect fit."

Such stories are a dime-a-dozen among devotees. Precious because they are delighted by the leelas of their lord, but prosaic because mir-

Vibhuti apparation on Sai Baba photo at Wilma Bronky's house in Grant's Pass, OR.; Shirdi Sai Bab figurine below. (Photo by Parfrey.)

189

acles are ostensibly a common occurrence around Sai Baba.

If it's all just abracadabra, Sai Baba's a highly proficient con. He's convinced fifty million souls that he's God. One big goof in his daily materializations in front of thousands of followers and the jig is up.

What makes the case of Sai Baba so curious is that many believers report strange materializations in their own homes. A not uncommon phenomena is the materialization of *vibhuti* or *amritha* on pictures of Sai Baba. In researching this article I was able to view two separate examples of these ostensibly miraculous apparitions. In an elderly devotee's home in Grants Pass, Oregon, scented *vibhuti* appears on a couple dozen images of Sai Baba. Aluminum foil dams are jerry-rigged below the pictures to catch the runoff. And in a cup presented to the devotee by Swami, *vibhuti* is said to replenish itself and never run out. At the Sathya Sai Book Center of America, located in a modest, one-story building on a busy street in Tustin, two images of Sai Baba are streaked with *amritha*. "When we take the pictures out of the work room," says Book Center manager Mary Keene, "and put them in the meditation room the amritha stops flowing. As soon as we put them back in the work room, they start flowing again."

Stranger still is that Baba believers — unlike Christians from Fatima to El Monte — are content to keep the so-called miracles under wraps. Could these manifestations be the result of devotees suffering from Munchausen's Syndrome, a disease in which the patient, in a kind of trance, fabricates miracles for the conscious self? Wilma Bronky, the aged devotee from Grants Pass, tells me nobody in town knows about the mysterious events taking place in her home. "They wouldn't understand." Wilma has been so circumspect about the Swami's "blessing" that the usually well-informed SoCal Babaites expressed surprise when I told them about the Grants Pass *"vibhuti* storms." "Whenever the *vibhuti* stops flowing for a time," says Wilma, "it means that Swami is displeased. And I've got to figure out why." Despite health problems, Wilma Bronky is planning her 30th trip to see Sai Baba.

Dr. Sandweiss, the psychiatrist, says, "I've seen the most extraordinary things, right here in San Diego. I've seen pictures with the *amritha*. I've seen a house where all the pictures fill with *vibhuti*. I've seen experiences that were just mind-boggling. I mean, a person, a 28-year-old rather naive person who doesn't know any foreign language would feel that [Sai Baba] would come to her in her mind's eye, and she would start chanting Sanskrit, and *vibhuti* would materialize on her body and her pictures. I mean, it was just so extraordinary.

"A friend told me one day she wanted to go to India. I discouraged her because she had a lot of responsibility here. She said, 'Come let me show you something.' She showed me a picture which was materializing *vibhuti*." Sandweiss looks me in the eye, perhaps trying to gauge whether I believe these stories, and continues, "Those kinds of dramatic expressions give a charge to believers but wreak havoc with people who don't believe."

An article in the August 15, 1993 issue of *India Today* reveals that *vibhuti* apparitions are a common trick of fakirs that can be duplicated by spraying lactic acid over picture frames. Ash is produced when dried lactic acid comes into contact with moisture. It's comforting to know that a parlor trick can perhaps replicate the mystical experiences of Sai Baba devotees, but a disturbing question remains. How can a true believer remain a true believer when he's loading the dice?

In his official biographies, presently collected in four volumes, Sai Baba is described as raising the dead, manipulating time and space, transmuting energy into matter and matter into energy. In a country where cows are treated with more consideration than most individuals, modernist Indians are practically driven mad by what they perceive to be the regressive reverence of godmen like Sai Baba.

One frustrated rationalist went so far as attempt to take God to court.

In 1985, B. Premanand, Chairman of the Indian chapter of the Committee for the Scientific Investigation of Claims of the Paranormal (CSICOP), initiated a court claim against Sai Baba for contravening the India Gold Control Act, which prohibits the manufacture of gold articles without registering proper permissions from the central government. A judge dismissed the Premanand's writ, finding, "An article or an ornament which was admittedly materialised from air in a split second by the use of spiritual powers or otherwise cannot be said to have been 'made, manufactured, prepared or processed,' within the meaning of Section 11 of the [Gold Control] Act."

Premanand and rationalists accused the Indian government of coddling and protecting the godman, an accusation that may hold some merit considering leading politicos and jurists profess to be Sai Baba devotees. According to the July 15th issue of *India Today,* among "the godman's staunch believers includes the President [and] The Prime Minister [of India]." Their professed belief may simply be good politics. Sai Baba's teachings are a sedative for the excitable millions. He blessed the military on several occasions, preaching unquestioning allegiance to parents and the state.

Deepening the controversy was the mysterious June 6, 1993 attack on Sai Baba's living quarters, in which the holy man's cook and driver were murdered, and four assailants — all longtime Sai Baba devotees — were cornered in a room and killed by police. *India Today* magazine clucked that Sai Baba, alerted by a burglar alarm, cowered in his bathroom while the killers were taking down his close associates. Finding sport in the mysterious bloodbath, *India Today's* July 15th account was titled "Intimations of Mortality."

Several days later, Sai Baba finally explained to his anxious followers that the attack was simply a case of jealousy, that the plotters were envious of the cook and driver's access to the avatar. Police investigators fingered the plot on the four murdered devotees, a canteen worker and the head of ashram security. A large quantity of cyanide, capable of spiking the ashram's water supply, and three explosive devices, powerful enough to destroy a building, were discovered by police.

In America, devotees heard news of the June attack but did not get an official explanation until the Fall 1993 publication of the American *Sathya Sai Newsletter,* which reprinted a speech titled "Bhagawan Speaks of Ancient Truth and Recent Events." Under the subhead, "What Really Happened," Sai Baba unfolds a kind of shaggy dog story in which he shares a glass of buttermilk with his ill-fated driver Radakrishna, but the driver, in his impulsiveness, ignores Swami's entreaties to follow him upstairs out of harm's way. In the official newsletter, Sai Baba neglects to inform anybody about the four dead devotee-assassins, the cyanide, the explosive devices, or his own conduct when bloodbath was taking place. He concludes the story about the buttermilk and Radakrishna's willfulness with an admonition: "Swami gives instructions for one's own good. Whatever Swami says is sacred." Case closed. At the weekly meetings in Grants Pass, the lack of concern about the particulars of the case seemed eerie. Despite the bloodbath, the devotees seemed quite satisfied with their god's explanation of the matter. Their articles of faith could remain undisturbed.

The Holy Man and the Psychiatrist

Every Thursday night Sam Sandweiss's home becomes the principal San Diego Sathya Sai Baba devotional center. Huge three-sheet sized posters of Swami shine through the vaulting living room windows of Sandweiss's tony Sunset Cliffs estate. Custom calls for shoes to be left by the front door. Devotees greet one another and drift into the devotional room, segregate themselves by gender, grab a cushion, and assume a lotus position on the floor. "Hugging and kissing is discouraged at our meetings," reads the welcoming instructions. "This is a very different custom than what we are used to in America. Sai Baba teaches us that we are not aware of the impact physical contact with other people may have on us."

Facing the altar of Baba photos, the several dozen devotees are led in a group "OM," which is followed by forty minutes of *bhajans*, the traditional call-response songs of devotional praise in Sanskrit, Hindi and English. But when the congregation sings about Rama, Krishna and Siva, it's obvious that they're directing the songs to Sai Baba, who is said to embody all God forms. Decorum precludes shows of exhibitionist religiosity. The zeitgeist of this primarily boomer crowd, some in suit and tie, is more Unitarian than Fundamentalist. These people are unlikely to spasm, possessed by the Holy Ghost, or chant and wheedle money at the airport.

After *bhajans*, monitors distribute the holy cow dung ash, which some devotees streak on their foreheads and others throw into their mouths. "Perfectly safe," whispers a man to my left. He motions for me to eat the ash.

193

All eyes turn toward Dr. John Hislop, who is to conclude the meeting with a discourse on Sai Baba and love. At eighty-eight years of age, *vibhuti* smudging his third eye, Hislop's regal bearing is reminiscent of the Grand Lama in Lost Horizon. Devotees politely listen to Hislop's account of the time at Puttaparthi when he had seen *saris* exude water — "they are weeping," explained Swami — because they were rejected by Baba. On Hislop's finger is an ungainly ring on which the profile of Swami's future incarnation, Prema Sai Baba, can be vaguely made out on the black stone.

After the meeting, Sam Sandweiss finally makes himself available to talk. For weeks, phone calls and faxes had been flying back and forth regarding his wavering commitment to an interview. Sam was worried about how badly I'd sensationalize his beloved Baba, worried about how his cooperation with me would affect the Bhagawan Sri Sathya Sai Baba organization; he was also concerned about how the article would affect his professional standing as a psychiatrist.

"Did you dream of Him? Did Swami come to you in a dream?" Sandweiss asks.

I don't think so, I tell Sandweiss.

Sandweiss smiles nervously. "You'd remember if you dreamt of him. He calls many people to Him in this manner. People often want to dream of Baba, but can't. It really doesn't matter how you come to him. Just the fact that you're inquiring probably means that he's calling you."

Was I hearing right? As far as I knew, psychiatrists were not the sort of folk to put their faith in avatars and miracles that defy the laws of science as we knew them. Whither Freud? Fenichel? Ferenczi? Were dreams no longer the property of the dreamer's own consciousness? Was the consciousness now owned or guided by an ochre-robed holy man from South India?

"There were four psychiatrists here this evening," observes Dr. Sandweiss. "Computer engineers, physicists, and educators. All high-caliber individuals." I notice Baba believers are quick to point out that their co-religionists are "high-caliber." This tendency, however, pales in comparison an almost neurotic compulsion to see Sai Baba in everything. Any coincidence, any peculiar event, even any perfectly normal and conventionally explainable occurrence is seen as an example of the avatar's object lesson to his disciple. Sandweiss, in his self-published book *The Holy Man and the Psychiatrist* recalls the dislocating feeling when he meets Indra Devi, an elderly Russian yogi from Tecate, Mexico, who speaks incessantly of Sai Baba, and little else. "It seemed that no matter what I asked, her mind was channeled to Sai Baba. Sai Baba this, and Sai Baba that, until I began to consider how unusual it was for a woman in her seventies to have such a reaction."

Essentially a diary of his conversion experience, *The Holy Man and the Psychiatrist* is reminiscent of those E.M. Forster novels of Westerners seduced by the exotic incomprehensibility of India. "My belief in [miracle] stories is growing," writes Sandweiss. "I hear them from everyone, miracle after miracle, and now I have seen up close with my own two eyes a very dramatic example myself. People tell me of Baba's ability to know everything in their past and present, what they are thinking and what will happen in detail in the future. ... Amazing! Unbelievable! Unthinkable! The most mind-blowing, extraordinary experience — as if the most far fetched science fiction were actually seen to be true...

"There is no doubt in my mind that Sai Baba is divine. I astound myself to say such a thing. What must have I experienced, a rational scientific man, to say such a thing? I believe I can't even communicate the experience. I know all this isn't hypnosis, mass delusion, hallucination, hysteria, an effect of cultural shock or drug intoxication. It's too simple to say I saw a materialization and then all of a sudden changed."

After his encounter in India with Sai Baba, Sandweiss returned to the States with the eagerness and reformist vigor of the proselyte. "Soon after I got home I threw a party. I wanted to tell everyone about my amazing adventure in India — and that was my undoing... something fell flat. I lost my credibility and most of my friends. Psychiatric residents I taught in medical school were contacted to see if I had gone crazy. ... I could see the humor in it. I left for India as a modern, successful psychiatrist going on an adventure — and returned home almost as if in rags and covered with ash."

GOD, CHRIST, SATAN, OR CON?

The main tenet of Hinduism is that earth is a purgatory from which the soul may finally able to obtain release from cumulative acts of righteousness. Service, helping the less fortunate, is an opportunity to get incrementally closer to that cosmic Get Out of Jail Free card. In the Kali-Yuga age, says Sai Baba, release from the vicious cycle of karma may be achieved in chanting his name.

In the Kali-Yuga, as Sai Baba explains in his 43rd birthday address, we are all sinners. In other eras:

> Avatars like Rama and Krishna had to kill one or more individuals who could be identified as enemies of the dharmic way of life, and thus restore the practice of virtue. But now there is no one fully good, and so who deserves the protection of God? All are tainted by wickedness, and so who will survive if the avatar decides to uproot? Therefore I have come to correct the buddhi, the intelligence, by various means. I have to counsel, help, command, condemn and stand by as a friend and well-wisher to all, so that they may give up evil propensities and, recognizing the straight mark, tread it and reach the goal.

"To attain enlightenment [release from the physical world]," Dr. Hislop tells me, "you have to see that you are under illusion. Fortunately, you can disperse that illusion more easily in the Kali-Yuga than in the other yugas. To disperse that illusion you must learn about detachment. You think that you're the body — and if you examine it carefully you can be detached from the body, and you see that you're not the body or the mind at all."

The Sai Baba sarva dharma symbol is a lotus composed of petals with logos from the five major religions in India: a cross, a star and crescent, a Buddhist wheel, a Zoroastrian bowl of fire, and the Hindu Sanskrit OM. In the West, the Magen David was added to the symbol at the request of Baba's Jewish adherents. In all the symbol reflects the godman's ecumenical aspirations. He instructs devotees to

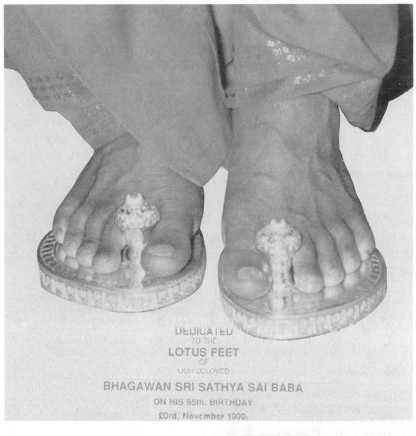

DEDICATED
TO THE
LOTUS FEET
OF
OUR BELOVED
BHAGAWAN SRI SATHYA SAI BABA
ON HIS 65th. BIRTHDAY
20rd. November 1990.

Top: Baba's Lotus Feet

Right: Detail of crucifix
materialized by Sai Baba
for Dr. John Hislop.

worship "in the way it is comfortable for you." In so doing, he says, they will come to him, since, of course, Sai Baba is God of all.

It is difficult to find Sai Baba devotees, at least in the San Diego area, who also continue to practice Judaism or Christianity. "I think I'm a fairly devout Catholic," says Mike Congleton, insecurely. "St. Francis is a favorite saint, and so is St. Teresa. At one time in my life I went on a lot of pilgrimages to Catholic shrines." The hardest thing to swallow about Sai Baba, Congleton says, was the concept of reincarnation, but he was reassured when he discovered "the bible mentions reincarnation a couple times."

When Congleton visited Puttaparthi and was witness to Sai Baba's miracles, he worried about not having enough faith. "I was basically confronted with the divine. Sai Baba says trust in the divine. Have faith, and everything will be taken care of for me. That's also message of St. Francis."

Sai Baba announced that the bible predicted his return. Does Congleton believe that the Swami is the second coming of Christ? "Can you have faith?" he muses. "I wondered that if I had lived in the time of Christ, I would have known Christ. I would have abandoned everything, right?"

The Lost Years of Jesus, a documentary filmed by a devotee named Richard Bock, proclaims that Jesus was initiated into the Vedic teachings by a Himalayan guru, traversing India under the name Isa. Jesus is not the son of God, but another manifestation of the God current, a human being who evolved into enlightenment.

Fundamentalists, predictably, who consider Hinduism a form of Satanism, are convinced this kind of esoteric Christianity the ultimate blasphemy.

A former devotee and born-again Christian Tal Brooke, wrote *Avatar of Night: The Hidden Side of Sai Baba* (1982, Tarang Paperbacks) to accuse Sai Baba of repeated homosexual molestations. A particularly strange chapter charges that Baba is a hermaphrodite who catches the semen of his sexual partners on handkerchiefs in order to perform occult rituals. Such bizarre stories would appear to cast doubt on their verity, but the charge of homosexual molestation has been publicly repeated by several former devotees, including Malaysian student Hariram Jayaram. In a letter to the Indian skeptic B. Premanand, Jayaram wrote: "I was until recently [1981] an ardent follower of Sathya Sai Baba. To my surprise and that of the surprise of his many devotees in Malaysia, Sathya Sai Baba carried out homosexual activities on the Malaysian students studying in his Colleges. When I came to know of the same, I dropped out from the Sai movement." John Worldie, whose photographs were printed in several devotee publications, rants in an epilogue to Brooke's *Avatar of Night:* "I never could figure out why he played with my penis so I rationalized it as he was 'purifying' me. I sent him a telegram and said I'd purify him American style if he came here. ... He has the mark of the beast on his forehead. ... I'm sure he must be a form of Satan or whatever."

San Diego devotees feel blessed to live near the holy relic produced by Sai Baba for Dr. Hislop. It is said to illustrate an exact likeness of Christ; the cross, Baba says, is made of the wood from the original crucifix, and "shows Christ as He really was at the time when He left his body. No writer or artist has imagined him this way before." Swept away by the emotion of the materialization, Hislop pronounces that the crucifix is one of the most exquisite works of art he has ever seen; others seem to find it a more prosaic item. Dr. William S. Dale, professor at the University of Western Ontario remarks in Dale Beyerstein's *Sai Baba's Miracles: An Overview:*

> From the photograph it is quite clear that the metal figure closely resembles those on crucifixes of the 19th and 20th centuries. As is normal with these, the suppedaneum is cast in one piece with the figure. Its small scale suggests that it may once have been attached to a rosary. Contrary to Sai Baba's claim, there is nothing unusual about the iconography of the piece."

Dr. Dale goes on to describe the evolving iconography for crucifixes through the centuries, in which this particular piece represents a fairly modern form. Judging from the quantity of air bubbles on the surface, antique expert Uno Langmann surmises that the figure is a cheap reproduction, cast in lead.

The crucifix's owner, Dr. John Hislop, is a living legend in Baba circles, not only for his access to Sai Baba, which is recounted in his two books, but for his many years as an associate of Krishnamurti, Maharishi Mahesh Yogi and Paramahansa Yogananda. Hislop was working for the Theosophical Society in India when Krishnamurti was being groomed by Annie Besant to become the avatar, the human form of the mysterious "Hidden Masters" of the Himalayas that Madame Blavatsky had supposedly contacted through clairvoyant means.

Although Hislop was favorably impressed by Krishnamurti, Yogananda and Mahesh Yogi, he eventually discovered that Sai Baba was "more than a philosopher."

How does one determine divinity, I ask the spry and amiable Hislop. Through his magical powers?

"Many yogis have *siddhi* powers," he says. "Any yogi who goes into that line of endeavor can gain *siddhi* powers. But it takes long work and extreme discipline of the mind. With Swami it was no work and no discipline, just natural to him. He never studied those disciplines whatsoever to get all these powers. With the avatar, most things are just natural. I've been places where *amritha* would flow off pictures. The *vibhuti* would fall off in a steady stream."

Miracles unrelated to Sai Baba?

"Not related to Swami at all, no. There was a chap who would move his hand and create what people would want, just like Swami. It was no problem at all for him. But the governor of Goa, told me this chap could only do it after he prayed to the goddess Durga. Why, I couldn't tell you."

The watch that Sai Baba had materialized for Sam Sandweiss is a Citizens brand.

"I have one too."

Citizens?

"Uh huh. Over the years Swami has materialized many watches. In the past years he used to give out extremely expensive Swiss watches. Of course, the question in you mind is, how are those watches secured? There are two methods whereby the watch can appear. One is transporting them. The other is their creation. It could be that Swami does both. When Swami was giving these expensive Swiss watches to his students, people were saying Swami was taking these watches from stores and not paying for them. And so a couple of devotees decided to check it out. They took the number off the Swiss watches and contacted the maker in Switzerland, and found out the store that number had been shipped. And they went to this jewelry store, 800 miles from Prasanthi Nilayam [Sai Baba's ashram], and gave them the numbers, and asked if they remembered about the watch. They said they remembered because they don't sell many watches that expensive. The manager of the jewelry store said that a man came in the store, looked at several watches, chose them, paid for them, and walked out of the store. Now that was some 800 miles away from where Swami was, and happened at exactly the same date and time as when Swami materialized the watch, we know that for sure because those fellows in the store had the invoice book. So there you have a transaction that takes several minutes and 800 miles away, and Swami walks by some student and the thought occurs to him that he'll give the student a watch, and he produces it in a matter of seconds. I don't know how you explain that."

Any ideas on how the materializations occur?

"Swami has said recently that he does not now apport watches. That his workmen manufacture them. Now, how can that be? I really can't tell you that either. We know that so-called solid objects are just masses of vibrations, different frequencies and different wavelengths. A solid object is just energy. So apparently it's possible for the mind, then, to, I suppose, change the wavelength and the frequency, and here appears an object."

Skeptics say that Sai Baba is an accomplished magician. For that reason he can't materialize objects larger than he can palm."

"I've seen him materialize over a hundred of objects in every possible kind of circumstance. Some years ago, whenever Swami went someplace, He'd take me with him. I saw many manifestations of things, in the car, walking, sitting, every possible way you could think of. So if someone tells me it's all my imagination, I don't say anything."

And so, Sai Baba is God?

"I accept on faith that's the case. If you want to find out if he's God, you're going to have to pay attention to the second half of his formula. If people ask him, he says, 'Yes, I am God,' but then he continues and says, 'But so are you. The only difference is, I know it, and you don't know it."

Are there other Gods running around?

"I asked Swami about those people who have realized themselves, recognized themselves as absolute. I asked, 'Are there such people today?' And he said, 'Oh yes, of course there are. You don't see them, they're in the foothills of the Himalayas, and they keep to themselves. ' I asked Swami if there were people like that in America. He said, 'Oh yes, but they keep a very low profile. You would never know who they were.'

I ask Hislop about an incident in which Sai Baba is said to have saved his life from a bungled prostate operation in the city of Bangalore.

"People [in the operating room] saw Swami's hands. They said I talked during the operation, saying, 'Don't bother me. Swami's here, I'm talking to him.' After the operation I had to stay at the hospital for ten days because I was very sick. Swami would come every day to see me. I was puzzled why all this happened to me. Finally it dawned on me that must have been my normal time for death. I figured out, this was my time of death. I should have died. So I told Swami, 'I think I've figured it out. That was my normal time of death, and you gave me extended life.' And he laughed and said, 'You've figured it out. That's correct.' That was one episode. There were car incidents in which he saved our lives, those are recorded in my book."

If he's God, why doesn't Sai Baba end all the misery?

"Swami said, 'I could do that. There would be no trouble. No poverty. No problems in the world at all. But tomorrow morning people would be at each other's throats again. The way that humanity can be changed is not through miracles, but from the raising of consciousness.'"

What about contradictory statements that he'll make?

"He'll make contradictory statements because you have to understand that any statement you make is based on duality. The ancient sages used to tell their devotees, 'Forget everything. Forget everything, don't remember anything.' Anything you know has a tremendous quotient of error because it's based on duality and the perception of duality is false."

You wrote that you saw Sai Baba become Krishna.

"Oh yes, I sure did."

Was he like the Krishna pictured in Indian wall hangings?

"I just suspected he was Krishna. Because when I looked back in the car and saw him, Swami was no longer there, but this person who was so beautiful, he would just twist your heart. There's no way to describe it. A dark, dark blue. And it lasted about twenty minutes. The others in the car were saying, 'Hislop, what's wrong with you?' You see, they didn't see anything. I asked Swami about the dark color. He said, 'Whenever you look at something with immeasurable depth it has that dark blue color, as the sky or the ocean.'"

As with most yogic teachers, Sai Baba calls for destruction of the ego, utter servitude. While in *darshan,* devotees prostrate themselves before him, vying for the opportunity to touch the avatar's feet. The biggest jolt of bliss, apparently, is delivered through the big toe. "You heard the story at the meeting tonight," says Richard Del Maestro, "about sitting in front and touching Baba's lotus feet. It is a feeling of indescribable joy, being indescribably fulfilled. You could describe it as drinking divine nectar. In one interview I got to massage his feet. I was sitting there. There were three of us. His feet were there and I just took a hold of his foot and massaged it. Everyone would love the opportunity to do that. It wasn't like I was really working on his foot, I just gently started to rub on the bottom of his foot. I was so worried about doing it, the moment he withdrew his foot just slightly I immediately stopped. It's hard to describe the experience, but it was very powerful, overwhelming."

I ask Hislop if people visit Sai Baba and walk away unimpressed.

"Oh yes, very often. In the past, the distant past, perhaps, they established a karmic savings account. When they come to see Him, they draw on this account. So these people must have exhausted their savings."

Postscript

This article is a miracle of restraint. Devoting a preponderance of space to the comments of Baba's followers, I found it fascinating that so-called professionals would become fair game for unquestioned devotion of this religious figure.

Despite my reluctance to make light of the Baba-believers, many wrote angry letters, misperceiving the article to be a simple hit piece. Their angry missives drove home the point that true believers lack the saving grace of humor.

Much has been made of Sai Baba's miracles, and his continued refusal to be tested by skeptics. I am more interested in discovering just how much influence Sai Baba wields in the military and the Parliament.

GIMME GIMME SHOCK TREATMENT

[Stalin is not alone in using psychiatry to control the political process. Lobotomy and shock therapy was commonly employed by psychiatrists in the 1950s to make housewives more compliant and transform bohemians and dissidents into "productive" members of capitalist society. Leonard Frank, author of the recent *Influencing Minds* and *The History of Shock Treatment*, suffered a battery of insulin and electric shock simply because his parents were displeased by his "beatnik-like" behavior.

Inspired by *One Flew Over the Cuckoo's Nest,* laws were passed in the '70s to protect prisoners and mental patients from shock therapy imposed without their consent. Around this time, shock therapy became increasingly rare. It's taken a decade for shock therapy to become trendy once again. A recent campaign, complete with celebrity testimonials and strategically-placed articles extolling shock therapy's benefits, has effectively revived the procedure. Every passing year sees increasing numbers of shock patients.

Appealing to budget-conscious bureaucrats, shock proponents sold Clinton's Health and Human Services Department on shock as a cost-effective treatment for depression. If Clinton's Health Care Program became law, shock therapy, reinforced with a regiment of psychiatric drugs, would become the treatment of preference. Talk therapy and social programs are now considered expensive and ineffective solutions to the condition of depression and general feelings of hopelessness.

Many patients praise shock therapy as an effective though temporary treatment for debilitating bouts of depression. Unfortunately, many patients have also reported side-effects such as permanent memory loss, which conjures its own depressive side-effects. In some cases, intelligent professionals have been shocked into vegetative states, unable to accomplish the simplest tasks.

Pro-shock propagandists I interviewed were so defensive in their praise of ECT they resorted to making hubristic and easily-refuted statements. One arrogant psychiatrist insisted that shock is absolutely without controversy, with a success rate that approaches 100%. When the shock propagandist was confronted with articles from professional journals refuting these claims, he countered with an emotional attack on dissident psychiatrists, calling them "crazy."

ECT is extremely profitable for many hospitals across the country, as well as for the psychiatrists who administer the procedure. New York, the epicenter of psychiatric power, is the home of *Convulsive Therapy,* the professional journal devoted to ECT. It's not surprising that the *New York Times'* Sunday Magazine as well as *New York* magazine surfaced with articles reiterating pro-shock propaganda.

The following article examines the position of boosters, skeptics, victims and those said to be helped by shock treatment. Scientists have yet to discover just how electricity affects the brain for good or ill.

Since differing versions of this article appeared in the *San Diego Reader* and *Hustler* magazine, I learned that shock equipment is used as a torture device in Central and South America. Is it too far a stretch to imagine shock equipment used once more to punish American dissidents? ECT's capacity to erase one's memory — arguably the most precious aspect of being human — demands continued strict oversight rather than reckless expansion. Playing fast and loose with the human mind in the pursuit of profit may well become the ugliest side-effect of the New World Order. Pay close attention to the man behind the curtain.]

When Dick Cavett came out of the closet last year to praise shock therapy as the miracle cure for a long-term depression, it got him prominent ink in *People* magazine and major newspapers. Whether the rodent-like TV talk show host's confession was a publicity stunt or a brave testimonial for the public welfare, the revelation was part of an ongoing media rehabilitation for a psychiatric cure that only a decade ago seemed as barbaric and outdated as bloodletting.

Despite the state-mandated hearings, form-filling and bureaucratic delays that rendered involuntary use of shock treatment increasingly difficult, the controversial therapy has escalated in recent years among patients who have been coaxed by their psychiatrists to consent to its use. It now appears that electroconvulsive treatments have received the green light from the Clinton Administration. In April, 1993, the Health and Human Services Department issued guidelines recommending shock therapy, powerful anti-psychotic drugs and "broad-spectrum light therapy" as the preferred treatments for depression.

By giving ECT — the clinical acronym for Electroconvulsive Therapy — a clean bill of health, the Clinton Administration has chosen to unquestioningly follow the dictates of the APA (American Psychiatric Association). The APA is a powerful trade association formed to protect the privileges of its wealthy members. Enshrined on the APA seal is Benjamin Rush, the "father of psychiatry" and inventor of a torturous restraining device called the tranquilizer chair. Rush was a believer in bleeding cures and rather notoriously bled George Washington to death — William Jefferson Clinton, take note.

Mindful of his public image and standing among their peers, a psychiatrist privately admitted to me that ECT has been a hard sell ever since *One Flew Over the Cuckoo's Nest* and *Frances* alarmed moviegoers with the spectacle of evil psychiatrists wielding electroshock to punish free spirits. The same psychiatrist admitted that while it was true that ECT was once brandished as a kind of weapon, it didn't happen anymore.

Torquemada had nothing on shock propagandist Dr. Gary C. Aden, the San Diego psychiatrist whose American Society for Electrotherapy was formed to combat anti ECT sentiment. In 1989, Dr Aden dealt his fellow shock advocates a stunning setback when regional newspapers revealed that he had sex with his patients, beat them with a riding crop, penetrated them sexually with foreign objects, and branded two women with an iron that bore his initials. To forestall an embarrassing public trial, Aden was allowed to quietly forfeit his license. It is rumored that Aden has changed his name and now sells used cars somewhere in Arizona.

The entire purpose of running electricity through the brain is to induce a *grand mal* convulsion in the patient, but ECT practitioners are quick to tell you that the original method of inducing this convulsion, which inadvertently broke the bones of thousands and led to the deaths of hundreds of patients, is no longer practiced.

Muscle relaxants are now introduced intravenously to prevent the harrowing full-body paroxysm. Pain is no longer a concern since the patient is KO'd with anesthetic prior to treatment. Until the mid-1960s, many patients were forced to endure insulin shock therapy in tandem with the trauma of unmodified (read: old style) Electroconvulsive treatments. Insulin therapy, which involved plunging the victim into a convulsive hypoglycemic coma, was discontinued after too many patients were killed by the cure. In the 1940s and 1950s, shock was commonly prescribed as a cure-all for a variety of conditions ranging from alcoholism to zoophobia. Now ECT is largely prescribed for those suffering from depression, and to a lesser extent, those exhibiting signs of catatonia, mania and certain schizophrenic syndromes. In its non-modified form, patients received dozens, hundreds, and in some cases, even more than a thousand shocks, instead of the series of six to twelve treatments given three days a week that is today's therapeutic norm.

An instructional video shown by shock docs to their patients as part of the state-mandated informed consent procedure presents a rosy picture of modified Electroconvulsive Therapy. Sponsored by the Somatics Corporation, an East Coast manufacturer of shock equipment, the video is intended to allay unfounded fears about the controversial procedure. Indeed, as viewed through Somatics' boosterish lens, modified ECT seems like a walk through the park in contrast to the torture device seen in *Cuckoo's Nest*.

In a dull medium shot, the video first shows a catheter inserted into the patient's arm, through which an anesthesiologist pumps in knock-out drops and muscle relaxant. With electrical wands in hand, the psychiatrist applies one to the patient's right temple and the other one is set on top of the head. This configuration is called unilateral ECT, a recent addition to the shock repertoire, which is supposed to cause less damage to memory than bilateral ECT, the traditional method.

Then the shrink flips the toggle switch on the Somatics shock machine; when the juice hits the patient's forehead we hear a dull thud. The patient grimaces and wiggles his toes as an orderly pumps

high potency for

shock therapy

ILETIN (INSULIN, LILLY) made U-500

from Zinc-Insulin Crystals

Provides a convenient means of administering the extremely high doses required for shock therapy in schizophrenia.

Iletin (Insulin, Lilly) made from Zinc-Insulin Crystals, U-500, should be used only under the direction of a physician familiar with shock therapy.

Lilly

Available in individual 20-cc. vials.

QUALITY/RESEARCH/INTEGRITY

ELI LILLY AND COMPANY · INDIANAPOLIS 6, INDIANA, U.S.A.

air into his lungs. (The muscle relaxant eliminates the patient's ability to breathe.) In several minutes the muscle relaxant wears off and
the patient once again breaths on his own; in thirty minutes or so he
comes to, and is wheeled into a waiting area to recuperate.

It should be pointed out that only medically trained doctors have the
power to medicate and shock. Current research pegs mental illness on
biological factors — the "medical model" or "broken brain" hypothesis. Freudian talk therapy has more or less fallen out of fashion except
for those wealthy enough to pay for it. Regarding mental distress as a
biological problem justifies the psychiatrist's imperative to prescribe
drugs and other mechanistic treatments, including drugs, shock treatment and psychosurgery (lobotomy).

Shock dissidents reject the premises of the medical model. Thomas
Szasz, M.D., the author of *The Myth of Mental Illness,* portrays psychiatry as a messianic ideology that foists its authoritarian presump-
tions on those it considers its social inferiors. The psychiatric diagnostic manual, at time of writing the DSM-IV, is seen by Szasz as a
modern *Malleus Malleficarum,* the medieval witch-burning guide-
book, with shock therapy the contemporary equivalent of the torture
devices of the Inquisition.

ECT advocates are quite convinced that the modern method of
administering shock is safe and effective — pro-shock literature
describes the procedure as less traumatic for the patient than visiting
a dentist. Sensitive to years of negative publicity, some members of the
psychiatric community are so intent on reining in dissident sentiments
that they deny such a thing exists. Dr. Alan Bergsma, a tightly-wound
San Diego psychiatrist, bristles when I suggest ECT is controversial.
"ECT is not controversial," says Dr. Bergsma. "That is a media mis-
representation. There is no disagreement over ECT among knowl-
edgeable psychiatrists." Despite Dr. Bergsma's certitude, a 1992 con-
sensus statement issued by his peers at the National Institute of Mental Health acknowledges "Electroconvulsive therapy [as] the most
controversial treatment in psychiatry."

Dr. Ari Albala, an Israel-trained administrator at Southwood Hospital
in Chula Vista, California, reassures me that "the [shock] treatment
done today is extremely clean, surgical, if you will, in terms of its pre-

cision. The main side effect, the memory problem, has become much less frequent in the last ten years. We have positioned the electrodes differently than we have before. We position them usually now in one side of the head. One hemisphere, in the so-called non-dominant hemisphere. We use a machine that generates a wave form that is different than the one used before. Now it is pulse instead of sine wave, so the energy delivered is much less. These changes have resulted in dramatic improvement."

Richard Danford, a patients' rights advocate who for years helped administer shock therapy as a psychiatric assistant, challenges Dr. Albala's assertion that ECT is now a kinder or gentler treatment. "I've seen it before. When you see psychiatry get in touch with its inability to prescribe effective [drug] treatments, then they revert back to ECT. They say it's different than it used to be. I have trouble with that. It doesn't look quite so bad, because the patient does not go into arm-flailing and back-spasming convulsions, but the treatment is absolutely identical. It's running current through someone's brain."

Modern, "modified" ECT is actually more dangerous for the patient's brain fears Leonard Frank, a writer who survived a chilling battery of insulin coma and shock treatments that permanently destroyed his memory. His book, *The History of Shock Treatment*, has become a standard reference for the anti-psychiatric community. "What the psychiatrists don't tell you," says Frank, "is that today they are forced to use more electricity, not less. Because of the muscle relaxant and single hemisphere shocks, more electricity is required for a longer length of time. It used to be the case that one-tenth of a second was adequate to produce the convulsion; now it takes one second or more." As proof of his argument, Frank points to an editorial by Dr. Harold Sackeim in the Winter 1991 issue of the professional journal *Convulsive Therapy* which argues for "the next generation of ECT devices [to] have significantly higher upper output limits, perhaps at least double what is available with the current [sic] generation." ECT foes claim that higher-wattage shock devices increase the potential for inflicting permanent brain damage.

Advertising in psychiatric journals conveys the sense that even modified ECT is not without its hazards. In *Convulsive Therapy* an advertisement for the Somatics Corporation's synthetic rubber "Mouth Guard" reveals cases in which "... a tooth was dislodged ... two upper incisors split in a longitudinal plane ... as the electric current was passed ... the patient's right upper incisor fractured horizontally and flew into the air." The advertisement also warns that loose teeth or fragments could be aspirated and that the "tongue and buccal surfaces can be severely bitten."

The number of shock patients has been estimated at between 50,000 to 100,000 annually. Although there is no national clearinghouse that collects statistics, figures supplied by San Diego County hospitals reveal that among those who receive shock treatment, nearly two-thirds are women over the age of 50. Dr. Bergsma reminds me that depression, for which ECT is said to be an effective treatment, more often plagues elderly women than men. Antidepressant drugs, shock therapy's competing treatment, are also notoriously hard on hearts. Dr. Peter Breggin, a dissident psychiatrist, called a "fanatic" by Dr. Bergsma, finds a more sinister motive in the shocking of elderly women. In his 1992 exposé *Toxic Psychiatry*, Dr. Breggin writes, "Frail, despairing, desperately needing emotional support, elderly women often have no one to defend them or to stand up for them, and they are unlikely to find the strength in themselves to defy their doctors."

Memory loss, a major ECT bugaboo, is portrayed by shock proponents to be only temporary. Dr. Bergsma informs me that out of the hundreds of patients that he's administered ECT, none had any memory loss more severe than a five month gap. "There is a loss of memory for perhaps a week or two after treatment, but then memories invariably return. Patients who undergo ECT are usually quite depressed, which reduces the quality and quantity of memory retention. ECT is 100% safe and effective, and studies show that over 90% of patients who undergo ECT show a marked improvement."

Counters patients rights advocate Richard Danford, "To say that 90% of [ECT] treatments are beneficial, my experiences do not reflect that at all. I would say at the top end, in which the patient was restored to a higher level of functioning, my experience was 50% at the top end. A number of patients were substantially impaired. No doubt about it.

"I'll give you an example. There was this successful advertising and marketing executive; we're talking six figure income. He was in his mid-30s, went through a divorce and was very depressed. They decided to do ECT. Even after the first couple of treatments, he showed a level of confusion that was absolutely incredible. And that was in done in the recovery room at a general care hospital under the modern modified ECT circumstances. After the treatments he was completely disoriented. I mean he couldn't remember anything, short term and long term. He had so little recall of anything it was almost impossible to work with him. It was a major task to get him to his room. He got so agitated he would wind up in seclusion in four-point leather restraints. He never came back. We took a clinically depressed person, and at the end of the experience the guy went to the state hospital."

As a medical intern at Bethesda Hospital in Denver, and at the now-defunct Clairemont Hospital in the late 1970s, Danford assisted in many Electroconvulsive treatments. "At Bethesda we were doing the shock therapy in a little room off the nurse's station. It would take two or three treatments to get the proper amount of muscle relaxant. If they gave the person too much muscle relaxant, you couldn't tell if they were having a seizure. They'd just be out. The other side, and this is where I came in, was when they didn't give a person enough muscle relaxant. They would literally fly off the table in a full-blown seizure. My role was to hold the person down.

"There was a special hold for it. You put your hand underneath their body in a certain way, and over across the top of the body in a certain way, usually right at the abdomen. It's a bizarre experience, literally holding on to this person as electricity would course through their brain.

"The way it's done today in most of the facilities is that electroshock takes place in a recovery room or an ICU [intensive care unit]. They usually have an anesthesiologist involved, at least to determine proper dosages [of muscle relaxant and anesthetic]. At Clairemont Hospital I had the responsibility not of holding people to the table but getting them ready for treatment. Telling them what was going to happen, what to expect, making sure they didn't have tight clothes on, necklaces or jewelry. They also had to remove all metal."

"Before my first day at Bethesda," Danford recalls, "I was very anxious about the procedure, about holding people down. My co-workers said, 'You've got to get big rubber boots, you have to wear gloves.' You need some levity, some release. I tried not to think too much about what I was participating in. Today, with what I know, I would not agree to participate in ECT."

Neurologists, who have less to lose than psychiatrists in pushing lucrative shock therapy, have their own theories on how shock treatment affects the brain.

Dr. Sidney Samant, a neurologist, noted in the March 1983 issue of *Clinical Psychiatry News,* "I have seen many patients after ECT, and I have no doubt that ECT produces effects identical to those of a head injury. After multiple sessions of ECT, a patient has symptoms identical to those of a retired, punch-drunk boxer ... After a few sessions of ECT the symptoms are those of moderate cerebral confusion, and further enthusiastic use of ECT may result in the patient functioning at a subhuman level. Electroconvulsive therapy in effect may be defined as a controlled type of brain damage produced by electrical means."

Unlike the media-wary ECT boosters of today, early users of shock quite openly acknowledged shock treatment as a way to permanently alter or damage a sick person's brain. H. L. Gordon's 1948 article, "Fifty Shock Therapy Theories," provides a number of guesses by ECT users on how shock does its job: "Because ... lobotomy improves the mentally ill by destruction, the improvement obtained by all the shock therapies must also involve some destructive processes"; "the resulting amnesia is healing"; "Threat of death mobilizes all the vital instincts and forces a reestablishment of contacts with reality"; "the treatment is considered by patients as punishment for sins and gives feelings of relief"; "the personality is brought down to a lower level and adjustment is obtained more easily in a primitive vegetative existence than in a highly developed personality. Imbecility replaces insanity."

Why are psychiatrists so insistent that imbecility or low-level functionality is preferable to insanity? Could this notion have authoritarian roots? The first researcher to introduce electroshock into the field of psychiatry was an Italian Fascist by the name of Ugo Cerletti. Possessed of the idea that schizophrenia never touches epileptics, Cerletti toured a slaughterhouse where he observed pigs convulsing after being shocked by an electric prod.

Anxious to test his hypothesis that such a paroxysm would cure madness, Cerletti contacted the Fascist police for a suitable human guinea pig. On April 15, 1938, the Police Commissioner turned over to the doctor a vagrant found on the streets of Rome mumbling to himself. If he died he would not be missed.

Cerletti strapped down the hapless bum and delivered an 80 volt shock to his head, which did not provoke the desired grand mal convulsions but a painful and frightening "missed seizure." Before Cer-

letti could apply a stouter jolt of electricity, the vagrant screamed, *"Non una seconda! Mortifiere!"* ("Not another! It's going to kill me!") Undeterred, Cerletti carried on with his experiment; this time the 110 volt discharge provoked the grand mal seizure without the death blow the doctor feared might occur.

Present at these historic applications of shock treatment was Lothar Kalinowsky, a Jewish doctor who earlier fled Nazi Germany to Fascist Italy, where he joined Cerletti's staff. Forced to leave Italy after an Axis pact was signed calling for the extradition of German Jewish nationals back to the Nazis, Kalinowski proselytized the treatment in France, Holland, England and finally in the United States. Recently deceased, Kalinowsky kept shocking patients at Gracie Square Hospital in New York City until he reached the ripe old age of 90.

In off-the-record comments, a psychiatrist whispered to me about a certain intolerance within his profession against dissent. Psychiatrists who have turned against the modus operandi of their professions, like Dr. Peter Breggin and Dr. Thomas Szasz, are derided by their peers as "nut-cases." One psychiatrist, again off-the-record, suggested that Breggin and Szasz were themselves deserving of shock treatment.

The several former shock patients I encountered believed, like Dick Cavett, that ECT had saved their lives. Through quiet and halting speech a 47-year-old San Diego resident we will call Carol credits ECT for her recovery from depression. "My husband calls it a miracle." Carol tells me that she isn't troubled by much memory loss, and that the shock treatment has given her a renewed interest in "being a good homemaker."

Licking his dry lips and crossing and uncrossing his legs frenetically in his modest Santee flat, 57-year-old Jim Albright tells the story of undergoing a nervous breakdown while laboring as an engineer at Eastman Kodak in Rochester, New York. When a company psychiatrist diagnosed him as schizophrenic, Albright was told to report to the hospital where he was subjected to a series of shock treatments.

"They were short-handed in the patent department," recalls Albright. "ECT was the fastest way to get me back."

Albright experienced ECT with a religious sense of awe.

> [ECT] was like Christ making the blind man see.
> I felt that my experience was like seeing some-
> thing for the first time and not having a history of
> perception. Being amazed and awed by the extra-
> ordinary vision of light filtering through a venet-
> ian blind. On to the white walls of the hospital. I
> saw the sun but didn't have a word for it. It was
> like God. Like a Sun God.

Since receiving his initial shock treatment in Rochester, Albright has
received only one other Electroconvulsive treatment, a modified uni-
polar shock. "It didn't do me much good," says Albright. "Only the
bipolar shocks seemed to be strong enough to reorder my synapses."
Albright is currently maintained on injections of Prolixin, though his
psychiatrist, Dr. Stanley Nadel, concerned that his patient was showing symptoms of Tardive Dyskinesia, a common unpleasant side-effect
of neuroleptic drugs, has tried to switch his patient to daily doses of
Lithium Carbonate. Despite the unpleasant muscular tics caused by
Prolixin, Albright has so far resisted the change.

Though he hasn't drawn a paycheck for nearly twenty years and lives
off of SSDI checks, Albright is active and (in the words of so many
psychiatrists) "marginally functional." He's very active in promoting
his New World Order cosmology, in which regional interests are bal
anced by the governing body of the United Nations. "It's the extinc-
tion of the bi-polar world," says Albright, curiously reflecting the language of shock therapy. He attends classes at Grossmont College, fires
off policy suggestions to political leaders, and is active in the field of
community outreach programs for the mentally ill. In 1985, Albright
importuned members of NAMI (The National Alliance for the Mentally Ill) to open a San Diego-based outreach program. The psychiatric referral service was named, after its conceptual founder, The
Albright Center.

Jim Albright shows me his camera, a transparent Instamatic in the late
1960's style, one that allows you to see its electronic guts. Jim
designed the clear camera when he was quality control engineer for
Kodak. "The camera is kind of like a fetish for me. I took it with me

everywhere I went because I had the delusion that the camera was like my heart, and that people can see inside of me — I linked my body with my camera."

His last major breakdown occurred after the doctor who injects him with Prolixin flew to Kuwait during the Gulf War. Shock survivor Leonard Frank suggests that Albright might not have been suffering from a so-called schizophrenic relapse, but a simple case of drug withdrawal. Albright acknowledges that that is a possibility, but is insistent that shock therapy is a miracle cure that must continue to be shared with the depressives and schizophrenics of the world.

White foam flecks the corners of Jim Albright's mouth. "ECT is a wonderful thing, a wonderful thing. It saved my life." If D.C. bureaucrats have anything to say about it, ECT may save your life, too.

Convulsion of Hystero-Epilepsy, circa 1872.

G. G. Goes to Heaven

[At the request of the Portland publication *PDXS,* I followed up a five-year-old article on G.G. Allin in *Apocalypse Culture* with a new interview to coincide with a Murder Junkies tour through town. It was to be his last.

Despite my insulting questions regarding prison rape and his inability to make good on his long-declared promise to kill himself, G.G. sounded chipper and treated me with respect. Several days later, he was to suffer the ignominious end he declared in *Apocalypse Culture* would never happen to him. Snorting four bags of New York white, he went out like a light, choked on his puke, and expired.

After years of bragging about the way by which he would achieve "rock and roll immortality," G.G. started to have second thoughts when fans reminded him to respect his words. I told G.G. that he could easily bring some of these morbid fanboy masochists along with him, should he decide it was time to make his mark.

As before, G.G. impressed me as a dyed-in-the-wool Romantic who believed in the redemptive value of rock's Dionysiac ritualism. G.G. became obsessed with ridding rock of its hypocrisy-inducing genuflection before Mammon. In these Irony-drenched times, such naivete seems comical. As demonstrated in the comedy documentary, *Hated,* G.G. Allin was nothing less than an Andy Kaufman-type stand-up act. G.G.'s self-mythologizing worked only through potential energy, the possibility of wreaking havoc. His end was poetic justice, a suburban kid's end. G.G. was simply too much of a fuck-up to achieve mythic stature.]

When did you get out of the pokey?

Got out on March 11th, this year [1993].

Was that for the beating of the girl? [Allin was handed a two-year sentence for beating and carving a groupie, whom, he claims, was a masochistic consensual partner.]

It was actually a parole violation. I did the two years for the [girl beating] incident. I got out on parole and got arrested on tour about seven or eight times and then they violated my parole for what I did on stage, and I ended up doing another year.

Are you currently on parole?

No, I maxed out. I'm done with Michigan.

Are you up on any other charges?

I think there's about eight or nine states where I have warrants but nobody will extradite unless I come into those states, so yeah, I'm not by any means completely clear, and with this upcoming tour I'm sure there'll be a few more states to add to the fucking list.

You have any fights in the yard?

The first day I got there. I was in quarantine and I was walking back in, and, what happens is, all the niggers gang up on whitey in prison, especially in quarantine. A guy hits me on the head as hard as he could from behind. He didn't realize it, but I break Jim Beam bottles over my head, six at a fucking time. So here it's like Peter Pan. I turn around and look at him and say, "Hit me again, and maybe I'll feel it this time." He never fucked with me again. I had to do two years, so it's like kill me now, or let's get on with it. After that they thought I was fucking crazy so they didn't fuck with me. I'd let you hit me in the face as hard as you want and I'd probably bleed, but I'd laugh. I like it. That shit don't bother me.

You got any problems in public now?

Nobody wants to fuck with me cuz of the way I smell, probably.

Now why do you want to keep a sorry ass old form like rock and roll alive?

I don't look at rock and roll the same way other people look at rock and roll. I look at it as a terrorist movement. When I grew up rock and roll was the only weapon that I had against people, and it was a great weapon to have. It's not like, "how do I look?" and "who do we hang out with?" and "how many scenesters are going to be there?" Now rock and roll is just bullshit. I want to bring nonconformity, the

G.G. GOES TO HEAVEN

KEVIN M. ALLIN - - - - 89-24090FH

amounts of pain, suffering and disfigurement. Throughout Monday evening and night Mr. Allin exhibited violence upon me in an espisdic fashion. Each episode seemed to entail a specific theme. Each time Mr. Allin would enter my room it would begin the same. I would struggle with him until he would physically dominate me. At which point he would put his hands around my neck and choke me into a semi-conscious state of exhaustion. Mr. Allin did not seem to want me to be unconscious. He would arouse me if you will by burning me with lit cigarettes. Once somewhat alert Mr. Allin would verbally indulge me with his intentions.

I remember Mr. Allin being atop me and he was shoving cigarettes into my mouth. He had one hand up around my throat and with it he would choke me. When I would gag he would put them into my mouth. I would spit them out at him and he would choke me more. He would hit me about my head.

Adventually I would pass out.

While atop me again Mr. Allin had his hand on my neck and in the other he had a large glass of liquid. In the glass there were a lot of mashed up cigarettes. He would choke me and when I would gag he would pour it down into my mouth. He kept saying I should drink it because I liked to smoke and drink so much. I clenched my teeth really tight even when he was choking me so he poured it all over my face.

I remember Mr. Allin being atop me and he was teasing me with a lit cigarette. He would put it close to my face and then pull it back. Saying, "Oh you really think I'm going to burn your precious face?" He tried to put a lit cigarette into my mouth. He had his knees on my upper arms so I couldn't get him off of me. I wouldn't open my mouth. He burned my right cheek twice with a lit cigarette.

I remember Mr. Allin being atop me again choking me. I was rather limp. He began cutting at me. He was cutting at my chest. He said it was beautiful. Like painting a picture. He wanted my breasts to bleed more. He googed at my left breast with I think a piece of broken glass. When it began to bleed more he said again how beautiful it was. That my breast looked like crying eyes.

I remember him cutting my right thigh. He was sort of digging at it. He was using this black metal dagger. He kept going over it.

The last time I remember Mr. Allin atop me he was choking me. I was done. No more fighting. I was very calm. I shut my eyes and at that point I was sure death was a good possibility. I remember Mr. Allin slapping at my head. He kept saying "Wake up, wake up you fucking bitch wake up". I just drifted off.

From the affidavit of the girl G.G. assaulted.

Now rock and roll is just bullshit. I want to bring nonconformity, the true rebellion.

What would you like to see done to MTV?

Murder all those fucking vee-jays. I think people should go into all the major record companies and drop bombs and fly over Lolla-palooza with bombs and machine guns. That would be great, the greatest thing of all, if you could build an army to do those things. Wipe out the fucking industry.

What about rap?

I don't see living in Beverly Hills and singing about the ghetto. If you're going to sing about something you should go out and do it.

Are you still doing a rock and roll show, as before?

It's not really a show. It's really kind of what I feel like doing at the time. I've got a band, if that's what you mean. I don't consider it to be entertainment. I would consider it to be feelings of revenge.

When are you finally going to kill yourself?

The biggest question that everyone keeps asking me is about the sui-cide thing. For me right now to say I'm going to commit suicide is just way too premature because there's too many battles and it seems like there's too many people who want me to do it now, so as long as I've got the battle and the fight, and as long as I got some enemies, I gotta keep going to fuck these people up. To end it now is what the government would want and what society would want, and as long as I can be that dagger in their back and as long as I can be the enemy of the people then I've got to stay alive.

People are saying you're not a man of your word.

People who say that don't know what I am. Those are the fucking people I'm fucking up. I'm seriously fucking them up. They have no idea of what I'm about. In 1989 I was like fucking death anyway. Any-body that has to say that is definitely an ignorant motherfucker and has no idea. All they wanted to see me do is commit suicide. That's not what I'm all about. I'm here to fight the system, and I'm here to fuck with the goddamn music industry, and I'm not done yet. In '89 I was dying every day. It was like, am I going to die on this rooftop? Am I gonna die on the streetcorner? Or am I gonna die on stage and take some motherfuckers with me? Now the prison has just opened more doors for my anger, so for me to commit suicide right now would be to play into their hands, so absolutely not. If people think that I just said that ... absolutely not. I would have carried out that, and I still plan on it. I may be killed on this tour or the next tour. When we go out on tour, it's not a question of when we come home, it's like, where are we going to end up in jail? What hospital will I be in? Will I even make it home? This really pisses me off when I hear people say [I'm not a man of my word] because I was absolutely ready to do it. I mean I had it all planned out, and if the club wasn't going to let me do it I was gonna do it on the street.

Who do you want to revenge on? Anyone in particular?

Everybody. The fucking government, the system and everybody, everybody that's walking around. I follow what I believe in and fuck everybody else. I'd just as soon see them dead.

How do you revenge a record industry by doing...

You have to be a powerful source. You have to gather a bunch of powerful allies. I mean I like to see people walk into the fucking Warner Brothers records with bombs, just blow the fucking place up. I'm very independent, I'm not going to sell out to any major label....

Did you get any offers from any major labels?

Naw, they're all afraid of me, are you kidding me? They're not going to fucking sign me. They want something they can market, they want something they can tell you, "This is dangerous, but we can keep it under control." They can't keep me under control. I've never gotten involved with music for money anyway, or for fame or for women or for fucking any of that, I'm not into that at all. That's not my purpose.

So you weren't anybody's punk in jail?

Fuck no.

What did you see go on in there?

All sorts of shit going on. I see people get their heads cracked open, people getting stabbed, people getting fucked, guys with tits and cunts.

Guys with tits and cunts?

Oh there were guys in there with tits and guys with sex change operations...

They put the sex changes in with the men?

They had like "sex unknown," but I guess they had to put 'em in with the men.

Did you get along with the guards?

I stayed away from all those people. I did my time my own way and was the stronger for it. I formed a group in their called PAC or Prisoners Against Conformity. We would meet on the yard. I was the leader of this group — we were all going to see the psychiatrists together. It was mandatory that I go to sex therapy and all this ...

What was sex therapy like?

Oh, you know, what you did was wrong, and this is not normal, and you have to admit, like, your remorse. The typical bullshit.

Anything like the Clockwork Orange *"Ludovico technique?"*

Oh absolutely. We had to see films.

What kind of films?

Films on human behavior, then we'd have to talk about our crimes, and I had to write a letter to the victim. All these questions and answers and all this shit. All this time when you go in there you tell them one thing but you don't believe anything you say. You don't let it penetrate.

What else were you up to?

I was doing a lot of writing, I was trying to form as many noncon-formist groups within the system that I could. I was helping this other guy in there; we were doing lawsuits against the state. Anything that I could keep myself busy with, to fight against the system. The more I fought the system, the stronger I became. I just would not let them ever get to me, ever, at all. It didn't matter what they did, I was gonna come out of this a much stronger person, which I think I have. I learned how to become a better criminal. I learned some good tricks from a lot of great people.

Give me an example.

I'm not going to give away any of my secrets. I've lived with mur-derers and rapists and child molesters and arsonists and bank robbers, and the whole lot, so I talked with these people, ate with them ...

You learned a trick from a child molester?

Well, I knew a lot of those tricks anyway. Absolutely. If I want to have sex with somebody young I'm going to continue.

You find it difficult getting booked for shows now?

It's always been difficult. People seem to think now that I'm just starting out or something. It was fucking hard for me to get gigs 15 years ago. It's harder now because it's more publicized. Fifteen years ago when I started out with the Jabbers, we were banned all over New England; we couldn't get shows in Boston. Our philosophy was go and fuck the club up and fuck the people up, and we didn't give a shit about getting paid.

You living in New York now?

I'm living in Chicago. My band's in New York. I'm pretty much back and forth.

You have any records out?

We just recorded a brand new album with Don Fury here in the city. I don't think it's going to see daylight until the fall. The movie *Hated* just came out. A documentary film.

What's that?

Todd Phillips shot it. It's a documentary film about the Murder Junkies and myself. It's going to be shown around the country in theaters. They're working on a package now with a couple other movies. They premiered it in New York and it got great reviews. *Screw* said *Cocksucker Blues* looked like *Bambi* compared to it.

What's in it?

It pretty much documents the year I was on parole, and it interviews bandmates. Gacy's in it, shit, a bunch of people. I've only seen it once, and I was really drunk when I saw it.

What's going on with you sexually?

I'm not looking for any relationship or anything. Just a girl to piss in a cup or shit in a bag for me and I can take it home and get off on that and I don't have to deal with her.

There's videotape floating around of you doing some queer stuff.

I'm into anything, basically. Anything that gets me off.

You get any new tattoos in the joint?

No. I got some more before I went back in. I got three on my head. I got like a snake on the front of my head, and on that side I got a rat sitting on my ear, and then on the other side I got a snake skull, and then I got a Murder Junkies logo I'm putting on the back of my head. I got so many scars anyway. My whole body is like a scar tattoo.

How's your teeth?

I've got a few on the bottom.

How do you eat meat?

I just gum everything. I don't wanna get teeth. When something falls out I'll keep going on with what I got. I don't want to get any artificial shit. It's like scars. I never get any stitches cuz I like the way scars look. If I get new teeth I'm going to get them knocked out so what's the sense in it?

How did you grow up? Middle class?

I grew up in a cabin with no running water. No heat, no electricity. In the mountains of New Hampshire and shit.

That's your brother there in New York?

Merle's a Murder Junkie, he hasn't been with me the whole time.

You have anything to say to the world?

I don't have anything to say except that I'm doing things my way. Rock and roll in general, there's nothing left to it, it's all fucking entertainment now. You got the frauds and phonies and a bunch of bullshit people trying to make it on labels and the so-called alternative scene, these Lollapalooza corporate-sponsored events. It's all fucking bullshit. And I think when people come to see us they're probably going to see the only real underground thing that's happening right now, because it's not really a show and it's not something you're going to see be the same night after night. One night you might see 15 people get carried out of the club on stretchers and the next night maybe we won't even show up or maybe we will. It's just kind of an extension of life offstage. I don't give a fuck. I don't care if we suck. We're not interested in what other people think.

G.G.'s wake, surrounded by his life's artifacts.
(Photo courtesy Nick Bougas.)

Form out of chaos photographed by
James Shelby Downard of snow on his television set.
(Photo courtesy James Shelby Downard.)

RIDING THE DOWNARDIAN NIGHTMARE

> Never allow anyone the luxury of assuming that
> because the dead and deadening scenery of the
> American city-of-dreadful-night is so utterly
> devoid of mystery, so thoroughly flat-footed, ster-
> ile and infantile, so burdened with the illusory
> gloss of "baseball-hot dogs-apple pie-and-Chevro-
> let" that it is somehow outside the psycho-sexual
> domain. The eternal pagan psychodrama is esca-
> lated under these "modern" conditions precisely
> because sorcery is not what twentieth century
> man can accept as real. — James Shelby Downard,
> "King-Kill 33°."

While the sleepwalking millions glut themselves with the daily brainwash, becoming all the more glutted and dazed, James Shelby Downard lives by his wits to elude the Masonic hit squads that would like nothing better than hang him like a contemporary Captain Morgan, for "revealing the [Masonic] method" which he believes underlies all reality. He rubber-stamps his correspondence with a quote from Bierce: "My Country 'Tis of Thee / Sweet Land of Felony."

Among the believers, James Shelby Downard is an almost mythic fig-ure. In homage to a Downard essay, an Atlanta punk rock band calls itself "King-Kill 33°." Feral House receives letters from filmmakers and just plain folks on a daily basis begging for Downard's address. Downard was prone to spend most of his time driving across the country in his Airstream trailer, exploring geomantic magic, but for several years now, Downard has settled down in his sister's home in Memphis, Tennessee. He says he's too old to get around — his eye-sight is bad enough to make typing a real strain. But you can't keep the man down. He recently convinced his niece to drive him to

Kansas City to explore underground caves. Upon their arrival, the spelunking society told Downard and niece that there was no such thing as a cave under Kansas City. He makes friends with a helpful librarian who spent many hours leafing through maps, consulting with city employees and other bureaucrats. The librarian discovered that, indeed, huge caves *do* exist below the city.

Memphis, home of Graceland, occult temple, reflecting the King's quest for eternal life. The Memphis Convention Center is a huge glass pyramid, where developer Isaac Tigrett hangs photographs of Hindu Godman Sai Baba and is said to have found a Mayan crystal skull. Memphis is a power vortex of the New World Order ... and it makes perfect sense for James Shelby Downard to reside there.

It's summer, '94, the first time I've ever visited Shelby Downard. His sister's home is an upper-middle-class, brick, two-story affair located near a man-made lake in an exclusive part of town. Shelby's sister, an elderly, D.A.R.-type woman, greets me at the front door with Southern hospitality, invites me into the living room for a whiskey sour. Downard, an octogenarian full of tics, wattles, and liver spots, comes down from his upstairs office, eyes dancing with excitement. Sis hands me the whiskey, and Downard takes me aside, whispers in my ear: "She thinks she's my sister, you know, but she's not. She was adopted."

Around Shelby Downard, things are never what they seem. I had expected his library to be filled by thousands of obscure books. Instead there's an old set of World Books, a dictionary, an abused set of *Man, Myth and Magic,* and a couple dozen tomes that could probably be found in any large used bookstore. Downard does not rely on secondary materials for his research, but instead upon topological and city maps to focus his personal visits to weird and significant sites. All he needs is a dictionary and a batlike intuition for navigating the dark to amass the kind of data which amazes his coterie of admirers. In the middle of an oak desk lay a 1940s-issue Royal typewriter on which he types his drafts. Thick magnifying lenses perch upon his nose.

The unimpressive nature of his library makes his research all the more amazing. Or so I tell him. He's abashed by praise.

Not used to hosting company, Downard seems for the moment at a loss for things to do, so I ask him whether he's seen a new pair of stamps, a commemorative celebrating deaf sign-language. "Either it's my imagination," I tell Shelby, "or the U.S. has issued a couple stamps celebrating the devil's horns."

"Is that right?" says Downard a little dubiously. I flash him the symbol, and suddenly he's excited. "Cuckold, the sign of the horns! You sure now? This I've got to see"

We enter a standard issue East German-style post office. Cataleptic clerks work in slow motion, foggy-eyed hominids stand in line and gape beyond a cracked, polarized shade duct taped to a thick greenish glass. Even the young ones seem dull and soulless. By contrast, an excited and chatty Downard seems the epitome of life.

A growling clerk barks us ahead to his window, and Downard requests the "devil stamps." "Don't know what you mean," says the clerk. "The hell you don't," says Downard. "He means the deaf stamps," I intervene. The clerk tears out ten pairs for our inspection. Downard lets out a war whoop, a gutbucket howl of gleeful recognition I've never heard anywhere, much less from a post office, much less from an 85-year-old man examining stamps in a post office.

"You're right, you're right, by golly! The sign of the horns, the cuckold, the devil," he shouts triumphantly. "And it's printed there that it means 'I love you.' I love you! I *love* you! That's the way *they* love you alright." And he laughs again, and stamps and snorts.

Later we stop for lunch, read the afternoon newspaper which prints a wire story about the National Reconnaissance Office (NRO), an intelligence agency that remained a secret until 1992. Apparently a few members of Congress were upset that no one would tell them why and for whom a half-billion dollar, million square-foot "Taj Mahal" was being constructed near Dulles Airport. NRO was forced to publicly admit that their huge complex, nearly half the size of the Pentagon itself, will store and analyze information gleaned from satellites and phone wiretaps. Information about whom? The Cold War is over. And the U.S. government expresses most of its worry about domestic critics.

Spy satellites are today capable of photographing objects as small as an inch in dimension, even through cloud cover. The satellites can even listen to a conversation conducted in somebody's home. So says the Associated Press. Tracking individuals implanted with a homing device is the latest wrinkle. Servicemen were injected with such experimental devices during the Persian Gulf War without their knowledge. New transponder devices have been constructed with two-way mechanisms, not only able to receive information, but transmit whatever information the secret agencies wish the implant to hear, says Colonel John Alexander.

This two-way transponder and satellite is the cutting edge of Air Force / NRO mind control technology, developed at places like Buffalo's CalSpan laboratory, the complex where Timothy McVeigh spent six months as a security guard before quitting after complaining of being implanted with a "mind control device."

Welcome to dead and deadening scenery of spookland. With $35 billion spent yearly on intelligence agencies, the dissemination of misinformation, the secret murder of enemies or friends who know too much, shall we curtly dismiss James Shelby Downard as a kook?

When an individual brings up the possibility of a government plot on the net, dozens attack him as a "paranoid" and a "kook." The same thing happened when people in Argentina spoke up about the disappeared. The scaredy cats screamed. "Paranoid!" "Kook!" Fearing their own disappearance, they became the government by turning in the "kook" who spoke the truth.

An admission — like everyone else, I first became interested in the writings of James Shelby Downard simply because he seemed so delightfully insane. On closer inspection I noticed that his "madness" had its own undeniable logic.

In Downard's writings, the products of his subconscious bubble to the surface and catalyze painstaking research. The collision of the poetic against the logical works especially well in the field of conspiracy; it remains the freshest approach to a field of inquiry where ego, logic, faith and fealty fight for possession of the "Ultimate Truth." How can a researcher produce a smoking gun when the gun has long ago been smelted into metal ingots? Cops facing a logical dead-end are known to hire psychics to solve crimes.

Michael A. Hoffman II assisted me in bringing "King/Kill 33°" to print. It's remarkable that JFK's assassination, by 1987 a thoroughly tired and over-examined subject, could receive such an astonishingly fresh treatment. Who but Downard would think of examining the symbolism behind Jack Ruby (neé Jacob Rubenstein). To paraphrase Downard: the gem business calls a fake ruby passing itself off as the real thing a "jack ruby." A ruby is a blood-red gemstone, and is sometimes referred to as a bloodstone. Since the facts behind JFK's assassination must be concealed from the public, it makes sense that the man whose job is to silence the patsy by spilling his blood would change his name to "Jack Ruby."

With his emphasis on government crime, why does Downard pick on the Masons? Aren't they merely a clownish fraternity of small businessmen? Downard says he isn't interested in tenderfoot recruits, or the window dressing of Masonic philanthropy. He's interested, as others should be, by the inner elite.

For many years Downard moved about in his Airstream trailer to avoid becoming a Masonic "Pharmakos," or scapegoat. To this day he keeps a loaded .45 Colt by his bedside. He takes his claims about Masonry seriously.

Scottish Rite Freemasonry, the most popular American Masonic organization, has 33 degrees in its hierarchy. A Mason revealed to me that the top two degrees are known as the "Illuminati." Aleister Crowley's sex-magical OTO organization reputedly swiped its own rituals from the top Masonic initiations. It's no longer such a well-observed secret that the highest degrees of freemasonry involve sex magic.

Masonry enjoins the oath-taker that death will greet those who spill secrets. The costumes of the Knights Templar and other elite Masonic factions are littered with skulls and bones and knives. Talk about mysteries: Death, the greatest one of all.

Downard hands me a file of old newspaper clippings. Photographs of presidents and cabinet members decked out in ritual wardrobe. So what? Isn't Masonry as American as apple pie? Didn't Masonry pull

Upper Left: Shelby
Downard rendered by
Anton Mueller.

Upper Right: Downard
today. (Photo by Adam
Parfrey.)

Right: Photo of
Adam Parfrey for *Nose*
magazine by
Anne Greenwood.
Evidence of Parfrey's
unwitting compliance
with the cryptocracy,
says Downard.

off the American Revolution? Didn't G-Man J. Edgar Hoover boast of being a 33° Mason? What about the Skull and Bones society, which counted CIA head and Commander in Chief George Bush as one of its members? Didn't George Bush leave the press room when members of the White House Press Corps question him about his membership in the secret society? Isn't there a secret restaurant in Disneyland called the "33 Room?"

The All-Seeing-Eye (adopted as a symbol of Sarnoff's CBS network as well as for the Pinkerton security corporation) finds its rightful place in the Masonic pyramid on the back of every dollar of U.S. currency. Study the symbol closely. It isn't the All-Smelling-Nose for a reason. The eye represents the monitoring and control of society; the pyramid represents the building of monuments to honor the Pharoahnic elite.

European historians understand the influence of Masonry upon politics and international banking. They can read morning papers about the Masonic P2 (Propaganda Due) group, which infiltrated the highest arena of Catholic power and assumed control of the Vatican bank before hanging Roberto Calvi under a bridge and murdering John Paul I only a month after taking office because he expressed an interest in "cleaning house."

Tim O'Neill, a former Rosicrucian, traced the origin of Masonry from the Assassins. Parallels with Hasan-I-Sabah's cult are noteworthy: try terrorism, cryptography, drug-running, slave-trading and ritual murder for political purposes.

"Scottish Rite" was invented by Confederate General Albert Pike, and codified in his manual *Morals and Dogma*. The burly-bearded Pike helped put together another Masonic structure: the Ku Klux Klan, an organization Downard claim burned down his family home when he was a mere four years old.

A General invented American Masonry; no wonder it's popular among career militarists. Why was a Pentagonal shape chosen to house the military? Satanic protection? Roosevelt, Eisenhower, Johnson and Harry Truman all shared an interest in Masonry, but it was Truman's atomic bomb that fulfilled the Masonic ritual of splitting the monad. John Kennedy, whose allegiance to the Catholic church overshadowed his allegiance to Masonry, was, according to Downard, sacrificed in the pagan ritual of the Killing of the King to usher in the New Secular Order.

As far as the American public is concerned, Masonry remains something of a joke. The *Illuminatus Trilogy,* pulp written by Robert Shea and Robert Anton Wilson, may have copped more than several ideas from Downard. Shea and Wilson's pulp novels interweave astonishing but commonplace coincidence, puckishly propagandizing the Downardian religion of intentional coincidence. Wilson mentioned in *Cosmic Trigger* that Downard's JFK thesis is "the most absurd, the most incredible, the most ridiculous Illuminati theory of them all."

The skeptic, with his dust-dry religion of logic, will dismiss Downard's revelations as cherry-picking from the garden of fact in order to confirm his preconceptions. Similarly, a New Ager views the quatrains of Nostradamus as an accurate register of modern times, while a Dispensationalist will transform the morning headlines into proof of Revelation's prophecies.

The skeptic will likewise argue that once a scientist buys into a thesis, his data usually proves that theory. This sympathetic transformation of data occurs even in the physical sciences. If the scientist is not merely fudging data, this principle supports a magical conception of reality. If a mind believes it so, then reality follows. Perhaps this is the real lesson of Aladdin's Lamp. You had better be clear about what you want. You just might get it.

Downard's life story, confided to me in person, on the phone, and through several autobiographical epics published at Kinko's, combines elements from Sir Richard Burton, James Bond and the *Terminal Man*. Only a few of his later stories have been corroborated to me by a couple Downard cronies; none of his peers from the early days are alive to verify stories from before the Great Depression.

So much of Downard's autobiography is reminiscent of abduction stories, tales of generational satanic groups that eat babies, and those who believe the government tampers with their mind and body. All three of the above have forwarded their manuscripts to me. Out of curiosity I've talked at length with a number of these desperate souls. Every one of them is convinced of the truth of their witnessing: they've seen things with their "own eyes." No obvious financial or social incentive guided their claims; to the contrary, they all suffered ridicule and loss of income. They do not write for financial remuneration; many of these people urged me to publish their book for free. Their motive was pursuit of relief. They felt that if they were able to tell their stories, the evil entities would lay off.

Young Shelby Downard walked into a crypt and was nearly decapitated, but discovered several hundred impossibly high denomination gold certificates. His alarmed father rings up the Treasury Department. Downard and dad are invited straightaway to J. Edgar Hoover's office, who deputized young Downard in exchange for the gold certificates. From then on, Downard's life becomes a never-ending succession of narrow escapes from Masonic hitmen.

In between sharp-shooting episodes with the feds, Downard falls for a breathtakingly beautiful woman he calls the "Great Whore." The Great Whore is documented in a scrapbook of photos still owned by Downard. Captured in a ten-year succession of photos in the 1930s to the war years, the woman is definitely built for comfort and lives up to her advance billing.

The photographs make clear that Downard once owned the allegiance of this girl, and later lost her. The intensity of that loss informs his world-view. In a moody voice, Downard discusses his intimate relations with the Great Whore, telling about her drugging him with "abulic" and "amnesiac" drugs while she ran off to perform "sex rites" with famous and infamous men. "I don't blame her for for her nymphomania," says Shelby. "They had her wired up. One day I found [a wire] sticking out of her ass. I pulled it out. It's a long, thin wire, and connected to the end of it is some microelectronic contraption. This was to get her in a constant state of sexual excitation. They implanted me, too."

"Shah-raid," he says, emphasizing the first syllable in definitive Memphis inflection "Their entire program is an ah-cult shah-raid."

Once Downard sent me photographs, reproduced "Separated at Birth"-style, of a teenage Anton LaVey and an acquaintance of Downard's from Key West he called the "huckster witch." In both photos, LaVey and "huckster witch" sneer at the camera in zoot suits with scars slashing across their cheeks. The pose is identical. Downard asks me to question LaVey about said "huckster witch." Looking Downard's package over, LaVey seems perplexed by the similarity of the photographs, and he reveals the coincidental fact that a member of the Church of Satan had given him a "huckster witch" sculpture that occupied his "ritual chamber" for over 25 years. About this coincidence, Downard chuckles, "Don't you see? They were part of the sex and death ritualism. Both were implanted in the pudendum. About that I have no doubt."

Several weeks after meeting Downard, I dreamt portentously, reflecting a peculiar Downardian perspective. I spoke to Downard about the dream, from which he concluded that I was undoubtedly a mind control subject. I told him of a photo shoot for the defunct *Nose* magazine, for which I wore a Knights of Pythias uniform purchased in a Seattle thrift store. After I mailed him proofs of the shoot, he took special notice of the apron which covered my crotch. "Look at the apron you're wearing. Oh, boy, oh boy, that's all I can say. Sex and death, that's what they're all about. Sex and death."

∞ ∞ ∞

Ever get the feeling your life is mapped out in advance? I often do. Downard tried to convince me that this feeling reflected a sinister recognition of mind control. I prefer Jung's idea of this sensation: that your brain is marshalling higher forces to work for you. That it is a kind of power. It seemed to me that rebelling against my "path" would lead to disaster. I sincerely hope that, concerning this point, Downard is monumentally wrong.

Downard has influenced me to look with interest upon the details and the fantastic convergences of life; I once again take stock in the magic aspects of life. It does not matter that much to me if his autobiography seems more and more like Walter Mitty.

The underlying assumptions of Downardian theology can be summed up as follows:

- THEY are a demonic "other" that delights in controlling your destiny.

- There is no such thing as coincidence.

- Accidents are purposeful.

- Nothing happens by chance.

- Order created out of the formless void is a fetish of sorcery; the object of sorcerous "Chaos Theory" is to devalue the creator and revalue man as the ultimate creator.

- THEY have infiltrated the system for so long that every word, intonation, tone, meter, rhythm, melody, numeric measure has its subterranean meaning and symbolism. Correspondingly, every operatic confluence of symbols, whether in a parade, play, movie, sporting event, political convention, anything televised, radio-waved or printed, commands a complex array of perverse forces of sex and death to concentrate power to the masters and weakness to the slaves.

- The three-tiered plank of the New Age has nearly been attained. The moon shot, symbolic of the marriage of the earth and moon, was preceded by the killing of the king ritual. The last project remains the resurrection of Solomon's Temple in Jerusalem. For Solomon's Temple to rise, the Dome of the Rock, an Islamic sacred site, must fall, likely resulting in a world war.

While putting together this essay, I discovered a forgotten file in my computer — a dream I had written down shortly after visiting Downard.

The Downardian Nightmare

A hypoglycemic episode wakes me from a dream, at once disturbing realistic and disturbingly surreal. Going downstairs to pee, I decide to input the dream into my computer.

I wander through a city devoid of people. It's like the aftermath of a neutron bomb, without the evidence of dead bodies. I find an odd emporium containing record bins. I comb through the bins and discover a soundtrack with a picture of my father on the cover.

Walking out the store, I see a face emerging in the clouds, looking a lot like a kitsch Jesus.

Evidently, a killer is on the loose. How do I know? It's a dream, damn it, I know. The first humans I see are two cops. They're after this killer, or so it seems. I hear a homing signal. To my horror I find that it's coming from me. Perhaps it's some sort of signal to the killer. Frantic with fear, I run the deserted streets.

I find temporary safe haven in a recording studio. The place is familiar, as if I'm an employee. Engineers and a producer are present. I'm supposed to record a jingle of some kind. I rebel at the concept, which seems incredibly repellent. Nevertheless, I acquiesce, slave-like. After I complete the jingle I'm rewarded with a sweet drink that I know controls me, but I swallow it nonetheless.

Speaking to me through omnisciently over the sound system, the producer insists I record an additional jingle. I want out. The omniscient voice over the intercom insists that I comply, threatening me with murder.

At this moment I wake.

PROJECT MONARCH
HOW THE U.S. CREATES SLAVES OF SATAN

by Fritz Springmeier

[Project Monarch is an example of conspiracy theory *en extremis.* The article below, written by a Portland-based Christian, is the best summation of the conspiracy I have found. Monarch is discussed quite thoroughly in *Contact,* the magazine communicated through Hatonn, a Pleiadean entity who speaks through Doris Ecker regarding the terrible secrets held by our terrestrial leaders. The major proponents of the Monarch theory are Mark Phillips, an apparent "deprogrammer," and Cathy O'Brien, a self-styled former sex slave at the White House. I felt the urge to inform Mr. Phillips that the welcoming bushes at Michael Jackson's ranch in Santa Barbara are flanked by Monarch butterflies. Phillips and O'Brien offer hundreds of pages of reputed evidence taken from hypnotic sessions with Cathy O'Brien; they go into very specific detail, naming names of major Congressional leaders and their propensity to mutilate the sexual organs of their slaves, their sexual and drug appetites, and their use of slaves as barter or political gifts. It's also claimed that the entire Country-Western business is a power node of Monarch slavery. Whether Monarch is complete disinformation to discredit legitimate research, or simply a money scam, or true but exaggerated to create a curtain of public discredit, it is undoubtedly the strangest conspiracy tale going.]

One of the best kept secrets in history is the Monarch mind control programming which uses trauma-based mind control along with state of the art mind control to create humans who are totally controlled by a handler without even knowing that they are controlled. This is accomplished by sophisticated use of the brain's ability to disassociate, which is used to the extreme to create structured multiple personality-disordered minds.

241

For an extremely technical definition of what the Monarch program was, it was used as U.S. Department of Defense code name for a subsection of the CIA's Operation Artichoke which is also known as Project MK-Ultra. However, this technical definition is misleading because the Monarch Programming has been going on since the Nazis called it "Marionette Programming."

HOW IT WORKS

The Monarch Program is the sophisticated manipulation of a child's mind, which tries to protect itself from extreme trauma by engaging Multiple Personality Disorder. Severe, inhumane torture is used on children to create extensive MPD. Then the various alters (personalities) are discovered and programmed using state-of-the-art mind control. Harmonics and sound waves manipulate the RNA covering of neuron pathways to the subconscious. Harmonic generators codenamed "ether-wave" are able to imbed detailed commands linked to audio triggers. This is a standard feature of the Monarch program. It controls the slaves by trigger words which seemingly make no sense or transmit alarming connotation to outside listeners. For instance, the phrase, "Mr. Postman wait and see," may well set off an access sequence so that a slave is signaled to go to his *master* (also called a *handler*).

Some slaves are turned into *sleepers*. Seemingly normal, sleepers have been known to carry assignments to be carried out decades down the road, or when signaled by a pre-arranged trigger. Some of the Illuminati hierarchy have been turned into sleepers so that they can be available when the Anti-Christ begins ruling over a large influx of new converts to the Illuminati and satanism.

Electric shock is yet another basic component of Monarch. Stun guns and staffs with hidden electric prods are frequently used on the slaves in order to help create MPD. Shock is employed to erase memories once the slave has carried out a mission; it's also used to instill obedience in reluctant slaves through the negative reinforcement of fear. Slaves generally carry horrible body memories of electroshock tortures applied to various regions of their body. The deprogramming process will generally recover these horrible memories of electroshock training, among many other associated traumas.

Dangers Involved

Every Monarch slave is programmed with thousands of internal safeguards to prevent slaves from fleeing or freeing themselves of their programming. IF YOU DISCOVER A MONARCH SLAVE — BE CAREFUL NOT TO TELL THEM WHAT YOU KNOW OR YOU MAY CAUSE THEM TO COMMIT SUICIDE. If any of the readers of this article find a Monarch slave, I suggest they call and talk to me about any steps they plan to take. Suicide programs are rampant within a Monarch slave. Do not mistakingly think you can tamper with the programming. Do not think that you can merely tell the slave that you want to free the person, and expect that they will automatically want your help. Working with Monarch slaves (also called Marionette survivors) is as touchy as handling a live bomb. It calls for extreme dedication and patience.

OUR WORK TO EXPOSE MONARCH PROGRAMMING

In the summer of 1991, I decided to pass out a chapter I had written for a book on mind control. This particular chapter concerned the Monarch project. I have mailed out this chapter free of charge to hundreds of people. Subscribers received the chapter in their newsletter.

Soon after I wrote this chapter on Monarch, a man named Mark Phillips started providing me additional information on the sinister program. Mark's information dovetailed with my own findings, and gave me greater perspective on the subject. Mark Phillips has deprogramed Monarch mind-controlled slaves. One such slave is Cathy O'Brien, who has written over 76 papers on her history as a presidential model slave. Mark is currently deprogramming at least six Monarch slaves. As for myself, I find myself working with a similar number of Monarch slaves as more of a friend than deprogrammer. Above all, I try to be supportive of these people. I'm currently writing a book-length exposé of the Monarch Project. Contact me for details.

HISTORY OF MONARCH PROGRAMMING

Trauma-based mind control should be considered an outgrowth of Mystery Religions practiced in deep secrecy. Satanism has been alive and well for centuries through the auspices of generational satanists, but they remain unexposed behind a variety of fronts. Many of the European kings were satanists who had MPD. The royal families of Denmark, the Netherlands, Spain and England are all involved with the occult and satanism. The Romanov family, which had branches in Prussia and Russia, was also deeply into the occult. An examination of Romanov jewelry reveals an occult bent, though the autocrats outwardly presented a Christian front. Unless a satanist develops Multiple Personality Disorder the possibility exists that they will go insane due to the terrifying events that accompany high-level satanists. In other words, only satanists with MPD have the capacity to handle the horror. It goes without saying then that people in the higher levels of the Illuminati have MPD, but that does not mean they are highly structured MPDs such as the Monarch slaves.

Monarch slaves are the equivalent of human computers or human robots; they are in a sense zombies with the ability to hide behind a front that seems so reasonable they look and act like a normal individual. Monarch refers to the variety of butterfly. Children who are traumatized have their legs tied and are electroshocked and tortured until the alters (personalities) believe they are butterflies. This MPD personality is the basis for the designation Monarch as referring to trauma-based mind control.

Nazis refined the creation of multiple personality slaves. Following the Second World War, Nazi and Italian scientists were drafted into U.S. intelligence, particularly specialists in MPD or Marionette programming. The idea was to create perfect human puppets. The combined research of German, Italian, British and American scientists further refined Monarch programming until mind-controlled slaves became nearly impossible to detect

Since the 1940s, over one million Americans underwent Monarch programming, although only 40,000 are surveilled by the intelligence agencies in cahoots with the Illuminati. Extremely detailed records are kept on the 40,000 slaves; they presently exist on a computer database.

Access to the Monarch database is limited to the elite. Reprogramming centers found around the country ensure the continued brainwash of every slave. The possibility of a mind-controlled slave eluding their masters is exceptionally small. The programming has near-total dominance over the slave, and is consequently difficult to counteract.

MEETING PLACES

Not all Monarch slaves live with their masters. Those who live and work apart from their masters are accessed through the use of cryptic keys. For example, the entire country-western music industry is a major access point for Monarch slaves, and also serves as a hotbed of drug-running activities. Many country tunes are utilized as programming triggers. Karaoke is yet another method to access slaves for reprogramming and assignments. Monarch slaves become acquainted with one another through Karaoke mind control. Even a cursory glance at the Pioneer Karaoke version of the song "White Rabbit" reveals triggering mechanisms for Monarch Slaves with Alice In Wonderland programming. Both Alice in Wonderland and The Wizard of Oz remain popular mind control programs, and are still in use today. Children's films created by Walt Disney productions are being deliberately constructed with Monarch triggers and keys.

Churches and fraternal orders are likewise utilized by the Illuminati for accessing Monarch slaves. The configuration of lights in churches sometimes reinforce Monarch programming. Leaders of cover churches utter buzz words and employ hand signals to interact with slaves ordered to attend these churches.

In the Portland area, a young man named Rex accesses Monarch slaves and herds them into one of the five local reprogramming centers. I have already discovered the location of a number of these centers. One local programmer, named Ed, uses his day job as a meat salesman as cover for his involvement in Monarch.

Rex Church, Monarch Slave-Herder?

(Photo by Ted Soqui.)

WHITHER THE SLAVES?

The Monarch Slave's primary duty is to perpetuate the secrecy surrounding the Illuminati's satanic activities. Due to his or her programming, the Monarch slave lacks even the instinct of self-preservation or human empathy. They are thus ideal candidates to carry out such things as snuff films and other inhuman acts.

Slaves are also common in the entertainment industry since they are devoid of moral compunctions. Professional and collegiate sports are common haunting grounds for Monarch slaves. Their usefulness in military missions should not be underestimated. Slaves remain indispensible to the CIA, which uses Monarch subjects for spying, drug running, money laundering, prostitution, pornography and acting. Slaves make ideal "gun nuts" like Francisco Duran, whose white house target practice ensured public hysteria and reactionary anti-gun legislation. Bo Gritz is one of several Monarch slaves who are currently infiltrating the opposition to the New World Order.

Younger slaves I'm seeing have been programmed to believe that they are communicating with aliens in their heads. This programming is part of a vast scheme to inculcate almost religious belief in aliens that will culminate in a mock alien invasion, whose real purpose is to create a ruthless One-World Government.

COVER-UP

Atrocities carried out by Monarch slaves are covered up by a CIA project known as "Operation Armageddon." This cover-up operation is designed to convince people that Monarch slaves are demonically possessed, victims of dark, apocalyptic forces. Satan is indeed putting in long hours during the end times, though it is misleading to believe that new demonic forces have flown in through the ether. It is more accurate to say that evil has strengthened itself through its consolidation.

It is not surprising that the CIA targets psychologists who are trying to deprogram Monarch victims. So far, psychologists have lost an overwhelming majority of Monarch victims who seek their help. To date, only a handful of individuals have been successfully freed from

Monarch programming. A difficult task becomes nearly impossible when the Illuminati and intelligence agencies choose to interfere.

The secrecy that covers Monarch programming is extraordinarily smooth and professional. Suspicion of such programming is rarely aroused, even by mental health professionals.

MARIONETTES VS. BUTTERFLIES

Marionette programming differs from Monarch programming in several important ways. You can trigger a Marionette at any time. Even radio and television programs can do the trick. It's all a matter of hearing the proper cue phrase.

It's more difficult to trigger something as drastic as suicide. A three channel trigger is required for suicide.

The trick behind deprogramming is talking to the programmers as well as the victims. Codes, keys and triggers are the three vital aspects of Monarch, and must be learned to combat its programming.

Om, Shalom
Roads End

Reprinted from *A Newsletter from a Christian Ministry,* Dec., 1993
5316 S.E. Lincoln
Portland, OR 97215

THE BIBLE

HANDBOOK FOR
SURVIVALISTS, RACISTS,
TAX PROTESTORS,
MILITANTS AND
RIGHT-WING EXTREMISTS

By Pastor Pete Peters

Bo Gritz interviewed in his Sandy Valley, Nevada home.
(Photo by Scott Lindgren.)

GUNS, GOLD, GROCERIES
GUTS 'N' GRITZ

O n this dark, chill evening, a mere fortnight before a Trilateralist named Clinton got the nod, a peculiarly modern type of patriot has come to hear their Presidential candidate, Lt. Col. James "Bo" Gritz (rhymes with "rights"), lay out war-room strategies to combat the elite string-pullers who, we are told, are planning to insert a subcutaneous microchip into the right hand of every man, woman and child — the literal Mark of the Beast.

A large screen television is wheeled on the church stage: we are to commune with the videotaped image of the retired Lieutenant Colonel, in business suit this time, positioned in front of Old Glory, playing the crowd in the practiced give-and-take of a Baptist preacher.

"Things are serious today. All the things that our founders warned us about, guaranteed our rights. Do the rights come from the Constitution?"

"NO!" yells the throng on videotape.

Gritz continues. "No. They're inalienable rights. They come from where?"

"GOD!"

"From God. What is the Constitution?" Gritz holds aloft a copy of the "divinely-inspired document." "You see, here it is in one page. My heavens, remember? We used to have ten rules to live under, didn't we? There was a person 2,000 years ago that set an excellent example. He went into the Temples and he overturned the moneychangers' tables. That's precisely what we need to do today. We need to turn the tables of the moneychangers over!"

"As President of the United States, I am going to have on the very first day in office, a pot metal coin, and it is going to be struck, and it will say four trillion dollars, and it will say, 'Debt of the United States Paid in Full,' and it will also say, 'In God We Trust!'"

The faithful clap, shake their heads. If only, if only...

"People say, 'Well, Bo, what about the chaos you would cause? I mean the Emir of Kuwait owns eight billion dollars of this debt.' You know where the Emir of Kuwait can go to collect? Let him go to the Federal Reserve where he borrowed it from. I'm sure they'd be more than happy to carve him out a little piece of their coin."

Squalid Viet vets and scrawny Gritz grannies rise to their feet, cheering and hooting and stamping. Deliverance has come!

∞ ∞ ∞

At the age of 53, Bo Gritz is a powerfully-built man with bulging, Popeye-like forearms. Though he could take you out with one karate blow, Bo's heart-on-a-sleeve sentimentality remains disarming. A kind of military Tom Bodett, Gritz uses his folksy drawl to charming effect. It is said that the Rambo movies were inspired by Gritz's Vietnam and POW-rescue exploits. His daredevil rescue of a U-2's black box deep behind enemy lines was written up in General William Westmoreland's book, *A Soldier Reports*. Francis Ford Coppola asked to use the photograph of Gritz and his Cambodian mercenaries that appeared in Westmoreland's book for *Apocalypse Now*. "Colonel Kurtz was commanding a Cambodian army and I commanded a Cambodian army," says Gritz. "Matter of fact, I was the first to do so."

And like the Robert Duvall character in *Apocalypse Now*, Gritz conveys the sense that he is untouchable. Gritz claims that bullets bounce off his head, a spring miraculously appears to slake the thirst of seriously parched combatants, helicopters on crash course suddenly find enough lift to clear Gritz and crew from certain death. He figures that he had personally killed over 400 in combat.

"Combat is the most honest place on earth," writes Gritz in his self-published autohagiography, *Called to Serve*. "Men take on Christ-like qualities of selflessness. A pure unspoken language communicates a single message: 'You and I are one. What happens to you happens to me. We will live or die together.' It is a sweetness of spirit that few will taste, but once experienced, it causes profound changes in your life that the uninitiated do not understand."

Joining the rarefied ranks of the Special Forces, or Green Berets, reinforced a sensibility of maverick warrior mysticism. Think of Toshiro Mifune in Yojimbo. "They taught me to pick locks and crack safes, fall through thin air from 26,000 feet in the dead of night, breathe underwater, fly airplanes, bust a half-dozen bricks with my bare hands, blow things to kingdom come, shoot every kind of firearm made, communicate in Swahili, Mandarin Chinese, Morse Code and several other languages, travel the world over and be decorated for doing things that otherwise would have landed me in jail."

Singled out for his audacious leadership, Gritz was on the fast track to Joint Chiefs when he retired from Special Forces to hunt down POWs in Southeast Asia as a civilian. The various POW rescue missions throughout the '80s, culminating in a *Parade* magazine cover story, were responsible for the creation of Gritz's public persona, the balls of-brass moral crusader bent on pantsing "the Good Ole Boy circuit" in D. C.

"I'm very glad that things went the way they did," reflects Gritz. "I wouldn't want to be a general in the Pentagon today with no goo-nads, sitting there having been castrated of my initiative. There are soldiers like myself who are not staff pukes. We didn't come up the ranks slow-stroking the generals. Instead we came up in the foxholes and the field. We will not sell our time, our talent, our resources to anyone regardless. But we'll give them, if the cause is right."

His POW-MIA crusade, Gritz discovered, was just the emotional moral issue that makes the staff pukes squirm. Even the recent U.S. Senate Select Committee on POW-MIA Affairs concluded, after 17 months of hearings, that nothing has been proved for or against the presence of live POWs in Southeast Asia. Absent from its final report was Bo Gritz's oral deposition before to the Select Committee on November 23, 1992 detailing his excursions into Laos at the behest of the DIA (Defense Intelligence Agency) and the ISA (Intelligence Support Activity), a super secret intelligence arm of the Executive branch created by Jimmy Carter and used by the Reagan administration, yet hidden from Congress for years.

As Gritz explains it, General Eugene Tighe, Director of the DIA, asked H. Ross Perot to initially fund Gritz's rescue mission as a "private sector" operation. Gritz describes his first meeting with Perot in *Called To Serve:*

"In Perot's outer office was a large-scale bronze figure of 'The Marshal' — True Grit at full gallop with Winchester extended. Perot's inner office was lined with glass display cases containing stuffed birds in various habitats. Hanging on the wall behind his chair was a sign which read, 'Eagles don't flock.' On the side wall to the right was his U.S. Naval Academy diploma.

"Perot was to the point: 'General Tighe has asked that I send you to Southeast Asia in search of POWs. I want you to go over there and do everything necessary. You come back and tell me there aren't any POWs left alive. I don't believe there are and I'm not interested in bones.'"

Perot appreciated Gritz's expertise in black ops, outlining an ambitious scheme to choke the flow of dope:

"He added: 'When you get back I have an additional task for you. Governor Clements and the head of the DEA have given me permission to have one man operate outside the law. I know you have extensive contacts in Central America. I want you to uncover and identify everyone dealing cocaine between Columbia and Texas. Once you're sure you've got them all I want you to wipe them out in a single night like an angel of death. Is that clear? I know you have the capability to do this.'"

Gritz's POW rescue plan, which, naturally enough, resembled a Rambo adventure involving the use of inflatable rubber airplanes, wasn't greeted with enthusiasm by Perot, who begged off from bankrolling the scheme. But "Operation Lazarus" was eventually set in motion with financial help from Fred O'Green of Litton Industries and a cool 30 G's from none other than Clint Eastwood.

CPA
DEFENDING THE REPUBLIC

THE PATRIOT REVIEW

"Unless the American Patriot is Christian Liberty cannot be Restored"

VOL VI, NO.2 September 1992   12 Issues $24.00

Randy Weaver

THE SIEGE AT RUBY RIDGE

By Des Griffin

Ruby Creek, Idaho - What caused this multi-million dollar eruption of law-enforcement activity? On Friday, August 21, Randy Weaver, 44, his 14-year-old son, Sam, and Kevin Harris, 24, a family friend who lived with the Weavers, were working around their mountain-top cabin when they heard one of their dogs barking. Believing that a deer " one of the family's staple sources of food " had been flushed out of the undergrowth by the dog, Sam and Harris, with hunting rifles in hand, ran down the hill toward the disruption. As they neared the dog, an unidentified man, wearing camouflaged clothing, sprang from the undergrowth and ordered them to freeze. A shot, fired by another man in camouflage nearby, killed Sam's dog. Angered, the teenager turned, screamed at the unidentified intruder who had just killed his dog, and fired his 30-30 rifle at the intruder. Harris also shot at the uninvited visitors.

It was later revealed that U.S. Marshal, William Degan,

Presidential candidate Bo Gritz, reports to reporters and supporters of Randy Weaver at the Ruby Creek roadblock

of Quincy, Massachusetts, was apparently killed by one of the shots.

Randy Weaver, who was nearby and heard the shots, fired his own gun into the air and shouted for his son and Harris to get back to the cabin. Responding instantly, they turned and headed towards the safety of the cabin. As they ran another shot rang out and the teenager " shot through the back by one of the intruders " fell dead. Harris paused long enough to determine that the 14-year-old wasn't breathing, then resumed his race for safety.

What was apparently unknown until later was the fact that the Weaver dog had flushed out a group of U.S. Marshals who were on a reconnaissance mission, checking out the Weaver property in preparation for an assault. Weaver is alleged to have sold two 12-gauge shotguns to a federal informant in October 1080. In December 1990, he was indicted on firearm charges. After being set free pending a court appearance, he

continued on Page 1

The Christian Patriot Association's account of Bo Gritz's heroism in the Weaver affair. Gritz solidified his standing within the Patriot movement with anti-government rhetoric. Few Patriots were aware that Gritz flew to Ruby Ridge at the request of the FBI, and worked closely with Eugene Glenn, the FBI official who later became the fall guy for his commanding officer, Larry Potts. Glenn retaliated by telling the press that Potts approved Vicki Weaver's murder.

"Each time Bo's operation got underway," recalls POW-MIA activist Colonel Earl Hopper, "he was sabotaged by the U.S. government. In one case he was in Laos at the time the Voice of America broadcast to the Lao people that he was there. This was a stab in the back, a perfidious act, in my opinion."

From 1981 to 1985, Gritz and team undertook four risky trips across the Mekong river into Laos, and each time were thwarted due to leaks by the Thai press and Voice of America. On one mission, a POW-rescue team member, Chuck Patterson, made off with a briefcase carrying sensitive documents, selling the information to *Soldier of Fortune* magazine for $5,000.

Scott Barnes, the quixotic gadfly who fed H. Ross Perot peculiar information regarding Vietnamese hit squads at the tail end of 1992 Presidential campaign, looms prominently in the early miscues of Gritz's POW operations. Smarting from an early termination from the Gritz-led operation in 1981, Barnes began feeding the press the story that Gritz's actual mission was a CIA-sponsored plot to assassinate two POWs. He also told the FBI that Gritz had been planning to assassinate President Reagan in league with a Libyan hit squad.

Flakes, sabotage and perfidy aside, the only tangible proof of Gritz's proximity to POWs, dead or alive, exists in a MIA's Air Force Academy ring and the photograph and signature of MIA Major Walter H. Moon handed to Gritz by a Vietnamese contact. This evidence, without given benefit of examination, was denounced by Assistant Secretary of Defense Richard Armitage as fake.

Ted Sampley, now editor of the *U.S. Veterans News and Report,* was tapped by forces in the Reagan administration to track Gritz's activities. "I was approached by Special Forces Colonel Chuck Allen to infiltrate a Veterans group that were hanging out by the Vietnam Veterans memorial, and spy on Bo Gritz. Gritz became the victim of a smear campaign. He challenged the U.S. government and found himself being called a fruitcake, an idiot, a charlatan..."

By the mid-'80s, the star-crossed POW rescue campaigns involved excursions to the Golden Triangle, where through contacts in the Chinese Mafia Gritz met the notorious Golden Triangle druglord,

Khun Sa, who dropped a verbal bomb — that certain yet-to-be-named officials in the U.S. government had been among his best customers for high-grade heroin.

A highly-connected friend phoned a warning to Gritz: "They say you're in for a real shit-blizzard unless you knock of all current activities ... You've got no option ... You're going to be 'taken care of'... You've got to erase and forget everything ... You are going to hurt the government and get hurt unless you do exactly as I say."

"I found myself not in the shadows, but out in the open," explains Gritz, "not in verbal judo, but in real terms, where the government was saying, 'You erase and forget or we're going to bury you.' It made me angry. If you want me to do something, tell me I can't, and that's exactly what I'm going to start to do."

So Gritz went back to Khun Sa and pointed a camcorder at him. Through an interpreter, Khun Sa spills the beans on Americans who participated in drug trafficking, names like mafia don Santo Trafficante, CIA agents Daniel Arnold and Jerry Daniels, CIA Deputy Director for Covert Operation Theodore Shackley, and lastly, Richard Armitage, who is said to handle the financial arrangements, funneling drug money to Nugan Hand Bank of Australia.

The Khun Sa videotape was proclaimed by Gritz as red-handed evidence of the shadow government drug mob. But Daniel Sheehan, who was cobbling together the Christic Institute's ill fated La Penca lawsuit, thought the videotape seemed "a little too pat. Sure enough, [on a table in front of Gritz in the Khun Sa videotape] there was my affidavit open to the very page where I had named those same guys, based on a source I had that was the former CIA liaison officer to Vang Pao."

As Gritz repeatedly claims, "If you're catching flak, you know you're hitting the target." After the Khun Sa revelation, the "shit-blizzard" began to rain down on Gritz in earnest. For two years, from Spring, 1987, to Spring, 1989, Gritz would be entangled in a legal quagmire over "using the passport of another." It was a twinkie charge: working under the ISA, Gritz was supplied a variety of passports, one black diplomatic, one red official, and one blue tourist variety. In the end it was discovered that the U.S. Attorney, William Maddox, had brought the wrong charge against Gritz.

Following the dismissal, reporters crowd prosecuting attorney Maddox asking him why he had initially pursued the case.

Maddox answers, "George Bush called me up and told me to get Bo Gritz."

A CRISIS OF FAITH

Denouncing governmental chicanery on talk radio programs in the late '80s attracted to Gritz a coterie of freelance conspiracy researchers, including Lars Hansson. "Bo revealed to me one night," says Hansson, "that his full-time occupation now was to extract his cranium from his anal orifice."

Gritz became an avid student of conspiracy literature, at times latching on to a more speculative realm of conspiracy, a twilight area where shadowy politics melted into metaphysics. "One morning Bo wakes me up, all excited," says Hansson, "reading me passages from *The Gods of Eden.*" The book, by the pseudonymous William Bramley, postulates that an extraterrestrial superrace called "The Custodians" has enslaved the human race in warlike bondage through the intercession of evil secret societies, which Bramley traces back to ancient serpent cults.

Over 100 pages of Gritz's autobiography weave a network of conspiracies in varying shades of plausibility. The Kennedy Assassination was a coup d'etat masterminded by ex-Nazis turned munitions makers. The AIDS virus was a Federal project. Jonestown was an MK-Ultra-type CIA operation gone haywire. In fact, Gritz maintains that he knew Special Forces soldiers that had gone down to Jonestown to perform "exterminator" operations to "destroy the evidence." The conspiracy sections in *Called To Serve,* titled "Profiles In Conspiracy," "The Third-World War," and "One Nation Under Gog," are also informed by Gritz's Christian readings, to wit, the barcode is a Satanic ploy to coerce the population to accept the Mark of the Beast.

The talk show circuit revealed Gritz's strength as a charismatic Populist orator, a kind of contemporary William Jennings Bryan. When Willis Carto of the Liberty Lobby called Gritz in late 1987 to run alongside David Duke as the Populist Party's Vice-Presidential candidate, he accepted. Gritz soon drops out of the race, repudiating Duke as "bigoted garbage dumped into a perfectly good container." About Duke, Gritz pleads ignorance: "You got to realize a soldier is not into this kind of thing the way people are who are not in the military. I didn't know anything about JBS [John Birch Society] or Carto or Ku Klux Klan." But Gritz's admission was disturbing in its own right: why would he go so far as to sign himself up as a Vice-Presidential candidate without knowing about his running mate?

That question pains Lars Hansson: "This guy, who has so much strength and decency and courage and conviction, tripping on his dick almost every turn he makes. So many people who have so much reverence for the guy agonize over watching him do these things that are, and there's no other word for it, stupid."

After bailing from the 1988 Presidential race, Gritz makes a run for a Congressional seat from the Las Vegas area, an opportunity for further dick-tripping. "Bo really had a chance to win that Congressional race" remembers Hansson. "The other candidates were lightweights and non-entities. But Mike Triggs, his manager, is a real screwball. In the middle of the campaign Triggs goes to jail for thirty days for misuse of a rental car and writing bad checks. Bo totally alienates the Republican hierarchy. They went out in a special news conference to publicly endorse the other Republican candidate before the primary."

RIGHT WOOS LEFT?

Seething with "banksters'" plots to destroy America, Gritz discovered a role model in Old Hickory, Andrew Jackson, who shot down the privately-owned U.S. Bank and its cabal of foreign interests. For the Presidential campaign of 1992, Bo Gritz molded himself as the millennial reincarnation of Andy Jackson, God's own warrior, to sweep clean Washington's Augean Stables.

The 1992 Populist Party campaign, dependent upon the Gritz's "America First Coalition," was something less than a well-oiled machine. Few advertisements found their way into newspapers. Fewer still appeared on television. Supporters were forced to buy their own campaign material and were limited to distributing it at gun shows and church outings.

Throughout the campaign Gritz was fond of repeating the story about a Minnesota professor who says to him after a lecture, 'You look like Attila the Hun to me, and I probably look like a pinko commie faggot to you, but we're marching to the same drummer here.' I said, 'Professor, we've got to stop being right and left and liberal and conservative. We've got to start being Americans together before we lose what we have.'"

The folksy appeals to anti-establishment types on the right and left incensed his critics. "Bo had hoped that I would directly endorse his Presidential bid," says Daniel Sheehan. "The secular left community started really getting furious. They began to demand that I come out and publicly condemn Bo. That the Christic Institute wouldn't condemn Bo was seen as a kind of betrayal." A *Soldier of Fortune* slam piece sought to devalue Gritz among his own jingoistic constituency. Political Research Associates' Chip Berlet weighed in with a 70-page report, "Right Woos Left: Populist Party, LaRouchian, and Other Neo-fascist Overtures to Progressives, and Why They Must Be Rejected," in which he wrote: "Bo Gritz is the point man in an effort to build a coalition of white supremacists, anti-Jewish bigots, neo-fascists, and paranoid gun nuts."

Berlet need not have worried. Few people left-of-center were attracted to Gritz despite his anti-establishment rubric. If leftists weren't put off by the blinding glint of Gritz's medals, they were surely dismayed by his invocations for a return to a Christian nation, tough talk about homosexuals, and his stand against abortion. But some of Gritz's supporters belonged to a more exotic orbit.

On various weeks of the 1992 campaign the *Weekly World News* supermarket tabloid showed candidates Clinton, Perot and Bush shaking hands with a space alien. Bo Gritz may have been the only Presidential candidate to actually attempt to enact such an event. Gritz's claims that his Vice-Presidential candidate, Cyril Minett, had convinced him in the midst of the campaign to fly his Cessna to the Tehachapi mountains north of Los Angeles to meet with "Hatonn," an eight-and-a-half foot reptilian creature.

Recalls Gritz, "We got to this little storefront and Cy says, "Now, I just want to verify this. Hatonn himself is going to walk in and meet with us?' And a person said, 'Yes, he'll be here momentarily.' I had this vision in my mind of a person in a lizard suit walking across a parking lot, but momentarily [a woman who] calls herself 'Dharma' sat down at the table, and said very quickly without any fanfare, 'I am present.' And I thought, 'Shoot, we got a channeling thing going on here.' Cy said, 'Are you eight-and-a-half feet?' She said, 'No, no, I'm actually nine-and-a-half feet.'

"Hatonn's" tabloid mouthpiece, *The Phoenix Liberator* (now called *Contact* following internecine battles between the channeler and former associates) endorsed Gritz's campaign. It is not the first linkage of alien cultures to nativist politics. William Dudley Pelley, leader of the American Nazi Silver Shirts and the mystical "Soulcraft" group, was a friend of Guy Ballard, founder of the influential I AM cult. I AM is directly responsible for many a millennialist contactee organization. Elizabeth Clare Prophet's Church Universal and Triumphant, obviously fearing a Waco-type invasion, recently struck a deal with federal law enforcement to unload most or all of its weapons tucked away in underground bunkers near Yellowstone. Other I AM organizations merely invoke the Great White Brotherhood to fill them in on future catastrophes. One such organization sells maps and globes of the post deluge world, which we're told will take place before the year 2000. Alien contactee George Van Tassell, builder of the mysterious "Integratron" near 29 Palms in the Mojave desert, shared curious views on racial genealogy with Reverend Wesley Swift, co-founder of Aryan Nations.

Conspiracy paranoia was infectious among workers in the Gritz campaign. Many spoke of having their phones tapped and their mail opened. Gilbert Martinez, a building contractor who served Gritz as his campaign coordinator in San Diego County, whispered several weeks before the November 3rd election, "The CIA shot at my house. They're trying to get rid of me."

Top: I AM America's map of post earth-change America.
(© Lori Adaile Toye, Seventh Ray Publishing,
PO Box 1958, Socorro, NM, 87801.)

Below: Bo Gritz's personalized airplane
outside his Sandy Valley, NV, home.
(Photo by Scott Lindgren.)

While Gritz was stumping through San Diego, Martinez pressured him to meet a man named Andy Nicolaw, who represented himself as controlling a major piece of a "huge" corporation named COSMOS. Nicolaw had apparently promised Martinez that COSMOS would pour two billion dollars into Gritz's campaign if Bo would only "visit a little house in Illinois."

For the past dozen years Gritz has quartered his family in the high desert 50 miles Southwest of Las Vegas in a sparsely-populated region known as Sandy Valley. Two Cessnas are parked in the front yard; horses are penned in the back. It's a comfortable home, impeccably neat. There's an entire display case full of books on Karate (he met his current wife Claudia as a black belt Karate instructor), walls chock-a-block with Special Forces memorabilia, all the many medals under glass, portraits of Christ, a Confederate flag standing at the ready.

Bo Gritz and Claudia are practicing Mormons active in their local LDS church and "sealed in the St. George, Utah Temple for all eternity." (Gritz was finally excommunicated from the Mormon church two years after this article was written; apparently the hierarchy was none too thrilled with Gritz's frequently blasphemous comments.) Both Bo and Claudia, however, welcomed an invitation to camp out at Pastor Peter J. Peters' Christian Identity outpost in the Rocky mountains in Summer, 1987. Peters is one of the most notable proponents of what is known as the Christian Identity movement, an American offshoot of British Israelism. Identity holds that Anglo-Saxons are the true Israelites and Jews, Satanic impostors.

Members of the Christian Identity and Christian Patriot movements mix an almost Rabbinical fascination with the minutiae of bible and constitutional law with millennial fervor. To this day Gritz remains closely aligned with Oregon's Christian Patriot Association. Identity groups are not precise carbon copies. Some refer to God, others, "YahWeH." All Identity groups share a fierce opposition to Zionism, the IRS, The Federal Reserve System, and the perceived sinister plot of The New World Order.

"[Peters'] camp was a delight," recalls Gritz. "They had Catholics, they had Mormons, they had all kinds of folks, and it was a very healthy meeting, I thought. And I got to know Pete, and he invited me twice again to come to his camp and I spoke in those summers, and with no offense."

Pastor Peter Peters and Bo Gritz differed, however, on at least one question: whether homosexuals should be put to death. Pastor Peters' booklet, "Death Penalty For Homosexuals Is Prescribed in the Bible," is dedicated to "my Colonel friend [Gritz] who inadvertently inspired me to write this." In a phone interview, Peters stated that publishing the booklet was necessary since "Bo Gritz told me that he would 'fight to the death to allow anyone their rights, including homosexuals.' As far as I was concerned, that bordered on blasphemy."

Gritz has since toughened his views: "There are first-degree homosexuals who probably should be skinned alive. You find them in San Francisco making ads that say, 'We're going to pervert your sons and daughters, we're going to commit these atrocities.' Those are the first degree. Take 'em out, far as I'm concerned."

(Since his excommunication from the Mormon Church and a tightening of relationships among attendees of his SPIKE survival training seminars, Gritz purchased a large plot of land near Kamiah, Idaho, for subdivision into plots bought by those who wish to follow Gritz into a Christian Covenant Community called "Almost Heaven." The underlying idea is to create a completely self-sustaining community in order to exist during the time when Americans will be forced to accept the "Mark of the Beast.")

The Identity taboo on interracial marriage marks Gritz as somewhat of a pariah, since he has two children by his second wife, who is Chinese. He gets around his previous marriage by adopting the view that intermarriage is wrong. "If my daughter, who is Amerasian, were to come to me and say, 'Dad, I met this person and he is from India, what do you think about our getting married?' I would probably say, 'Melody, I'm advising against it, there's cultural problems you're getting into.' ... I support staying within your nation, within your language, within your race, within your religion."

The biggest and most defining event of Gritz's Presidential campaign was the "Ruby Ridge Massacre," a massive police action involving an

Identity family holed up in a plywood shack near the Sandpoint area of Northern Idaho. The family's patriarch, Randall Weaver, had decided that he wasn't going to respond to a warrant accusing him of selling shotguns with too-short barrels. Weaver accused the FBI of setting him up because he had refused to spy on Aryan Nations, the neo-Nazi compound located in nearby Hayden Lake.

When camouflaged U.S. Marshals crept onto the Weavers' property they accidentally caught the attention of Randall, his 13-year-old son, Samuel, and a family friend named Kevin Harris. An exchange of gunfire took the life of young Samuel, who was shot in the back. A U.S. Marshal named William Degan also died in the exchange. The following morning, government snipers shot Randall's wife Vicki in the face, killing her instantly. Randall and Kevin Harris were also wounded in the attack. With his three young daughters inside, and his dead wife lying on the kitchen floor, Weaver sealed off various openings in his house.

Hundreds of law enforcement troops — from the Bureau of Alcohol, Tobacco and Firearms, the FBI, and even U. N. troops training in Western Montana — descend on the Ruby Creek area, sealing off a two mile radius around the Weaver cabin. Invited to Ruby Creek by the FBI, Bo Gritz arrives to the cheers of anti-ZOG [Zionist Occupation Government] protesters camped out at the roadblock. It takes several days for Gritz to mediate a peaceful conclusion to the siege, just the way, Gritz tells me, he had prophesied in a dream.

The national media, with their cameras and microphones trained on Gritz after the surrender, capture him delivering a Nazi salute — or was it a wave? — at several skinheads in the crowd. Gritz claims he was conveying Randall Weaver's thanks to the skins for a letter he had delivered, and was simply trying to get their attention. "If I wanted to give a Nazi salute," Gritz maintains, "I certainly would know how to give it and I would have given it in a fashion that any good Nazi would have been proud of."

While the press latched on to Gritz's alliances with the white separatist movement, some Identity Christians began to doubt that Gritz was really on their side. In an article titled "The Ruby Creek Sa'Bo'tage," printed in the Ayran Nations newspaper, writer J. B. Campbell labels

Gritz a Freemason and a "political pied piper" bent on destroying the white racial movements. A cartoon accompanying the article shows a haloed, uniformed Gritz held aloft by a crane labeled "Central Government." The caption reads, "The Phony Savior."

"The Aryan Nation people were mad," explains Gritz. "They wanted Randall Weaver dead. They would have had their martyr. The media was mad. They wanted the Weavers up there in that little clapboard cabin as nothing but charred bones. That would have made a wonderful story. The truth is, a number of Weaver's neighbors were mad because they hated Weaver. And it just happened to be my misfortune that I got the Weaver family out alive with no more bloodshed."

Circling the Wagons

Gritz did not make the ballot in California or most states of the union, but he nevertheless managed to win 106,000 votes in the November 3rd general election — and that's not including the write-in statistics. His support was particularly strong in Mormon regions of the country. According to Hugh Delios of the *Chicago Tribune*, "In Utah, Gritz received 28,000 votes on Nov. 3, and residents say it was hard to find a car bumper in Central Utah without a Gritz sticker on it."

Several months after the election, Gritz campaign volunteers are burnt-out. Many had taken time off from there jobs and are now furiously trying to catch up with missed wages. A vocal few are disgusted.

Gilbert Martinez would rather not think about the whole thing. "I haven't talked to Bo. I'm not going to talk to Bo." Martinez's wife is even more adamant: "Everybody's talking for this, against that. We're not going to have anything to do with it, Bo Gritz or anybody else, ever again." Oh, and about the shooting up of their house by the CIA? Mrs. Martinez snaps, "Who told you that? That's a lot of bullcrap. It was gang members."

The Gritz Campaign Chairman in Colorado, Devvy Kidd, complains of gross mismanagement or chicanery. She says that Gritz "cancelled an appearance on *Larry King Live* to speak to 50 people at the Liberty

Lobby in Washington. That doesn't make any sense at all. Come November 4th, the son of a bitch evaporated out of the patriot movement. What Bo Gritz does now is hawk his book and survival literature. Instead of getting in the face of Congress he tells people how to go and hide and store food."

Mrs. Kidd faxes me the Federal Election Commission report on Gritz's campaign, circling a rather peculiar entry. A Jeb Bush of the CIA has contributed $400 to the campaign. Somebody somewhere must have a wry sense of humor.

"I'd rather have my mouth tied around the exhaust pipe of a bus and be drug all the way to Los Angeles than get into any political arena," complains a weary Gritz shortly after the conclusion of his Presidential crusade. "I hate politics, I hate politicians. They belong on the bottom of the ocean with whale manure. In 1994 there's a governor's campaign in Idaho. I don't want America five years from now to open their arms to an empty sky and say, 'Why, God, have you done this terrible thing to us?'

"The Northwest is touched by the palm of God. Idaho is a good place, strategically. It has access to Canada and probably has more water under its soil than any other state in the union.

"There are four phases that Americans that would continue to live as free individuals will face. The first phase is Awareness — that's what we did during the election. People have to know what's going on before they can be expected to act. The second phase is Preparation. I'm going to be doing for the next year to come, and that is helping people to prepare, to live self-reliant in spite of the government.

"Bill Clinton is even more of a globalist than Bush. I think it means a loss of the United States as a separate nation, and our Constitution will eventually come under the U. N. charter. Maybe there are enough people in Idaho who think we ought to maintain our identity. If there aren't it doesn't make any difference. We'll have a Neighborhood Watch program if we have to. Meaning if there's only five of us, we'll say, 'Look, we're not going to hurt anybody, but don't you come in here and tread on us.

"Eventually, people may have to relocate if they want to do that, and that's the third phase. There could even be a fourth phase, and that's a defense phase. I can see a time when we may have to circle our wagons, so to speak, in order to say, 'Look, if you want to come in and take our Constitutional rights, you can try, but we're going to defend what is ours.'"

Gritz is currently touring the states with his day-long "SPIKE" preparedness seminars, teaching self-defense, first aid, and "everything from getting a trust to protect your finances to secure a zone in your home so that if the police get the 'wrong' address you may not be hit by ammunition."

Preparedness is necessary, says Gritz, for the ultimate showdown with the Satanic New World Order. "I think it will come to the point. It's biblical. I think we're going to see a literal mark of the beast. On your right hand. I think it'll be a part of the globalist cashless system. If you do read Revelations you will see that if you accept this system that the smoke of your torment rises forever."

(Photo by Scott Lindgren.)

SWAT in Theme Park Land

Imagine waking up at 6 am in a cheap motel room, drawing aside the curtains and seeing nothing but cops, hundreds of 'em, and not your ordinary flatfoots either, but SWAT troops outfitted in Kevlar vests and black paramilitary gear, H & K MP5's slung around their shoulders, sidearms peeping from their holsters.

I had to remind myself they weren't storming the Orlando, Florida, Quality Inn but gathered for the "SWAT Round-Up," the largest get-together of elite tactical law enforcers in the U.S. Dozens of SWAT teams, from Los Angeles to South Florida, are here to negotiate obstacle-and-shooting competitions, attend seminars conducted by international tactical experts, browse state-of-the-art ordnance and accessories, and most importantly, hoist a few in pursuit of good fellowship. As I heard later from an East Coast Medic, some of the guys got a little overexcited and were bounced from Hooters, the restaurant chain known for its waitresses who serve up chicken wings in tights and miniskirt.

My tour guide to the world of Special Weapons and Tactics, a wiry, intense man by the name of Dick Kramer, waits for me, alternately chain-smoking and carbo-loading a breakfast buffet in the motel coffee shop. Kramer is the pre-eminent illustrator of tactical teams in action poses, and attends many such SWAT conventions to sell t-shirts and lithographs to the men in black.

A SWAT guy, friendly and sunbeaten, who posed for Kramer in his Collier County tactical duds, comes by to pay his respects. "Hello Dick," he says, quietly. Kramer pumps his hand, a ball of enthusiasm. "Howyadoin!" he shouts. "You gotta love these guys," Kramer says to me with his trademark enthusiasm. "You won't meet a greater bunch of guys in the world."

∞ ∞ ∞

To get to the Orange County Sheriff's range, home of the Round-Up, you've got to take a bumpy dirt road past the county dump. As you bounce past the sanitation site, odiferous in the sultry Florida humidity, the flashing tower of a local nuclear plant looms into view.

"It stinks and it glows, and I wouldn't miss it for the world," beams Dick Kramer, whose minivan is waved into the Sheriff's range, where hundreds of police cars are parked. For the moment they're not worried about serving warrants on drug dealers or doing an explosive entry.

The Orange County Sheriff's Range is really little more than an open concrete causeway with a metal roof facing a couple open fields. A shooting area extends to a 20-foot high berm designed to absorb a multitude of bullets. On the other side of the walkway, a four-story tower has been constructed for SWAT competition. On the walkway several dozen vendors display their wares to SWAT teams waiting their turn to compete.

The Round-Up Coordinator, Jeff Hopkins, himself a part-time SWAT officer for the Orlando police department, tells me that the event was calculated to build camaraderie and encourage the sharing of information among SWAT teams. "We realized there was a real void in agencies talking to each other. If we had we could have prevented some tragedies." And to get them to talk, Hopkins got them to compete. "SWAT team people are by nature competitive. This was a hook to get teams together."

SWAT guys are shoving money at Dick Kramer for his drawings and t-shirts that reflect an almost mythic adoration of domestic paramilitary forces. Other vendors, hawking body armor, night vision goggles, scopes, guns, training services, targets, magazines, holsters, "riot extinguishers" (huge fire extinguishers full of pepper mace), "distraction devices" (known as "thunder flashes" or "flash bangs"), are also doing a good business.

Cybergenics, the company that makes pills for bodybuilders, has come to the right event to put on its display. Many SWAT guys are into body-building, and move like steel doors on bank vaults.

SWAT ROUND-UP '93 PROGRAM

INSIDE:

Educational Schedule	Event Schedule
Area Map	Participating Agencies
Individual Event Schedule	Participating Vendors
Trophy Sponsors	Last Year's Team Results

"Seems to me," I tell Jeff Hopkins, an Orlando SWAT team member and coordinator of the Round-Up, "that a lot of the guys are pretty bulked-up."

"The wiry fast-mover works better on an obstacle course," allows Hopkins. "But that isn't to say there aren't bulked-up guys who don't go through the course fast. It's not bulk that gets you through the thing. It's stamina. I see a place for that bulk. I've done a lot of warrants where the guys would literally rip the door off its hinges. They are extremely good at that. Very few people want to physically challenge someone like that."

Today the troops are competing in "Survival City," an ersatz urban situation built with movie set-like fronts. A bombed-out phone booth sits disconsolately amid the bullet-frayed fronts like a high-tech scarecrow. Hopkins explains the game. "First, a sniper has got to run up to a platform, set up and shoot a one inch target at 75 yards. ... Once he does that he leaves the weapon, goes on out to meet his other people, and they all have to shoot one target with their handgun. Then they run down to this box, which is four feet by four feet by eight feet, and they have to pop up one at a time and engage targets outside of the box through a hatch.

Survival City. (Photo by Adam Parfrey.)

"Another competition is called Officer Rescue. They have to wear gas masks and cross a canal on a rope. They go do a shooting exercise, which in this case involves handguns, shotguns and sub-machine guns. They have to rig a dummy and move the dummy and themselves back across the canal.

"Then we have the Tower Scramble. On the word go two snipers scramble to the top of the tower, shoot a four inch target at 100 yards. Then the rest of the team go on a shooting course called Rolling Thunder, thirty targets these guys have to knock down. Plus they got to shoot a shotgun about fifty yards. ... Then they come back and join the snipers up at the top of the tower ... and then rappel down to the finish line."

A monsoon begins to sweep across the playing fields. Amid the grunts and the gunfire, the competitors are taking pratfalls in the mud. Dick Kramer surveys the scene and shakes his head in bemusement. "They play as hard as they work, and vice-versa. What a bunch of guys."

If he sounds like a broken record about his love for SWAT members, Dick Kramer has got his reasons. For many years a commercial artist in the New York corporate rat-race, he retired to the scenic splendor of Florida's Marco Island and began his business depicting tactical law enforcement in action. His photo-realistic styling can be found on material promoting Heckler and Koch's SWAT training division, and many Round-Up event posters.

NEW FROM DICK KRAMER

America's best known S.W.A.T. artist keeps expanding the finest in quality art lithographs and T-shirt art. A catalog of Dick Kramer's complete line is available on request.
All prices quoted do not include postage and handling. Add $3.50 for the lithographs which includes the mailing tube, and $2.50 for the shirts.

One of Kramer's better-loved lithographs has two SWAT members suiting up in their patented black outfits, fitting gas masks on themselves. The caption, "Time To Take Out the Garbage."

The caption captures the attitude of SWAT members at the Round-Up, who see themselves as a specially equipped and rigorously trained good guys out to clean up a manifestly dirty society. Through hard experience, some veterans have developed an even more hardboiled view. Cops are the forgotten heroes, taking the heat while the coddled millions snooze away in front of the television sets.

"Cops are the only real people left," rues Al Baker, who for 21 years was a key man in the NYPD Emergency Service Unit or ESU — New York City's version of SWAT. He repeats himself, "Cops are the only real people left. These cops are out there in the streets of the cities every day witnessing day after day the rapes, the child molestations, the violence, the murders, the drugs, the guns, the whole litany of degradation of society, of the degeneration of society. They're the first ones to see it, and they're the first ones to feel it. Cops are very sensitive. They're very sensitive to the precious things in life. A lot of people don't realize that."

"There's two schools of thought in SWAT," says Jeff Hopkins. "The West Coasties and the East Coasties. Really it's L.A. versus New York. New York's idea is that if someone is in a building with five hostages and he's shooting hostages — well, eventually he's gonna run out of hostages. They're not going in, they're not going to enter that building. They'll talk a man to death, but they won't go in and shoot him."

"Isolate, contain and negotiate," remarks Al Baker of East Coast SWAT tactics. "Jokingly, we say negotiate with malnutrition. ... In those early years after the so-called success of hostage negotiation on the East Coast, and after the so-called birth of SWAT on the West Coast ... NYPD developed the posture of 'SWAT We're Not.' It was almost as though we didn't want to be seen as black faced camo dressed people who would take you out, so to speak, in a heartbeat. But yet on the West Coast that was the way they were going. And today the ESU is still not called a SWAT team."

The West Coast SWAT cops are more likely to consider an aggressive, pro-active stance, Jeff Hopkins tells me. "The West Coast considers forced entry a very viable option. Sniper shots, also."

The entire concept of SWAT, that is, of facing domestic terrors like urban guerrillas, was originally a West Coast idea, created in Los Angeles as a response to the 1965 Watts riots. It was born in the mind of former LAPD chief Daryl Gates, who then was Commander of the Metro Squad, at the time a small unit of "special forces," who were used mainly to, as Gates puts it in his book *Chief,* "handle labor disputes and to 'shake, rattle, and roll' — that is, roust — anything strange that moved on the streets." Gates' mandate was to create military-style teams consisting of a leader, a marksman, an observer, a scout and a rear guard. There would be one sergeant for every two five-man teams. By 1967 Gates consolidated 220 SWAT-style raiders in his Metro Squad, but they were still without a name.

Gates first name for his new military style Metro Squad was "Special Weapons Attack Teams," but higher-ups vetoed that in favor of "Special Weapons and Tactics." The acronym SWAT was born. In keeping with SWAT's mythic reputation, Gates' men trained for several years in Universal Studios' backlot.

SWAT was first unveiled to the public in December 1969, on an operation against Black Panthers barricaded in a house in South Central Los Angeles. The Panthers surrendered just before Gates was to use a military grenade launcher borrowed from the military in order to blow their safe house "to kingdom come."

In 1974, SWAT graduated to prime time when the L.A. chapter engaged in a massive shoot-out with the Symbionese Liberation Army that ended only when its bungalow home burned to the ground. By Gates' count, the SLA fired 3,772 rounds of ammunition, and the SWAT teams, 5,371.

The SLA siege was a portent of things to come in regard to future actions against political subversives. In a similar effort against the black power group MOVE in the mid-

Daryl Gates

'80s, a full city block in Philadelphia was incinerated. An FBI action against white separatist Robert Mathews resulted in his burning to death in a standoff in a Whidbey Island cottage. And, of course, who could forget the conflagration in Waco against David Koresh and the Branch Davidians.

Despite these well-publicized incidents of destruction and a short-lived television series in the 1970s that pictured SWAT as a trigger-happy, confrontational bunch, SWAT forces on both coasts are quick to tell me that the purpose of SWAT is to save lives. A long-time LAPD SWAT member, who now sells body armor, explains, "Let's say you use untrained police in a hostage situation. Cops are used to acting as individuals or a two-man environment. In this case you might have indiscriminate firing. SWAT uses minimum force.

"In the time I was with LAPD SWAT we had 1,200 armed call-ups and only about 20 deaths or so, including seven from the SLA shootout. If you look at the percentages, that's damn good."

I ask Jeff Hopkins what the difference was between a military operation and the domestic deployment of SWAT:

> When you say Special Weapons and Tactics ... there's no acceptable casualty ratio, unlike the military. We don't go into anything to get hurt. The military says, "We have an objective, and if we have only five percent casualty, this is a success." It doesn't happen that way in SWAT, where there are no acceptable casualties.

> The other side of that is, if anybody gets hurt, it better be the bad guy. But we don't want to kill the bad guy, that's why you call SWAT. For instance, we got a call on a guy holding a gun on himself. He put the gun down on the car seat he was on, he was distraught, and moved his hand away for a second, and that was the opening we were waiting for. Immediately a thunder flash went off in front of his windshield. One of us broke the back right window of his car so that he

> had to startle. If he wasn't startled out front, the back would startle him. While all this was going on, two guys would come in on him. One guy would grab his hand, the other guy would grab his head and yank him out the window. It worked fine. That's why you call SWAT. In real life, the guy would have walked off, and the officers would have eventually had to shoot him because they'd think he was threatening somebody. But you don't want to have to do that, so you bring in a team that's used to working together as a team that has a bigger armamentarium with them.

The goal of no acceptable tactical casualties was breached in the initial raid on the Branch Davidian compound in February 1993 in which four officers of the ATF, Steven Willis, Robert Williams, Conway LeBleu and Todd McKeehan, were killed. When the FBI finally moved on Rancho Apocalypse with tanks, delivering CS gas into the flimsy walls, the compound went up in flames, burning to death nearly 80 members of the renegade Seventh Day Adventist sect. Reports issued by the Treasury Department and the Justice Department investigating the siege concluded that initial raid was poorly planned and poorly executed. Stephen Higgins, chief of the ATF, offered his resignation. Experts tapped by the Justice Department, all friends of law enforcement, were not favorably impressed with the final results of the siege, suggesting that the FBI listen with more alacrity to experts in the Behavioral Sciences, beef up its Hostage Rescue Team, and set up a more sophisticated training, including the use of virtual reality.

The SWAT guys I spoke to seemed a little resentful of the attitude of the Feds toward municipal SWAT teams. "If you ask the ATF and the FBI," says Al Baker, "they're the best hostage rescue units in the world."

> They're a little impressed with themselves, a little bit oversophisticated. They lack a lot of the common street knowledge and street techniques that the average street cops have. NYPD's Emergency

Services Unit doesn't really train all that much, but they handle over a hundred thousand calls a year. ... The people at the ATF and the Hostage Recovery Team at the FBI train, have all the advanced, state-of-the-art equipment, they don't have the number of call-ups, don't have the hands-on experience like New York or L.A. has.

Whoever made the decision to go in [the Branch Davidian compound] guns ablaze, that was a wrong decision from the beginning. If you go back in history, David Koresh was arrested by one of the local sheriffs. The local sheriff had enough smarts to get the guy on the phone. I think the ATF needed to say, look what a great tactical team we are, look at all the illegal guns we got.

Despite the chafing between local and federal agencies, Jeff Hopkins believes that there is now a trend toward greater cooperation.

The FBI, the Federal Marshall, the ATF and the IRS have all been working very hard to reverse ... the image of coming down with the tablets from on high.

Federal agents are signing up with the NTOA or National Tactical Officers Association, a group founded in 1983 to promote better communication between SWAT units. NTOA's quarterly magazine, *Tactical Edge,* available only to accredited members of tactical forces has, says NTOA president Larry Glick, "the cherriest informational magazine reference for SWAT tactics." Glick estimates that there are at least 20,000 SWAT officers nationally affiliated with 350 major metropolitan police offices. In keeping with the philosophy of strengthening ties between federal and local SWAT officers, the NTOA presented its 1993 Valor Award to agent Tim Chisholm of the ATF for bravery in the raid on the Branch Davidian compound.

In addition, the FBI's Special Operations and Research Unit (SOARU) will be working with 75 law enforcement agencies to establish a "crisis management database" to share with SWAT units across the country.

Al Baker, formerly of NYPD's Emergency Services Unit, comments:

> There has been a rapid deployment of SWAT teams throughout the country. We have SWAT teams in every major city and many of the smaller cities, where they're getting involved in more sophisticated weapons, more sophisticated tactics, more sophisticated training. ... The disease or the [crime] epidemic has now stretched out to Paducah, Kentucky. ... The only thing that makes New York different from Paducah is that we have more people and we have more opportunities.
>
> There's been an explosion of training and equipment. Laser sights. Diversionary devices have become more professional and more understood. Suppressors on machine guns. Years ago, people would have said, 'Why would you put a silencer on a submachine gun? What are you trying to do? Be like James Bond?' Recall the time in France when a SWAT team came in when a group of schoolchildren were being held hostage ... and they took out the suspect without the sound of gunfire going off. It reduces and lowers the whole state of panic that you would ordinarily experience when a gunshot is fired. Secondly, the SWAT team going in, when they hear a gunshot, they know immediately it couldn't be their own.

America's SWAT troops look to the military for their technical advances, and so the most logical development for domestic tactical forces will be the Soldier Integrated Protective Ensemble (SIPE), which turns every footsoldier into a computer-aided "terminator" by integrating a thermal sight that provides instant smart targets for their rifle fire. This sophisticated technology will be available to military and police organizations by the year 2000.

The recent governmental move to suppress silencer technology, so-called "assault rifles" and Black Talon ammunition, is part of an ongoing strategy to give the police the upper hand in armed confrontations. Most SWAT members I talked to supported the civilian ban on sophisticated weapon technology, but were ambivalent on the concept of banning guns altogether. "The only thing that restricting guns is gonna do is restrict the constitutional rights of those who deserve to have guns," complains Al Baker.

On the other hand, a former long-time member of the LAPD SWAT force who requested anonymity made it clear that

> Citizens are going to have to lose the right to possess guns. It's cheaper to ban these things than register them. If the government comes to my house with 50 millimeter weapons and Humvees I'm going to comply with their order to give up my guns. I'm not going to shoot it out with them. I'm not going to fight the military.

President Clinton's Omnibus Crime Act of 1994 provides for 100,000 new police officers nationwide and further restrictions on firearms. One would think that violent street gangs are the nation's most pressing law enforcement problem, but the erstwhile LAPD SWAT member tells me that future confrontations will most likely be avid gun owners who formerly may have been staunch law-and-order types.

> The biggest threat that faces law enforcement is the radical right. They've got guns, and they know how to use them. They are strict constitutionalists, and think that the right to bear arms is a concept direct from God. They're very dedicated and are likely to shoot it out to the death.

HOW TO FRAME A PATRIOT

TIME MAGAZINE DECONSTRUCTED

ANALYSIS OF CHRISTOPHER JOHN FARLEY'S ARTICLE ON MILITIAS

by Barry Krusch

On December 13, 1994, a journalist posted a message on the Internet (to the newsgroup TALK.POLITICS.GUNS), and invited public comment on an article he wrote for *Time:*

> This is Christopher John Farley, a staff writer at TIME magazine. I wrote a story in this week's TIME on the growth of the militia movement. Has anyone read it? Does anyone have any comments or criticisms? It's available on newsstands, but, in the spirit of the internet, if you want to read it for free (TIME has an web site at www.time.inc.com where several of the featured articles in TIME are posted for all to read, including my piece on militias.)
> Message-ID: <AB12999B44014756 @chris_farley.timeinc.com>
> Date: Tue, 13 Dec 94 00:21:47 GMT

You have to hand it to Farley. Considering the nature of his article, this was a gutsy move. The first reply to his message came five hours later, but it wasn't the last. A flood of comments were posted in reply, and they weren't flattering. Phrases like "hatchet job," "statist liberal paranoia," "lots of supposition without underlying factual support,","suspicious of your motives and your professionalism," "the constant effort to arouse fear" and "sleazy," among many others, peppered the commentary, and by the tone of things, you could tell that there weren't a lot of happy folks out there. Three days later, Farley came back on line to reply to these criticisms:

A lot of the people that have posted notes here have been calling my article biased. I don't think it was. I tried to keep my opinions out of the piece as much as possible (absolute objectivism is perhaps achievable only by supernatural beings). In almost any news piece dealing with a controversial subject, a responsible journalist will and should quote a range of people. So I quoted not only militia members, but their critics as well. The militia members were allowed to make their case — that they wanted to protect the second amendment, that they were nonracial, that they were family-oriented etc. And the militia critics were allowed to state their case. If what you were looking for was a pro-militia or pro-gun article, then sorry, that's not what I set out to write. I also didn't set out to write an anti-militia story either. What I wanted to write and what I did write was a story that presented the pros and cons of militias and patriots so intelligent readers could make up their own minds.
Message-ID: <AB172D1B7A014756@chris_farley.timeinc.com>
Date: Fri, 16 Dec 94 11:40:11 GMT

Farley says that he "didn't set out to write an anti-militia story". Rather than take his word for it, I took instead his implicit advice to "make up [your] own mind [ ]", my curiosity piqued by the criticisms in the newsgroup.

I went to my local library and photocopied the article, and after reading it was not surprised to discover the obvious bias present. For the last fifteen years, I've been reading about (and tolerating) media manipulation of reality, but most of the books I've read have given examples from the "left-wing" point of view. Few of these writings launched their in-depth analysis from the "right-wing" point of view.

I was glad to be made aware of this piece, and I'm in Farley's debt. The article gave me a chance to exercise what I've learned about media analysis on a horse of a different color. Throughout this analysis, I was amazed at Farley's sophistication. I can't escape the feeling that he had a little help from a fatherly "editor".

In the interests of helping people see "how the media does it", I'm posting my analysis on the Internet. "Reading" the media is a valuable skill, particularly in this day and age, when the power of the media to frame the way we think (and thus control the way we act) is truly awesome.

The following piece is Farley's article line-by line, with no words omitted or added, followed immediately by my analysis. After you read this piece, you be the judge. See if you think Farley's article is unbiased.

Farley's article appeared in *Time* on December 19, 1994, pages 48-9. The article was illustrated with three pictures, with these captions:

> WEEKEND WARRIOR: California militiaman Dean Compton says he's ready for the worst

> LINE OF DEFENSE: In the unlikely event that the U.N. invades northern Michigan, the local militia will be ready

> FAMILY FUN? Militia training includes obstacle courses, long marches and even playing capture the flag with the kids

Under the first photograph was the title of the article:

> PATRIOT GAMES

This is a reference to the recent Harrison Ford movie made from the Tom Clancy bestseller, but there's another subtext here: these patriots are playing a "game". Thus, they are not serious. The only difference between these "men" and boys are the size of their toys. If you didn't know that only "men" were involved, let the subtitle of this article explain:

> Irate, gun-toting white men are forming militias.
> Are they dangerous, or just citizens defending
> their rights?

Farley/*Time* tells us how we are to think of these "men": they are "irate" (irate people, as we all know, are irrational), "gun-toting" (the use of the word "toting" from the rural lexicon calls up images of hillbillies against the revenuers), and "white" (thus "racist" by implication, even though there are many black members of the movement).

These terms, standing alone, have a "negative spin", but when conjoined one after the other create a far greater and enhanced "negative spin" derived from their mutual "confirmation". This illegitimate bootstrapped credibility flows from the presence of a unifying negative spin that cuts across diverse substantive domains ("irate": EMOTION, "gun-toting": VOLITION, "white": DEMOGRAPHIC); the whole is greater than the sum of the parts, and the whole sends a clear message of minus-value.

Having thus begun by framing the movement with minus-value (the mark of all journalists who try to keep their "opinions out of the piece as much as possible"), we are then presented with the following "either/or" alternative (there are no other views possible): are these patriots "dangerous" (minus-value), or "citizens defending their rights" (plus-value)? The answer is obvious: since minus-value = minus-value, the patriots must be DANGEROUS. Note that this identification is implicit in the framing of the article. The facts presented will flesh out this frame, as we'll see.

Now let's go to the article proper:

> In a remote meadow in northern Michigan, inside
> a large tent heated by a wood stove, 50 white men
> dressed in combat gear and wielding rifles talk
> about the insanity of the outside world.

"[W]hite men . . . wielding rifles" in a "remote" area. Sounds scary! These "white men" use a "wood stove", so they are unsophisticated (this echoes and thus confirms the rural implication launched by "toting"). And what do these men talk of? "[I]nsanity." This word "insanity", floated into the conceptual ether, will find a resting place soon.

> The men, civilians all, see threats everywhere.
> There are reports of foreign soldiers hiding in salt
> mines under Detroit, some of the men say. Oth-
> ers speak of secret markings on highway signs
> meant to guide conquering armies.

Since these white men "see threats everywhere", they must be "paranoid", and therefore "nuts". This is proven by the "secret markings"
which "others speak of." Of course, it's a characteristic of the insane
to think that everyone else ("the outside world") is insane, isn't it?

> The men's voices subside as "General" Norman
> Olson, a Baptist minister, gun-shop owner and
> militia leader, enters the tent. He tells the men
> they are the shock troops of a movement that's
> sweeping America, that the "end times" are com-
> ing, and civil wars are two years away. "People
> think we are the ones who bring fear because we
> have guns," Olson says. "But we are really an
> expression of fear."

The "voices subside" when the "leader" enters — sounds like a cult
to me! Since the "leader" of this group is not a "General", but only
thinks he is (quotes around the word "General"), he is just one of
those loonies playing a game (one of the characteristics of the insane
is thinking that they are someone more grandiose than they are, e.g.
Jesus, Napoleon, etc.). Thus, Farley's first named example of the average patriot is someone the average reader of *Time* has already mentally discredited. Note that Farley doesn't focus instead on the members of the movement who communicate on the Internet, members
who presumably aren't insane, but rational. These members will be
discussed later, after the frame has been set.

> In dozens of states, loosely organized paramilitary
> groups composed primarily of white men are
> signing up new members, stockpiling weapons
> and preparing for the worst.

"[L]oosely organized", as opposed to "well-regulated" — how can
these people think that the Second Amendment could possibly apply

to them? This is the third time the word "white" has appeared. Farley is "paving the way" for an upcoming framing.

> The groups, all privately run, tend to classify themselves as "citizen militias." They are the armed, militarized edge of a broader group of disgruntled citizenry that go by the label of "patriots."

"[P]rivately run", as opposed to "State" militias — how can these people think that the Second Amendment could possibly apply to them? They "go by the label of" patriots, but they really aren't. They're just a bunch of disgruntled citizens.

> The members of the larger patriot movement are usually family men and women who feel strangled by the economy, abandoned by the government and have a distrust for those in power that goes well beyond that of the typical angry voter.

Thus, their views, motivated by personal concerns, must be the illegitimate expression of negative emotion ("General" Olson said so himself), and could not possibly be derived from an historical analysis of examples of totalitarianism such as Stalin's Russia, Hitler's Germany, Batista's Cuba, Somoza's Nicaragua, the Shah's Iran, the Khmer Rouge's Cambodia, etc. etc.

> Patriots join the militias out of fear and frustration. Says Jim Barnett, leader of a Florida militia: "The low-life scum that are supposedly representing us in Washington, D.C., don't care about the people back home anymore. We're grasping at straws here trying to figure out what we can do to get representation, and this is our answer."

These people are desperate, "grasping at straws". Look out!

> Patriots claim to be motivated differently from other fringe groups that have sprung up in America and taken up arms.

They "claim" to be motivated from "other" "fringe groups", but of course they aren't. Thus, they too are a "fringe group", with the same (presumably) illegitimate motivations of all the other fringe groups that have taken up arms.

> The Ku Klux Klan, for example — born as a social club and quickly evolving into a militia, recruiting members through appeals to patriotism — still thrives on hatred of blacks, Jews, Roman Catholics and foreigners. The moribund Posse Comitatus, a militant group based in the Farm Belt, wanted to wipe out the tax collectors.

Now we know why "white" has appeared three times. Subconsciously, you were supposed to be thinking of the Ku Klux Klan. Now your suspicion is confirmed. No matter how noble the present motivations of the patriots, they will eventually degenerate into just one more racist, "militant" organization. What else could we expect from "gun-toting white men" "grasping at straws" by a "wood stove" in a "remote meadow", all the while talking of "the insanity of the outside world"?

> The patriots, by contrast, have a more generalized fear of Big Government, which they say is rapidly robbing individuals of their inalienable rights, chief among them the right to bear arms.

Now *Time* has to get some credibility back. Just in the nick of time, too! Here's the "balance" that is supposed to make this an "objective" article.

> Patriots were particularly enraged when Congress passed a crime bill last August that banned assault weapons. Complains Henry McClain, the leader of another Florida militia unit: "The Federal Government has taken it upon themselves to regulate everything you can think or touch or smell."

And more "balance":

> Patriots also fear that foreign powers, working through organizations like the United Nations and treaties like the General Agreement on Tariffs and Trade, are eroding the power of America as a sovereign nation.

This "balancing" sentence shows a different, and more plausible side of the patriot movement, a view not grabbed out of thin air or based on fear, but one based on evidence one might be exposed to if one had a subscription to *Time*.

Take, for example, the case of Strobe Talbott, a former "editor-at-large" of *Time* who was nominated on December 28, 1993 to be Warren Christopher's Deputy Secretary of State. Both Talbott and Christopher were members of the Council of Foreign Relations. In a July 20, 1992 *Time* essay entitled "The Birth of the Global Nation", this CFR member/former editor of *Time* (now government official) wrote the following in his column "America Abroad":

> All countries are basically social arrangements, accommodations to changing circumstances. No matter how permanent and even sacred they may seem at any one time, in fact they are all artificial and temporary.

Prior to making this observation, Talbott had stated this:

> I'll bet that within the next hundred years ... nationhood as we know it will be obsolete; all states will recognize a single, global authority. A phrase briefly fashionable in the mid-20th century — 'citizen of the world' — will have assumed real meaning by the end of the 21st.

No such evidence for patriot views was quoted in Farley's article, even though Farley not only had access to this quote, but copyright privileges as well. Instead, we go to Farley-style "balance," where we are given views that are to be seen as mere opinions based on "fears", not views based on facts available to anyone who subscribed to the writings of Farley's employer:

> On a home video promoting patriot ideas, a man who gives his name only as Mark from Michigan says he fears that America will be subsumed into "one big, fuzzy, warm planet where nobody has any borders."

Here's "balance" for you. This is a "home video," so this is the work of amateurs, not researchers who cite evidence which appeared in, of all places, *Time*. What's more, these amateurs are clandestine, since the individual in the video is not "named" Mark; rather, this individual "gives his name only as Mark" — so the "name" is really an "alias" (what criminals use). Maybe that's why they hang out in "remote meadows".

> Samuel Sherwood, head of the United States Militia Association in Blackfoot, Idaho, tells followers, absurdly, that the Clinton Administration is planning to import 100,000 Chinese policemen to take guns away from Americans.

Back to the thrust of the article. These guys are nuts!

> Such wild allegations have proved to be an effective method of grabbing the attention of the disaffected and recruiting them into militias.

Ahh, that explains it. All this talk of GATT and the U.S. government robbing people of supposedly inalienable rights are nothing more than "wild allegations", just like the story of 100,000 imported Chinese policemen. But it turns out that these "wild" allegations, which are ignored by the rational among us, are "effective" on the members of the patriot movement (not surprising, since the movement is primarily composed of the "abandoned" and "disgruntled" who have been made gullible by their fears). So, if you meet someone who's in this movement, the chances are excellent he's there because he's an intellectual bimbo who's been sucked into the movement by "wild allegations" the rest of us rational people have dismissed out of hand. Thus, the "balancing" sentences are re-framed with minus-value. Well, it was nice while it lasted.

Most experts agree that the groups are multiply-
ing and their membership is expanding, though
estimates vary. Chip Berlet, who studies militias
for Political Research Associates, a Massachusetts
think tank, says militia units exist in 30 states,
including large organizations in Michigan, Montana and Ohio, and he suspects there may be units
in 10 other states. Although there may be hundreds of thousands of people who identify with
the patriot movement, Berlet estimates that only
about 10,000 people have actually joined the
armed militias.

If "only 10,000 people" have joined armed militias out of "hundreds
of thousands" who identify with the movement, why focus on them?

On their wilderness training excursions, these
would-be warriors give themselves a vigorous
workout. In Michigan the members of a local
militia build their endurance by running army-
style outdoor obstacle courses or tramping long
distances across rugged-terrain while holding
heavy semi-automatic rifles.

Oh, that's why. Note that we don't read, "many concerned individuals post information on USENET regarding the failure of the American government to actually represent the people who finance it, a
government which has willfully and wantonly disregarded clear constitutional directives against its actions, and a government which day
by day seems to grow more and more remote from the concerns of
the average American". We won't talk about the set of people we
don't typically fear, concerned people who express their views on-line
— we're going to talk about the set of people upon whom fears can
plausibly be projected, the minority set of people who "tramp [ ] long
distances … while holding heavy semi-automatic rifles." We'll talk
about the people on-line later, once the well has been suitably poi-
soned. Note also the conceptual no-win for the militia: if they don't
train, they're "amateurs wielding rifles" (and therefore "dangerous")

— but if they do, they're "exhibiting militant tendencies" (and therefore "dangerous").

Here we find yet another example of an ages-old pattern in American media discourse: not only are the activities of the more militant subgroups of larger anti-establishment groups focused on at the expense of their more pacifist brethren, but in addition, these more militant activities will be ripped from the web of history; the spotlight will focus on the falling of dominoes M and N, but not dominoes A through L which occurred prior in time, and which help to explain (and legitimize) the actions in question.

This "decontextualization" of events by the media is a classic tactic. We aren't given any direct contact with the thoughts of these men who are holding the rifles, men who obviously have concerns about the way things are going in the United States. We're only to view what they do, and react accordingly.

Of course, this image is a frightening one, and is preparing us for a frame of "incipient revolution is headed our way". But *Time* has more than one ace in the hole; these people aren't that influential yet, so it doesn't need to step up to direct accusation of nascent revolutionary tendencies at this time (though *Time* reserves the right to utilize [and is paving the way for utilization of] this frame in the future). *Time* is going to "go to the bench," and introduce a subtle frame shift.

When we started the article, the frame was supposed to be MINUS-value ("dangerous") vs PLUS-value ("citizens defending their rights"). That was supposed to show us how "balanced" and credible *Time* is: "You can trust us! Come on in!" But the use of the word "games" clued us in (and prepared us for) another possible framing, which we're to be presented with here. Now that we're deep in the bowels of the article, the frame will magically shift to MINUS-value ("dangerous") vs. MINUS-value ("boys 'n' toys") — VOILA! Another conceptual "no-win" for the patriots! The frame having shifted, we'll enter it by moving to the story of "boys 'n' toys".

> John Schlosser, coordinator of Colorado's Free
> Militia (claimed membership: 3,000), admits that
> his group's doomsday preparations sometimes

289

> amount to no more than "playing games in the
> woods." Militia members, sometimes with their
> families in tow, play hide-and-seek and capture
> the flag, all to build conditioning in case of an
> armed conflict.

Not "membership", but "claimed membership". We're to be wary of
these militia "claims", except when a militia coordinator inadvertently happens to follow the *Time* line, and therefore gets an "admits"
(not "claims") inserted before the report of his *Time*-echoing view
that these "doomsday preparations" are "games". Well, *Time*/Farley
is right after all! Look, they play "hide-and-seek" and "capture the
flag" — that proves the subsidiary *Time* frame is legitimate.

> When it comes to organization, however, the
> troops go high-tech. The militia movement, says
> Berlet, "is probably the first national movement
> organized and directed on the information high-
> way." Patriot talk shows, such as *The Informed
> Citizen*, a half-hour program broadcast on public-
> access TV in Northern California, spread the
> word that American values are under attack from
> within and without.

Looks like balancing, but watch out.

> Militias also communicate via the Patriot Net-
> work, a system of linked computer bulletin
> boards, and through postings in news groups on
> the Internet. One recent posting by a group call-
> ing itself the Pennsylvania Militia, more specifical-
> ly the F Company of the 9th Regiment, asked for
> "a few good men" to join up and "stand up to the
> forces of federal and world tyranny."

When patriots/militias communicate over "linked computer bulletin
boards", they don't exchange historical analysis of the Second
Amendment, revelations of government hijinks, or in-depth analyses
of media framing techniques. Rather, they use the power to communicate to recruit armies (and that doesn't surprise us, given the prior

discussion of the "heavy semiautomatic rifles" brigade). "F Company" calls up *F Troop,* a 60's television sitcom. Maybe this army is the "Keystone Kops."

> The patriot movement was galvanized by two events: the bloody face-off in rural Idaho between white separatist Randy Weaver and law-enforcement officials in 1992 and the fiery siege of the Waco, Texas, compound of cult leader David Koresh in 1993.

Balancing, but note that while Farley throws in the word "cult", he frames the event as a siege on "Koresh", and not the other people in the "compound". There WERE other people in the "compound" (house?).

> The violent confrontations helped convince many would-be militia members that the U.S. government was repressive as well as violently antigun and untrustworthy. "The Waco thing really woke me up," says Frank Swan, 36, a trucker who is a member of a militia in Montana. "They went in there and killed women and children."

Balancing (though we still don't know how many women and children were killed, nor the motivations for Koresh and his "followers". Farley spares us any dissertation of the factual background of the case). Maybe these people aren't nuts after all.

> Critics of the militias say the genuine concern on the part of patriots for second-amendment rights could, in many cases, turn into something more menacing. In October the Anti-Defamation League of B'nai B'rith issued a report titled *Armed and Dangerous* which charged that militias were "laying the groundwork for massive resistance to the Federal Government and its law-enforcement agencies."

Now, the counter-framing. Sure, these concerns are "genuine", but they could turn into "something more menacing". Turns out that these genuine concerns are just tools to carry out the real agenda of the patriot movement: they are to "[lay] the groundwork" for massive resistance to the Federal government. Our one last flirtation with the minus/plus frame just leads us back to "dangerous" again — it's how *Time* makes a lemon out of lemonade.

Note also that the Anti-Defamation League of B'nai B'rith, a Jewish organization, is opposed to this movement. Well, we all know what group was opposed to the Jews (it starts with an "N"). *Time* implies (in the same way it implies that a handful of patriots represents a larger movement) that one Jewish organization (note: not characterized as a "fringe" organization) speaks for Jews in general, with a very subtle painting of the larger patriot movement with a tainted brush, because supposedly all Jews are opposed to them (and we know who opposed the Jews, don't we?). This subtlety will now be made explicit.

> But most militia groups claim to be nonracial, nonpolitical outfits interested only in preserving the Constitution and core American values. Dean Compton, a real estate agent and California militia member, says members aren't consumed by ideology: "I still play with my kids. I still go to the movies. It's not all gloom and doom." Compton also says neo-Nazis and white supremacists were purged from his militia, and they're not welcome back: "If they're crazies, we don't want 'em."

Your subconscious thoughts of "Nazis" are now echoed in print. The "militia groups" (and by extension, the larger non-militia patriot movement) "claim to be" nonracial, but since they are composed of "white" men (as were the Nazis), this could not possibly be true. And we get yet another subconscious echo when we read Compton's quote, where we re-learn that the choice for patriots is only "play[ing] [games]" or "gloom and doom". So the subsidiary frame IS true after all. You can see how, for *Time*, "balancing" facts are just cakes to be iced with minus-value: in this case, a ton of it.

> But analyst Mike Reynolds of the Southern Poverty Law Center says some of the people

emerging as militia leaders have ties with hate-mongering groups. "They are being very canny about it," says Reynolds. "They aren't going around lighting torches and burning crosses at these meetings. They are using code words. Instead of talking about the Zionist occupation, they talk about the new world order. It's the same old stuff dressed up for the '90s."

Watch out for those false claims! Don't be fooled — these people are "canny". When they dress in three-piece suits and cite footnoted articles, this is just part of the act. Really, this is just camouflage, "code words" for the "same old stuff".

Note what *Time* has adroitly done here. We already knew that "General" Olson was illegitimate, as were the men in the "remote meadows", not to mention the ones carrying the "heavy semiautomatic rifles". Now *Time* tells us that when we meet a person in a three-piece suit (or on-line) who talks in the standard academic dialect, we're actually to see this individual as a smooth talker using "code words". So, the entire spectrum of members of the patriot movement, from alpha to omega, is SUSPECT. The message is clear:

THERE ARE NO LEGITIMATE MEMBERS OF THE PATRIOT MOVEMENT, NOT EVEN THE ONES WHO APPEAR LEGITIMATE! "You can't trust anyone!" *Time* sternly warns. Gosh, *Time*, you're starting to sound a little paranoid yourself! Better watch out, before those militia recruiters come after you to suck you into their Koresh-style cults.

> Militia recruiters have no shortage of fears to play on. Recently, members of the Militia of Michigan stopped by the Veterans of Foreign Wars meeting room in the town of L'Anse to scout for new members. The local timber and mining industries are fading, and an area Air Force base is set to close next year. Residents, looking in vain for new solutions to old problems, were good targets for the militia message. Said logger and school board member Sonny Thoren: "I can't tell the differ-

ence between Democrats and Republicans anymore."

"No shortage of fears to play on" — now that's objective reporting!
Since the "recruiters" are just "play[ing] on" fears, this proves this is
just a game, albeit a dangerous one. Can infantilized adults (who play
"hide-and-seek" and "capture the flag") really be trusted with arma-
ments? The people who receive information from these groups on
bulletin boards (their minds turned to Spam by threats of unemploy-
ment) better watch out — they're "targets". Oh, and by the way . . .
if YOU too "can't tell the difference between Democrats and Republicans anymore", better start worrying — that's one of the warning
signs of a mind turning to mush. You're becoming just like them!

> The patriots, to him, seemed to offer a clear alter-
> native. They had bold ideas and big guns. After
> the meeting, Thoren and four others stood next
> to a flag in the corner of the room, underneath a
> gun case filled with vintage M-1 rifles, and took
> the oath to join the militia. A new brigade was
> born.

38 words away from the word "targets", we find the word "guns",
which cements our subconscious thinking. Those "big guns" re-frame
those "bold ideas" — we're talking revolution here! Look out, everybody! Well, here's the good news: only about 5 million people read
this article. Now here's the bad news. Two weeks after this article
appeared, Phil Donahue did a show on this movement. Believe it or
not, Donahue's framing beamed to millions more people! Here were
some of the titles overlaid over the images of the men on the show as
they tried to talk over Donahue's incessant interruptions ("yeah",
"yeah", "yeah") and loaded questions:

READY TO SHOOT TO KEEP THEIR GUNS

MICHIGAN MILITIA PREPARING TO
FIGHT U.S. GOVERNMENT

ARE YOUR NEIGHBORS PREPARING TO
FIGHT OUR GOVERNMENT?

ARE AMERICANS CREATING THEIR OWN PRIVATE ARMIES?

OHIO UNORGANIZED MILITIA PREPARING TO FIGHT U.S. GOVERNMENT

This show also had a Jewish representative to argue against these people, and yes, Nazis were discussed. Perhaps the worst offense of this show was a digital card displayed on the screen, a card which was supposed to contain the text of the Second Amendment. Here is what was broadcast to over ten million Americans as the text of our written Constitution:

> A well-regulated militia being necessary to the security of a free state, the right to keep and bear arms shall not be infringed.

Check your copy of the Constitution, and see if YOU can find the missing words! Just a harmless error? A tiny boo-boo that somehow managed to slip past the producer? Somehow I doubt it.

FURTHER READING:

ON-LINE

MASS MEDIA 101
ftp.netcom.com /pub/kr/krusch/media.txt
A survival guide for the DisInformation Age, this 67-page article contains much hard evidence for media distortion — dozens of framing techniques are discussed (with examples), along with information "behind the scenes" (memoranda, laws, and what not) which serves to explain why this distortion of information is so pervasive.

THE ROLE OF FRAME ANALYSIS IN ENHANCING THE TRANSFER OF KNOWLEDGE
ftp.netcom.com /pub/kr/krusch/frame.dp
This paper contains extensive discussion of issues related to frame analysis, including schemas, encoding, and decoding.

OFF-LINE

The Whole World Is Watching, Gitlin (University of California: 1980)
The Persian Gulf TV War, Kellner (Westview: 1992)
Seeing Through the Media, Jeffords and Rabinovitz (Rutgers: 1994)
By Invitation Only, Croteau and Hoynes (Common Courage: 1994)
The Myth of Soviet Military Supremacy, Gervasi (Perennial: 1986)

LANGUAGE AND PSYCHOLOGY

Telling It Like It Isn't, Rothwell (Spectrum: 1982)
How We Know What Isn't So, Gilovich (Free Press: 1991)
Logic and Contemporary Rhetoric, Kahane (Wadsworth: 1980)
Metaphors We Live By, Lakoff and Johnson (U. of Chi.: 1980)
Teaching Thinking Skills, Baron and Sternberg (Freeman: 1987)
The Social Animal, Aronson (Freeman: 1980)
Thinking, Problem Solving, Cognition, Mayer (Freeman: 1992)

CD-ROM

Time Almanac, 1994. A superb collection of texts on which to practice media analysis, all downloadable to a word processor. The trick is to go for articles which are likely to be embedded with bias. You might try searching for terms like "Persian Gulf," "Gun control," "abortion," "Perot," "fringe group," etc.

The latest version of this article is archived at ftp.netcom.com, /pub/kr/krusch. This is version 1.4. Farley's reply to my article is archived at ftp.netcom.com /pub/kr/krusch/reply_to_frame.txt

Thanks to Drew Betz for posting the e-text.

AMERICAN POLICE STATE

Don't tread on Linda Thompson.
(Photo by C. T. Wemple.)

LINDA THOMPSON'S WAR

[A version of this article was featured in the October 11, 1994 issue of the *Village Voice*. When I completed a first draft, in May '94, Linda Thompson still vowed to march armed militiamen on Washington, D.C. in September of that year. By August, Thompson called off her march. But calling off her march revealed more than Thompson's bluster.

A whole new grassroots element had emerged from anti-gun control groups, strict Constitutionalists, and Libertarians: the so-called Patriot or Militia movement. Six months after the *Voice* article appeared, and the Murrah building went up in smoke, the militias had become a public pariah, a scapegoat for "domestic terrorism." Whether she is an *agent provocateur* or simply a concerned attorney, Linda Thompson played an integral — if questionable — role in the rise of Constitutional nationalists on the post Cold War stage. Many thanks are due Jim Redden for his invaluable help in putting this piece together, including flying to Indianapolis to interview Linda Thompson when she denied me access, claiming that I was CIA. After the article was printed, she informed people that I work for the Anti-Defamation League. Whatever works.]

> Most of the people with balls in this country late-
> ly seem to be women. — Linda Thompson

Speaking that good-old-boy drawl, the caller stammers a few words about a conspiracy even older than the John Birchers still around to talk about it — centuries old, as a matter of fact — waiting for that once-every-thousand-year moment, the new millennium, to impose Satan's New World Order. Like so many other callers these days lighting up the call buttons on talk radio, the good-old-boy is talking Revolution. A Second North American Revolution.

The talk show host, Art Bell, broadcasting at 2:30 am in the morning from his home studio in Pahrump, Nevada, breathes heavily. You might even call it a sigh. Several months ago he gave the patriot conspiracists a lot of airtime, particularly after Waco, but by now he is beginning to get concerned for his sanity. The panicked are calling in to spread rumors of apocalyptic desperation: ten thousand black males were either abducted or killed during the L.A. riots; gang members, deputized by the United Nations, are to be employed as mercenary armies to confiscate guns from citizens; a cabal of luciferian elitists will try to force the unwary to accept a subcutaneous barcode numbering 666, the proverbial "Mark of the Beast"; foreign U.N. troops will enforce dictatorial Presidential fiats, while resisters to the New World Order will be whisked off to FEMA-operated concentration camps.

"Boy oh boy," says Art Bell sarcastically. "You missed the black helicopters, the unmarked choppers that have got nothing better to do than scare the daylights out of good law 'biding citizens like yourself. Not to mention the Russian tanks rolling down American streets. A fax just came in here that told me about an Alaskan concentration camp, biggest in the world, so this fax says. What I want to know is, why do so many of you guys believe this stuff?"

∞ ∞ ∞

Every age has its own style of revolt. Haymarket and its mad bombers. Joe Hill and the Wobblies. Rock and psychedelic hysteria. With all the Woodstock nostalgia bruited about by the likes of *Time/Life*, it may be fair to wonder who the anti-government revolutionaries are these days. One thing is certain. It's not the longhairs — they're on MTV rocking the vote. Leftist activism confines itself to issues of sexuality and gender, while a self-described "dumpy broad from the Midwest" — Indianapolis attorney Linda Thompson — rattled the alarums for Revolution, 1990's style.

As "Acting Adjutant General of the Unorganized Militia of the U.S.A.," Thompson announced that she would command militiamen to march into Washington, D.C. on September 19, 1994. Her stated mission: hang congressional traitors (and their media lackeys) who refuse to abolish the Federal Reserve System, the Internal Revenue Service, the Brady Bill, and a laundry list of anti-constitutional horrors that horripilate the flesh of all good patriots.

Word of Thompson's "Ultimatum" spread like prairie fire among a certain restless demographic — those tens of thousands of orthodox constitutionalists who call themselves Patriots, Populists or Libertarians. On the Internet newsgroups alt.conspiracy, alt.politics.batf, talk.politics.guns, talk.politics.civil-liberty, "Are You Prepared for the Next American War?" became a heavily posted thread, discussing the feasibility of Linda Thompson's war. Would this woman actually lead her retinue, carrying rope, gibbet and musket, to Pennsylvania Avenue?

To the relief of the John Birch Society, which warned its members against the armed gambit, Linda Thompson called off her kamikaze campaign. But she has not given the New World Order any quarter. "We are at war right now," she portends. "Make no mistake about it."

If Linda Thompson's brinksmanship seems hysterical and over-wrought it befits the mood of the Patriots, a burgeoning movement largely — but certainly not altogether — composed of apocalyptic Christians who believe a cabal of evil internationalists are bringing the United States and its divinely-inspired Constitution under the heel of the godless New World Order.

The Patriot view of world events is not guided by a lack of information, but rather by a panic-stricken deluge of news, extrapolated by rumor and innuendo to fit a large, intricate and infinitely sinister conspiracy. Patriots are information junkies, combing newspapers, magazines, books, internet newsgroups, lawbooks, fax networks, railyards, gun shows, executive orders, and biblical concordances. But even though their information gathering seems indiscriminate, the Patriots raise legitimate questions ignored by the blithely apathetic. Privacy is quickly eroding; the crime bill provides draconian punishments for drug crimes and political dissidents; America is close to bankruptcy; over 80 Branch Davidians, including 17 children, were subjected to a crippling form of tear gas outlawed by the Geneva Convention and burned alive on Mount Carmel.

"It's the Wizard of Oz terrorism campaign," says Thompson tying in Waco to the New World Order conspiracy. "If you have a tank on your corner, it doesn't take much to get your compliance. Look at what they did in the Soviet Union. They kick one guy to smithereens, splatter his blood out in the neighborhood, terrorize everybody, and the rest of the neighbors whimper in the corner. That's the Wizard of Oz terrorism philosophy. Pay no attention to the man behind the curtain, it's the all-powerful Oz. ... I'm trying to beat that ... through educating people to the sheer fact that this Wizard of Oz stuff is garbage. United we stand, divided we fall."

Because she spends such long hours giving the scarecrows and cowardly lions a lot of information to chew on, Thompson has put aside her law practice to concentrate on her dissident activities. Thompson's Associated Electronic Network (AEN) computer bulletin board, echoed nationally on Fidonet, is daily filled with extraordinary helpings of news and chat. Her weekday diatribes on 5810 megahertz shortwave radio and guest shots on other radio programs have generated a vast amount of anti-Government publicity. In concert with dozens, maybe as many as one hundred patriot bulletin boards, and with the shortwave and AM radio programs of Chuck Harder, Tom Valentine and William Cooper, the Patriot message is reaching millions.

To the public at large, Thompson is best known for the video shockumentary *Waco: The Big Lie,* which became the watershed samizdat document of the past year, reaching hundreds of thousands of viewers on public access cable stations. At just 34 minutes in length, *Waco: The Big Lie* includes contested footage of a tank backing up from Ranch Apocalypse with what seems to be a burst of flame jetting out from the tank's boom, apparently making a lie out of the FBI's contention that the tanks merely delivered non-incendiary tear gas into the compound. Fearing the deleterious impact of Thompson's video, the Department of Justice spent several pages of its official report on Waco debunking her footage. *Waco: The Big Lie, Part II,* also making the rounds on the public access cable circuit, is Thompson's attempt to debunk the debunkers, taking on not only the Department of Justice report but also a mysterious public release from a private organization called the California Organization for Public Safety (COPS) which was taken up by *Soldier of Fortune* magazine to explain away the tank flames as merely a chunk of gypsum wallboard.

Professionally editing raw Ku-band satellite downloads topped with effective omniscient narration, *Waco: The Big Lie* is a get-the-bastards motivational wonder. The video is Linda Thompson's calling card and convincer, attracting turn-away crowds at speaking engagements in the South and Midwest. She described her typical audience on Chuck Harder's populist radio program back in February: "When I go talk around the country, I'm talking to groups of 3,000 to 5,000 people, everywhere I go. And these are not redneck, Bubba, crazy people. These are people that are, for the most part between 35 and 55 years old, middle-class Americans, across-the-board normal, everyday, average, tax-paying type citizens that are coming, that know the truth, that are doing everything they can to get the truth out. And I have received, at my office, no less than 200 to 400 letters every day. We get 300 phone calls every day. These are people that do know what's going on, and there is such a huge number of them out there that it's amazing to me that the media has completely ignored this. But they are!"

> We who love liberty more than security seek no quarrel with any man. But, neither will we wear the chains of subjugation. Take our weapons and we will take your life. Take warning, the line has been drawn. If blood is to be shed, let it begin here. Should the flames of violence consume us, history will mark for future generations the courage and passing of free men. If the Almighty grants an undeserving people mercy once again before the light flickers into darkness, free men and women will take their weapons in hand, place the point of the sword against the throat of the enemy and no quarter shall be given. — James Jarrett, from Linda Thompson's AEN computer bulletin board.

> There is no retreat, but in submission and slavery! Our chains are forged. Their clanking may be heard on the plains of Boston! The war is inevitable — and let it come! I repeat, sir, let it come! It is in vain, sir to extenuate the matter.

> Gentlemen may cry, peace, peace — but there is
> no peace. The war is actually begun! The next
> gale that sweeps from the north will bring to our
> ears the clash of resounding arms! Our brethren
> are already in the field! Why stand we here idle?
> What is it the gentlemen wish? What would they
> have? Is life so dear, or peace so sweet, as to be
> purchased at the price of chains and slavery.
> Forbid it, Almighty God — I know not what
> course others may take; but as for me, give me lib-
> erty or give me death! — Founding Father
> Patrick Henry, quoted on the AEN computer
> bulletin board.

Like most of the individuals who tune into her daily shortwave program, flock to her public speaking engagements and dial up her electronic bulletin board echo, Linda Thompson views Waco as certain
proof that the republic has been usurped by elite fascists. She admires
the Branch Davidians for standing up to the government, and believes
they were perfectly within their rights to defend themselves against
"armed tyrants." In Thompson's view, Koresh's clan was an innocent
target, a true church smeared by establishment propaganda and razed
to the ground to cover up establishment crimes.

> Make no mistake, the negative social stigma
> attached to the hippie movement by the media is
> now being pointed directly at us. Your perception
> of a hippie was formed by the media experts and
> will probably remain with you the rest of your life.
> Long after both of us are gone, whether we pre-
> vail or not, we will be thought of as red-necked,
> knuckle dragging, gun nuts. Or possibly much
> worse. — posted by a Christian Patriot on the
> AEN computer bulletin board.

The adoption of such rhetoric confounds pigeonholing of the Patriot
movement. So what are they? A spokesman for the Southern Poverty
Law Center confusedly tells us that Linda Thompson's American
Justice Federation is found on their 1993 hate group rap sheet under

the "tax protest" category. It's true that Thompson's AJF is a hate group — it hates policemen and bureaucrats — but it should be pointed out that Thompson discourages the posting of racist or anti-Semitic sentiments on her bulletin board, and invokes the Third Reich only as a pejorative, as in "The ATF are a bunch of Nazi bastards." Thompson's stylistic kinship with '60's radicalism doesn't end with the spelling of Clinton's name with a K. Like the Weathermen, Thompson and her supporters freely discuss armed conflict with the "police state." Posted on her bulletin board are fictitious scenarios, reminiscent of the white supremacist wet dream *The Turner Diaries,* of armed battles between patriot militias and the government.

∞ ∞ ∞

Conservatism could have been invented in Indianapolis. Tree-lined streets, grassy parks and well-preserved neighborhoods, milquetoast and mayonnaise, an Imperium of bland stolidity. The ghetto, relatively small, is relegated to a containable area on the "other side of the tracks." In its previous eight elections Indianapolis has voted in a Republican mayor. It is the sort of place that gives Dan and Marilyn Quayle comfort and nurture. It is also the nerve center of Linda Thompson's war.

Sandwiched between a Domino's Pizza and an Italian take-out restaurant in a depressingly generic single-story mini-mall, Linda Thompson's American Justice Federation battles for the soul of the free world. In the front window Adolf Hitler throws out a stiff armed *sieg heil.* "All in Favor of Gun Control, Raise Your Hand," reads the caption. Red, white and blue bumper stickers crowd the remaining window space.

JOIN THE MILITIA / GIVE ME LIBERTY OR GIVE ME DEATH / BAN GUNS. MAKE THE STREETS SAFE FOR A GOVERNMENT TAKEOVER / YOUR GUN PERMIT: THE SECOND AMENDMENT / IS YOUR CHURCH ATF APPROVED? / REMEMBER WACO: YOU ARE NEXT! / SUPPORT THE MILITIA: IF YOU CAN'T JOIN OR FIGHT, LEAVE FOOD ON THE PORCH. / FEAR

THE GOVERNMENT THAT FEARS YOUR
GUNS / DICTATORS LOVE GUN CONTROL

Within these conventional low-rent law offices hang three versions of Revolutionary War era "Don't Tread on Me" flags. Six-full time employees or volunteers (Thompson won't say for sure) monitor 20 phone lines that are used for voice mail, fax machines, and the AJF bulletin board. A boy, perhaps 11 or 12, fill orders for videos, stickers, militia information, post cards, "traitor files" (on the Clintons, the Council on Foreign Relations, and patriot enemies), and the cassette recordings of patriot folksinger Carl Klang, featuring the songs "It's Dangerous (To be Right When the Government is Wrong)" and "17 Little Children."

Listening to Indianapolis talk radio, one begins to wonder why the city's patriots are gripped by fear. On AM 950, Stan Solomon inveighs against gays for the AIDS epidemic and blacks for being too violent. But unlike the orotund Rush Limbaugh, he's also attacked federal police agencies for Waco, and was at least, in part, fired by the Indianapolis FM station WIBC for having Linda Thompson appear as a guest "too often."

"Linda believes everything she's told, and that the time to resist the government is now or never," says Solomon. "But if only eighty percent of what she's hearing is true — she's right."

With graying hair, neatly trimmed beard, and a silver semi-automatic shoved inside his belt, the constantly in-motion Solomon discusses plans to install a mainframe computer to link all sorts of right-wing groups and individuals; he's already collected 27,000 names for the database. "The government is warning against religious fanatics with guns, but this country was founded by religious fanatics with guns," says Solomon, repeating a popular Patriot mantra.

Last spring, Indianapolis' weekly alternative paper, *Nuvo,* ran an article by black community activist Richard Bottoms on racist bulletin boards, and singled out Linda Thompson's "Motherboard" as tolerating a certain kind of cyberhate. Convinced that Thompson's bulletin board is her most potent propaganda tool, Bottoms asked rhetorically, "How many people were in the Weather Underground in the '60s? Dozens, maybe. But now thousands of people with guns are talking to each other about fighting the government. I'm not really worried about a mass uprising, but about the loner who decides it's time to kill the mayor."

"It's my feeling that Linda Thompson wants to be the Margaret Thatcher of the far right — the iron lady that everyone looks to for advice," says *Nuvo* editor Steve Hammer. Hammer was exchanging e-mail with Thompson on her bulletin board at the time Richard Bottoms' article appeared in his newspaper, and was bitterly flamed for what Thompson considered a smear job. "Everything [Linda Thompson] says," says Hammer, "she believes on some level. If she believes something, she'll say it, but I think down the line she's headed for a violent confrontation with somebody. ... Indiana breeds weird, violent people. Jim Jones started here. Charles Manson was a product of the state's juvenile justice system. Linda Thompson is very much a product of her state, and that may be the scariest thing of all."

In person, Linda Thompson looks like Madge the manicurist, and that is perhaps a source of her credibility and comfort to the patriot common folk. But similarities to the lumpenproletariat end there. According to her resumé, Thompson served in the Army between 1974 and 1978, including a stint as "Assistant to the U.S. Army Commanding General, NATO, Allied Forces Central Europe" with a "Cosmic Top Secret/Atomal security clearance." Interestingly, her military training included an "Adjutant General Officer Basic Course"; Thompson signed her Ultimatum to Congress as "Acting Adjutant General" of the Unorganized Militia. Thompson's military career did not end with her Honorable Discharge in 1978, but continued for another decade in the Army Reserve. After investigating her military record, an Indianapolis television news station attempted to discredit Thompson with the charge that she had not served as an "assistant" to the commanding general, but simply as a secretary. The news station may have been better advised to put Thompson's claims of "expert marksmanship" to the test.

For all her venom unleashed at the federal police, Linda Thompson looks nostalgically on her Vietnam War-era career, and reserves a

warm place in her heart for the army and local cops. In the preamble
to her Ultimatum to Congress, Linda Thompson writes:

> We have support from many state, city and coun-
> ty police agencies and US military. This is the
> country and the Constitution, that all of us have
> sworn to uphold and defend against all enemies,
> and the enemies are corrupt leaders who have
> duped our police into being cannon fodder — to
> disarm America — while these same corrupt lead-
> ers have reduced our Army's strength from 18
> divisions to 11, and sent them out of the country,
> to weaken our numbers.

After 14 years with the army, Thompson started her private practice
in 1989, concentrating on cases involving criminal and constitutional
law. Her highest profile case involved defending manufacturers of
grow light fixtures from seizures under George Bush's War on Drugs.

Thompson's hatred for federal police combined with her love for the
military is as enigmatic as her legal defense of accused "pot growers"
amidst all the anti-abortion rhetoric that Thompson dishes out on her
daily shortwave radio show. But Thompson's schizoid ideology cannot be fully explained by strict readings of the Constitution. Her
stand against abortion may be a recent development. A disgruntled
follower, complaining on Thompson's computer bulletin board about
Thompson's "flip-flop" on abortion, recalls that Linda once wrote,
"fetuses are parasites" and "pro-lifers are racists wanting more white
babies to adopt." Responding to the dismayed pro-lifer, Thompson
didn't deny making those characteristically rash comments. But now,
after having viewed pro-life horror literature, showing abortion doctors sucking the brains out of third-trimester fetuses, Thompson
claims, "I've always been against abortion, but nobody ever asked my
opinion." In an interview, Linda remembers falling in love with Al,
her husband of ten years, by trading fannish remarks about the blas-
phemous/scatological musician Frank Zappa on a computer board.
Although Linda's three teenage children by a previous marriage are
schooled in the anti-Government Indianapolis Baptist Temple, Pastor

Greg Dixon reports that the Thompsons rarely if ever attend church services there.

It is difficult to imagine earthy Linda Thompson sitting through a stuffy church service when she could be taunting pacifists on her bulletin board as "dickless cowards." Admirers who think they can perhaps "change the system from within," are the recipients of stinging ripostes. "Working through 'the system' is absolutely useless," wrote Linda Thompson on her bulletin board. "It is controlled by the enemy. If you don't know enough to know that, then start reading." Those who dared to question the strategy of her armed march on D.C., were dismissed as disinformation agents, *agents provocateur* and traitors. This elaborate game of chicken forced a wide swath of patriots to hide behind their bible quotations that instructed them not to follow a woman to battle.

All the furor played into the hands of the Acting Adjutant General of the Unorganized Militia of the United States of America. She floated the concept of a confrontational action, and the patriots bit. Big time. Outsiders began to ask: What the hell is the Unorganized Militia? How many of them are there? Do they jump at Linda Thompson's command?

Militias composed of civilians (called "unorganized" to distinguish them from organized militias like the National Guard) do in fact exist, and are growing by the day. None are directly affiliated with Linda Thompson or American Justice Federation, though the Michigan militia, named the "Wolverines," are frequent posters on her bulletin board. Word on the militias is getting out. A feature article in the August 15, 1994 edition of *U.S. News and World Report* profiled the Montana militias with their usual pry-the-guns-out-of-my-cold-dead-hands rap. In an unusual twist, Planned Parenthood presented a video to the Department of Justice in August, 1994, because a man active in the anti-abortion movement (Jon Salvi) also advocated milita-type sentiments.

The militias are largely a response by citizens to gun control measures, and are based upon readings of the Second Amendment and other constitutional provisions from the early days of the country — provisions meant to allow governors to call up citizens for civil defense.

Most of these contemporary militias are nothing more than social clubs of perhaps a dozen individuals who swear to protect the Constitution from enemies foreign and domestic, and enjoy marching formations through a public park. There have been only halting efforts to organize militias on a statewide level. No national organization exists.

It was Linda Thompson's idea to transform these Second Amendment social clubs into something akin to latter-day Minutemen. Thompson's Ultimatum was formulated without the various militias' knowledge or consent. While plans for the armed march were in full flower, none of the dozen militiamen interviewed for this article thought the confrontation was a good idea. Not one.

In order to log on to Thompson's "Motherboard," one must type in one's name, address, phone number, vow to battle the wicked, and answer questions regarding the supply of a safe house, guns or ammunition — damning evidence if the government decided to use this information in a conspiracy or RICO charge against patriots. And although Thompson boasts that the FBI is likely bugging her bulletin board, she attacks other patriot bulletin boards as being a method for the government to suck up names, addresses and phone numbers.

When she first proposed her Ultimatum, many people asked: "Linda Thompson, kook or spook?" In the 1960s, FBI COINTELPRO operations placed *agents provocateur* in the Black Panthers, SDS, MOVE and the Minutemen in order to goad those groups into divisive and extreme actions that would provoke a heavy-handed police reaction. Lots of people squawked about the armed march bringing on Martial Law and total disarmament. Now that she's called off her Ultimatum, the spook charge wilts under scrutiny, though nagging questions remain.

Thompson is quick to call most Patriot/Populist leaders and organizations "government fronts," particularly if they publicly disagree with her.

The weekly conspiracy tabloid *The Spotlight* published by the right-wing, anti-Zionist Liberty Lobby peddled the Waco video, highlighting Thompson in a double-truck interview. But after getting wind of her armed march, the periodical discouraged its readers from taking part in it. Thompson is now convinced the newspaper is a "government operation." Ditto the John Birch Society, which expressed a negative view of Thompson's planned march in a hand-wringing position paper. The American Patriot Fax Network, which disseminates news to approximately one thousand Patriot fax machines nationally, is characterized by Thompson as a government con-job. Similarly, Thompson believes *Contact,* the weirdo alien-channeling Patriot newspaper is a CIA front. Populist Presidential candidate Bo Gritz, radio host Ron Engleman, and Branch Davidian defenders Ron Cole and Gary Hunt are all government stooges, contends Linda Thompson.

It's rare to hear Thompson say a good word about anybody in the Patriot or Populist hierarchy, save for a very peculiar exception: author and radio personality William Cooper. Linda Thompson calls William Cooper "one of the best patriots in the country" and recommends Cooper's book, *Behold a Pale Horse,* as essential reading. She took time off from her busy schedule to team up with Cooper for a five day August conference in Arizona that instructed paying students on the gathering of intelligence and the care and feeding of long-range rifles. But Cooper says so many outlandish things that he merited an entire chapter in Donna Kossy's *Kooks.* Among other consistently astonishing claims, Cooper tells us space aliens signed a treaty with President Eisenhower that formally allowed them to abduct humans in exchange for technological advice, and that 600 aliens work hand-in-glove with scientists and CIA agents at the Groom Lake, Nevada, defense facility. Cooper's conspiratorial tome, *Behold A Pale Horse,* includes a reprint of the hoax document, *Protocols of the Elders of Zion,* with instructions to substitute "Illuminati" for "Jews" and "Cattle" for "Goyim." Recently Cooper has propounded the notion that the U.S. government has bombarded Jupiter with plutonium explosions — the true origin of the Shoemaker-Levy comet — a theory that Linda Thompson has echoed on her bulletin board.

After she returned to Indianapolis from Cooper's conference, Linda Thompson called off the September 19 armed march on Washington. Some followers thought it was a hoax, since the encryption that fol-

311

lowed the announcement as "verification" was not Linda's signature, but this was, alas, only a slip-up.

Thompson explained the about-face as a I-know-what's-best-for-all-of-you Machiavellian strategy: "Has anything," she writes, "in the history of this country, since the Revolutionary War, accomplished this much towards actually solving our current problems, mobilized so many, so quickly or so effectively, or done so much to literally scare the absolute bejeebers out of the opposition, as the public announcement, by a dumpy broad in Indianapolis, that, enough is enough, we are going to arrest the traitors, man the weapons?"

Some supporters go ape on the AEN board:

> HA HA HA HA HO HO HO HO HA! Thanx Linda, for brightening my day. You are so totally, completely full of shit that it's pathetic. Just a few days ago you blasted a caller, basically calling him a pussy and challenging him to DO SOME-THING and now you say that all along, you weren't planning to go. ... So now you're telling people that you've lied to them all of this time and you expect them to believe ANYTHING you say from now on.

Linda Thompson continues to SYSOP her bulletin board, host a shortwave program, and sell videotapes, but refrains from announcing any future coup d'etat. "I accomplished what I intended to accomplish," explains Thompson about her blown credibility. "If I have to spit quarters naked in the town square to get people to listen, that's what I'll do. If my credibility was the issue, then I wouldn't have done any of this." (For the first time she has started to beg contributions from her supporters, announcing monthly expenses as being close to $12,000, not including her own salary.)

The most interesting fallout from Thompson's call-to-arms were strange offers she received of neutron bombs, stinger missiles and all sorts of exotic weaponry by shadowy thugs. "A group of scientists [had] some very interesting weaponry that was developed by black op budgets. They're no longer with black ops and are kind of independent entrepreneurs, I guess you'd say. One had a real interesting weapons that I don't think is well-known, actually. It's an electromagnetically operated laser type of weapon... It's kind of a damning statement of the condition of the world that these folks could be out trying to sell this stuff to every Tom, Dick and Harry on the street."

Neutron bombs? Stinger missiles? I hear a Hollywood screenwriter making a pitch. "A bunch of flag-wavers from Indianapolis discover a government plot to kill all the good Christians. You know, *Red Dawn meets Mad Max in the year 2000.*"

∞ ∞ ∞

At AJF headquarters, Linda Thompson pops a video cassette into a VCR. "This video more than anything else I've done," says Thompson, "shows where I stand and what I believe." To Carl Klang's "Seventeen Little Children," with its "Puff the Magic Dragon" melody, snapshots of Branch Davidian children are intercut with a little blond boy who places daisies on tiny graves marked with homemade crosses.

Just in case you don't remember
Let me jog your memory
In a church they called the Waco Compound
Back in April '93
Seventeen little children
All so helpless and so small
Died a senseless death of gas and flames
How many names can you recall?
Seventeen little children
Don't it make you wonder why
Seventeen little children
How could they deserve to die?
Maybe we should stop and ask ourselves
Have we become so blind?
Seventeen little children
Finally open up your mind.
How did you sleep last night Bill Clinton
Tell me did you feel their pain?
Seventeen little children

Cried out and perished in the flames
Attorney General Janet Reno
I accept your offer to resign
How can you stand for law and order now
When you won't answer to your crimes?
Seventeen little children ...

The video is pure corn, but it's affecting nonetheless. As the names of dead Branch Davidians scroll on screen at the end of the video, tears well up in Linda Thompson's eyes. No crocodile can cry this well.

A memorial for the Branch Davidians was proposed on Thompson's bulletin board by an AJF member. There is no better illustration of the Patriot mind:

I think the memorial should be designed to elicit responses of OUTRAGE at the murder of innocent children, SHOCK people out of their apathy, and SHAME them for standing by and doing nothing. Instead of making it look like an ad for a Rambo movie, let's make it a representation of people screaming out in pain and confusion, children crying for their parents, parents holding their children tight, with expressions of total despair. A testimony to their helplessness. Something that would break even the hardest hearted.

... I have an image in my mind of a portion of wall, the corner of a room, with a mother crouched in a corner, holding a child, while another child lies dead in rubble scattered on the floor in front of them. ... The tops of the walls are jagged and burnt. A ruins type of look. The mother is sitting crouched in the corner with her child, the floor in front of her is scattered with big chunks of concrete, and smaller pieces of debris, with a child laying face down among them. The mother is crying out to the child, leaning out and reaching her arm out desperately, but it is obvious the child cannot hear and will not get up and run to its mother.

... I also think the memorial should be made to stink somehow, a very strong odor of something burnt and dead. That would stay in people's minds for a long time, and cause an immediate gut-level reaction.

I also think their [sic] should be a testimony to their religious beliefs:

"And I looked, and behold a pale horse: and his name that sat on him was Death, and Hell followed with him. And power was given unto them over the fourth part of the earth, to kill with sword, and with hunger, and with death, and with the beasts of the earth. And when he had opened the fifth seal, I saw under the altar the souls of them that were slain for the word of God, and for the testimony which they held:

"And they cried with a loud voice, saying, How long, O Lord, holy and true, dost thou not judge and avenge our blood on them that dwell in the earth?" — Revelations 6:8-10

Many patriots responded enthusiastically to the memorial concept, adding their own gruesome details, such as adding casts of seventeen children, buried head-first into the ground.

America Under Siege is Linda Thompson's just-completed video project, an attempt to describe and document her New World Order conspiracy theory. Here are shots of pesky black helicopters, the spy cameras on highway lightpoles, the FEMA concentration camps disguised as Amtrak repair yards and the stickers on the back of road signs that lead U.N. troops to the concentration camps — all being set up to suppress armed uprisings when international bankers bankrupt the economy. The video is the familiar mix of amateur video clips, personal testimonies and news footage used to create a baffling but ominous view of the future.

In battling the New World Order, the damnedest things seem to happen to Linda Thompson. Electronic sweepers find bugs on the phone lines, the mail is drenched in fish juice, UPS men ask to pee at the office, unmarked cars buzz her on freeways, electrical burps short out all the appliances at home, wolverines growl in her backyard, strange burns appear on one breast, bullets whizz by at all hours, a guy with a distinct New Orleans accent calls and asks, "Why ain't you dead yet, darling?" But Thompson is, at least, philosophically secure. "Mentally you make that adjustment," Linda says, "you just say that they can have all [my belongings], I don't care, then you're free, you're really free. Remember Janis Joplin's line, 'freedom's just another line for nothing left to lose.' That's actually very true. If you don't care about your stuff, nobody can make you do things you don't want to do."

Oh ... about those black helicopters Thompson is fond of talking about: White House Press Corps reporter Sarah McClendon has just received confirmation from Army Public Affairs that a Black Helicopter Unit, headquartered at Fort Campbell, Kentucky, is currently equipped to do a lot of "low flying country surveillance" as part of a three billion dollar a year domestic counter-terrorism campaign.

Terrorism? In Kentucky? Now that the Cold War is over, it seems the U.S. Army has surveyed its enemy, and decided, like Pogo Possum, that it is us.

Linda Thompson's "Ultimatum"

All MILITIA units will convene in Washington, D.C. the second full week that the Congress is in session in September. All units will be armed and prepared to enforce this mandate. This is exactly what it sounds like.

NOTE:
MILITIA UNITS MUST WEAR IDENTIFYING INSIGNIA.

If you wear a military insignia identifying you as a member of a military unit, if captured, you must be treated as a Prisoner of War, not as a criminal arrestee, by law.

We have five months to get in shape and be prepared to restore this country's liberty. Mentally and physically, we must be ready, willing, and able, to do the job.

I have personally signed the ultimatum to be delivered to Congress, as John Hancock said, in handwriting so large that the King cannot mistake my identity. No other persons are or will be identified.

A copy of the ultimatum follows in the next message.

An additional initiative includes the delivery of signed Declarations of Independence to the White House on the day the militia convenes in Washington, D.C. in September.

These Declarations are as follows in the next message. Circulate these Declarations for signature throughout the country immediately.

We will be airdropping these blank Declarations, as well as leaflets detailing the militia information, and a point paper on what this is all about, throughout the country, from airplanes, at churches, gun shows, etc.

Please do the same, immediately.

More pilot volunteers, printers, and funding for the distribution of the Declaration of Independence is needed.

Whether I am arrested or killed in the interim has no bearing on the preparations of the militia units or the Declarations of Independence throughout this country.

Proceed as planned, plan accordingly, and God bless us all.

Linda Thompson
Acting Adjutant General UMUS,
pursuant to 10 USC 311
Articles I and II, Bill of Rights,
Constitution of the United States of America

* Forwarded from "AEN_NEWS"

* Originally by Linda Thompson

* Originally dated 17 Apr 1994, 18:20

A copy of this ultimatum is being delivered this week to each member of the U.S. House of Representatives and U.S. Senate, as well as to all national media.

ULTIMATUM

WHEREAS, the federal government of the United States of America is constrained by the law of the United States Constitution, the Supreme law of this country, to limited jurisdiction, and limited power; and

WHEREAS, the federal government of the United States of America, through unlawful Executive Orders, and through legislation passed without quorum and without proper ratification or otherwise unlawfully enacted under mere color of law by members of the legislative branch, have usurped the Constitutional authority of the sovereign states and sovereign citizens of this country, and laws which are unlawful and unconstitutional have been enacted in voluminous number which have outrageously exceeded the boundaries of law and decency; and

WHEREAS, the people of this country have been exploited and subjugated to an unlawful authority by an unlawful system of loans from a private banking institution, known as the Federal Reserve, and been forced, even at gunpoint, to submit to an unlawful federal income tax which is not and never has been within the authority of the federal government to enact or enforce, all to the benefit of private individuals and corporations at the expense of the liberty, lives, and property of the citizens of this nation; and

WHEREAS, persons acting under color of law as federal agents, under the direction of those claiming to be elected officials operating under color of law, sworn to uphold and defend the Constitution of the United States, have infringed upon the rights of citizens to keep and bear arms, have conducted unlawful warrantless house to house searches and seizures, have assaulted and killed sovereign citizens of this country on the false pretense of "gun control," "child abuse," "the war on drugs" and a plethora of unlawful statutes enacted to unlawfully control the lives and liberty of the citizens of this country;

WHEREAS, elections are now controlled through the power of committees and lobbies wielding the most money to obtain electoral votes or sway the nomination of candidates and persuade the enactment of legislation that has made it impossible for the common citizen to participate as a candidate in an election or for the vote of the common citizen to be meaningful; and

WHEREAS, through an unconstitutional and unlawfully enacted "income tax," the federal government has created a "carrot and stick" that has seduced and coerced the elected officials of the several states to submit to the unlawful incursion of the federal government and its agents into the sovereign territory of each state, as a trade off for the receipt of these ill gotten proceeds;

Therefore, YOU ARE COMMANDED to uphold your oath and duty to the citizens of this country, to uphold the Constitution and the rights of the citizens of this country, and in so doing, you are commanded to personally initiate legislation and do all things necessary to:

REPEAL the Fourteenth, Sixteenth, and Seventeenth Amendments to the Constitution of the United States and to publicly acknowledge that the federal government has no jurisdiction to make or enforce criminal laws outside its territories, limited to the area of Washington, D.C., and the property and territories actually owned by the United States, which does not include any State within the several states of the united states, and

REPEAL the Brady Bill and NAFTA;

REPEAL the Drug Interdiction Act and any laws which allow the use of military equipment or military personnel against United States citizens. Presently, these laws provide a backdoor method to fund "national guard" and "drug enforcement" using military troops and equipment against U.S. citizens, while claiming these aren't "really" military troops, they are "merely" national guard, or worse, "federal law enforcement," but all are trained in military tactics, possess military weapons, and military equipment. These laws must be repealed and you must publicly acknowledge that the federal government may not, through any means, use military force, weapons, or equipment against any person on U.S. soil or upon the soil of any sovereign state, except in the event of an actual invasion by troops of a foreign country within the boundaries of the United States of America, and only then, against such foreign troops, not citizens or residents of this country; and

IMMEDIATELY remove any and all foreign troops and equipment and to immediately identify each and every federal military troop and federal law enforcement or tax enforcement agent and all equipment now located within the boundaries of any and every state, including all assets of military or task force "special operations" units, CIA, NSA, or any other covert law enforcement, quasi-law enforcement or military agency or activity; and

DECLARE that the United States of America is not operating under the authority of the United Nations or if it is, to immediately renounce and revoke any and all agreements binding the United States to such authority; and

DECLARE the federal debt to the Federal Reserve null and void, unconstitutional, and without effect and order that currency no longer be printed by the Federal Reserve or any entity other than the Treasury of the United States, backed by gold within the possession of the United States; and

DECLARE that the federal government does not now have and never has had the legal authority to enact or enforce criminal laws outside the area of Washington, D.C., or outside its territories or its own property, such as military bases, and never upon the soil of any sovereign state, and that all such laws are null and void and without effect;

CONVENE a full Congressional inquiry, to be conducted publicly, by an independent prosecutor selected from a person who has no association in any way whatsoever with any agency of the federal government, into the events in Waco, Texas, from February 28, 1993 through the present, at the property known as Mt. Carmel, with the special prosecutor to have the full power to convene a grand jury from the citizens of all the 50 states, obtain indictments, and issue subpoenas duces tecum and subpoenas for testimony before a grand jury, and to prosecute any and all persons, regardless of their position in government, for any crimes for which a true bill of indictment is returned.

NOTICE: You have until 8:00 a.m., September 19, 1994, the Monday following the second full week that the Congress reconvenes in September, to personally initiate legislation to this effect and to do all things necessary to effect this legislation and the restoration of a Constitutional government within this country.

IF you do not personally and publicly attend to these demands, you will be identified as a Traitor, and you will be brought up on charges for Treason before a Court of the Citizens of this Country.

> Linda D. Thompson
> Acting Adjutant General
> Unorganized Militia of the United States of America

Postcard, with commentary, from Thompson's
American Justice Federation.

Top Left — Child standing out front during ATF raid.

Top Center — ATF beginning their military-style assault.

Top Right — ATF agent shooting at his own men

Center Left — Military helicopter equipped with .50 caliber machine gun used during the siege.

Center — FBI sniper's nest outside Mt. Carmel.

Center Right — Flame-throwing tank.

Bottom Left — Only petroleum-based fuel can make this black smoke.

Bottom Center — Mt. Carmel after the fire and before it was bull-dozed.

Bottom Right — ATF victory flag.

NEWSPAPER

April 24, 1995

Advertising Age

Crain's International Newspaper of Marketing • In Two Sections • Section 1• $3.00 • In Canada $3.50 ♻ Printed on recycled paper

NEWSPAPERS
Feeling the paper cost bite
Special Report follows Page 24

The End OF Innocence

By James Brady

Half a century ago Rodgers & Hammerstein, as they usually did, caught the mood of an innocent American heartland, grasped its spirit, got it right. Their words and their music still today tell us the kind of country this once was and in ways still is, the sort of people we are, our capacity for wonder, our confidence that no matter how bleak it looks, somehow everything will turn out.

Listen to the lyrics. Listen

"Oklahoma! Where the wind comes sweepin' down the plain/ And the wavin' wheat can sure smell sweet/ When the wind comes right behind the rain."

Last Wednesday morning in Oklahoma City rather
(Continued on next page)

INSIDE

■ **"Invisible enemy":** Exclusive Shapiro survey compares consumer reaction now and during Persian Gulf War. **Page 3.**

■ **"Fear and stereotyping":** Arab community in U.S. responds to media coverage of bombing. **Page 4.**

■ **"Prolonged mourning, aftermath of grieving":** Business as usual shattered for Oklahoma City ad community. **Page 43.**

■ **"Anytown USA":** Foreign media report on the bomb that ended the complacency. **Page 4.**

■ **"America has a gaping wound":** But the carnage in Oklahoma City will galvanize us. **Editorial, Page 18.**

■ **"Loose lips sink ships":** How about stirring public with World War II theme? **Page 42.**

■ **"This changes nothing":** Bob Garfield says Americans will let their guard down again. **Page 43.**

FINDING OUR WAY OUT OF
OKLAHOMA

Ken Stern of the American Jewish Committee faxes a special warning to "members of the press, AJCers, legislators, prosecutors, attorneys general, federal officials," regarding a possible terrorist attack that will strike the U.S. on "April 19 ... the anniversary of Waco ... THE KEY event for the militias, and for the hard core April 20 is Hitler's birthday." The page-long communique is received by federal Judge Redden of Portland, Oregon on April 10, '95, a prophetic week prior to the bombing of the Murrah building.

Judge Wayne Alley, whose office is located directly across the street from the devastated Alfred P. Murrah building, tells a reporter that "security officials" warned him to take "special precautions" several days prior to the April 19 bomb blast. Reported April 20 in the Portland *Oregonian*, Judge Alley's warning is never again mentioned even when it's reported that he has been assigned the case.

Edye Smith, whose two children died in the Oklahoma City bombing, is interviewed by CNN correspondent Gary Tuchman on May 23, '95, the day FEMA officials bring down the ruins of the Murrah building. The childless mother tells Tuchman she was told to "keep your mouth shut, don't talk about it," when she asked officials why BATF agents were "given the day off" on April 19. Although we're told that the BATF was the primary target of the bombing, which kills and maims hundreds, no BATF officer suffers injury in the attack.

> I am an American military man, and I can tell you categorically that if one of you militia drones or one of your crackpot units started any kind of half-witted shooting war, that I would unhesitatingly blow all of your asses into the netherworld. Not even one split second of hesitation, because

you're goofy, dangerous examples of twisted delayed adolescence..." [Post taken from the internet newsgroup "misc.activism.militia"]

SETTING MINDS AGAINST TERRORISM

"Setting Minds Against Terrorism" was the headline of an article relegated to the back pages of the April 24, 1995 "terrorism" issue of *Advertising Age*. Though its placement would seem to indicate that news, advertising and public relations executives might consider its content filler-like or possibly redundant, the article's implications are, to my mind, startling.

In the bloodless manner of the faceless hack, author Joe Mandese reveals how propaganda, here called "public policy," and mind control, here called "behavioral science,"[1] is cooked up by high-level "policy makers" in the National Security Council, and then passed down to the CIA and FBI for dissemination through Madison Avenue and onwards through print and electronic media.

Mandese's bureaucratese is designed to lull the outsider to sleep, but translate his article into plain language and one is left with a schematic diagram of how the media juggernaut collaborates with the highest levels of government intelligence to decide how and where the sheep are to be herded.

Notice that the executives Mandese interviews are not interested in relaying or even cushioning the truth, but how to best tell a lie in order that U.S. subjects will regard the government as a loving benevolent entity. It's not 1995, it's 1984. This isn't the New World Order, it's *Brave New World*.

"There used to be a day when Americans looked around and reported suspicious things to the FBI, or the local police," says Bob Dilenschneider, president of the Dilenschneider Group in the final paragraph of Mandese's article. He continues, devoid of irony. "Of late, [turning in suspicious characters to the FBI] has been regarded as Big Brother is watching, and carries the overtones of a fascist state. We have to get back to the thinking that the police are there to help us and the FBI is there to protect us."

Despite all the hoary lies told about our "free press" and "objective journalism," the *Advertising Age* article reveals how the media "implements strategies" instead of reporting the facts. Mandese's article asks "how shall the government be served?" rather than "how shall citizens be served by their public servants?" Mandese suggests that brain massage can best be accomplished by ad hoc committees comprised of marketing experts and intelligence agencies. The Persian Gulf War seemed like a dress rehearsal in media's lockstep goosestep with the NSA. Oklahoma City is further proof of capitalism's cooperative Total War against the consumerist mind. For another precedent of media-approved or media-created foreign escapades, see history books on the Spanish-American conflict, known as Hearst's War.

When the *Los Angeles Times* building burned in 1910, killing dozens of printers and other low-level workers, the nascent labor movement was buried by *agents provocateur* from the Burns Detective Agency working behind-the-scenes for *Times'* owner, General Otis. The day his building exploded, General Otis and staff had previously fled the office. One day earlier, General Otis made sure to raise his insurance premium. Though workers complained of a bad gas smell, nothing was done to correct the problem. Despite a sterling defense by Clarence Darrow and labor hero Job Harriman, the blame fell to the McNamara brothers, declared guilty by the best jury money could buy. Shedding crocodile tears for the victims of the fire, General Otis had his pompous prose chiseled into a monument purchased by insurance money, while he built himself a great new building on the present site of the *Times*.2

Advertising Age's paradigm for creating the proper framing around events is nothing new. Christopher Simpson's *Science of Coercion* (Oxford University Press, 1994) tells us how private corporations, foundations, and universities intermingle with government to create an interlocking network in which capitalist propaganda could be disseminated.

Fifty years ago Assistant Secretary of War John J. McCloy established "Psychological Warfare" as a "highly secret" branch of the War Department. According to Simpson's book, McCloy is "probably better known today for his later work as U.S. high commissioner in

Germany, chairman of the Chase Bank, member of the *Warren Commission* [my emphasis], and related posts." Though his book stops short of J.F.K.'s Kennedy assassination, *Science of Coercion* establishes beyond the shadow of a doubt that private think tanks and University tenured social scientists advised policy-makers and police agencies how to better deploy Psy War propaganda.

Not only do Psy War units inhabit the Pentagon, but they also perform important roles in the NSA, FBI, CIA and NSC, as well as the ATF, Secret Service, U.S. Marshal Department, et al. White House Press Corps journalist Sarah McClendon has even received official confirmation that Psy War receives a slice of a $3 billion/year domestic anti-terrorism program created in 1987 during the Reagan Administration. Was this expensive program ever spoken of in news media during the debate on the 1995 Anti-Terrorism Act? Not anyplace I can find.[3]

The Psy War payroll extends to private corporations like Wackenhut, Rand and TRW. Private corporations are even less subject to oversight than their brethren than FLEAs — the all-too-appropriate acronym for Federal Law Enforcement Agencies. A contractor that "takes care of business" without dirtying the hands of the government, Wackenhut can be seen as the interstice between the government and the mob; such connections were being drawn by journalist/novelist Danny Casolaro before he died under suspicious circumstances. Air Force contractor CalSpan plays a part in the evolving Oklahoma City bombing, about which, more later.

Non-profit foundations also field their own intelligence organizations. The Anti-Defamation League, knuckle-rapped with a $75,000 fine for illegal possession of police files, bribed San Francisco police officer Tom Gerard to gain extensive and sensitive information on not only racists, but politicians, leftists, and anti-apartheid groups. Information on anti-racist protesters would be of intense interest to the formerly apartheid South African Republic, which supplied Israel, a direct ADL conduit, with nuclear weapons.[4] The Southern Poverty Law Center,[5] presided over by the telegenic Morris Dees, was exposed in a five-part *Montgomery Advertiser* investigation as the second wealthiest non-profit organization in America. Its own wealth and preoccupation with fundraising belies SPLC's eponymous objective to battle poverty. *The Advertiser* revealed that the organization's few high-profile lawsuits have resulted in little or no compensation for the "victims" of their legal crusades, but have in fact yielded millions of dollars in fees paid to Morris Dees for television movies and a ghostwritten autobiography that was criticized by *Publishers Weekly* for its rampant self-aggrandizement.

The ADL and SPLC boast that they are the media's primary sources on information regarding militias and patriot groups. Their information is usually absorbed whole into establishment news stories as unimpeachable and objective news sources. In truth, the coffers of the ADL and SPLC bulge when constituents are led to believe they're fighting an enemy of enormous evil and mounting strength. Despite their altruistic charters, the ADL and SPLC profit directly off the sensationalism that acts as a spark plug for Hollywood and the weekly tabloids. Their information ought to be regarded with skepticism greeted a docu-drama or the *National Enquirer.*

Another non-profit organization media star, Political Research Associate's John Foster "Chip" Berlet, has become something of a ubiquitous presence on establishment news shows and so-called progressive magazines, as an expert on the "extreme right-wing." Berlet stumps for the division of anti-establishment rightists and leftists at a time when even Republicans see the "Democratic" President as "Bush Lite." His pooh-poohing of "conspiracy theories" serves to question government skeptics rather than the government itself. Even though he's a prolific contributor to leftist magazines, Berlet's passionate defenses of Janet Reno and Bill Clinton protect rather than "question authority." Targets of Berlet's smears and criticism include Daniel Sheehan of the Christic Institute, Daniel Brandt, whose NameBase software is a leading resource for tracking government misdeeds, and Ace Hayes, the prolific Portland-area researcher. Both Brandt and Hayes insist that Berlet's past associations seem to render him a chip off of John Foster Dulles' block. Hayes and Brandt contend that the true division in the country is not between left and right, but between up and down, the haves vs. the have-nots.

The wedge Berlet drives between left and right critics of the elite is exemplified in the treatment of a book written about the Trilateral Commission by leftist Holly Sklar. Acquiescing to Berlet's demands, Sklar denounces all readers of her book if they do not subscribe to crypto-Socialist theology. Berlet's ideological purification creates divisions between individuals thoughtful enough to glean knowledge from a book. A right-winger reading Sklar on Trilateralism might well empathize with Third World victims of the New Order economy. Similarly, a leftist reader of Carroll Quigley's *Tragedy and Hope,* purchased at a John Birch Society bookstore, might open his eyes to the many so-called liberal politicians who uphold Eastern Establishment elitism. Reading Quigley seems particularly urgent in light of Bill Clinton's reference to Quigley as an ideological mentor in his Presidential acceptance speech.

A Berletian smear tactic against government critics was also taken up by Michael Kelly in his "Road to Paranoia" article featured in the June 19, 1995 issue of *The New Yorker.* Kelly tells us about a dangerous new trend that combines elements of both left and right into a variety of conspiracy theory he calls "fusion paranoia." I can speak of this phenomenon with some degree of depth, since Mr. Kelly includes Feral House in his short list of publishers ratcheting up the millennial perversity of "fusion paranoia." Kelly, like Berlet before him, implies that it is lunatic to come to the conclusion that a powerful minority of elitists direct the economy and other significant social trends to expand profits and power.

Imagine, Kelly sniffs, "fusion paranoids" say that Bush started the Gulf War for his own gain. The writer should have consulted a back issue of *The New Yorker* for a Seymour Hersh investigation that revealed the many millions of dollars received by President Bush, his sons, and cabinet members as postwar tribute from Kuwait. He should have also examined a transcript of pre-war conversations between U.S. Iraqi ambassador April Glaspie and Saddam Hussein, in which Glaspie declares that the U.S. would not involve itself in an Iraqi border dispute with Kuwait.

The roots of "fusion paranoia" are firmly planted in the Iran-Contra affair, says Kelly, where both leftists and rightist conspiracy theorists

MILITIA ACTIVITY IN THE UNITED STATES

Number of 🔫 indicates level of activity in 27 states with known Militia groups.

Information from ADL Fact Finding Report, *Armed & Dangerous: Militias Take Aim At The Federal Government* (October 1994), and subsequent research.

© Anti-Defamation League, April 1995.

Top: Intelligence from the ADL report, *Armed and Dangerous.*

Bottom left: Photo from June, 1995 issue of *Soldier of Fortune* with the Timothy McVeigh *doppelganger,* who is called an "unidentified agent ... who sat in press section of court with burp gun under his trench coat" by the *SOF* caption. Agent on left is Robert Rodriguez, and Davy Aguilera, center.

believed the tale peddled by "liars" that a shadow government operated behind the scenes to negotiate a bombs-for-hostage deal with Iran. Kelly contends "fusion paranoids" are so deluded as to believe that George Bush personally flew to Paris to negotiate with Iranian representatives months prior to Reagan's inauguration.

Bush's itinerary for the days he allegedly spent in Paris are still missing from his diaries. According to the erstwhile Israeli intelligence operative Ari Ben-Menashe, who helped set up the Iran-Contra negotiations on behalf of Israel, Bush was directly involved with the hostages-for-arms negotiations, a charge backed by Richard Brenneke, found innocent of charges brought against him by the U.S. government for backing Menashe's allegations. The deal had the Iranians holding the hostages until after Jimmy Carter lost re-election and the Republicans assumed power. The hostages were released the very day of Reagan's inauguration.

WILL THE REAL MILITIAMAN PLEASE STAND UP?

Militias are largely a white and middle-class movement, and though the movement has been joined by Jews, blacks, Indians, and Asians, it is fair to estimate that at least 60% of militias are Christian, of which a much smaller percentage subscribe to Christian Identity beliefs, a minority sect of racialist Christians who think Anglo-Saxons are the original Israelites. The usurpation of Hebrew identity by the Christian right-wing is correctly identified as a threat to Jews, since Identity types believe Jews to be Satanic impostors. Unfortunately, the sensationalizing of Identity groups by watchdog organizations and their persecution by government authorities, have simply justified the Identity Christians' own persecutorial and millennial beliefs. In my opinion, Identity Christians are best left alone in the same way adherents of Nation of Islam ideology are allowed to practice their own religion without the same level of harassment. Continued friction can only increase the likelihood of causing a volatile reaction.

Militias continue to grow as a response to the creeping internationalization of the economy, with the passage of international trade treaties such as GATT and NAFTA, which reward multinational corporations at the expense of domestic wages and employment. Squeezing the middle class with the highest per-capita tax burden while large corporations, foreign and domestic, are granted tax breaks and corporate welfare contributes to the perception that George Bush and Bill Clinton's New World Order is rewarding the multinational elite while giving the shaft to the working man.

Though it's been repeated a million times, there is no evidence that militias were involved in the Oklahoma bombing. While Timothy McVeigh and Terry Nichols have been spotted at two militia functions as far apart as Florida and Michigan, we don't know if their presence is due to government infiltration, the use of doubles (see photo), or the result of two men's idle curiosity. McVeigh and Nichols were said to have spouted off about bombing buildings at a meeting of the Michigan militia, whereupon several militia members reported the terrible two to the FBI! Either these militia members were hip to the COINTELPRO tactic of *agents provocateur,* or became so nonplused by potential violence that they ratted out supposed ideological allies to a government agency bent on the destruction of militia organizations.

Although the establishment media has portrayed militia men as either paranoid gun-toting geeks or the current incarnation of Nazi-like evil, Militia membership has sustained steady growth, even after the Oklahoma bombing. According to a militia leader who wishes to remain anonymous, "The bad publicity justifies all the bills they're trying to pass, but when the average American listens to what we're saying on the tube, it doesn't sound so unreasonable. To them, we look like their next door neighbor who helped them fix a flat. As a matter of fact, we ARE the guys who helped them change their tire. That makes an impression. And the phony politicians who come on in with their Armani suits and say we're terrorists, it makes some people think. Next week they might be the terrorists. TV brainwashes people, but no matter how they edit the tape, we're still the friendly neighbor with the car jack."

Charles Schumer (D-NY) would like to ban guns. Entirely. This has made him unpopular with gun owners, militias particularly. On July 10, 1995 Schumer held a press conference in which he put several government workers before microphones to tell the world about the miserable and inhuman conduct of militias. Much of the press conference consisted of recycled news about judges threatened by Montana racists (not militia members). A female County Tax Assessor told of being cut with a knife and threatened with a gun. Her assailants were said to be "tax protesters" — with apparently no connection to a militia organization. This distinction was lost on reporters, who dutifully told of the terrible behavior below quailing headlines ("WORKERS SPEAK OUT ON MILITIA BRUTALITY") The news articles chided Republicans for failing to attend Schumer's show, suggesting their apparent appeasement of militia criminals.[6]

The FBI now claims that it has successfully infiltrated the militia movement. Militias, are, in fact, rife with slippery individuals like Linda Thompson, the subject of a full-length article in this book originally printed in the October 11, 1994 edition of the *Village Voice*. In Spring '94 Thompson sent an "Ultimatum" (see following article) to every member of Congress, demanding elimination of the IRS, Federal Reserve, Brady Gun law, several constitutional amendments and so on, announcing that as "Adjutant General" of the U.S. Militias she would come marching in with guns and lynching rope on Washington D.C. on September 7, 1994 if Congress did not comply with her demands.

Thompson got a lot of attention for her efforts, but negligible support from militias themselves despite Thompson's self-adopted title of "Adjutant General." Frantic about Thompson's misleading stunt, militia men called up Thompson's American Justice Federation computer bulletin board, posting messages about the "suicidal" nature of such a march. Thompson used the opportunity to divide the militia community, accusing nearly all extant leaders as being government agents, and insulting and inciting militia men who revealed they weren't thrilled with the armed march concept. "Dickless coward" was a favorite comeback. Anyone who logged on to Thompson's bulletin board was compelled to complete an on-line questionnaire. How would they help the movement? With guns? Safe houses? Training? Though Thompson boasted that the FBI constantly monitored her board, she insisted that bulletin board users implicate themselves with possible charges of conspiracy or worse, by simply filling out these incriminating questionnaires.

Thompson canceled her notorious armed march after returning home in August, '94 from the Arizona high desert, where she assisted the bizarre William Cooper[7] with a seminar on the fine art of propaganda and long-range rifle sniping. In a public announcement, Thompson claimed the march was nothing more than a publicity stunt, but people should realize that even though the march was canceled, the "war is on."

Perhaps Michael Kelly's "fusion paranoia" theorem should not be disposed of too quickly. The phrase seems to accurately fit an individual by the name of Craig Hulet, aka K.C. DePlace. In the late '80s, Hulet made the rounds, speaking on radio talk shows and appearing at seminars to disseminate information on executive orders known as "Rex '84," that would, in time of "emergency," turn the U.S. into a virtual police state and transform emptied military bases into concentration camps. One leg of the "Rex '84" plan has come to fruition: the closure of military bases. After his high-profile presence in the late-'80s, Hulet dropped out of sight, particularly after articles appeared linking him to past associations with far-right or racist organizations. Hulet has again emerged, this time supplying screeds to the August, 1995 issue of *Soldier of Fortune,* in which he turns about-face from his former position to insult "conspiracists" (a neologism derived from Chip Berlet) and declaring there is no such thing as a "sinister" project emanating from an imperial elite.

Cui Bono, Oklahoma City?

Does it really matter who blew up the building in Oklahoma City? Such knowledge is only useful for purposes of punishment. History tells us to pay attention to the aftermath, not to the puny distractions of trials and culpability. What is in store for us?

At his first post-bomb press conference, Clinton swaggers to the podium, radiating anger and confidence. Clinton's hate rant, invoking the perpetrator's execution, is rewarded with the highest approval ratings of his term.

For this first time in memory, Clinton drops his I-feel-for-you whine. His righteous anger reflects Mussolini-like vitality rather than his usual wan, comforting equivocations. Flying high in the polls, Clinton invokes a hostile "love it or leave it" refrain when Dianne Sawyer informs him citizens are concerned about Waco. Later, in a speech at Michigan University, Clinton throttles non-establishment views of history as the "peddling of paranoia," a sowing of distrust in the benevolent institutions known as federal government. "You have the right to say what you please in this country," explains Clinton, "but that doesn't give people the right to tear down this country."

News programs took Clinton's bait and started to report about "conspiracy theorists." With clear astonishment in his voice, *Dateline's* Stone Philips tells us "some of the conspiracy theorists actually believe the U.S. government was responsible for the Oklahoma City explosion!" "Even worse," says Philips to the eye of the camera, "millions of Americans actually believe them." To demolish these Establishment-Deniers, *Dateline* interviews popularizers of three unlikely stories. Former FBI man Ted Gunderson says that a four pound aerially dropped "pineapple bomb" invented by Michael Riconosciuto of Iran-Contra fame is responsible for the blast. Another scenario features a sharp-featured computer expert, Debra Von Trapp, who tells us Oklahoma City was Japan's retribution for the subway gassings, which were executed by the U.S. government as punishment for Japanese spies in the White House. The final "kook factor" was supplied by jailbird Ron Jackson, who produced an incoherent, typewritten document as "proof" of the government's involvement.

By offering only the most unlikely scenarios, *Dateline* de-legitimizes every alternative reading of Oklahoma City. Never mind Gunderson, Von Trapp, and Jackson, the kookiest tale is currently being told by the FBI, and presented to us in daily doses by the compliant corporate scabs employed in establishment media. Why doesn't *Dateline* or any other news program ask the following questions?

• If the bombing of the Murrah building was a terrorist reprisal for Waco, why weren't ATF or FBI agents injured? How many ATF personnel took the day off? Why were Judge Alley and others warned by special agents about impending violence on April 19. Who were these special agents?

• By definition, a terrorist must take credit for his violence, or else there is no compelling reason to commit a crime. The specific purpose of terrorism is gaining leverage on a specific political objective through the ability of threatening future terrorist acts. No one has claimed credit for the Oklahoma City bombing. Militia groups produced particularly vehement public statements condemning the crime.

• Did the Murrah building warehouse documents regarding the Branch Davidians? Are these documents missing? Will the missing papers affect Ramsey Clark's suit against the ATF and FBI on behalf of the remaining Branch Davidian survivors?

• Why did the director of University of Oklahoma's Geological Survey, Dr. Charles Mankin, say that according to two different seismographic records, there were two blasts. Dr. Mankin reports that "the news media even reported two bomb blasts initially, but later changed their story."

• A pre Oklahoma City bombing issue of *Soldier of Fortune* featured a James Pate article on Waco with a photograph of three BATF agents. One of these agents, the only agent unidentified, looks like the spitting image of Timothy McVeigh. Is this merely coincidental? Or was there a second "Timothy McVeigh" roaming the country, appearing at militia meetings? (The use of doubles is not a James Bond fantasy but an everyday aspect of intelligence work.)

• According to a *New York Times* chronology, Timothy McVeigh was said to have worked as security for the defense contractor CalSpan in Buffalo. CalSpan, owned by the Fortune 500 company Arvin Industries, is actively involved in the research and development of microwave technology and telemetric devices for the Air Force. Telemetry can chart the location of individuals implanted with a microchip, or, quite possibly, send the telemetric device further information by satellite. An executive for CalSpan told the New York Times that McVeigh was a model employee, that the company was disappointed that he "dropped out of sight," because they were planning to promote him. After McVeigh "dropped out of sight" from his security job at CalSpan he began complaining that the government was "controlling his mind" through a microchip implanted in his buttocks.

• Who is John Doe #2? Why did the FBI entertain the possibility that he was a pre-pubescent relative of Terry Nichols, and yet they profess no interest in a John Doe #2 photographed at the crime scene, and then rediscovered in Oklahoma City by the local television station KFOR?

• Retired Air Force Brigadier General Benton K. Partin, former commander of the Air Force Armament Technology Laboratory, a 25-year expert in the design and development of bombs, urged Senators and Congressmen to delay destruction of the Murrah building crime site. Partin disseminated information to the John Birch magazine, the *New American:* "When I first saw the picture of the truck bomb's asymmetrical damage to the federal building in Oklahoma, my immediate reaction was that the pattern of damage would have been technically impossible without supplementary demolition charges at some of the reinforced concrete bases inside the building — a standard demolition technique." Partin further explained that "reinforced concrete targets in large buildings are hard targets to blast. I know of no way possible to reproduce the apparent building damage through simply a truck bomb parked outside.... The evidence indicates there was an inside bomb effort." General Partin's request to examine the possibility of a second bomb in the concrete bases fell on deaf ears. The building was brought down on May 23. Researcher Alex Constantine tells me that Partin's information is suspect due to blaming the bomb on a peculiar coalition of "international leftists." Perhaps more troubling was Constantine's insistence that McVeigh's former employer, CalSpan, subcontracted the devlopment and construction of mind control devices for the Air Force, where Partin was and perhaps still remains a major player.

• Why was the bomb first reported as a car bomb, then reported as a bomb similar to the one that struck the World Trade Center (a one-half ton model)? The FBI raised their estimate of the amount of explosive to 4,800 pounds, and the truck size to the largest model rented by Ryder, Inc.

• FBI agents were said to have tracked down McVeigh's truck rental agency by finding a vehicle identification number (VIN) one the truck's rear axle. This axle was found either in the bomb crater, according to the mayor, or three blocks away, if one is to believe the FBI. But there is another problem to the tale. No rear axle is imprinted with a vehicle identification number, even after recent legislation forcing manufacturers to place multiple VINs on the engine, firewall, and frame to discourage chop shops. When queried, a spokesman for Ryder told me that it does not imprint additional VINs on its trucks. The only conceivable number available on a rear axle is a part number, but a part number couldn't lead to the identification of a specific vehicle. Where did the VIN story come from? And why?

• Did McVeigh use fake i.d. or real i.d. to rent the truck? The FBI tells us both versions.

• If he committed such a heinous crime, why did Timothy McVeigh make the mistake of driving 81 miles per hour without a license, and why didn't he shoot the highway patrolman who stopped him?

• The story is told that Timothy McVeigh would have been released from jail on the day of his capture if he had produced sufficient bail money. Why couldn't he contact the Nichols brothers or other friends or family members to obtain bail? Why did he choose to stick around long enough for the sketch of John Doe #1 to reach his small town courthouse, resulting in his arrest for the Oklahoma City explosion?

• The FBI claims that Michael Fortier, McVeigh's friend from Kingman, revealed that he and McVeigh snooped around the Murrah building several days before the bombing, asking many people where BATF agents could be found. Why, then, did McVeigh bomb the building on the opposite side from the BATF offices?

• Why did Fortier tell CNN news on May 8 that "I do not believe Tim McVeigh blew up any building in Oklahoma"?

• U.S. Government, Technical Manual No. 9-1910 from the Departments of the Army and Air Force titled *Military Explosives,* which specifies that ANFO, the acronym for the Ammonium Nitrate and Fuel Oil bomb said to be used on the McMurrah building, requires a greater than 99% purity of Ammonium Nitrate, as well as a specific dryness before it can be mixed with diesel fuel to create an explosive substance. The manual further spells out that even under ideal conditions (not often reached, even by experts) 4,800 pounds of ANFO explosive would create a much smaller crater than the one left in front of the McMurrah building, and its shockwave could not possibly wield the force necessary to compromise the building's concrete supports.

• The FBI claimed the ANFO charge was made from 50 bags of fertilizer. Ammonium Nitrate fertilizer comes in much weaker concentrations than the 99% plus required for explosives. Creating concentrated amounts of Ammonium Nitrate is quite complex, and would require many more than 50 bags of fertilizer.

• Accredited explosives experts who wish to remain anonymous for fear of retribution, agree that the explosion could have only been created with professional explosive detonators and professional explosive. Such things are highly regulated in non-military use. The military is supposedly even more strict about its explosive inventory.

• If the explosion is too strong to have been created by 4,800 pounds of ANFO, if the explosive could only have been detonated by professional materials rather than bags of fertilizer, what sort of explosive was used, and why is the FBI supplying public statements that do not support the government's own manuals?

AN AMERICAN REICHSTAG?

Ridicule is an everyday event for researchers who have compared the Oklahoma City event to the burning of the Reichstag. Researcher Ace Hayes believes the Reichstag analogy is appropriate because its burning was the pivotal gambit that permitted the Nazis to unleash the emerging police state on political enemies prior to their total seizure of power.

The Reichstag, much more than a simple federal building in Oklahoma, was something of a sacred national symbol — though the current regime wants to live down its Nationalist mythology by allowing the Bulgarian artist Christo to toilet-wrap the monument under mylar for his personal profit. The burning of the nationally symbolic site spurred on the Nazis to characterize the attack as "terrorism. The Communists, early on accused by the Nazis of perpetrating the attack, produced their own conspiracy theories, turning the Nazi's accusation back on them. A dim-witted Dutch anarchist named Marinus Van Der Lubbe became the official "lone nut" terrorist, convicted of burning the huge building with a gas-soaked jacket. Even the popular Ballantine histories of the Second World War blames Van Der Lubbe for the attack, supporting neither Nazi nor Communist conspiracy theories.

The U.S. government likewise blames the destruction of a federal building on "terrorism" inspired by its most vocal opponents, the militias. American dissidents, far fewer in number and much less active or powerful than the Nazis' Communist opposition, generally believe that those in power had more to gain by the blast.

Whoever or whatever burned down the Reichstag, the Nazis seized the moment to beat, kill or imprison their political enemies. Hitler induced Hindenburg to sign a decree suspending German civil liberties. The Clinton Administration used the pretext of the blast to unleash SWAT teams against militias and gun-owners in Michigan, Arizona, Montana and elsewhere, and in the process arrest and seize assets from dozens of anti-government dissidents for various crimes. Multi-Jurisdictional Task Force (MJTF) attack teams terrorized communities in Ohio, Pennsylvania and other states in live-fire attacks against imaginary urban dissidents in abandoned buildings. The most alarming comparisons of Oklahoma City to the Reichstag Fire can be found in newly-passed and newly-proposed legislation. Recent anti-crime and anti-terrorist bills have already eliminated or diminished portions of the first, second and fourth amendments, and has dismantled the Posse Comitatus Act, which is supposed to prevent the use of military forces against American citizens. President Bush had already chipped away at Posse Comitatus by allowing the use of military weapons for the "War on Drugs." *Soldier of Fortune* correspondent James Pate discovered that the ATF lied in telling the army that David Koresh was running a methamphetamine lab in order to procure military training and weapons for its initial raid. New anti-terrorist laws have loosened requirements, so that the ATF and other federal police agencies will not have to lie to obtain military training, personnel and materiel for their adventures.

The Executive Branch is now invested with the authority to declare any group or anyone it doesn't like as "terrorist." The terrorist designation amounts to immediate deportation, if a foreign national, or imprisonment, if a U.S. citizen persists in his or her belief. Private property can be seized at will, and there is no appeal process to the terrorist designation.

Sound bad? You ain't heard nothin' yet.

Currently proposed before congress, the "Domestic Insurgency Act of 1995 (HR-1544)," a bill sponsored by Gerald Nadler (D-NY) borrows from the "sample legislation" appended to an ADL scare report, as a legal method to snuff out the phenomenon of militias, which the ADL claims are nothing more than "racist, extreme right-wing hate groups." HR-1544 stipulates:

> (a) Whoever knowingly participates in a paramilitary organization shall be fined under this title or imprisoned not more than 10 years, or both.

> (b) As used in this section, the term 'paramilitary organization' means two or more individuals acting together, organized in a military or paramilitary structure, who knowingly —

> (1) possess firearms, explosives, incendiary devices, or other weapons or techniques capable of causing injury or death to individuals.

> (2) provide or participate in training in the use of any such weapons or techniques; with the intention that such weapons or techniques be used unlawfully to oppose the authority of the United States or of any State or for any other unlawful purpose.

Simply put, the "Domestic Insurgency Act" would clap citizens behind bars for ten years simply for observing the constitutional guarantees of free speech, the right to keep and bear arms, the right to wear goofy camouflage clothes, and the right to assembly. Unlawful intention is left for the federal law enforcement agencies to interpret. The definition of "paramilitary organization" is so open to interpretation that it could be used to imprison hunters, explorer scouts, or attendees of a church picnic, as long as two or more picnic-goers held Swiss army knives and discussed their unhappiness with the U.S. government.

If the ADL or Representative Nadler attempted to foist a "Domestic Insurgency Act" on the state of Israel, citizens would likely riot in the streets. Israeli nationals and settlers view weapons as their last protection against violent enemies.

In light of onerous legislation and the continued militarization of domestic police forces, the comparison of Oklahoma City to the Reichstag Fire is perhaps not quite so far-fetched. There are, however, several important distinctions. Weimar and early National Socialist-period Communists actively expressed political distaste in street brawls, assassinations, riots, large political assemblies, destruction of property, even capture of German territory. By contrast, militias remain largely defensive, chartered to protest the erosion of constitutional rights. The militias' paramilitary flavor is as much a statement of serious intent as a threat to the government. Like the Black Panthers, militias feel empowered with the ability to own and train with weapons.

The question remains: at what point will the militias use their weapons?

Militias are sure to react as the government continues to overturn the Constitutional, discarding the right to keep and bear arms, suffocating the right to free speech, or roping off the right to public assembly. If the rancid Domestic Insurgency Act targeting militias becomes law, the law's already-alarmed target will surely react. But I can only hazard a guess. Militias are unsophisticated, easily mislead by *agents provocateur* scattered throughout the movement; the militias' decentralization makes it difficult for the government to monitor and control most or all of the groups at once.

THE END OF AMERICAN INNOCENCE?

Accompanying news coverage of the Oklahoma City bombing were frequent and peculiar statements to the effect that America had lost its innocence. "It was an explosion of unimaginable magnitude," quailed a CNN anchorwoman. "You expect these kind of things to happen in New York or Jerusalem, but Oklahoma? If this kind of thing can happen in Oklahoma, it can happen anywhere, anytime. This is the end of American innocence." And so on, *ad nauseam...*

Was America innocent of running black ops in Laos? Innocent of gifting smallpox blankets to Indians? Innocent of selling drugs for guns? Innocent of raking off our share of the world's misery? To quote Malcolm X, the chickens have come home to roost.

Media coverage of the Oklahoma City incident was maudlin in the extreme, a kind of flip-side of militia fetishism for the children killed at Waco.

Two weeks after the bombing, a beaming President Clinton dons a yarmulke at a meeting of the American Jewish Congress celebrating liquor tycoon Edgar Bronfman, a vastly powerful Zionist leader with notorious mob ties. With great media fanfare, Bronfman's son had just purchased MCA, the Hollywood studio with long-established mob ties. Clinton lauds Bronfman Sr., a Canadian version of the politically avaricious Joe Kennedy, as a paragon of virtue. He then announces to the assembled guests, with no suppressed glee, that he has just decided to punish the "terrorist" state of Iran with economic sanctions in order to fight terrorism both here and abroad. Further, Clinton's domestic anti-terrorism legislation delivers the goods for Israeli hawks. Years after the King David Hotel was bombed by Begin's Irgun, resulting in the deaths of many British soldiers and diplomats, the word terrorist has instead come to indicate any activist opposed to capitalism or Zionism. According to Western news organizations, capitalists or Zionists never commit terrorism or even vigilantism, they are instead characterized as "preserving the peace."

The perception of terrorism emanating from the Arab community plays well in Tel Aviv, rekindling hate vibes lying dormant since the Persian Gulf War. It was almost a *fait accompli* that "swarthy, middle-Eastern types" were initially fingered by FBI agents as responsible for the Oklahoma City bomb. They detain a Lebanese-American at Dallas airport several minutes before he was to fly to London. "Forgetting" to search the Arab-American's bags, they fly on to London. While the FBI imprisons their Arab suspect, not allowing him to access to an attorney or relatives, his luggage arrives in London for Scotland Yard to rip open before news cameras. Without a shred of evidence to further detain him, U.S. officials release the Lebanese-American, who hops the red eye to London, whereupon Scotland Yard claps handcuffs on his wrists, and chains him to a door until another plane departs to Dallas, where the FBI barks at him to keep close to home, and not to talk to anyone.

MILITIAS: HOW LARGE A THREAT?

As of mid-July, 1995, researchers have failed to uncover the smoking gun that implicates any government entity for the bomb blast. Without direct evidence, one must proceed cautiously in assigning blame on any party That said, it's clear that the government continues to withhold and even cover-up evidence: lame excuses accompany the destruction of the crime site ... the relatives of three missing civilians need a death certificate to obtain insurance ... psychiatrists say the crime scene must be detroyed to provide "closure" to Oklahoma City residents. But like the Branch Davidian compound, crucial evidence is forever destroyed or "lost"; in this sense, the government bears comparison to a card sharp who blindfolds his competition. The sighted competitor will win every hand, but his winnings come at the expense of his credibility.

When McVeigh was fingered as the mastermind of Oklahoma City, a lynch mob bayed for the suspect's blood as he was exposed to the public, a standing target next to near-midget sized FBI men.

It may be advisable at this point to admit my own biases. I own two guns, purchased for self-defense. My political beliefs combine skepticism of authority tempered with libertarian-style economic self-reliance. Unlike hardcore libertarians, I do not worship at the altar of a free market economy for the simple reason that unlimited economic growth along with unchecked procreation seems incompatible with long-term survival of the species. I am more of an agnostic than Christian, though I appreciate much in the legacy of Christian music, art and architecture.

Why then do I feel compelled to defend the militia man with his Manichean conspiracies and apocalyptic dreams? Because quite simply, the Christian militia man has become a scapegoat, a justification for intelligence agencies' headlong rush into technocratic dystopia, where every opinion voiced over the phone, modem and fax is evaluated, where every financial transaction is instantly monitored by computers operated by Fortune 500 and its omnipotent police force. Waco and Randy Weaver are harbingers of this spin-controlled, *1984*-like world in which paramilitary goons stage theatrical assaults against contentious targets to instill fear into dissidents or make a televised action picture whenever they need to pad their budget.

On the most pragmatic level, militia men and their pea shooters are no match for electronic or subsonic "non-lethal" weaponry devised to put down civilian uprisings. Anti-gun propaganda has become so intense that all advocates of private gun ownership have become vulnerable to smear campaigns by skittish elements of the left who demand government protection from crib to coffin. Although the militia movement is supposed to take advantage of a Constitutional provision that states that all men between the ages of 18 and 45 not belonging to an organized militia shall be considered members of an "Unorganized Militia," the law was enacted in order to allow the government to draft citizens in a national emergency. Furthermore, many states have already banned private paramilitary organizations back in the 1930s, primarily as a strategy to control the Klan's extracurricular activities.

Alfred McCoy and others have published scholarly tomes linking U.S. intelligence with large-scale sales of opium and cocaine in order to fund illegal insurgent actions. While a small elite within the U.S. military have become *de facto* dealers of tons of hard drugs that find their way to the streets of America, the Executive Branch makes a big show of eliminating the rights of citizens under the so-called War on Drugs. Similarly, the ever-increasing hysteria regarding militias translates into further onerous damage to the Constitution. Is it simply a coincidence that militias are largely composed of ex-military, or do they know things the average ignorant citizens aren't aware of?

The government and media have characterized the Murrah explosion as unreconstructed terrorism. The word terrorist has been cultivated to create an emotional reaction, an unreasoning fear that provokes an instinctive reflex to provide the government with anything it asks for to rid the citizen of his fear. Society has consequently become frantic to do away with "suspicious" characters without due process. Communism no longer haunts post Cold War America; consequently the federal police and intelligence agencies have become a bad parody of Stalin's NKVD or Honecker's Stasi.

Without an enemy, without terrorism, there would be no justification for police, no rationale for expanded police powers, no reason whatsoever to give into laws providing the police legal access to one's personal business, no possible justification for eviscerating the Posse Comitatus Act, designed to protect citizens from governmental attack by its own military.

Militia men, correctly distrusting the establishment line, have not developed a nose for bad information, which once embraced, discredits the militia's entire plank of beliefs. For this reason, it is important for researchers to reveal the disinformation along with the good information. Only a fanatical adherence to truth can hope to change the face of political opportunism.

A Brief Career as Media "Expert"

James Ridgeway, the usual Voice staffer who covers right-wing phenomena, was caught by surprise when I submitted a query to the *Village Voice* regarding a story on Linda Thompson and her ill-fated militia march. My query was accepted by the editors, despite Ridgeway's objection that the militia phenomena was a minor sociological burp, not worth the trouble of an article. Unfortunately, the Oklahoma City bombing and government scapegoating got in the way of Ridgeway's opinion. And so, six months after the article appeared in the October 11th issue of the *Voice,* my phone began to ring. *New York Times, Washington Post,* Associated Press. Everyone wants a quote regarding militias and their possible involvement in the Oklahoma City bombing. I discover that the newspapers already had their quote formulated: they merely needed to attribute the quote to a so-called expert. "The militias — whoever the fuck they are" an addled staffer from the *Washington Post* tells me, "are a ticking time-bomb composed of paranoid lunatics." "Not quite," I object, giving him a more informed and balanced view of the topic. The journalists, unable to match my name to their pro-forma concepts, decide that perhaps I'm not worth quoting after all.

After the bomb, James Ridgeway starts covering the militias for the *Voice,* regurgitating information from SPLC, ADL and Klanwatch reports, using the bombing as a way to lay blame for the militia mentality on elements within the Republican Party. All the while a bi-partisan Congress ushers in totalitarian crime laws, as well as a one hundred million dollar a year raise for the ATF. And, while even the Department of the Treasury finds its men criminally culpable for events gone awry at Waco, a long-overdue Congressional investigation is attacked by Charles Schumer as the appeasement of the NRA and paranoid conspiracy theorists.

ENDNOTES

1.) John B. Watson's turn-of the century attempt to turn mind control into a science.

2.) See *Bread & Hyacinths: The Rise and Fall of Utopian Los Angeles* by Paul Greenstein, Nigey Lennon and Lionel Rolfe, California Classics Books, 1992.

3.) According to armed forces spokesman Harvey Perrett III, the $3 billion/year program fields a black helicopter base in Fort Campbell, Kentucky. McClendon's enlightening interview fairly demolishes the canard trumpeted by the press that black copters are the paranoid imaginings of all those extreme right-wing militias.

4.) The ADL would love to do away with militias for perceived anti-Semitic overtones in militia conspiracy literature. This perception is at least partially due to Jewish oversensitivity. When a militia man talks about international bankers, the ADL believes he is using code words to describe Jewish control of the monetary system. If a militia man criticizes specific congressmen for attempting to do away with the Second Amendment who also happen to be Jews, this is again taken as anti-Semitism. The presumption of anti-Semitism in the militia movement is overstated, especially when a number of Jewish libertarians, including Jews for the Preservation of Firearm Ownership, are movers and shakers within the militia movement. The JPFO have tried to engage the ADL in a debate, to no apparent success. The group is critical of both the ADL and gun control measures because of they believe genocide becomes practicable after the general confiscation of firearms.

5.) Director Morris Dees boasts of having files on more than 14,000 "populists."

6.) Schumer apparently had no interest in the threats, dead animals, or obscene effigies sent to conservative Congressmen, since these activities weren't the province of militias, but DOJ-protected activists protesting abortion rights and gay activism.

7.) Linda Thompson's championing of William Cooper at the expense of every other militia member or leader is peculiar, to say the least. In his magnum opus, *Behold a Pale Horse,* Cooper reprints the hoax document *Protocols of the Learned Elders of Zion,* stipulating that readers should change the word Jew to "Illuminati."

ANNOTATED BIBLIOGRAPHY

By no means exhaustive, this bibliography annotates a few items encountered while researching *Cult Rapture*.

Adams, Thomas. F., **Police Field Operations, Second Edition,** Prentice Hall, Englewood Cliffs, NJ, 1990. "Sometimes it is possible to determine in advance the potentiality of civil disturbance of major proportions."

Adorno, T. W., Frenkel-Brunswick, Else, Levinson, Daniel J., Sanford, R. Nevitt, **The Authoritarian Personality** (Abridged Edition), Norton, 1982. First published in 1950 by the American Jewish Committee, Adorno and company bring a distinctively political bent to the social sciences by merging sociology and psychology to winnow out those holding incorrect attitudes from the general population. A taste of social engineering to come?

Allen, Steve, **Beloved Son: A Story of the Jesus Cults,** Bobbs-Merrill, New York, 1982. "For the first time in my life I fully appreciated the beauty of the natural universe," writes Steve Allen of his LSD trip. Little did he expect his son Brian to become involved in Seattle's Love Family, whose Church of Armageddon worshiped the inevitability of death through toluene trips. The tv host accepts his son's transformation into a glue-sniffing Jesus head with equanimity, deciding his particular fate is not as dire as that facing converts to Children of God or Moonies. Allen summons a respectable amount of anger in regard to the heavy-handed "deprogramming" methods, which resulted in a Love Family member's repeated exposure to shock treatments and neuroleptic drugs as a method to "cure" him of his religious affiliation.

Arendt, Hannah, **The Origins of Totalitarianism,** New Edition with Added Prefaces, Harcourt Brace Jovanovich, San Diego, 1973, Meditations on Jewish history informed by World War II.

Badura-Triska, Klocker, Hubert, **Rudolf Schwarzkogler,** Ritter Veglag Klagenfurt, 1992. Photodocumentation of and illustrations by this crucial Aktionist.

Bamford, James, **The Puzzle Palace: Inside the National Security Agency, America's Most Secret Intelligence Organization,** Penguin, New York, 1988. A tip of the iceberg glimpse at the agency that monitors all American phone traffic, its computers alert for word-triggers, such as derogatory references to the present government. Yes, you are being watched.

Barnes, Harry Elmer, editor, **Perpetual War for Perpetual Peace,** Caxton Printers, Caldwell, ID., 1953. The original Historical Revisionist sees perpetual war as the inevitable outcome of capitalist culture.

Beaudrillard, Jean, **In the Shadow of the Silent Majorities ... Or the End of the Social and Other Essays,** Semiotext(e), New York, 1983. "Basically, what goes for commodities also goes for meaning ... "

Beaudrillard, Jean, **The Transparency of Evil,** Verso, London, 1993.

Bennett, David, H., **Party of Fear: From Nativist Movements to the New Right in American History,** University of North Carolina Press, Chapel Hill, 1988. Fair-minded, leftist assessment of nativist movements in American history.

Beyerstein, Dale, **Sai Baba's Miracles: An Overview,** Privately Published, Vancouver, B.C., 1992. Skeptic's revelations.

Bierce, Ambrose, **The Devil's Dictionary,** Dover, New York, 1958. "Freemasons, n. An order with secret rites, grotesque ceremonies and fantastic costumes, which, originating in the reign of Charles II, among working artisans of London, has been joined successively by the dead of past centuries in unbroken retrogression until now it embraces all the generations of man on the hither side of Adam and is drumming up distinguished recruits among the pre-Creational inhabitants of Chaos and the Formless Void..."

Bordan, Dana & Stoert, R., **Warten,** Volume 2, Berlin, 1992. Among the *Apocalypse Culture*-like eclecticism of its contents, a version of my Unarius article.

Boyer, Paul, **When Time Shall Be No More: Prophecy Belief in Modern American Culture,** Harvard University Press, Cambridge, 1992. Scholarly treatment of Dispensationalism in the world today.

Bramley, William, **The Gods of Eden,** Avon, New York, 1993. Scientological-type conspiracy of human origins.

Bremer, Arthur H., **An Assassin's Diary,** Harper's Magazine Press, New York, 1973. "Lone nut" who went after George Wallace. His diaries were found by police in his car after his assassination attempt. The lone-nut-with-diary echoes Oswald and inspired Taxi Driver and possibly many other intelligence frame-ups.

Brooke, Tal, **Avatar of Night: The Hidden Side of Sai Baba,** Vikas Publsihing House, New Delhi. "Baba called Patrick to his chambers for a private interview. At the end of the interview, Sai Baba collected Patrick's semen in a little white handkerchief and then told him that the whole 'world lay in the palm of his hand and that anything Patrick wanted he could have.' Phil, an ex-follower of Sai Baba, said 'semen is the most potent thing in heavy occult.... That is why there's such a heavy emphasis on sex in covens."

Bryan, Gerald B., **Psychic Dictatorship in America,** Harry J. Gardener Publishing, Los Angeles, 1940. First exposé of the I AM cult to be published; includes revelations of I AM's flirtations with Nazism.

Buie, Louis A., **Practical Proctology,** W. B. Saunders, Philadelphia, 1938. ... "I would gladly insert my finger into the rectum of a patient professionally, with whom I would not care to shake hands, socially."

Burton, Richard F., **The City of the Saints,** Knopf, New York, 1963. The British explorer's look at the exotic polygamous sect of Mormonism.

Canetti, Elias, **Auto-Da-Fé,** Jonathan Cape, London, 1962. Story of a bibliomaniacal scholar whose mind gives way.

Chambers, Whittaker, **Witness,** Random House, New York, 1952. God battles Communism. A devoted member of the latter faith becomes imbued with God's spirit, testifies against former comrade Alger Hiss. A more complex and interesting book than people would have you believe.

Childress, David Hatcher, **Lost Cities of North & Central America,** Adventures Unlimited Press, Stelle, IL, 1992. Anomalous archeological artifacts that raise the specter of advanced prehistoric civilizations. Whence did they come?

Church, Gene and Carnes, Conrad D., **The Pit: A Group Encounter Defiled,** Outerbridge and Lazard, New York, 1972. An executive encounter session run like a concentration camp leads to the psychic and physical battering of participants. An amazing indictment of how much brutality individuals will undergo for "job security."

Churchill, Ward & Vander Wall, Jim, **The COINTELPRO Papers: Documents From the FBI's Secret Wars Against Dissent in the United States,** South End Press, Boston, 1990.

Coleman, John, **Conspirators' Hierarchy: The Story of the Committee of 300,** America West Publishers, Carson City, 1992. Imbroglios of the Royal Family, Tavistock, Club of Rome, etc. A quote from Tavistock's chief theoretician, Kurt Lewin: "One of the main techniques for breaking morale through a strategy of terror consists in exactly this tactic — keep the person hazy as to where he stands and just what he may expect. In addition, if frequent vacillations between severe disciplinary measures and promises of good treatment together with the spreading of contradictory news, make the cognitive structure of this situation utterly unclear, then the individual may cease even to know a particular plan would lead toward or away from his goal. Under these conditions even those individuals who have definite goals and are ready to take risks are paralyzed by severe inner conflict in regard to what to do." In his book, Coleman charges Henry Kissinger of following this Tavistock training technique "to the letter" in order to unseat President Nixon.

Commander X, **The Ultimate Deception,** Abelard Productions, 1990. Strange ufological exposé chock-full of neo-Nazi and racialist overtones. The book holds that the U.S. government has forged an agreement with Extraterrestrial Biological Entities for the right to abduct humans and "plant monitoring devices in their brains, in exchange for technical and scientific data. Our only hope for survival, says Commander X, is a second group of benevolent extraterrestrials — most commonly referred to as the Nordic Types — who believe in the universal law of non-interference. Those aliens have taken our side in a cosmic spiritual war that pits the forces of Light and Darkness against each other for the virtual minds and bodies of humankind..." Martin Cannon's *The Controllers* is a necessary corrective.

Commander X, **Underground Alien Bases,** Abelard Productions, 1990. Contemporary "non-fiction" rendering of the age-old Aryan myth of subterranean worlds.

(Constable), Trevor James, **They Live in the Sky!: Invisible Incredible UFO Around Us,** New Age Publishing, Los Angeles, 1958. Reichian bions solve the riddle of UFO composition and propulsion.

Constantine, Alex, **Blood, Carnage and the Agent Provocateur: The Truth about the Los Angeles Riots and the Secret War Against L.A.'s Minorities,** Constantine Report, Volume 1, P.O. Box 791, Los Angeles, CA, 90078-0791, 1993. Interesting take on the "growth industry" of domestic counter-insurgency. Includes little-reported facts regarding the Beverly Hills Police catching National Guardsmen with arson materials. Constantine uses this and other troubling facts to bolster his thesis that the 1992 Los Angeles riots was at least partially instigated by *agents provocateur* of the National Security State.

Constantine, Alex, **Psychic Dictatorship in the U.S.A.,** Feral House, Portland, 1995. As publisher, I was privileged enough to view contents before they were shipped to the printer. The first major book to address the smarmy background to "Non-Lethal Technology."

Conway, Flo, and Siegelman, Jim, **Snapping: America's Epidemic of Sudden Personality·Change,** Delta, 1978. Examination of tactics employed by coercive cults to induce the conversion process. In so doing, the book also reveals anti-cult "deprogramming" process to be equally coercive.

Cooper, William, **Behold a Pale Horse,** Light Technology Publishing, Sedona, AZ, 1991. Linda Thompson's best friend, William Cooper claims to be ex Navy Intelligence. He makes a number of other claims, too, regarding the existence of aliens on military bases and his special knowledge regarding the death of J.F.K. Cooper knows practically everything. For good measure he includes the *Protocols of the Learned Elders of Zion* with the proviso that the reader substitute the word "Illuminati" for "Jew" and "Cattle" for "Goyim."

Creme, Benjamin, **Maitreya's Mission,** Share International, Amsterdam, 1986. The Second Coming of Christ as beheld by the New Age entrepreneur.

Daraul, Arkon, **A History of Secret Societies,** Citadel Press, New York, 1962. Skoptsi, Illuminati, Vehm. It's all here in capsule form.

Darwin, Charles, **Expressions of the Emotions in Man and Animals,** D. Appleton and Company, New York, 1896. Darwin's forgotten treatise on the utility of emotion. This book is likely forgotten because it takes Verdi out of the opera of emotion. Science transgresses the province of the great novelists and composers.

DeCamp, John W., **The Franklin Cover-Up: Child Abuse, Satanism, and Murder in Nebraska,** AWT, Inc, Lincoln, 1992. The strange activities of ex-Police Chief Wadman (yes, that is his name) and his friends in the FBI who helped cover up these extracurricular activities.

De Camp, Spencer, **Lost Continents: The Atlantis Theme in History, Science and Literature,** Dover Publications, New York, 1970. "The Mayas' downfall may have been hastened by their priests' habit of issuing gloomy prophecies ... the priests' object may have been to keep their own people in a state of apprehension to make them easier to control. But as a result, when the Spaniards came, although some Mayas fought like demons, others sighed 'This must be it' and stolidly awaited the end."

DeMeo, James, editor, **Pulse of the Planet: Research Report of the Orgone Biophysical Research Lab,** Issues 2 & 3, 1989 & 1991. The most important organ of contemporary researchers influenced by Wilhelm Reich's controversial "late" period.

DePugh, Robert Bolivar, **Beyond the Iron Mask,** Salon Publishing, Norborne, MO, 1974. Leader of the far-right guerrilla group publishes his treatise on survival in Leavenworth.

Deyo, Stan, **The Cosmic Conspiracy,** WATT Books, Kalamunda, Australia, 1978. Christian physicist explores anti-gravity, the Illuminated Council of Nine, Weather Control and other occult sources of conspiracy.

Deyo, Stan, **The Vindicator Scrolls,** WATT Books, Perth, Australia, 1989. Archeology, plate tectonics, perpetual energy devices, prophetic dreams of the author's wife, biblical readings, ALF (Alien Life Forms, not the television character), the authenticity of the ostensibly debunked Majestic 12 top secret document concerning captured alien life forms, and an urgent plea for Jews and Christians to put their religious houses in order since Rapture is just around the corner.

"Doe, John," **Report From Iron Mountain: On the Possibility and Desirability of Peace,** Dial Press, 1967. Probable hoax document from a supposed elite study group (like Rand) that discusses the desirability of perpetual war to ensure perpetual peace.

Domhoff, G. William, **Who Rules America Now?: A View for the '80s,** Prentice-Hall, Englewood Cliffs, NJ, 1983. Remnant of the days when leftists felt themselves estranged from the establishment, and attempted dissections of the "ruling social class" without fear of the stigma of being a so-called "conspiracy theorist." Those individuals who believe that there is such a thing as class in America and who employ data from researchers of the left and right are now called "fusion paranoids." Feral House was regarded as a "fusion paranoid" publishing company by Michael Kelly in a Summer '95 issue of *The New Yorker.*

Downard, James Shelby, **Skullduggery; Violence Is On the Wind and Blood Is In the Air; Flashbacks,** Published by the Author, Memphis, TN, 1992. A mixture of hair-raising autobiographical adventures and investigations into the cultic whirlwind for which he had been unwittingly indoctrinated. Three separate articles bound as one book.

Downard, James Shelby, **Carnivals of Life & Death,** Published by the author, Memphis, TN, 1991, Further autobiographical imbroglios in the inimitable Downard style.

Duncan, Malcolm C., **Revised Duncan's Masonic Ritual and Monitor; or, Guide to the Three Symbolic Degrees,** Behrens Publishing, Danbury, CT, 1922.

Dworkin, Andrea, **Mercy,** 4 Walls 8 Windows, New York, 1991.

Epperson, A. Ralph, **The Unseen Hand: An Introduction to the Conspiratorial View of History,** Publius Press, Tucson, 1985. Comprehensive overview of the Bircherite perspective of history, written by a Bircher. For those seeking an all-inclusive textbook of Nativist or populist history without the reductions or distortions of mass media or "progressive" critics, this 500 page tome is a good place to start.

Epperson, A. Ralph, **The New World Order,** Publius Press, 3100 S. Philamena Pl., Tucson, Arizona, 85730, 1990. Converges the Illuminati to contemporary Conspirators. A textbook example of the pitfalls of the Bircherite conspiracy crossing its wires with fundy paranoia. Occasional consequential research is difficult to pick out from obvious "kook" material. Why pay homage to the Constitution, when it was a masonically-inspired document, and then accuse those who would do away with it, as part of the Masonic conspiracy?

Farrakhan, Louis, **The Announcement: A Final Warning to the U.S. Government,** Final Call, Inc., Chicago, 1989. Farrakhan's vision of Elijah Muhummad second coming in a UFO revealing Bush's war against the Black people of America.

Ferris, Kirby, **A Mountain of Lies: The Apprehension and Arrest of Idaho's Randy Weaver,** Rapid Lightning Press, Stinson Beach, CA, 1993. Christian Identity point of view on the Weaver affair. Crying towels and hobby horses dear to the Christian Patriot movement.

Festinger, Leon, Riecken, Henry W., Schachter, Stanley, **When Prophecy Fails: A Social and Psychological Study of a Modern Group That Predicted the Destruction of the World,** Harper, New York, 1956. The classic study of ontological despair.

Ford, Brian, **German Secret Weapons: Blueprint for Mars,** Ballantine, New York, 1969. The near-miss that was Peenemünde.

Foreman, Dave and Haywood, Dave, **A Field Guide to Monkeywrenching,** Ned Ludd Books, Tucson, 1987. How-to-fuck-up incursions on nature by Earth First!

Frank, K. Portland, **The Anti-Psychiatry Bibliography and Resource Guide,** Press Gang Publishers, Vancouver, 1979. Activism from the standpoint of psychiatry as politically oppressive to capitalist dissidents.

Frank, Leonard Roy, editor, **The History of Shock Treatment,** published by author, San Francisco, 1978. Anti-psychiatric activist provides a useful and unbiased history of electroshock, insulin and metrazol treatments.

Frank, Leonard Roy, editor, **Influencing Minds: A Reader in Quotations,** Feral House, Portland, OR., 1995. Nuggets on Persuasion, Psychiatry, Conversion, Indoctrination, Brainwashing and Transformation.

Frazer, Graham and Lancelle, George, **Absolute Zhirinovsky: A Transparent View of the Distinguished Russian Statesman,** Penguin, New York, 1994.

Friedrich, Mattern, **UFO's Nazi Secret Weapon?,** Samisdat Publishers, Toronto, 1976. Neo-nutzies venerate Nazism's anti-gravity research.

Freud, Sigmund, **Jokes and Their Relation to the Unconscious,** Norton, New York, 1960. The will to power as exhibited in the telling of jokes.

Freud, Sigmund, **Totem and Taboo: Some Points of Agreement Between the Mental Lives of Savages and Neurotics,** Routledge & Kegan Paul, London, 1950.

Fuller, Captain J. F. C., **The Star in the West: A Critical Essay Upon the Works of Aleister Crowley,** Walter Scott Publishing, London, 1907. The military tactician wins Aleister's contest for the best essay on Crowleyanity. "Into the realms of sexual-neurasthenia Crowley takes us, and it is necessary that he should. His religion, his philosophy, and his psychology, all point to an ultimate blending of our extreme perfections and imperfections — vice and virtue — in one great monistic unity.

Fulop-Miller, Rene, **Leaders, Dreamers and Rebels: An Account of the Great Mass-Movements of History and of the Wish-Dreams that Inspired Them,** Viking Press, New York, 1935. Attempts a Spenglerian synthesis of history, technology and mass movements.

George, John & Wilcox, Laird, **Nazis, Communists, Klansmen and Others on the Fringe: Political Extremism in America,** Prometheus Books, Buffalo, 1992. Above all, a non-hysterical overview.

Gertz, Elmer, **Odyssey of a Barbarian. The Biography of George Sylvester Viereck,** Prometheus Books, Buffalo, 1978. Viereck, once Aleister Crowley's boss, was tried for sedition in 1942, and was as disliked for his championing of sex research as his outspoken Germanophilia.

Giedion, Siegfried, **Mechanization Takes Command: A Contribution to Anonymous History,** Oxford University Press, 1948. Architecture, furniture, gadgetry. Its influence on humans and vice-versa. A book of immense importance, a precursor to McLuhan.

Greenstein, Paul, Lennon, Nigey & Rolfe, Lionel, **Bread & Hyacinths: The Rise and Fall of Utopian Los Angeles,** California Classics Books, Los Angeles, 1992. How the *Los Angeles Times* killed the labor movement with a bomb much like that which exploded in Oklahoma City.

Gilman, Sander L., **Jewish Self-Hatred: Anti-Semitism and the Hidden Language of the Jews,** The Johns Hopkins University Press, Baltimore, 1986. "Jews are not the invention of the anti-Semite — or vice versa. It is a reciprocal relationship: each invents the other." — *London Review of Books.*

Glover, Crispin Hellion, **Oak Mot,** Volcanic Eruptions, Los Angeles, 1991. The lurking malevolence within the stiff and formalist language of turn-of-the-century potboilers is accentuated here through crucial excisions and replacements of phrase, sentence and paragraph of similarly tortuous syntax but with altogether more contemporary content. Glover's ink pen leaks varicose vein-like lines that sometime take flight into full-blown renderings of neurological malady. These neurotic assaults on the antique texts create a new contextual highway marked by the detritus of construction ... soft shoulders, narrow alleys, dead ends, quizzical loops, detours, and the odd region blocked off to traffic. Photographs and illustrations are pasted over old pages and even pop up within the text, leading the reader to a confusion of interpretative solutions. *Oak Mot* has something to do with nostalgia, will power, the friend-

357

ly menace of persuasion — all leading up to consideration of a mass movement which failed to enact its latent promise within a horror film milieu.

Goad, Jim and Debbie, **ANSWER Me!,** issues 1-4, Los Angeles and Portland.

Godwin, Joscelyn, **Mystery Religions in the Ancient World,** Thames and Hudson, 1981. Well-illustrated but schematic consideration of pre-Christian worship.

Gokak, V. K., **Sri Sathya Sai Baba,** Abhinav Publications, New Delhi, 1975. A narrative of Sai Baba's early life.

Goldberg, B.Z., **The Sacred Fire: The Story of Sex in Religion,** Horace Liveright, 1930. Pioneering account of the sex motif in religion. Seems to have influenced John Michell's work particularly.

Goodrick-Clarke, Nicholas, **The Occult Roots of Nazism: The Ariosophists of Austria and Germany 1890 - 1935,** Aquarian Books, Wellingborough, 1985. The least hysterical account on the origin of Nazi ideology.

Gould, George M. and Pyle, Walter L., **Anomalies and Curiosities of Medicine: Being an Encyclopedic Collection of Rare and Extraordinary Cases, and of the Most Striking Instances of Abnormality in all Branches of Medicine and Surgery, Derived From an Exhaustive Research of Medical Literature from its Origin to the Present Day, Abstracted, Classified, Annotated and Indexed,** Bell Publishing, New York, 1961. The original *Mondo* movie. Gould and Pyle's grand collection of bizarrarie must have been influenced by Barnum as well as Krafft-Ebing.

Grant, Kenneth, **Aleister Crowley and the Hidden God,** Weiser, New York, 1974.

Guenon, Rene, **The Reign of Quantity & The Signs of the Times,** Penguin, Baltimore, 1972. Hindu and Islamic spiritual traditionalism informs Guenon's vision of the accelerating, replicating, de-evolving "reign of quantity" currently engulfing the West.

Halsell, Grace, **Prophecy and Politics: Militant Evangelists on the Road to Nuclear War,** Veritas Publishing, 1986. The Christian Right and its penchant for conflict in Israel in order to bring on Armageddon.

Hamilton, David, **The Monkey Gland Affair,** Chatto and Windus, London, 1986. The humorous attempts of scientists to bottle youth.

Hansen, L. Taylor, **He Walked the Americas,** Amherst Press, Amherst, 1963. Indians of the American continents speak of the Great White Prophet and Healer.

Harris, Frank, **The Bomb,** Published by the Author, New York, 1920. A novelization of the Haymarket affair from the bomber's point of view.

Harrison, Ben, **Undying Love: A Key West "Love Story,"** Les Editions Duval, Key West, 1993. The story of Count Carl von Cosel, the eccentric gentleman whose love for late wife Elena was demonstrated to the public by exhibiting her taxidermied body to houseguests. Shelby Downard says Von Cosel was a sophisticated psychic operative (witch) who could kill individuals by thought alone.

Harrison, Ted, **Elvis People: The Cult of The King,** Fount Books, London, 1992.

Hatonn, Gyeorgos Ceres, **Tangled Webs "Gotcha" — Again: Just As With Disease — To Avoid Contact You Must Either Disperse the Disease OR you Must Learn to Protect Yourself From the Contagion. Either Way — You Must Know the Cause,** America West Publishers, Carson City, NV, 1992. Hatonn, come from the Pleiades to save earthlings from corrupt politicians, speaks through the grandmotherly medium "Dharma." Hatonn's conspiratorial maunderings are captured in the weekly tabloid *Contact* (previously, the *Phoenix Liberator*). Strangely, Hatonn must borrow his discoveries from emotionally imbalanced investigators on earth, and thus has been sued for plagiarism. Read the story on Bo Gritz for details regarding the Colonel's *Weekly World News*-like encounter with Hatonn.

Heckethorn, Charles William, **The Secret Societies of All Ages and Countries: Embracing the Mysteries of Ancient India, China, Japan, Egypt, Mexico, Peru, Greece, and Scandinavia, The Cabbalists, Early Christians, Heretics, Assassins, Thugs, Templars, The Vehm and Inquisition, Mystics, Rosicrucians, Illuminati, Freemasons, Skopzi, Camorristi, Carbonari, Nihilists and Other Sects,** Volumes 1 & 2, University Books, New York, 1965. First published in 1875 and revised in 1897, Heckethorn's work is the source for the popularizing editions about this subject, especially Daraul and MacKenzie.

Hill, Michael Ortiz, **Dreaming the End of the World: Apocalypse as a Rite of Passage,** Spring Publications, Dallas, 1994. The author believes in the Apocalypse as an "unveiling" of the mysteries, as a method to "re-vision" end-of-the-world nightmares into Jungian mythic drama. Perhaps being vaporized into itty bitty molecules is something of a transcendental experience? "Yah," says Dr. Strangelove. "You need to queue up for the ride only once."

Hinckley, Jr., John, **Letters to Jodie,** publisher and dates unknown. Chapbook features obsessive letters and poetry to Jodie Foster used as evidence in Hinckley's trial for his assassination attempt on President Reagan. Coincidentally, Vice President Bush (former head of the CIA) had dinner with Hinckley's parents the night before the shooting. "Hang onto my dream and we will fly to the netherworld of happiness."

Hindus, Milton, **The Crippled Giant: A Literary Relationship with Louis-Ferdinand Céline,** Brandeis University Press, Hanover, 1986. A Jewish admirer of the notorious anti-Semite visits Céline during his exile in Denmark. *The Crippled Giant* is a diary of their peculiar relationship.

Hirschfeld, Magnus, **The Sexual History of the World War,** Panurge Press, New York, 1934. Like Céline, Hirschfeld discovers war to be aphrodisiacal.

Hislop, John, **Conversations with Bhagavan Sri Sathya Sai Baba,** Bhagavan Sri Sathya Sevi Organization, Ratlam, 1976.

Hoffman II, Michael A., **Secret Societies and Psychological Warfare,** Wiswell Ruffin House, Dresden, NY, 1992. Hoffman's key essay, first developed in his introduction to James Shelby Downard's "King Kill/ 33°" from the first edition of *Apocalypse Culture,* that an occult cryptocracy utilizing secret symbolism and word magic underlies the entire capitalist establishment.

Holleman, Edith & Love, Andrew, principal writers, **Inside the Shadow Government: Declaration of Plaintiffs' Counsel Filed by the Christic Institute U.S. District Court, Miami, Florida, March 31, 1988,** Christic Institute, Washington D.C., 1988. Despite the loud clamoring against this document, it remains valuable for names and dates of specific incidents regarding drugs, guns, payoffs, murders and dirty deeds accomplished by what Daniel Sheehan believes to be an "off-the-shelf" extra-governmental authority operating within the government itself. The black helicopters mentioned here prove that they are not solely a canard of the far-right.

Hougan, Jim, **Spooks: The Haunting of America — The Private Use of Secret Agents,** William Morrow, New York, 1978. "The CIA itself maintains what may be the world's largest collection of espionage literature and fiction — literally tens of thousands of volumes, ranging from Sun Tzu's *Roots of Strategy — Art of War* (Peking, 500 B. C.) to Harry Murphy's *Where's What* and Fleming's *Dr. No.* The collection, housed in the CIA's campuslike compound near Langley, Virginia, is a musty rebuke to the immaculate world surrounding it.... This library ... is regularly perused by the Agency's employees, who may be looking for new technology worth inventing, a dirty trick worth resurrecting, or just a good 'read.'"!

Hubbard, L. Ron & Hubbard, **Mary Sue, The Book of E-Meter Drills: Clearing Series, Three,** Church of Scientology Publications, Los Angeles, 1965. Instructs the Scientological "auditor" how to read the "E-Meter," a device used to help locate a student's "engrams."

Jackson, Holbrook, **The Anatomy of Bibliomania,** Farrar, Straus and Company, New York. A non-fiction corollary to Elias Canetti's *Auto-Da-Fé.*

Jullian, Philippe, **The Symbolists,** Phaidon, Oxford, 1973. A reconsideration of works previously dismissed as degenerate and occult.

Kafton-Minkel, Walter, **Subterranean Worlds: 100,000 Years of dragons, Dwarfs, the Dead, Lost Races & UFOs From Inside the Earth,** Loompanics, Port Townsend, WA, 1989. Entertaining and exhaustive survey of the mythological touchstone of inner earth.

Kahane, Rabbi Meir, **The Story of the Jewish Defense League,** Chilton Book Company, Radnor, PA, 1975. "Every Jew a .22." The late Rabbi Kahane might well have supported Jews for the Preservation of Firearm Ownership, a group that circulates statistics on the coincidental relationship between disarmament and genocide. Kahane also published a book titled *Uncomfortable Questions for Comfortable Jews.*

Kauffmann, Friedrich, **Northern Mythology,** Suhal, Thame, 1992 (?). Brief treatment, from 1903, of the early religion and mythology of the Germans, Scandinavians and the Goths. "Even the gods must die."

Keane, Margaret and Walter, **Tomorrow's Masters Series,** Johnson Meyer Publishing, Redwood City, CA., 1964. Two-volume slipcased monograph of the two masters, complete with adulatory introductions. Walter's book was prefaced by a worshipful Tom Wolfe masquerading under the name "Eric Schneider."

Keane, Walter, **The Many Loves of Walter Keane,** La Jolla, CA, 1991. Author's pre-publication edition of his auto-hagiography.

Keel, John A., **The Flying Saucer Subculture,** The New York Fortean Society, New York, 1994. "UFOlogy has been a propaganda movement rather than a scientific movement. The ufologists began stumping for a myth in the late 1940s before the sighting evidence was empirical. Additional myths were gradually developed and absorbed into the main premise, the ETH (extraterrestrial hypothesis), while the mounting correlations between UFO and psychic phenomena were ignored or even suppressed by the ET believers, not by the USAF or C.I.A.".

Keith, Jim, editor, **Secret and Suppressed: Banned Ideas and Hidden History,** Feral House, Portland, 1994. Includes Downard article and extremely interesting and/or explosive ideas not usually available in bookstores.

Key, Wilson Bryant, **Media Sexploitation,** Signet, New York, 1976. Subliminal advertising deconstructed.

Khomeini, Ayatollah Ruhollah, **Ayatollah Khomeini's Mein Kampf,** Manor Books, New York, 1979. Post Islamic Revolution swipe at Fundamentalist Islamic dogma.

Kick, Russ, **Outposts: A Catalog of Rare and Disturbing Alternative Information,** Carroll and Graf Publishers, New York, 1995.

King, Dennis, **Lyndon LaRouche and the New American Fascism,** Doubleday, New York, 1989. Associate of PRA's Chip Berlet infiltrates the bizarre mechanisms of the Trotskyite turned techno-cultist. King defends Henry Kissinger from the LaRouchies' onslaught. "It is not necessary to wear brown shirts to be a fascist ... it is not necessary to call oneself a fascist to be a fascist. It is simply necessary to be one!" — Lyndon LaRouche, from his paper, "Solving the Machiavellian Problem Today."

King, Francis, editor, **The Secret Rituals of the O.T.O.,** Samuel Weiser, New York, 1973. Baby eating included.

Kingsmill, Hugh, **An Anthology of Invective and Abuse,** Dial Press, New York, 1929.

Kingsmill, Hugh, **More Invective,** Dial Press, New York, 1930. Kingsmill's volumes illuminate the art of the rant, later taken up by Bob Black and yours truly in 1989's *Rants & Incendiary Tracts.*

Kirban, Salem, **20 Reasons Why This Present Earth May Not Last Another 20 Years,** Riverside Book and Bible House, Iowa Falls, 1973. Kirban's current events-keyed prediction of imminent Apocalypse followed a *Life* magazine format adopted by many "Apocalypse Soon" religious tracts.

Kossy, Donna, **Kooks: A Guide to the Outer Limits of Human Belief,** Feral House, Portland, 1994.

Krafft-Ebing, Richard von, **Psychopathia Sexualis,** Bell Publishing, New York, 1965. The first unbowdlerized edition of Kraft-Ebing was translated as late as 1965, when the sexual case study was released from scientific oversight into the salacious hands of sensation-seekers.

Laquer, Walter, **Black Hundred: The Rise of the Extreme Right in Russia,** Harper Collins, New York, 1993. A scholar of political extremism swings his weight against the new xenophobic nationalism emerging in Russia.

Laquer, Walter, editor, **The Terrorism Reader: A Historical Anthology From Aristotle to the IRA and the PLO,** New American Library, New York, 1978.

Larson, Bob, **Dead Air,** Thomas Nelson Publishers, Nashville, 1991. Christians from Chicago's *Cornerstone* magazine revealed this book was actually ghostwritten by a secretary. The book predictably battles Satanism from the bully pulpit of radio.

Lasch, Christopher, **The New Radicalism in America 1889 - 1963: The Intellectual as a Social Type,** Knopf, New York, 1965. The reformer as tyrant.

Legman, G., **The Fake Revolt,** Breaking Point, New York, 1967. Hippieism as Hitlerism is the topic of this great little rant.

Legman, G., **Rationale of the Dirty Joke: An Analysis of Sexual Humor,** First and Second Series, Grove Press, 1968. A tremendous achievement of modern folklore. From a man whose own name elicits sexual humor, 1600 pages of off-color theme and variation. "I laugh, so that I may not cry." — Beaumarchais.

Leutcher, Fred, **The Leutcher Report: The First Forensic Examination of Auschwitz** with a foreword by David Irving, Focal Point Publications, London, 1989. American extermination expert gets over his head by taking up an offer by Holocaust Revisionists to forensically examine Auschwitz and Majdenek. Leutcher examines wall scrapings and declares that the gas chambers were nothing more than delousing rooms for prisoners and their clothing. The Anti-Defamation League has seen to it that Leutcher will not work again for the American penal system.

Lever, Maurice, **Sade: A Biography,** Harcourt Brace & Company, San Diego, 1991. "In the aftermath of World War II, the author of the *Cent Vingt Journées de Sodome* was faced with more serious accusations. The man who had been portrayed as a communist militant was now denounced as an apostle of the extreme right and even of Nazism, with some commentators going so far as to blame him for the death camps. Raymond Queaneau had this to say: 'It is undeniable that the world imagined by Sade and willed by his characters ... was a hallucinatory precursor of the world ruled by the Gestapo, its tortures, and its camps.'"

Lewinsohn, Richard, **A History of Sexual Customs,** Harper and Brothers, New York, 1958. Most interesting chapters: "Police State and Romance," "Prudery and Demi-Monde."

Lewis, Sinclair, **It Can't Happen Here,** Signet edition, New York, 1993. Lewis knew just how close Babbitt came to the totalitarian personality. Thinking the "impossible" in 1935.

Lombroso, Cesare, **The Man of Genius,** Walter Scott Publishing, London, 1905. Nordau dedicated *Degeneration* to Lombroso; *The Man of Genius* shows us why. "Professor Virgilio has furnished me with a very curious portrait of an insane patient at the moment of attack — the eyes rolling, the hair on end, the arms extended.

Under his feet is the epigraph: 'Deliria." This is the work of an alcoholic pederast. ... I think that a sane artist would have some difficulty in painting a closer likeness of delirium." Art criticism as forensic criminology.

London, Jack, **The Iron Heel,** Grosset and Dunlap, New York, 1907. "The captains of industry had turned upon the middle class. The employers' associations, that had helped the captains of industry to tear and rend labor, were now torn and rent by their quondam allies. Amidst the crashing of the middle men, the small business men and manufacturers, the trusts stood firm. Nay the trusts did more than stand firm. They were active. They sowed wind, and wind, and ever more wind; for they alone knew how to reap the whirlwind and make a profit out of it. And such profits! Colossal profits! Strong enough themselves to weather the storm that was largely their own brewing, they turned loose and plundered the wrecks that floated above them."

Lyman, Mel, **Mirror at the End of the Road,** American Avatar Publications, 1971. Cult leader crosses "the dark night of the spirit" to attain Godhood.

Lynch, David, **Ronny Rocket,** unpublished movie script, his most personal evocation. The script begins: "There is a dark land where mysteries and confusions abound, where fear and terror fly together in troubled cities of absurdities. Black clouds race by over a soot-covered city, where it is darkest night. Only a few tiny yellow squares of light in the old buildings and factories. Everything is so dark. Very little life is noticed except the tiny dark yellow squares. There are no cars seen from this high angle looking down over the city   no people out this night."

MacIntyre, Ben, Forgotten Fatherland: The Search for Elisabeth Nietzsche, Harper Perennial, New York, 1992. Journalist discovers the pathetic remnants of *Nueva Germania,* Elisabeth Nietzsche and Bernhard Förster's breeding ground for a new Aryan race.

MacKay, Charles, **Extraordinary Popular Delusions and the Madness of Crowds,** Harmony Books, New York, 1980. Now 150 years old, MacKay's popping of mass delusional balloons is even applicable today; as in the get-rich-quick chain letter.

McCormack, Win, **The Rajneesh Chronicles,** New Oregon Publishers, 1987. Hostile news articles collected together portraying Rajneesh's failed commune in Central Oregon.

McManus, Michael J., **Final Report of the Attorney General's Commission on Pornography,** Rutledge Hill Press, Nashville, 1986. McManus, a conservative columnist, attempted to shop around the Meese Commission Report with his introduction at its head but could not find an interested major publisher. McManus had no special dispensation to peddle the Report. Theoretically the Report's public domain status would enable any publisher to reprint the Government Printing Office's version at no cost. The McManus edition was nevertheless picked up by Rutledge Hill, a regional publisher. McManus subscribes to hang-em-with-their-own-rope tactics, hoping to fill the reader with revulsion of porn through a Ludovico-like overload of explicit titles and explicit descriptions of repulsive scenes. In 1992 McManus wrote that an article I placed in *Hustler* magazine inspired a grisly crime in Oklahoma. The sole evidence of this causality was a vague similarity between the crime and a quote I had featured taken from a gay author's "How to Torture" book. The culprit had not been found, nor was there any evidentiary connection between my article and the crime. This didn't stop McManus from pointing the finger at *Hustler* magazine, or stop him from quoting the offending sentences IN FULL. It did seem far more prurient spotlighted in a family newspaper than its original context in an adult magazine. Which brings me to my final thought on the Meese Commission Report. Susie Bright said that she masturbated for hours while reading it.

Mahdi, As Sayyid Issa Al Haadi Al, **The Book of the Five Percenters,** Original Tents of Kedar, Monticello, NY, 1991. 650 page appeal by the Nubian Hebrews to the elect members of the Nation of Islam, known as the Five Percenters, to convert to the absolutely black-run sect. The author includes a xerox of a *Washington Times* article revealing that the Elijah Muhammad claimed he was white on his arrest records.

Mahdi, As Sayyid Issa Al Haadi Al, **The Fallacy of Christmas: Santa or Satan?,** Original Tents of Kedar, Monticello, NY, 1987. Exposé of St. Nicholas, the Patron Saint of thieves and gangsters. Complete with reproductions of Anton LaVey's photograph.

Mahdi, As Sayyid Issa Al Haadi Al, **The Paleman,** Original Tents of Kedar, Monticello, NY, 1990. The Devil in all his incarnations. Possibly the first religious text to reprint choice articles from supermarket tabloids to bolster its remarkable beliefs.

Mangalwadi, Vishal, **The World of Gurus: A Critical Look at the Philosophies of India's Influential Gurus and Mystics,** Cornerstone Press, Chicago, 1992. Sai Baba is included in the chapter "The Thaumaturgic Guru."

Mantegazza, Paolo, **Physiognomy and Expression,** Walter Scott Publishing, London, 1904. Addresses the "defects" of Darwin's study of emotion and expression. The author seems insulted by Darwin's "too analytical" study of artistic temperament and emotion, to which Italians build shrines.

Mardi, S. Hussein, Nekoodast, N., Tinsinlier, S., editorial staff, **Echo of Islam: The Dawn of the Islamic Revolution,** Publication of the Ministry of Islamic Guidance, Tehran, 1981 (?). Excellent coffee-table edition by the propaganda department of Khomeini's revolution. Complete with posters of a snake-like Jimmy-the-Tooth.

Marks, John, **The Search for the Manchurian Candidate: The CIA and Mind Control,** McGraw Hill, New York, 1980. MK-Ultra, ARTICHOKE and other euphemistic programs undertaken by U.S. intelligence to construct a better zombie.

Mason, James, **Siege.** Edited and Introduced by Michael M. Jenkins, Storm Books, Denver, 1992. Revolutionary turns from George Lincoln Rockwell to Charles Manson. Political pornography.

Masters, R. E. L, **Eros and Evil: The Sexual Psychopathology of Witchcraft, Incorporating the Complete Text of Sinastri's Demoniality,** Matrix House, New York, 1966.

> Bad as he is, the Devil may be abus'd,
> Be falsly charg'd, and causelessly accus'd,
> When Men, unwilling to be blam'd alone,

Shift off those Crimes on Him which are their Own.
— Daniel Defoe

Mencken, H.L., **A Mencken Chrestomathy,** Knopf, New York, 1949. No one has replaced him.

Michell, John, **The Earth Spirit: Its Ways, Shrines and Mysteries,** Thames and Hudson, 1992. As with most of Michell's books, stimulating thoughts on the imprint of nature on civilization and vice-versa, especially the origins of religion as nature-worship.

Miller, Russell, **Bare-Faced Messiah: The True Story of L. Ron Hubbard.** Scientology sued to prevent this book's domestic release. For this reason alone, worth a look. More astounding than fiction.

Mishima, Yukio, **Sun and Steel,** Kodansha, Tokyo, 1970. Escaping the cult of the word to develop the cult of the body and its utility as a nationalistic instrument.

Mullins, Eustace, **The World Order: A Study in the Hegemony of Parasitism,** Ezra Pound Institute of Civilization, Staunton, VA, 1985. A rare individual: one who discards Pound's aesthetic for his economic theories. It's difficult to read this book without being a true believer; the names become something like an Enemies List.

Murphet, Howard, **Sai Baba: Man of Miracles,** MacMillan, New Delhi, 1972. The miraculous side of Sai Baba.

Netanyahu, Benjamin, editor, **Terrorism: How the West Can Win,** Avon, New York, 1986. The Israeli hawk collects writings of major establishment figures in order to plump for anti-terrorism legislation. "In none of the liberal democracies has the adoption of [...] strong anti-terrorist measures led to a significant or lasting curtailment of individual freedoms."

Nietzsche, Friedrich, **The Antichrist,** Walter Kaufmann translation, illustrated by Trevor Brown, Coup de Grace publications, Antwerp, 1988.

Nietzsche, Friedrich, **The Joyful Wisdom,** Thomas Common translation, Russell & Russell, New York, 1964.

Nordau, Max, **Degeneration,** Appleton and Company, New York, 1892. My copy comes from the library of Cecil B. DeMille. Nordau, below only Herzl in the Zionist movement, and who unsuccessfully bid to make Uganda (?!) the Jewish homeland, rants against modernism as the sure sign of insanity.

Norman, Ruth (aka URIEL), **Preview for the Spacefleet Landing on Earth in 2001 A.D.,** Unarius Academy of Science, El Cajon, 1987. The philosophy of Unarius is explained more concisely than any of their other publications. Includes a full-color photo of the Archangel Uriel dressed in the "cosmic generator."

Norman, Ruth (writing here as "The Interplanetary Ambassador"), **FACTS ABOUT UFOs,** Unarius Academy of Science, 145 S. Magnolia Ave., El Cajon, CA, 92020. 60 page giveaway introduction to the remarkable thrift store splendor of Unarius, informing the potential initiate about the impending landing of 33 spacecraft in San Diego County to form the interplanetary Unarius academy.

Norman, Ruth E & Spaegel, Vaughn, **Who is the MONA LISA?,** Unarius Academy of Science, El Cajon, 1973. Morphs Uriel and Mona.

O'Brien, Barbara, **Operators and Things: The Inner Life of a Schizophrenic,** Arlington Books, Cambridge, 1958. "'I am almost convinced,' said one biologist, 'that the schizophrenic is an attempt on the part of nature at forming a mutation.'" ... "A certain percentage of the population have minds so constructed that they can influence the mentality of others and dominate them. These individuals are known as operators and refer to the rest of the population as things. Upon these things they establish liens, chattels, and charters and so retain options over them."

Olson, Norman, Commander, **Michigan Militia,** Cass City Chronicle, Cass City, MI, 1994. Spiral-bound information kit for the curious.

Ostrovsky, Victor & Hoy, Claire, **By Way of Deception: The Making and Unmaking of a Mossad Officer,** St. Martin's, 1990. Insights on Middle East *realpolitik.*

Paine, Thomas, **The Life and Major Writings Of Thomas Paine,** Collected, Edited and Annotated by Philip S. Foner, Carol Publishing, New York, 1993.

Parfrey, Adam, editor, **Apocalypse Culture,** Amok Press, New York, 1987. First edition. Includes both Michael A. Hoffman's analysis and text of James Shelby Downard's "King Kill/33°."

Parfrey, Adam, editor, **Apocalypse Culture: Expanded and Revised Edition,** Feral House, Portland, 1990. Downard's "The Call to Chaos" expands his earlier article; 18 other additions appear in this expanded edition.

Parfrey, Adam & Black, Bob, editors, **Rants and Incendiary Tracts: Voices of Desperate Illumination,** Amok Press, New York, 1988. The rant as literary archetype.

Pelley, William Dudley, **The Door to Revelation: An Intimate Biography,** The Foundation Fellowship, Asheville, NC, 1935. The founder of I AM-type metaphysical group Soulcraft as well as the Nazi Silvershirts, Pelley peddled this prolix, mimeographed memoir himself on lecture tours. Pelley writes a lot about his days in Hollywood, seething with hatred for his bosses. "The fleshpots of Hollywood. Oriental custodians of adolescent entertainment. One short word for all of it — JEWS! Do you think me unduly incensed about them? I've seen too many Gentile maidens ravished and been unable to do anything about it. They have a concupiscent slogan in screendom, "Don't hire till you see the whites of their thighs!" I know all about Jews. For six years I toiled in their galleys and got nothing but money."

Pike, Albert, **Morals and Dogma of the Ancient and Accepted Scottish Rite of Freemasonry Prepared for the Supreme Council of the Thirty-Third Degree for the Southern Jurisdiction of the United States and Published by its Authority,** A. M. 5632, Charleston, SC, 1906. Pike was both a general in the Confederate Army and a founder of the Ku Klux Klan. His Scottish Rite Freemasonry was far more obsessed with degrees than its Grand Orient brethren. A dull read, *Morals and Dogma* has nonetheless been vivisected for its allusions to luciferian worship by Christian conspiracy theorists. *Morals and Dogma* does hint at solar worship and a return to Babylonian Mystery Religion, sans cannibalism and human sacrifice.

Pitkin, Walter B., **A Short Introduction to the History of Human Stupidity,** Simon and Schuster, New York, 1932. Attempt to address the errors, ignorance and outright stupidity exhibited by the navigators of human destiny.

Pound, Ezra, Ezra **Pound Speaking: Radio Speeches of World War II,** Edited by Leonard W. Doob, Greenwood Press, Westport, CT., 1978. A large collection of Pound's anti-Allied radio transmissions throughout the WWII from Italian soil.

Pound, Ezra, **Jefferson And/Or Mussolini: L'Idea Statale Fascism As I Have Seen It,** Liveright, New York, 1935. From Pound's Foreword: "The body of this ms. was written and left my hands in February 1933. 40 publishers have refused it. No typescript of mine has been read by so many people or brought me a more interesting correspondence." Pound found Mussolini's fascism an attractive cure for the war profiteering and usury of international bankers. Fellow Idahoan Randy Weaver fought against a similar enemy fifty years later.

Pritchard, John, **Reichstag Fire: Ashes of Democracy,** Ballantine, New York, 1972.

Proceedings of the Fifteenth Annual Conference on Explosives and Blasting Technique, February 5 - 10, 1989, New Orleans, LA, 1989. Interesting reading in light of Oklahoma City.

Prophet, Elizabeth Clare, **The Great White Brotherhood in the Culture, History and Religion of America,** Summit University Press, Los Angeles, 1978. The continuation of the Ballards' I AM cult by a woman whose proposed timetable for apocalypse has already passed.

Quigley, Carroll, **Tragedy and Hope: A History of the World in Our Time,** MacMillan, New York, 1966. The 1348 page Rosetta Stone of modern conspiracy. Interest increased considerably after Bill Clinton acknowledged Quigley in his acceptance speech at the Democratic Convention. From *Tragedy and Hope:* "There does exist, and has existed for a generation, an international Anglophile network which operates, to some extent, in the way the radical Right believes the Communists act. In fact, this network, which we may identify as the Round Table Groups, has no aversion to cooperating with the Communists, or any group and frequently does so. I know of the operations of this network because I have studied it for twenty years and was permitted for two years, in the early 1960s, to examine its papers and secret records. ... I have no aversion to it or most of its aims, and have, for much of my life, been close to it and many of its instruments. ... I have objected ... to a few of its policies... but in general my chief difference of opinion is that it wishes to remain unknown, and I believe its role in history is significant enough to be known."

Ravenscroft, Trevor and Wallace-Murphy, T., **The Mark of the Beast.** The popularizer of the *Spear of Destiny* fable, in which Hitler attains Satanic power by taking possession of the sword that pierced Christ's side, backslides in a weak effort to correlate the Book of Revelation with current events.

Reavis, Dick J., **The Ashes of Waco: An Investigation,** Simon and Schuster, New York, 1995. Freelance journalist writes the story the armies of establishment media failed to give us.

Reich, Wilhelm, **Contact With Space: Oranur Second Report 1951 - 1956,** Core Pilot Press, New York, 1957. Ostensibly the work of a madman, the book describes the denuding of the life-force with prose worthy of J. G. Ballard.

Reich, Wilhelm, **Listen, Little Man!,** Farrar, Straus and Giroux, New York, 1973.

Reich, Wilhelm, **The Murder of Christ,** Farrar, Straus and Giroux, New York, 1953. "Stalin is to Marx what Paul is to Christ."

Reich, Wilhelm, **The Sexual Revolution: Toward a Self-Governing Character Structure,** Orgone Institute Press, New York, 1951. "The first prerequisite for healthier human and sexual relationships is the elimination of those moral concepts which base their demands on allegedly supernatural commands, on arbitrary human regulations, or simply on tradition."

Robbins, Shawn and Susman, Edward, **Shawn Robbins' Prophecies for the End of Time,** Avon Books, New York, 1995. Psychic Shawn Robbins appears on cover in an intriguing photograph. One-half of her face is made to seem maniacal and Kali-like. The other half of the face looks like a sorority babe. Her predictions seem like intelligence briefings for the New World Order. Africa is gutted in a famine; the U.S. incorporates Canada, Cuba and Mexico; Christianity runs out of luck, the elderly snuff themselves at Kevorkian camps, and a group of movie stars and baseball players buy some Pacific Islands where they worship Baal. Yup.

Rogers, J. A., **Facts About the Negro Number 2.** Pamphlet illustrates such discoveries as Schubert's and Beethoven's dusky heritage.

Rokeach, Milton, **The Three Christs of Ypsilanti,** Vintage, New York, 1967. In a mental asylum, three self-styled Christs are made to confront one another.

Rosenthal, A. M., and Gelb, Arthur, **One More Victim: The Life and Death of an American-Jewish Nazi,** New American Library, New York, 1967. Auteur of *KILL!* magazine shoots himself in the head after his Jewish heritage is disclosed to fellow KKK members. A. M. Rosenthal, *New York Times* owner and columnist, and co-author Arthur Gelb conclude that Dan Burros' ambition to slaughter Jews is proof of his victimization by anti-Jewish bigots. The sad truth is that Burros was raised in a predominantly Jewish community and was considered an example of perfect Jewish boyhood by the rabbis of Queens. Burros' hatred of Judaism was a by-product of his continuing interaction with relatives and friends in the Jewish community. Burros' violent fantasies may well have been nourished by Kahane's JDL, had it existed in the early '60s. Burros was merely a victim of his fetishistic preferences.

Rosner, Joseph, **The Hater's Handbook. A Guide to the Wonderful World of Ill Will: The Catcalls, Abuse and Caustic Comment Flung at Persons of Note Throughout the Ages,** Dell, New York, 1965.

Salgado, Gamini, **The Elizabethan Underworld,** Dent and Sons, London, 1977.

Sandweiss, Dr. Samuel H., **Sai Baba: The Holy Man ... and the Psychiatrist,** Birth Day Publishing, San Diego, 1975. Psychiatrist reassesses Western attitudes in light of his conversion to Sai Baba.

Sarfatti, Margherita G., **The Life of Benito Mussolini,** Frederick A. Stokes, New York, 1925. Il Duce's Jewish mistress pens an early hagiography. "For Mussolini Freemasonry no longer had any charms ... Its pretenses of secrecy above all repelled him ... the secretive, the concealed, the surreptitious, is hateful and horrible to Mussolini.... At the Congress of Ancona he proclaimed that Socialists must no longer be Freemasons. Eight years later, in 1922, the same rule was enforced for Fascists."

Sargant, Dr. William, **Battle for the Mind,** Penguin, London, 1961. Techniques of conversion both political and religious. Relevant now more than ever.

Sargent, Lyman Tower, **Extremism in America,** New York University Press, New York, 1995. Documents gleaned from the Wilcox Collection. More from the right than left, however.

Saxon, Kurt, **The Survivor, Volume 1,** Atlan Formularies, Harrison, AR., 1987. Survivalist tips encompassed in reprints of 60-year-old *Popular Mechanics* articles.

Scott, Peter Dale, **Deep Politics and the Death of JFK,** University of California Press, Berkeley, 1993. Scholarly inquiry into the elite misdirections of the JFK affair. Scott is the most believable source on the assassination coverup.

Serrano, Miguel, **C. G. Jung & Hermann Hesse: A Record of Two Friendships,** Schocken, New York, 1968. Reminiscences of meetings with Hesse and Jung. Nearing his own death, Dr. Jung advises Serrano to follow the I Ching, for it is "never wrong."

Seymour, Cheri, **Committee of the States: Inside the Radical Right,** Camden Place Communications, Mariposa, CA., 1991. Christian Identity superstar Colonel Gale spills his story to a local journalist at a time when the U.S. government has set him up for a sedition trial under "Operation Clean Sweep."

Siepmann, Eckhard, **Montage: John Heartfield vom Club Dada Zur Arbeiter-Illustrieten Zeitung,** Elefanten Press Verlag, 1977. Fascinating German edition on the montage techniques of influential prop artist John Heartfield.

Simpson, Christopher, **Blowback: The First Full Account of America's Recruitment of Nazis, and its Disastrous Effect on our Domestic and Foreign Policy,** Weidenfeld and Nicholson, New York, 1988. Nazis imported the Cold War.

Sitchin, Zecharia, **The Lost Realms,** Avon Books, New York, 1990. Von Daniken redux.

Sklar, Holly, editor, **Trilateralism: The Trilateral Commission and Elite Planning for World Management,** South End Press, Boston, 1980. Sklar has disavowed use of this volume by militias and other perceived right-wing thunder. We don't hear much about the Trilats from liberals anymore, owing to their discomfort of ideological agreement with "radical right-wing conspiracy theorists."

Solanas, Valerie, **S.C.U.M. (Society for Cutting Up Men) Manifesto,** Olympia Press, London, 1971. Righteous anger emanating from the Magnetic North of the woman's movement.

Spear, Robert K., **Creating Covenant Communities,** Universal Force Dynamics Publishing, Leavenworth, KS, 1993. Veteran of Bo Gritz's SPIKE training seminars gets Patriots thinking about forming Christian communities in rural areas far away from the clutches of the Beast.

Spear, Robert K., **Surviving Global Slavery: Living Under the New World Order,** Universal Force Dynamics, Leavenworth, 1992. Practicalizing the Fundy fear.

Spence, Gerry, **From Freedom to Slavery: The Rebirth of Tyranny in America,** St. Martin's Press, New York, 1993. It's often touted that Spence never lost a case. He defended the shoe-fetishist Imelda Marcos, and, incidentally, Randy Weaver.

Spengler, Oswald, **The Decline of the West. Form and Actuality (Volume One) & Perspectives of World-History (Volume Two),** Knopf, New York, 1926 & 1928. With intellectual courage Spengler accused Hitler of demagoguery at a time when he could have very easily feathered his nest in the Nazi hierarchy.

Spengler, Oswald, **Selected Essays,** Regenery, Chicago, 1967. From "Is World Peace Possible?: A Cabled Reply to An American Poll (*Cosmopolitan,* January 1936)": "Life is a struggle involving plants, animals, and humans. It is a struggle between individuals, social classes, peoples, and nations, and it can take the form of economic, social, political and military competition. It is a struggle for the power to make one's will prevail, to exploit one's advantage, or to advance one's opinion of what is just or expedient. When other means fail, recourse will be taken time and again to the ultimate means: violence. An individual who uses violence can be branded a criminal, a class can be called revolutionary or traitorous, a people bloodthirsty. But that does not alter the facts. Modern world-communism calls its wars 'uprisings,' imperialist nations describe theirs as 'pacification of foreign peoples.' And if the world existed as a unified state, wars would likewise be referred to as 'uprisings.' The distinctions here are purely verbal."

Sprinzak, Ehud, **The Ascendance of Israel's Radical Right,** Oxford University Press, New York, 1991. Right-wing terrorists attempt to resurrect Solomon's Temple despite the existence of the second holiest Islamic shrine on the same ground. If Israeli fundamentalists succeed in their plans, a Muslim holy war could well be waged against Israel and its allies.

Stekel, Wilhelm, **Peculiarities of Behavior: Wandering Mania, Dipsomania, Cleptomania, Pyromania and Allied Impulsive Acts, Volumes 1 & 2,** Grove Press, 1964. Herr professor studies the war between civilization and instinct.

Stekel, Wilhelm, **Sadism and Masochism: The Psychology of Hatred and Cruelty, Volumes 1 & 2,** Grove Press, New York, 1965. Classic volumes of unexpurgated case histories. Makes for better reading than mysteries or other "creative writing."

Toye, Lori Adaile, **I AM AMERICA New World Atlas,** Seventh Ray Publishing, Socorro, New Mexico, 1991. The geographical configuration of the "New World" is communicated to I AM mystics by St. Germaine, grand poobah of the Great White Brotherhood. By the year 2000, great earth changes will have made an ocean of the

U.S. West Coast and a tropical forest of Canada. Fear not, dear ones. The calamities will initiate a great New Age!

White, John, editor, **Psychic Warfare: Fact or Fiction? An Investigation Into the Use of the Mind as a Military Weapon,** Aquarian Press, Wellingborough, 1988. Now a bit long in the tooth, White's survey treats the new advances in Non-Lethal technology. It's dedicated to Thomas Bearden and Trevor James Constable, two noted right-wingers roaming the UFO circuit.

Wilcox, Laird, **The Hoaxer Project Report,** published by the author, Olathe, KS, 1991. Documentation of the propensity of professional victims and those who indulge in insurance fraud to take advantage of the overly-solicitous treatment of those who claimed they suffered "hate crime."

Williams, Chancellor, **The Destruction of Black Civilization: Great Issues of a Race From 4500 B. c. to 2000 A. D.,** Third World Press, Chicago, 1987. Pragmatic suggestions for pan-African hegemony by the Nubian race.

Wood, Sterling A., **Riot Control,** Military Service Publishing Company, Harrisburg, PA, 1952. Military manual for the repulsion of civil disturbances.

Waterfield, Robin, **René Guénon and the Future of the West: The Life and Writings of a 20th-Century Metaphysician,** Crucible, London, 1987. The modern link between Islam and neo-Nazi metaphysics.

Welsing, Frances Cress, **The Cress Theory of Color-Confrontation and Racism (White Supremacy),** C-R Publishers, Washington D C., 1970. Dr. Welsing's concept is that white people are jealous of melanin, thus creating white supremacy. Her theory was touted by Public Enemy in 1992.

Wertham, Fredric, **Seduction of the Innocent,** Rinehart and Company, New York, 1953. The book that started the Comics Code.

Wood, David, **Genisis: The First Book of Revelations,** The Baton Press, Tunbridge Wells, Kent, 1985. A nearly Downard-like exploration of word and earth sorcery at Rennes-le-Chateau. The bible and Christ go Luciferian.

Yanker, Gary, **Prop Art: Over 1000 Contemporary Political Posters,** Darien House, New York, 1972.

Zepenauer, Mark, **The C.I.A.'s Greatest Hits,** Odonian Press, Tucson, 1994. Schematic history of The Agency's most notable PR disasters.